COMPARATIVE ANALYSIS OF ME

EUROPEAN STUDIES IN LAW AND ECONOMICS SERIES

COMPARATIVE ANALYSIS OF MERGER CONTROL POLICY

Lessons for China

Jingyuan MA

Cambridge – Antwerp – Portland

Intersentia Publishing Ltd.
Sheraton House | Castle Park
Cambridge | CB3 0AX | United Kingdom
Tel.: +44 1223 370 170 | Email: mail@intersentia.co.uk

Distribution for the UK:
NBN International
Airport Business Centre, 10 Thornbury Road
Plymouth, PL6 7 PP
United Kingdom
Tel.: +44 1752 202 301 | Fax: +44 1752 202 331
Email: orders@nbninternational.com

Distribution for the USA and Canada:
International Specialized Book Services
920 NE 58th Ave. Suite 300
Portland, OR 97213
USA
Tel.: +1 800 944 6190 (toll free)
Email: info@isbs.com

Distribution for Austria:
Neuer Wissenschaftlicher Verlag
Argentinierstraße 42/6
1040 Wien
Austria
Tel.: +43 1 535 61 03 24
Email: office@nwv.at

Distribution for other countries:
Intersentia Publishing nv
Groenstraat 31
2640 Mortsel
Belgium
Tel.: +32 3 680 15 50
Email: mail@intersentia.be

Comparative Analysis of Merger Control Policy. Lessons for China
Jingyuan Ma

© 2014 Intersentia
Cambridge – Antwerp – Portland
www.intersentia.com | www.intersentia.co.uk

ISBN 978-1-78068-245-7
D/2014/7849/91
NUR 820

British Library Cataloguing in Publication Data. A catalogue record for this book is available from the British Library.

ACKNOWLEDGEMENTS

The first time I heard of 'law and economics' was in 2008, when I was reading the book *Economic Analysis of Law in China* at the library of Beijing Foreign Studies University. At that time, I could never imagine that I would have the opportunity to do my PhD under the supervision of the editors of this book: two distinguished professors in law and economics, Prof. Dr Thomas Eger and Prof. Dr Michael Faure.

In 2009, after completing my bachelor's degree in economics in Beijing, I started my master's under the guidance of Prof. Dr Thomas Eger, who was the director of the Institute of Law and Economics at Hamburg University in Germany. Professor Eger introduced the magical world of competition law to me, and encouraged me to do in-depth research in this field. By taking Professor Eger's class, I developed my interest in competition law, and became motivated to write my master's thesis on economic analysis of competition policy.

It would have been impossible to accomplish my dream of doing PhD research on competition law without the invaluable help and support of Prof. Dr Michael Faure. Ever since Professor Faure accepted me as his student, he has offered me enormous help through my entire PhD journey. I am deeply grateful for his kind advice and honest criticism at each crucial stage of my research. This book could not have been written without his kind guidance and supervision over the last four years. I will never forget the over twenty meetings with him in Ghent, Bologna, Rotterdam, Beijing, Nanchang, Amsterdam, Maastricht, Paris, Hamburg, and St. Louis. On many occasions, he took so much time out of his extremely busy schedule to read hundreds of pages of my text within a week. It was always very touching for me to read the detailed comments and corrections that he gave me in several versions of the drafts. Being my Doktorvater, Professor Faure not only taught me the principles and disciplines of doing academic research, but also kindly guided me in entering the amazing world of academia by providing me with many opportunities for conferences and seminars, in particular involving me in the conferences that he organized on Regulation and Competition at Jiangxi University of Finance and Economics, and at China University of Political Science and Law. In addition to academic work, I am deeply grateful to Professor Faure and his family – his wife Dr Wang Hui and lovely son Haitao – for their extremely kind hospitality in many places. I will always remember the experience of celebrating the Chinese New Year in Maastricht, the wonderful lunch and dinner they invited me to in Beijing, and the amazing trip to St. Louis where we went on a conference together.

I also would like to express my sincere gratitude to my committee chair, Prof. Dr Roger Van den Bergh at the Erasmus School of Law. Being an internationally renowned expert on competition law, he has a busy schedule with academic commitments in many countries across Europe and Asia. However, he has never rejected my request for appointment. I am deeply grateful for the very kind help that he has offered me ever since the beginning of my research in 2011. My study on competition law would have been so much more difficult without his guidance and support, and I would never have been able to develop my understanding of EU competition law without the comments, suggestions and criticisms that I have received from him. I always appreciate the inspiring advice that he gave me during our meetings in Rotterdam. His classic book *European Competition Law and Economics – A Comparative Perspective* has been the most important guide for my study of economic analysis of competition law.

I owe special thanks to Prof. Dr Thomas Ulen and Prof. Dr Gerrit De Geest, who have helped me in various ways to develop a better understanding of law and economics. Professor Ulen's work on law and economic growth, behavioural law and economics and empirical legal studies taught me to understand legal issues from a multidisciplinary perspective. I am grateful to Professor Ulen for kindly hosting me during my visit to Champaign, Illinois. I was deeply impressed by his dedication to the teaching and research of law and economics, and it was his encouragement and support that motivated me to pursue an academic career in this field. I am also grateful to Prof. Dr Gerrit De Geest, who provided me with extremely helpful guidance at important stages of my study. I appreciate the very kind advice that he gave me when I was his student in Ghent in 2010. His work on comparative law and economic analysis of contract law always inspire me to understand legal issues in a philosophical and innovative way.

Thinking back over the last nine years of university life, I wish to thank many Chinese scholars and teachers who have helped me enormously. I thank my teachers at the Beijing Foreign Studies University, where I received a thorough training in economics. I am indebted to my bachelor's thesis supervisor, Professor Sun Wenli, who encouraged me to develop a research interest in competition law. I thank Professor Chen Ruohong, Professor Niu Huayong, and Professor Peng Long for their kind guidance. I owe special thanks to Professor Wu Tao at the Central University of Finance and Economics, and Professor Xu Guangdong at the China University of Political Science and Law, for their warm support of both my study and my career. I have also received help from many legal scholars and industrial organization experts. I am grateful to Professor Zhang Xinzhu, Professor Vanessa Yanhua Zhang, Professor Xu Chenggang, Professor Lin Ping, Professor Qiao Yue, and Professor Zhou Qi for their helpful suggestions.

I would like to thank professors who have helped me during my study in the European Master in Law and Economics (EMLE) and European Doctorate in Law and Economics (EDLE) programmes. I thank my committee members Professor Klaus Heine, Professor Vincenzo Denicolò, Professor Roger Van den Bergh, and my plenary committee members Professor Li Yuwen, Professor Xu Guangdong, Professor Anthony Ogus, and Professor Jonathan Klick for putting aside some of their precious time to assess my thesis. I am indebted to Professor Niels Philipsen and Professor Stefan Weishaar for their insightful comments and suggestions. My sincere gratitude also goes to Professor Russell Pittman from the US Department of Justice, who provided me helpful insights from industrial economics, and helped me understand competition issues under the US Antitrust Law. I want to wholeheartedly thank Marianne Breijer, Lisa Verniti, Frauke Schmidt and Jennifer Broocks for providing unconditional support in dealing with many urgent and complicated administrative issues. I am very grateful to Ann-Christin Maak and Rebecca Pound for their extremely kind and professional assistance in the publication of this book.

This research could not have been accomplished without the support from many colleagues and friends both in Europe and in China. I would like to thank Caspar for his constant guidance and encouragement through my entire undergraduate and postgraduate study. I thank Wei Hong, Xun Xiao, Xin Wen, Wenjie, Shao Yan, Vaia, Liu Jing, Wenqing, Wu Qiong, Katrin, Peng Peng, Wang Shuo and Jess for taking their time to share both the happy and bitter moments with me during my research. I thank Liu Quan for providing me with helpful literature. I thank my special friends Katya, Wanfei, Yumeng, Cheng Jie; my colleagues in Hamburg: Federico, Cicek, Ana, Rahul; and my EDLE 2010 class for the wonderful experience that we had in many cities in Europe.

I also want to thank my friends and host families who gave me care and help when I was studying abroad. I owe my deepest gratitude to Inge and Guy's family, the Schwalbe family, Talita and Neil's family, Romi and Peter's family, Lotte and Bent's family, and Jane and Peter's family for their kind hosting over the years.

Finally, this book is dedicated to my beloved parents. I would not be the person I am today without their unlimited love, support and encouragement throughout my life.

CONTENTS

TABLE OF CASES

UNITED STATES

Appalachian Coals, Inc. v. United States, 288 U.S. 344 (1933)
Brown Shoe Co., Inc. v. United States, 370 U.S. 294 (1962)
Brunswick Corp. v. Pueblo Bowl-O-Mat, Inc., 429 U.S. 477 (1977)
Chicago Board of Trade v. United States, 246 U.S. 231 (1918)
Cieri v. Leticia Query Realty, Inc., 905 P. 2d 29 (Haw. 1995)
Continental T.V., Inc. v. GTE Sylvania, Inc., 433 U.S. 36 (1977)
Federal Trade Commission v. University Health, Inc., 938 F. 2d 1206 (11th Circuit 1991)
Fortner Enterprises, Inc. v. United States Steel Corp., 394 U.S. 495 (1969)
Ford Motor Co. v. United States, 335 U.S. 303 (1948)
FTC v. Procter & Gamble Co., 386 U.S. 568 (1967)
Northern Pacific R. Co. v. United States, 356 U.S. 1 (1958)
Reiter v. Sonotone Corp., 442 U.S. 330 (1979)
Redwood Theatres, Inc. v. Festival Enterprises, Inc., 200 Cal. App. 3d 687 (Ct. App. 1988)
Standard Oil Co. v. United States, 221 U.S. 1 (1911)
Times-Picayune Pub. Co. v. United States, 345 U.S. 594 (1953)
United States v. Aluminum Co. of America (Alcoa), 148 F. 2d 416 (2d Cir. 1945)
United States v. Baker Hughes, Inc., 908 F. 2d 981 (D.C. Cir. 1990)
United States v. Columbia Steel Co., 334 U.S. 495 (1948)
United States v. Citizens & Southern National Bank, 422 U.S. 86 (1975)
United States v. General Dynamics Corp., 415 U.S. 486 (1974)
United States. v. LTV Corp., 1984 WL 21973, 14 (D.D.C. 2 August 1984)
United States v. Marine Bancorporation, Inc., 418 U.S. 602 (1974)
United States v. Falstaff Brewing Corp., 410 U.S. 526 (1973)
United States v. Philadelphia National Bank, 374 U.S. 321 (1963)
United States v. Pabst Brewing Co., 384 U.S. 546 (1966)
United States v. Topco Assocs., Inc., 405 U.S. 596 (1972)
United States v. United States Gypsum Co., 438 U.S. 422 (1978)
United States v. Von's Grocery Co., 384 U.S. 270 (1966)
United States v. Waste Management, Inc., 743 F. 2d 976 (2d Cir. 1984)

EUROPEAN UNION

DECISIONS OF THE EUROPEAN COMMISSION

Abertis/Autostrade (Case No COMP/M 4249) Commission Decision of 22 September 2006
Accor/Wagons-Lits (Case No IV/M 126) Commission Decision of 28 April 1992

Aerospatiale-Alenia/de Havilland (Case No IV/M 053) Commission Decision of 2 October 1991

At&T/NCR (Case No IV/M 050) Commission Decision of 18 January 1991

Bertelsmann/Kirch/Premiere (Case No IV/M 993) Commission Decision of 27 May 1998

British Telecom/MCI (II) (Case No IV/M 856) Commission Decision of 14 May 1997

Danish Crown/Vestjyske Slagterier (Case No IV/M 1313) Commission Decision of 9 March 1999

E.ON/Endesa (Case No COMP/M 4110) Commission Decision of 25 April 2006

Friesland Foods /Campina (COMP/M 5046) Commission Decision of 17 December 2008

Mercedes-Benz/Kässbohrer (Case IV/M 477) Commission Decision of 14 February 1995

MSG Media Service (Case IV/M 469) Commission Decision of 9 November 1994

Nordic Satellite Distribution (Case No IV/M 490) Commission Decision of 24 March 1995

Olympic/Aegean Airlines (Case No COMP/M 5830) Commission Decision of 26 January 2011

Panasonic/Sanyo (Case No COMP/M.5421) Commission Decision of 29 September 2009

Ryanair/Aer Lingus (Case No COMP/M 4439) Commission Decision of 27 June 2007

Schneider/Legrand (Case No COMP/M 2283) Commission Decision of 30 January 2002

Seagate/HDD Business of Samsung (Case No COMP/M 6214) Commission Decision of 19 October 2011

Smith & Nephew/Beiersdorf/JV (Case No COMP/JV 54) Commission Decision of 30 January 2001

Unicredito/HVB (Case No COMP/M 3894) Commission Decision of 18 October 2005

Volvo/Scania (Case No COMP/M 1672) Commission Decision of 14 March 2000

DECISIONS OF THE EUROPEAN COURT OF JUSTICE

Case C-67/96, *Albany International BV v. Stichting Bedrijfspensioenfonds Textielindustrie* [1999] ECR I-5751

Case C-309/99, *J.C.J. Wouters, J. W. Savelbergh and Price Waterhouse Belastingadviseurs BV v. Algemene Raad van de Nederlandse Orde van Advocaten* [2002] ECR I-1577

Case C-289/04 P, *Showa Denko KK v. Commission* [2006] ECR I-5859

Case C-209/10, *Post Danmark A/S v. Konkurrencerådet* [2012] ECR I-0000

Case C-52/09, *Konkurrensverket v. TeliaSonera Sverige AB* [2011] ECR I-527

Case C-95/04 P, *British Airways plc. v. Commission* [2007] ECR I-2331

Case C-62/86, *AKZO Chemie BV v. Commission* [1991] ECR I-3359

Case C-8/08, *T-Mobile Netherlands BV and Others v. Raad van bestuur van de Nederlandse Mededingingsautoriteit* [2009] ECR I-4529

Case T-168/01, *GlaxoSmithKline Services Unlimited v. Commission* [2009] ECR I-9291

Joined Cases T-213/01 and T-214/01, *Österreichische Postsparkasse AG and Bank für Arbeit und Wirtschaft AG v Commission* [2006] ECR II-1601

TABLE OF LEGISLATION

CHINA

Guanyu Kaizhan He Baohu Shehuizhuyi Jingzheng De Zanxing Guiding (关于开展和保护社会主义竞争的暂行规定) [Provisional Rules on the Development and Protection of Socialist Competition] (promulgated by the State Council on 17 October 1980, effective on 17 October 1980, and repealed on 6 October 2001)

Guanyu Jinzhi Gongyong Qiye Xianzhi Jingzheng Xingwei De Ruogan Guiding (关于禁止公用企业限制竞争行为的若干规定) [Certain Regulations on Prohibiting Anti-competitive Practices of Public Enterprises] (promulgated by the State Administration for Industry and Commerce, 24 December 1993, effective on 24 December 1993)

Guanyu Qiye Jianbing De Zanxingbanfa (关于企业兼并的暂行办法) [Provisional Regulation on Mergers and Acquisitions] (promulgated by the State Restructuring Commission, the State Planning Commission, the Ministry of Finance, and the State Administration of State-owned Assets, effective 19 February 1989)

Guowuyuan Guanyu Tuidong Jingjilianhe De Zanxingguiding (国务院关于推动经济联合的暂行规定) [State Council Provisional Regulations on Promoting Economic Coalition] (promulgated by the State Council, effective 1 July 1980]

Guowuyuan Guanyu Jinyibu Tuidong Hengxiang Jingjilianhe Ruoganwenti De Guiding (国务院关于进一步推动横向经济联合若干问题的规定) [State Council Provision Regulations on Enhancing Horizontal Economic Coalition] (promulgated by the State Council, effective 23 March 1986)

Guowuyuan Guanyu Jinzhi Zai Shichang Jingji Huodong Zhong Shixing Diqu Fengsuo De Guiding (国务院关于禁止在市场经济活动中实行地区封锁的规定) [Provisions of the State Council on Prohibiting Regional Blockade in Market Economic Activities] (promulgated by the State Council on 21 April 2001, effective on 21 April 2001)

Guowuyuan Guanyu Zhengdun He Guifan Shichang Jingji Zhixu De Jueding (国务院关于整顿和规范市场经济秩序的决定) [Decisions of the State Council on Rectifying and Standardizing the Order in the Market Economy] (promulgated by the State Council on 27 April 2001, effective on 27 April 2001)

Shangwubu Guanyu Pinggu Jingyingzhe Jizhong Jingzheng Yingxiang De Zanxing Guiding (商务部关于评估经营者集中竞争影响的暂行规定) [Interim Provisions on Assessing the Impact of Concentration of Business Operators on Competition] (issued by the Ministry of Commerce on 29 August 2011, effective on 5 September 2011)

Shangwubu Guanyu Waiguo Touzizhe Binggou Jingnei Qiye De Guiding (商务部关于外国投资者并购境内企业的规定) [Ministry of Commerce PRC on Promulgation of the Provisions on M&A of a Domestic Enterprise by Foreign Investors] (promulgated by the Ministry of Commerce on 22 June 2009, effective on 22 June 2009)

Waiguo Touzizhe Binggou Jingnei Qiye Zanxing Guiding (外国投资者并购境内企业暂行规定) [Interim Provisions for Foreign Investors to Merge Domestic Enterprises] (promulgated by the Ministry of Foreign Trade and Economic Cooperation, the State Administration of Taxation, the State Administration for Industry and Commerce, the State Administration of Foreign Exchange, issued on 7 March 2003, effective on 12 April 2003)

Zhizhi Jiage Longduan Xingwei Zanxing Guiding (制止价格垄断行为暂行规定) [Interim Provisions on Preventing the Acts of Price Monopoly] (promulgated by the State Development and Reform Commission on 18 June 2003, effective on 1 November 2003)

Zhonghua Renmin Gongheguo Fanlongduanfa (中华人民共和国反垄断法) [The Anti-Monopoly Law of the People's Republic of China] (promulgated by the Standing Committee of the National People's Congress on 30 August 2007, effective on 1 August 2008)

Zhonghua Renmin Gongheguo Zhongwai Hezi Jingying Qiyefa Shishi Tiaoli (中华人民共和国中外合资经营企业法实施条例) [Regulations for the Implementation of the Law of the People's Republic of China on Sino-Foreign Equity Joint Ventures] (promulgated by the State Council on 20 September 1983, effective on 20 September 1983)

Zhonghua Renmin Gongheguo Jiage Guanli Tiaoli (中华人民共和国价格管理条例) [Regulations of the People's Republic of China on Price Control] (promulgated by the State Council on 11 September 1987, effective on 11 September 1987)

Zhonghua Renmin Gongheguo Fanbuzhengdangjingzheng Fa (中华人民共和国反不正当竞争法) [Anti-Unfair Competition Law of the People's Republic of China] (promulgated by the Standing Committee of the National People's Congress on 2 September 1993, effective on 2 September 1993)

Zhonghua Renmin Gongheguo Xingzheng Fuyi Fa (中华人民共和国行政复议法) [Administrative Reconsideration Law of the People's Republic of China] (promulgated by the National People's Congress on 29 April 1999, effective on 1 October 1999, revised on 27 August 2009)

Zhonghua Renmin Gongheguo Xingzheng Susong Fa (中华人民共和国行政诉讼法) [Administrative Procedure Law of the People's Republic of China] (promulgated by the National People's Congress on 4 April 1989, effective on 1 October 1990)

Zhonghua Renmin Gongheguo Xiaofeizhe Quanyi Baohu Fa (中华人民共和国消费者权益保护法) [Law of the People's Republic of China on Protection of Consumer Rights and Interests] (promulgated by the Standing Committee of the National People's Congress on 31 October 1993, effective on 1 January 1994, revised on 27 August 2009)

Zhonghua Renmin Gongheguo Duiwai Maoyi Fa (中华人民共和国对外贸易法) [Foreign Trade Law of the People's Republic of China] (promulgated by the Standing Committee of the National People's Congress on 12 May 1994, effective on 1 July 1994, revised on 6 April 2004)

Zhonghua Renmin Gongheguo Shangye Yinhang Fa (中华人民共和国商业银行法) [Law of the People's Republic of China on Commercial Banks] (promulgated by the Standing Committee of the National People's Congress on 10 May 1995, effective on 1 July 1995, amended on 27 December 2003)

Zhonghua Renmin Gongheguo Jiage Fa (中华人民共和国价格法) [Price Law of the
    People's Republic of China] (promulgated by the Standing Committee of the
    National People's Congress on 29 December 1997, effective on 1 May 1998)
Zhonghua Renmin Gongheguo Zhaobiao Toubiao Fa (中华人民共和国招标投标法) [The
    Bidding Law of the People's Republic of China] (promulgated by the Standing
    Committee of the National People's Congress on 30 August 1999, effective on
    1 January 2000)

EU TREATIES, REGULATIONS AND DIRECTIVES

Treaty Establishing the European Economic Community, 25 March 1957, 298 UNTS 3
    (EEC Treaty or Treaty of Rome)
Council Regulation (EEC) No 4064/89 of 21 December 1989 on the Control of
    Concentrations between Undertakings [1989] OJ L 395/1
Council Regulation (EC) No 1310/97 of 30 June 1997 [1997] OJ L 180/1
Council Regulation (EC) No 139/2004 of 20 January 2004 on the Control of
    Concentrations between Undertakings (the EC Merger Regulation) [2004] OJ L 24/1
Council Directive 93/13/EEC of 5 April 1993 on Unfair Terms in Consumer Contracts
    [1993] OJ L 95/29
Directive 2005/29/EC of the European Parliament and of the Council of 11 May 2005
    concerning Unfair Commercial Practices Directive [2005] OJ L 149/22

US LAW

Sherman Antitrust Act, 15 U.S.C. §§1–7
Clayton Act §7, 15 U.S.C §18
The Federal Trade Commission Act of 1914 (codified as amended at 15 U.S.C. §§41–58)

US MERGER GUIDELINES

US Department of Justice, 1968 Merger Guidelines
US Department of Justice, 1982 Merger Guidelines
US Department of Justice, 1984 Merger Guidelines
US Department of Justice and the Federal Trade Commission, 1992 Horizontal Merger
    Guidelines (revised in April 1997)
US Department of Justice and the Federal Trade Commission, 2010 Horizontal Merger
    Guidelines

LIST OF ABBREVIATIONS

AAG	Assistant Attorney General
AIDS	Almost Ideal Demand System
AML	Anti-Monopoly Law
AMC	Anti-Monopoly Commission
CJV	Contractual Joint Venture
CCP	Chinese Communist Party
CLB	Cylindrical Lithium Batteries
CNPC	China National Petroleum Corporation
CPCC	China Petroleum & Chemical Corporation
CR	Concentration Ratio
DOJ	Department of Justice
ECMR	European Community Merger Regulation
EU	European Union
ECJ	European Court of Justice
ECSC	European Coal and Steel Community
EEA	European Economic Area
EEC	European Economic Community
EJV	Equity Joint Venture
FDI	Foreign Direct Investment
FIJSC	Foreign Invested Joint-Stock Company
FTC	Foreign Trade Commission
HDD	Hard Disk Drive
HHI	Herfindahl-Hirschman Index
HMT	Hypothetical Monopolist Test
ICN	International Competition Network
M&A	Merger and Acquisitions
MOFCOM	Ministry of Commerce
MOFTEC	Ministry of Foreign Trade and Economic Cooperation
MII	Ministry of Information and Industry
NDRC	National Development and Reform Commission
NiMH	Nickel Metal Hydride
NPC	National People's Congress
OECD	Organization for Economic Cooperation and Development
O.J.	Official Journal of the European Communities
PCAIDS	Proportionality-Calibrated AIDS

PRC	People's Republic of China
R&D	Research and Development
RMB	Renminbi (Chinese currency)
SAIC	State Administration of Industry and Commerce
SASAC	State Assets Supervision and Administration Commission
SAT	State Administration of Taxation
SAFE	State Administration of Foreign Exchange
SCP	Structure-Conduct-Performance
SETC	State Economic and Trade Commission
SME	Small and Medium-Sized Enterprises
SSNIP	Small but Significant and Non-Transitory Increase in Price
SOE	State-Owned Enterprises
TEU	Treaty on the European Union
TEC	Treaty on the European Community
TFEU	Treaty on the Functioning of the European Union
TVE	Township and Village Enterprises
USD	US Dollar
US	United States of America
UPP	Upward Pressure on Price
UNCTAD	United Nations Conference on Trade and Development
WFOE	Wholly Foreign-Owned Enterprises
WTO	World Trade Organization

LIST OF TABLES AND FIGURES

TABLES

FIGURES

CHAPTER 1

INTRODUCTION

1.   INTRODUCTION

After thirteen years of discussion, on 30 August 2007, the Anti-Monopoly Law of
the People's Republic of China ('AML') was promulgated by the 29th session of
the 10th Standing Committee of China's National People's Congress, and this law
came into force on 1 August 2008.[1]

Although China is not the first developing country to adopt a competition
law, there are several reasons which make this AML special. Given China's
incomparable level of involvement in international trading and investment, the
enactment of the AML raised the interest of both scholars and entrepreneurs
around the globe.[2] More importantly, differing from antitrust laws in many
jurisdictions, the AML plays an important role in laying the legal foundations
for a socialist market economy. This function gives the AML a challenging role
to play in balancing promoting competition with maintaining State control over
strategic industries.[3] This challenge not only delayed the drafting process of this
law, but also posed a few difficulties to the implementation of the AML.[4]

The merger policy under the AML can be used as an example to illustrate
this challenge. Prior to 1978, China remained a centrally controlled economy. In
1978, a market reform was launched to transform the centrally planned system

---

[1]   Zhonghua Renmin Gongheguo Fanlongduanfa (中华人民共和国反垄断法) [The Anti-
      Monopoly Law of the People's Republic of China] (promulgated by the Standing Committee
      of the National People's Congress, 30 August 2007, effective 1 August 2008), available at
      <www.gov.cn/flfg/2007–08/30/content_732591.htm> (in Chinese) and <http://english.
      peopledaily.com.cn/90001/90776/90785/6466798.html> (in English) accessed 28.03.2014.
[2]   H.S. HARRIS JR. (2006), 'The Making of an Antitrust Law: The Pending Anti-Monopoly Law
      of the People's Republic of China', *Chicago Journal of International Law*, vol. 7, p. 169;
      X. ZHANG and V.Y. ZHANG (2007), 'The Anti-Monopoly Law in China: Where Do We Stand?',
      Competition Policy International, vol. 3, no. 2, p. 185; for a comprehensive discussion of the
      substantive and implementation issues of the AML, *see* M. FAURE and X. ZHANG (eds.),
      Competition Policy and Regulation, Recent Developments in China, the US and Europe,
      Edward Elgar 2011; M. FAURE and X. ZHANG (eds.), *The Chinese Anti-Monopoly Law, New
      Developments and Empirical Evidence*, Edward Elgar 2013.
[3]   Y. HUANG (2008), 'Pursuing the Second Best: The History, Momentum and Remaining Issues
      of China's Anti-monopoly Law', *Antitrust Law Journal*, vol. 75, p. 119.
[4]   Y. HUANG (2008), *supra* n. 3, p. 119.

to a market economy.[5] In 1993, the goal of this market reform was clarified as to establish a 'socialist market economy'.[6] Policy makers in China learnt that competition laws in developed economies play an important role in supporting a market economy as well as in contributing to the economic development.[7] Therefore, the drafting process of a competition law in China started in 1993. However, it remained a debatable issue among Chinese scholars and policy makers with respect to the goal of the merger policy under the AML. One widespread view was against the promulgation of a merger law to regulate mergers between domestic enterprises.[8] The reason for this was that compared with multinational firms, these Chinese firms were still small, fragmented and often engaged in an 'excessive competition'.[9] The primary goal of the merger policy, it was claimed, was not to prohibit concentration; rather it was to consolidate small companies, and to establish more powerful companies in order to compete in the global market.[10] By contrast, seeing the increase in mergers and acquisitions by foreign investors, it was argued that a merger policy should be applied to regulate foreign investments which would affect national interests and national security.[11] As a result, there was a tension over the understanding of the function of the AML: on the one hand, there was the willingness to enforce the AML towards foreign investors; and on the other hand, there was a reluctance to apply this law towards domestic firms.

This tension has had two results. The first result is that the goal of the AML became ambiguous. The language of the AML tends to include a multitude of policy goals, with unclear definitions for each goal. Article 1 of the AML includes five objectives, namely, restraining monopolistic behavior, protecting

---

5   Zhongguo Gongchandang Dishiyijie Zhongyangweiyuanhui Disanci Quantihuiyi Gongbao (中国共产党第十一届中央委员会第三次全体会议公报) [Communiqué of the Third Plenary Session of the 11th Central Committee of the CPC] (adopted at the Third Plenary Session of the 11th Central Committee of the Communist Party of China on 22 December 1978), available at <http://news.xinhuanet.com/ziliao/2005–02/05/content_2550304.htm> (in Chinese) accessed 03.04.2014.

6   Zhonggongzhongyang Guanyu Jianli Shehuizhuyi Shichangjingjitizhi Ruoganwenti De Jueding (中共中央关于建立社会主义市场经济体制若干问题的决定) [Decision of the Central Committee of the Communist Party of China on a Number of Issues about the Establishment of the Socialist Market Economy] (adopted by the Third Plenary Session of the 14th Central Committee of the Communist Party of China on 14 November 1993), available at <http://cpc.people.com.cn/GB/64162/134902/8092314.html> (in Chinese) accessed 03.04.2014.

7   D.J. GERBER (2008), 'Economics, Law and Institutions: The Shaping of Chinese Competition Law', Journal of Law and Policy, vol. 26, p. 282; B.M. OWEN, S. SUN and W. ZHENG (2008), 'China's Competition Policy Reforms: The Anti-monopoly Law and Beyond', Antitrust Law Journal, vol. 75, p. 232.

8   B.M. OWEN, S. SUN and W. ZHENG (2008), supra n. 7, p. 247.

9   B.M. OWEN, S. SUN and W. ZHENG (2008), supra n. 7, p. 247.

10   B.M. OWEN, S. SUN and W. ZHENG (2008), supra n. 7, p. 249.

11   B.M. OWEN, S. SUN and W. ZHENG (2008), supra n. 7, p. 253 ('[u]nlike all of the controversial topics surrounding the debates on the AML, the necessity of limiting entry by foreign companies in key sectors is one of the few concepts on which China's policymakers have a near consensus.').

competition, promoting efficiency, protecting consumers' interests and public social interests, as well as contributing to the development of a socialist market economy. It is not clear, for example, whether the concept of the 'public interest' includes the interests of certain business operators.[12] In addition, Article 5 of the AML gives permission to mergers which aim at achieving economies of scale. Article 7 protects the State-controlled industries that are 'crucial for national economy and national security'. Article 31 of the AML requires concentrations initiated by foreign investors to undertake an additional test to examine the effects of that concentration on national security.

The second outcome is that economic analysis may only play a minor role in the decision of antitrust cases. Other policy goals, besides economic goals, may have to be taken into account, which would make the enforcement of the AML more uncertain.[13] For example, it has been criticized that the decision of the *Coca-Cola/Huiyuan* case was influenced by the concern of national interest and other political considerations, not solely based on competition theories.[14]

2. MOTIVATION

I have been fascinated by the discussion of the AML since I was a bachelor's student in Beijing. The research that I conducted during my master's study in Germany on the topic of comparative competition policy gave me a strong impression that this topic deserves a more comprehensive study by taking a multidisciplinary perspective. Therefore, I attempt to explore this topic by using a law and economics approach. Among all the fascinating issues of competition policy in China, I specifically focus on the Chinese merger control policy and I choose to compare this policy with the ones in the US and the EU.

There are two reasons for choosing the Chinese merger control policy as a research topic. The first reason is that the concern of regulating mergers by foreign investors in order to protect national interest is one of the most important driving forces for drafting the AML.[15] Ever since China started its market reform in 1978, the debate on the extent to which foreign investment should be allowed has continued. It was a widespread argument that foreign takeovers which will affect national interests should be prohibited and an antitrust law

---

[12] X. Wang (2008), 'Highlights of China's New Anti-Monopoly Law', *Antitrust Law Journal*, vol. 75, p. 142.

[13] B.M. Owen, S. Sun, and W. Zheng (2005), 'Antitrust in China: The Problem of Incentive Compatibility Antitrust in China', *Journal of Competition Law and Economics*, vol. 1, no. 1, p. 132; S.B. Farmer (2013), 'Recent Developments in Regulation and Competition Policy in China: Trends in Private Civil Litigation', in M. Faure and X. Zhang (eds.) *The Chinese Anti-Monopoly Law, New Developments and Empirical Evidence*, Edward Elgar 2013, p. 16.

[14] See discussion in Chapter 5.

[15] Y. Huang (2008), *supra* n. 3, p. 123.

would be the appropriate instrument for the authority to use.[16] By contrast, competition rules towards domestic enterprises should only be applied for the purpose of supporting them to fight against the powerful multinationals.[17] As the drafting process of this AML was deeply influenced by the progress of the market reform, the development of merger policies in China, including the ones before the enactment of the AML, shows to what extent foreign investment is welcomed. Therefore, the study of Chinese merger control policy is a critical starting point for understanding why the AML was enacted in China and what the goals of this law are. It is also the perspective to understand how this competition law in China is different from those in other jurisdictions.

The second reason is that after the enactment of the AML, among all the competition issues, merger policy has most effectively and frequently been enforced in practice. Shortly after this law came into force on 1 August 2008, a specialized office (MOFCOM) was immediately established. Following Chapter 4 of the AML, the MOFCOM implemented several guidelines which provided specific criteria to examine and to investigate concentrations between undertakings. The study of policy goals in Chapter 3 and Chapter 4 therefore provides a useful tool to understand the decisions of the published merger cases. The comparison between these decisions will draw a picture of how competition goals may affect merger analysis in the US, the EU and China.

3. RESEARCH QUESTION

As many scholars have argued,[18] one of the most critical issues concerning the development of an effective legal framework for market competition in China is identifying the ultimate aims that the AML strives to achieve. Moreover, the specific competition goals in China may also be an important starting point to understand the differences between merger policy in China and in other jurisdictions. In this book, I focus on the impact of competition goals on merger policy in the US, the EU and China. The hypothesis of the research is that the implementation of merger policy can be strongly influenced by competition goals. This hypothesis will be tested by reviewing the antitrust history in the US and the EU, as well as by investigating empirical evidence and merger cases. The central research question is: by comparing merger policy in the US, the EU and

---

16   Y. HUANG (2008), *supra* n. 3, p. 123.
17   Y. HUANG (2008), *supra* n. 3, p. 118.
18   For a discussion why policy goals are of primary importance in antitrust analysis, *see* R. VAN DEN BERGH and P.D. CAMESASCA, *European Competition Law and Economics, A Comparative Perspective*, Thomson/Sweet & Maxwell 2006; R. VAN DEN BERGH (2006), 'The Economics of Competition Policy and the Draft of the Chinese Competition Law' in T. EGER, M. FAURE and N. ZHANG (eds.), *Economic Analysis of Law in China*, Edward Elgar 2006; *See also* M. FAURE and X. ZHANG (eds.) (2011), *supra* n. 2.

China, what are the impacts of competition goals on merger policy? This research question will be investigated by taking four steps and each step is composed of one chapter. The first step (Chapter 2) is to understand the legislative history of the AML in China and to understand the specific competition goals in China. The second step (Chapter 3) is to investigate the debate on antitrust goals and to answer the question: what are the competition goals in the US and the EU. The third step (Chapter 4) is to focus on merger policy and to investigate how the efficiency goal has been incorporated in merger policy in the US and the EU. By applying the theoretical analysis in these three chapters, the last step of the investigation (Chapter 5) is to focus on the impact of competition goals on merger cases. The ultimate goal of this research is to understand Chinese merger policy from the perspective of competition goals, as well as to draw lessons for Chinese competition policy makers by learning from the experiences in the US and the EU.

The central research question will be discussed by following a few sub-questions in each chapter. As goals of merger policy are to a large extent influenced by the goal of antitrust law, the investigation will start by reviewing the debate on antitrust goals in the US and the EU. After presenting the debate on antitrust goals, particular attention will be paid to how the efficiency goal has been incorporated into merger policy. In the last part of this book, the theoretical findings will be applied in order to discuss to what extent different goals may lead to a different outcome of merger cases. Given the importance of competition goals, this book will conclude by suggesting policy implications for competition policy makers in China.

The sub-questions that will be answered in the following chapters include:

(1) How has the debate on antitrust goals in the US evolved from the early 20th century until today?
(2) How did law and economic scholars (in particular the Harvard School and the Chicago School scholars) perceive the goals of competition and how did these arguments influence court decisions?
(3) How did Ordoliberalism influence EU competition law?
(4) What are the major differences between competition goals in the US and the EU?
(5) How did the US Horizontal Merger Guidelines and the EU Merger Regulation incorporate the efficiency goal?
(6) Will competition goals affect the analysis of merger cases and will different competition goals lead to different merger case decisions in the US, the EU and China?

4. STRUCTURE

This book is composed of six chapters. After the introduction, the second chapter summarizes the drafting process of the Anti-Monopoly Law and the merger policy in China. This chapter focuses on the historical background of the market reform in China and attempts to explain why the Anti-Monopoly Law was enacted to pursue a multitude of policy goals. From a positive perspective, the drafting process of the AML in China shows that goals of the AML have been affected by several factors. In particular, the AML has been deeply influenced by the stage of the economic and political development of the society. Concerning goals of the merger policy in China, the study shows that there is a tension between the goal of supporting domestic firms and the goal of regulating foreign investors. I will conduct a positive study to investigate why this tension exists and how this tension has been reflected in the AML and in the merger policies. The objective of the positive study is to explain why the AML and the merger policy in China include multiple goals and whether the language of the AML and of the merger guidelines reflect various social and political goals. From a normative perspective, I will investigate how these goals were understood by Chinese and international scholars, as well as by policy makers in China, and according to their opinions, whether incorporating various non-economic goals in the AML is desirable for China.

The third chapter conducts a theoretical study and attempts to present the discussion of antitrust policy goals in the US and the EU. In the US, the evolution of the debate on antitrust goals led by populism, the Harvard School, and the Chicago School will be discussed respectively. The debate on antitrust goals in the US shows that there was an evolution of switching from social and political goals towards economic goals. However, a consensus has not been reached among US scholars regarding whether the consumer welfare standard or the total welfare standard should be prioritized. With respect to competition goals in the EU, this chapter will first discuss how Ordoliberal thinking has influenced the formulation of the EU competition policy in the 1950s. This chapter will also discuss how competition goals have been incorporated in the treaties, and how these goals have been interpreted by the Competition Commissioners.

In the fourth chapter, I focus on the influence of policy goals on merger policies in the US and the EU, and will investigate how the efficiency goal has been incorporated in merger analysis. In economic theory, efficiencies that a merger could generate can be divided into productive efficiency, allocative efficiency, and dynamic efficiency. However, these three types of efficiency may conflict with each other and can therefore not be achieved at the same time. Moreover, the Williamson tradeoff diagram developed in 1968 shows that a merger could be decided differently by taking a total welfare standard, or by taking a consumer welfare standard. This chapter discusses how the economic goal, in particular the efficiency goal, has been incorporated in the merger policy in the US and the EU.

The fifth chapter applies the findings of Chapter 3 and Chapter 4, and focuses on the question of whether competition goals will indeed matter in merger analysis, and if so, what the impact of competition goals is on merger cases. This chapter will take economic theories and modern economic techniques as the benchmark, in order to compare how competition authorities in the US, the EU and China apply economic techniques to merger analysis. It will first present an overview of the merger decisions published by the MOFCOM, and will discuss the main features of these cases. To deepen the analysis, in the following sections, the differences in merger analysis between the US, the EU and China will be discussed by investigating the empirical evidence and by conducting a comparative case study. This chapter will also discuss to what extent competition goals would matter in merger analysis. The last chapter will conclude, and will provide a few policy implications.

5.   METHODOLOGY

The methodology of this research is multidisciplinary. It investigates the historical debate on the goals of antitrust law by taking a law and economics perspective. The reason for focusing on the economic analysis of antitrust law is that the evolution of the goals of competition law and policy is to a large extent driven by the development of the economic theory.[19] At a theoretical level, the models of 'competition' and 'monopoly', which have been employed in antitrust statutes, are the inventions of economists, not sociologists or politicians.[20] In practice, competition law is one of the major legal domains which has been dramatically influenced by economic theories. This trend can best be illustrated by the fact that in the US, every major antitrust casebook includes an author with PhD training in economics.[21] Moreover, in the US, since the implementation of the Horizontal Merger Guidelines in 1968, economics experts

---

[19]   As Bork said, '[a]ntitrust is, first and most obviously, law, and law made primarily by judges... Antitrust is also a set of continually evolving theories about the economics of industrial organization'. R.H. BORK, *The Antitrust Paradox: A Policy at War with Itself*, Basic Books 1978, p. 10.

[20]   *See* R.H. BORK (1967), 'The Goals of Antitrust Policy', *American Economic Review*, vol. 57, no. 2, p. 245.

[21]   For example, P. AREEDA and L. KAPLOW, *Antitrust Analysis, Problems, Text, Cases*, 6th ed., Aspen Publishers 2004; A.I. GAVIL, W.E. KOVACIC and J.B. BAKER, *Antitrust Law in Perspective: Cases, Concepts and Problems in Competition Policy*, 2nd ed., West 2008; E.T. SULLIVAN, H. HOVENKAMP and H.A. SHELANSKI, *Antitrust Law, Policy and Procedures: Cases, Materials and Problems*, 6th ed., LexisNexis 2009. *See* R.D. BLAIR and D.D. SOKOL (2013), 'Welfare Standards in U.S. and E.U. Antitrust Enforcement', *Fordham Law Review*, vol. 81, p. 118.

have actively cooperated with lawyers in the analysis of merger effects.[22] In Europe, law and economics scholars have also applied an integrated approach to investigate competition law from an economic perspective.[23] In recent years, economic arguments have to a large extent been accepted by the Commission and the European Court of Justice in merger analysis.[24]

For this reason, this research focuses on the debate on the goals of competition law among law and economics scholars, for example, the Harvard School and the Chicago School in the US, and the Ordoliberal scholars in Europe. The analysis is centered on the question of how economic goals can be integrated in antitrust law. The issue of how to interpret such concepts as 'competition', 'welfare' and 'efficiency' from an economic perspective has also been addressed.

In addition, this research embodies two dimensions in its analysis: horizontally, it compares the competition policy in the US, the EU and China; vertically, it compares competition policy from the early 20th to the early 21st century. Naturally, given the scope of this research, it will not give a full overview of all the details. It will focus on the historical events and will provide a critical analysis of how the understanding of competition policy has evolved over time and across jurisdictions. The contribution of this comparative analysis is that it gives an unbiased explanation of the issue of implementing merger control policy in China. As a philosopher once said, 'Life can only be understood backwards; but it must be lived forwards';[25] thus studying the history of antitrust might be the best way for antitrust decision makers in China to understand their puzzles and doubts, and to prepare themselves to take up future challenges.

6.   LIMITATIONS

Given the scope of this research, there are a few limitations that are worth mentioning. The first limitation is that it particularly focuses on horizontal mergers. In theory, there are three types of merger: horizontal mergers, vertical mergers and conglomerate mergers. Horizontal mergers refer to the merger between two or more firms that operate at the same level and produce the same or substitutable products, for example, between manufacturers or between

---

[22]   J.E. Kwoka, Jr. and L.J. White, *The Antitrust Revolution, Economics, Competition and Policy*, 4th ed., Oxford University Press 2004, p. 2.

[23]   R.J. Van den Bergh and P.D. Camesasca (2006), *supra* n. 18.

[24]   *See* discussion in Chapter 4, section 5.3.2.

[25]   This is quoted from the Danish philosopher Søren Aabye Kierkegaard in S. Kierkegaard (1843), *Journalen JJ:167. See* S. Kierkegaard, *Soren Kierkegaards Skrifter 18 Journalerne EE FF GG HH JJ KK*, Gads Forlag 2001; *see also* R.A. Skitol (1999), 'The Shifting Sands of Antitrust Policy: Where it Has Been, Where it is Now, Where it Will be in its Third Century', *Cornell Journal of Law and Public Policy*, vol. 9, p. 266.

wholesalers. This type of merger occurs between two competitors in the given product and geographical market. Vertical mergers refer to the merger between firms in the same market but at different levels of production, such as a merger between a manufacturer and a supplier of the raw material or product components. The relationship between these two merging firms is usually complementary.[26] Conglomerate mergers are defined as mergers between undertakings in different markets. This type of merger will not reduce the number of competitors, but would increase the scale of the undertakings and make market entry more difficult for smaller companies.

This research focuses on horizontal mergers for the reason that horizontal mergers are the most frequent in the US, the EU and China; therefore, the effects of horizontal mergers are more easily comparable. In addition, the comparative study in this book focuses on substantive issues, and does not compare the procedures in merger review. This is because policy goals may have less influence on the procedure than on the substantive issues involved in merger control.

The second limitation of this research is that the selection of literature focuses on the evolution of antitrust thinking among law and economics scholars on competition policy goals. However, given the long history of the development of competition theory and the enforcement of antitrust law in the US and the EU, a rich literature has been developed in the field of both competition law and industrial economics. By taking a law and economics approach, this research gives primary attention to the influence of the Harvard School, the Chicago School, and the Ordoliberal School. Among the broad concepts in competition theory, this research focuses on the concept of efficiency. The interpretations of the legislative history and the development of competition policy in the US and the EU are largely based on the scholarly work of American and European scholars.

Nevertheless, to determine the goal of antitrust policy is an extremely broad topic. Throughout antitrust history, scholars and judges have attempted to approach this question from various perspectives, for example the perspectives of why it is necessary to enact an antitrust law, what the functions of an antitrust law are, how the function of an antitrust law can be understood, and more generally, how the concept of 'competition' can be interpreted from both a scientific and a practical view. Therefore, the comparative study that this research will conduct is only limited to the scope of the theoretical debate between law and economics scholars, and to what extent this debate has influenced court decisions. This debate focuses on how economic analysis can be integrated and whether an antitrust law should prioritize economic goals. The purpose of presenting this debate, however, is not to investigate the details of over one hundred years of antitrust history; instead, it is only to argue that the

---

[26] A. JONES and B. SUFRIN, *EU Competition Law, Texts, Cases and Materials*, 4th ed., Oxford University Press 2010.

choice of policy goals will be important for establishing an effective competition system in China.

In addition, a few limits for the discussion in this book concerning competition goals should be mentioned. First, this research does not attempt to make a judgment on which goals should be prioritized and which goals are more desirable from a normative view. The author holds the opinion that to give a normative judgment on the goals of competition law requires a neutral benchmark and the choice of this criterion is dependent upon the purpose or objectives of the research. This study attempts to draw conclusions on the influence of competition goals on merger policy by taking a comparative view. However, the normative question of whether the choice of goals in one jurisdiction is desirable is beyond the discussion. Second, the perspective of policy goals is only one way to explain the differences between competition laws in different jurisdictions. Moreover, this research does not aim to provide an explanation of the question of why these differences exist. The hypothesis of this research is only that the goal of merger policy can be counted as one of the reasons for these differences. Third, the enforcement of merger policy in different jurisdictions is affected by several factors. The prediction of merger cases would be particularly challenging when there is a conflict between the competition goals that are mentioned in the law and the goals that the enforcement agency is willing to pursue in a particular case. Although this book attempts to draw a conclusion that the choice of competition goals may affect the analysis of merger cases, to predict how merger cases would be decided will require further research.

CHAPTER 2

THE DEVELOPMENT OF
COMPETITION LAW AND MERGER
CONTROL POLICY IN CHINA

1.   INTRODUCTION

After 13 years of discussion, the Anti-Monopoly Law of the People's Republic of China ('AML') was promulgated on 30 August 2007[27] and entered into force in August 2008. A first look at the AML and its merger rules gives the impression that the enactment of the AML is based on the foreign influence.[28] In particular, the language of the AML sounds similar to EU competition law.[29] The AML in China also deals with abuse of dominant position, monopolistic agreements and concentrations. However, several implementation issues arise when this law is investigated in a more careful manner. There is probably no other law in China that has been negotiated for more than a decade before approval,[30] with the drafting of the AML taking 13 years. The legislative process of this law coincided with the market reform in China, which aims at establishing a market economy.[31] Therefore, the AML not only establishes the legal foundations for a competitive market, but also fulfills several social goals, such as the protection of the public interest and the pursuit of a socialist market economy. The tension between different policy goals makes the enforcement of the AML and the

---

[27]   This law was promulgated by the 29th session of the 10th Standing Committee of China's National People's Congress on 30 August 2007.

[28]   D.J. GERBER (2008), *supra* n. 7, p. 281; p. 284.

[29]   D. WEI (2011), 'China's Anti-monopoly Law and Its Merger Enforcement: Convergence and Flexibility', *Journal of International Economic Law*, vol. 14, no. 4, p. 812; *see also* D.J. GERBER (2008), *supra* n. 7, p. 289; Y.J. JUNG and Q. HAO (2003) 'The New Economic Constitution in China: A Third Way for Competition Regime?', *Northwestern Journal of International Law and Business*, vol. 24, p. 124; J.R. SAMUELS (2007), '"Tain't What You Do" Effect of China's Propsed Anti-Monopoly Law on State Owned Enterprises', *Pennsylvania State International Law Review*, vol. 26, p. 184; W. ZHENG (2010), 'Transplanting Antitrust in China: Economic Transition, Market Structure and State Control', *University of Pennsylvania Journal of International Law*, vol. 32, no. 2, p. 648.

[30]   D. WEI (2011), *supra* n. 29, p. 809; *see also* Y. HUANG (2008), *supra* n. 3, p. 118.

[31]   D. WEI (2013), 'Antitrust in China: An Overview of Recent Implementation of Anti-Monopoly Law', *European Business Organization Law Review*, vol. 14, no. 1, March 2013, p. 120.

---

merger policy more ambiguous. Since its enactment, there has been a considerable debate over how this law could be effectively implemented.[32]

This chapter discusses how the development of competition policy and merger control rules in China has been affected by the concerns of policy goals. The main finding of this chapter is that merger rules in China tend to incorporate two different goals for domestic companies and for foreign investors. For mergers between domestic firms, the goal of the merger rules is to consolidate the small firms in order to encourage them to compete with international companies on a global market. This is because one important concern among the Chinese legislators and scholars at that time was that domestic enterprises were still small and fragmented; hence it would not be necessary to apply merger rules to fight against concentrations as they were not powerful enough to compete with multinationals.[33] Moreover, it was even argued that promoting competition for non State-owned, small and medium-sized enterprises would not be needed, because the problem for small and medium-sized enterprises in China was that the 'excessive competition' between them, which leads to the destructive results of repetitive investments.[34]

In addition, it was argued that another goal that the AML should pursue was to contribute to the establishment of a socialist market economy. This function would require the State to have a dominant control over strategic industries.[35] For this reason, in the 1980s, mergers between State-owned enterprises ('SOEs') were often led by the State and guided by administrative regulations.[36] Moreover,

---

[32]   R. Van den Bergh and M. Faure (2011), 'Critical Issues in the Enforcement of the Anti-Monopoly Law in China: A Law and Economics Perspective', in M. Faure and X. Zhang (eds.), *Competition Policy and Regulation, Recent Developments in China, the US and Europe*, Edward Elgar, pp. 54–72.

[33]   Y. Huang (2008), *supra* n. 3, p. 118.

[34]   B.M. Owen, S. Sun and W. Zheng (2005), *supra* n. 13, p. 132.

[35]   Y. Huang (2008), *supra* n. 3, p. 119; p. 127.

[36]   For example, Guowuyuan Guanyu Tuidong Jingjilianhe De Zanxingguiding (国务院关于推动经济联合的暂行规定) [State Council Provisional Regulations on Promoting Economic Coalition] (promulgated by the State Council, effective on 1 July 1980), available at <http://law.people.com.cn/showdetail.action?id=2598297> (in Chinese) accessed 04.04.2014; Guowuyuan Guanyu Jinyibu Tuidong Hengxiang Jingjilianhe Ruoganwenti De Guiding (国务院关于进一步推动横向经济联合若干问题的规定) [State Council Provision Regulations on Enhancing Horizontal Economic Coalition] (promulgated by the State Council, effective on 23 March 1986), available at <http://news.xinhuanet.com/ziliao/2005–02/06/content_2554208.htm> (in Chinese) accessed 04.04.2014; Guanyu Qiye Jianbing De Zanxingbanfa (关于企业兼并的暂行办法) [Provisional Regulation on Mergers and Acquisitions] (promulgated by the State Restructuring Commission, the State Planning Commission, the Ministry of Finance, and the State Administration of State-owned Assets, effective on 19 February 1989), available at <http://law.lawtime.cn/d599827604921.html> (in Chinese), accessed 04.04.2014. *See also* B. Song (1995), 'Competition Policy in a Transitional Economy: The Case of China', *Stanford Journal of International Law*, vol. 31, p. 397. These regulations did not mention the pro-competition or anti-competitive effects of mergers, nor did they separate horizontal mergers, vertical mergers and conglomerate mergers. *See* B. Song (1995), p. 399; The translation of these regulations is based on S.K. Mehra and Y. Meng (2009),

in the 1990s, concentrations between SOEs were strongly encouraged by the government, as it was believed that mergers would facilitate market integration as well as increase economies of scale.[37] Given this reason, it is unclear how the AML will be applied to SOEs in State-regulated industries.[38] Notably, the AML has granted several exemptions for SOEs, and listed 'contributing to the development of the socialist market economy' as one of its goals.[39]

For foreign investors, legislators in China attempted to implement merger rules to regulate transactions which would have negative impact on national interest and national security.[40] The reason for this goal is that after the 1978 market reform and China's entry into the World Trade Organization ('WTO') in 2002, foreign investment in China has dramatically increased. Both the public and the lawmakers held the opinion that foreign investment might be over-concentrated, and that their dominant control of national assets in certain industries might affect national economic interests.[41] Moreover, as domestic companies were still small and inefficient, policy makers in China were also concerned that international competitors would drive local companies out of business.[42]

These two opposing attitudes towards mergers between foreign companies and domestic enterprises were among the most debated issues during the drafting process of the AML.[43] There is a clear tension between these two forces: on the one hand, there is the willingness to enforce the merger policy for foreign investors, and on the other hand, there is the reluctance to apply competition rules to domestic firms.[44] To find a solution, the goals of the AML were formed in an ambiguous way by incorporating several social and political goals. For example, Article 5 of the AML permits business operators to merge for the purpose of achieving economies of scale. This article reveals the first concern of encouraging SOEs to grow more powerful and to compete with multinationals.[45]

[ ] 'Against Antitrust Functionalism: Reconsidering China's Anti-Monopoly Law', *Virginia Journal International Law,* vol. 49, p. 388.

[37] Y.J. JUNG and Q. HAO (2003), *supra* n. 29, p. 150.

[38] Y. HUANG (2008), *supra* n. 3, p. 127.

[39] AML, Art. 1.

[40] Y. HUANG (2008), *supra* n. 3, p. 123; Wu stated that when the AML draft was reviewed by the Standing Committee of the 10th National People's Congress, many of the members at the Standing Committee argued that the AML should serve as a legal instrument to prevent foreign investments from affecting national security in China. Z. WU (2008), 'Perspectives on the Chinese Anti-monopoly Law', *Antitrust Law Journal,* vol. 75, p. 101.

[41] Y. HUANG (2008), *supra* n. 3, p. 129; B.M. OWEN, S. SUN and W. ZHENG (2008), *supra* n. 7, p. 252.

[42] J.A. BERRY (2005), 'Anti-Monopoly Law in China: A Socialist Market Economy Wrestles with Its Antitrust Regime', *International Law and Management Review,* vol. 2, p. 144.

[43] B.M. OWEN, S. SUN and W. ZHENG (2008), *supra* n. 7, p. 232; L. HAN (2004), 'The Opportunity to Establish a Competition System – Foreign M&A as the External Pressure for the AML' (创建反垄断制度的契机–对外资并购催生我国反垄断法的思考), *International Trade* (国际贸易), no. 1, p. 45.

[44] B.M. OWEN, S. SUN and W. ZHENG (2005), *supra* n. 13, p. 132.

[45] Y. HUANG (2008), *supra* n. 3, p. 129.

Article 7 of the AML reveals the second concern of protecting SOEs in the industries which are 'crucial for national security and national economy'.[46] Article 31 of the AML reveals the concern of regulating foreign investors. According to this article, an additional examination on national security may be applied for concentrations which include foreign investors.[47]

The central message that this chapter attempts to convey is that the formulation of the competition law and the merger policy in China is affected by the concerns of policy goals. In the positive study, this chapter attempts to give an answer to the question of why the AML contains a multitude of policy goals and how they have been incorporated into competition and merger policy in China. In the normative study, this chapter will also summarize how scholars and policy makers in China interpret the competition goals that have been included in the AML. The debate shows that from a normative perspective, scholars, legislators and policy makers in China have different opinions on the goal of competition policy in China.

The structure of this chapter is as follows. After the introduction, the remaining sections can be divided into three parts. The first two parts will conduct a positive study and the last part is the normative study. The first part (sections 2–4) will present the background and history of merger policy in China, in order to answer the question of why merger policy in China consists of different goals. The discussion focuses on how these two different attitudes were developed since the market reform in 1978. Section 2 will first introduce the market reform that started from 1978. The third and fourth sections will discuss the merger policy towards domestic firms (section 3) and towards foreign investors (section 4). The second part of the chapter (sections 5–6) discusses how various competition goals are reflected in the competition policy. Section 5 presents an overview of the competition law and the merger policy in China, including the Chinese competition policy before the AML, an overview of the AML, the enforcement of the AML and the guidelines implemented after the enactment of the AML. Section 6 analyzes how different goals are reflected in the AML and in other merger guidelines. The last part (section 7) presents the debate on the competition goals of the AML among Chinese and international scholars, and Chinese legislators and policy makers. Section 8 concludes.

2. THE 1978 MARKET REFORM

Shortly after the ten-year 'cultural revolution', and upon seeing the importance of participating in the international market, China initiated the 'reform and opening up policy' after the Third Plenary Session of the Eleventh Central

---

[46]   Art. 7, AML.
[47]   Art. 31, AML.

Committee of the Communist Party of China in December 1978. The central government had decided to change the economic structure, not only by transferring a controlled economy to a market mechanism internally, which is included in the 'reform' element, but also by opening the borders to participate in international trade, which is referred to as 'opening up'. This transition started by generating incentives for developing agriculture, establishing economic zones with special industry policy to attract foreign investment and relaxing the strict control over SOEs. From 1978 to 1992, a carefully planned economy and a limited level of market openness coexisted.[48] In October 1992, the 14th National Congress of the Chinese Communist Party clarified that the goal of the 1978 Market Reform is to establish a 'socialist market economy'.[49] The concept of 'socialist market economy' was formally incorporated in the amendment to the Constitution of the People's Republic of China ('PRC') on 29 March 1993.[50]

Before the 1978 Market Reform, the Chinese economy was organized through a system of national planning.[51] SOEs, which played a dominant role in almost all industries, were under the direct control of the central authority.[52] Prior to the market reform in 1978, most firms were owned by the State and were operated according to the State's plans. In 1978, the total assets of SOEs accounted for 92 percent of the total assets of all industrial enterprises.[53] Learning from the former Soviet Union, prior to the 1978 reform, in every major industry in China there was a 'corresponding ministry'[54] to ensure the

---

[48] It was referred to as a 'dual-track' approach. Z. Liu and Y. Qiao (2012), 'Abuse of Market Dominance Under China's 2007 Anti-Monopoly Law: A Preliminary Assessment', *Review of Industrial Organization*, p. 78; *See also* L.J. Lau, Y. Qian and G. Roland (2000), 'Reform without Losers: An Interpretation of China's Dual-track Approach to Transition', *Journal of Political Economy*, vol. 108, no. 1, pp. 120–143; C. Xu (2011), 'The Fundamental Institutions of China's Reforms and Development', *Journal of Economic Literature*, vol. 49, no. 4, pp. 1076–1151.

[49] Zhonggongzhongyang Guanyu Jianli Shehuizhuyi Shichangjingjitizhi Ruoganwenti De Jueding (中共中央关于建立社会主义市场经济体制若干问题的决定), *supra* n. 6.

[50] *See* Article 7 of the Amendment to the Constitution of the People's Republic of China (adopted at the First Session of the Eighth National People's Congress in March 1993), available at <www.npc.gov.cn/englishnpc/Constitution/node_2828.htm> accessed 06.04.2014; *see also* Y. Huang (2008), *supra* n. 3, p. 121.

[51] M. Shang (2009), 'Antitrust in China – a Constantly Evolving Subject', *Competition Law International*, vol. 5, p. 4.

[52] Y.F. Lin, F. Cai and Z. Li (1998), 'Policy Burdens, and State-owned Enterprise Reform', *American Economic Review*, vol. 88, no. 2, p. 423.

[53] *See* Y. Chen, 'Uneasy Road for SOEs' (国有经济一路走来不容易), *XinHuaNet News*, 3 October 2008, available at <http://news.xinhuanet.com/mrdx/2008–10/03/content_ 10144853.htm> (in Chinese) accessed 03.04.2014.

[54] According to Yang (2002), in most of the traditional utility sectors, natural monopolies hold dominant positions. These natural monopolies are State-authorized operators; for example the telecommunications industry has been operated by only one enterprise (China Telecom) for 45 years. It is owned by the former Ministry of Post and Telecommunications and managed by the China Telecommunications Bureau. In 1999, the former China Telecom was divided into four companies: China Telecom, China Mobile, China Sat and China Netcom. However, this spin-off was only related to product lines. Each of these companies still holds a monopoly

---

government control and management.[55] The State directly regulated production, price, supply of raw materials, entry and exit into the market, even the salary of enterprises' managers and employees.[56] SOEs had to produce according to the central plans, and to deliver all the outputs and revenues to the State.[57] The tight control over industries was gradually relaxed after the 1978 market reform. SOEs were allowed to retain part of their profits. Non State-owned enterprises, such as township and village enterprises ('TVE') and private enterprises, were allowed to sell products in the market and to get access to the raw material, equipment and capital.[58]

An essential feature of the reform on SOEs lies in the fact that SOEs in different industries were reformed in different ways. For SOEs in 'non-essential' industries that may not create a 'natural monopoly' and do not affect national security, such as machinery, electronics, chemicals and textiles, the direct supervision from the ministries was dissolved, and 'industrial associations' were established to represent the interest of these industries.[59] Meanwhile, for SOEs in industries that were considered critical to national security and the development of the economy, such as electricity, petroleum, banking, insurance, telecommunication, railroads and aviation, the direct supervision from the government ministries remained, and the government-dominated SOEs still played an important role.[60]

In addition, a series of company laws and administrative regulations were promulgated, which paved way for the establishment of foreign invested enterprises and the accommodation of foreign direct investments ('FDI'). The first law concerning the establishment of foreign invested enterprises, the Law on Chinese Foreign Equity Joint Ventures, was adopted on 1 July 1979,[61] and shortly after, a regulation for the implementation of this law was enforced.[62] In 1986, the Law on Foreign Capital Enterprises (Wholly Foreign-owned Enterprises) was

---

position in one business area. *See* J. YANG (2002), 'Market Power in China: Manifestations, Effects and Legislation', *Review of Industrial Organization*, vol. 21, pp. 170–171.

[55] B.M. OWEN, S. SUN and W. ZHENG (2008), *supra* n. 7, p. 240; *see also* J.A BERRY (2005), *supra* n. 42, p. 133.

[56] Y.F. LIN, F. CAI and Z. LI (1998), *supra* n. 52, p. 423.

[57] Y.F. LIN, F. CAI and Z. LI (1998), *supra* n. 52, p. 423.

[58] Y.F. LIN, F. CAI and Z. LI (1988), *supra* n. 52, p. 424.

[59] B.M. OWEN, S. SUN and W. ZHENG (2005), *supra* n. 13, p. 129.

[60] B.M. OWEN, S. SUN and W. ZHENG (2005), *supra* n. 13, p. 129; W. ZHENG (2010), *supra* n. 29, p. 665.

[61] Shan made comments on this law that '[t]his law signaled Chinese new era of Open-door Policy and Economic Reform'. W. SHAN (2000), 'Towards a New Legal Framework for EU-China Investment Relations', *Journal of World Trade*, vol. 34, no. 5, pp. 157–159.

[62] Zhonghua Renmin Gongheguo Zhongwai Hezi Jingying Qiyefa Shishi Tiaoli (中华人民共和国中外合资经营企业法实施条例) [Regulations for the Implementation of the Law of the People's Republic of China on Sino-Foreign Equity Joint Ventures] (promulgated by the State Council on 20 September 1983, effective on 20 September 1983), available at <www.gov.cn/gongbao/content/2011/content_1860719.htm> (in Chinese) and <http://english.mofcom.gov.cn/article/lawsdata/chineselaw/200301/20030100064563.shtml> (in English) accessed 03.04.2014.

enacted and in 1988, the Law on Chinese-Foreign Contractual Joint Ventures was adopted. According to a report by *Business Week*, from 1979 to 1983, 4,119 laws and regulations were promulgated in China, and from 1996 to 2000, this number increased further to 37,775.[63] By 2004, 94,288 laws and regulations were enacted. This report states that by 2006, '[v]irtually every area of business life in China is covered by a modern statute or regulation.'[64]

The trend of mergers and acquisitions ('M&A') only became apparent in China nearly two decades after the 1978 Market Reform. There are two types of M&A activities – one is M&As between SOEs, which were often led and regulated by the State. The other is M&As of foreign investors. Several competition and merger policies were implemented particularly for the purpose of regulating M&As by foreign investors. This section presents these two types of M&As separately. The first part summarizes the reform on SOEs and the second part deals with merger rules towards foreign investors.

3. MERGER AND ACQUISITION BETWEEN SOEs

3.1. REFORM OF SOEs

The reform of SOEs consists of three steps: commercialization, corporatization and consolidation.[65] From the late 1970s to the early 1990s, the reform of commercialization focused on the management structure of SOEs. Managers of SOEs, instead of the government, were allowed to make decisions on the choice and quantity of products, technology, exports and the wages.[66] Following this reform, in the 1990s, SOEs were controlled in a two-tiered price system, in which market prices and government-controlled prices for important goods coexisted.

The second step of the reform was to convert SOEs to corporations ('corporatizing'), starting from the enactment of the Company Law in 1993.[67] According to the Company Law, there are three types of companies that SOEs can be converted to – wholly State-owned companies, limited liability companies and joint stock limited companies.[68] The direct control over SOEs was changed to a system of 'the State regulates the market, and the market in

---

[63] XINHUA NEWS (2007), 'Business Week: China Makes Remarkable Progress in Civil Law Making', 4 December 2007, *Xinhua Net*, available at <http://en.ce.cn/National/Local/200712/05/t20071205_13816882.shtml#> (in English) accessed 28.03.2014.

[64] XINHUA NEWS (2007), 'Business Week: China Makes Remarkable Progress in Civil Law Making', *supra* n. 63.

[65] W. ZHENG (2010), *supra* n. 29, p. 662.

[66] W. ZHENG (2010), *supra* n. 29, p. 662; *see also* L.C. XU (2000), 'Control, Incentives and Competition: The Impact of Reform on Chinese State-owned Enterprises', *Economic Transition*, vol. 8, p. 151.

[67] W. ZHENG (2010), *supra* n. 29, p. 663.

[68] W. ZHENG (2010), *supra* n. 29, p. 663.

turn guides the enterprises'.[69] Moreover, to achieve the goal of establishing a 'socialist market economy', an increasing number of legal rules have been developed in the fields of corporation, banking, contracts, insurance, the exchange market, and these rules have gradually taken the place of administrative plans.

The third stage of the reform is consolidation, which was initiated in the early 1990s. When the control of price and manufacture was lifted, the central government had to reconsider how to reform the ownership of SOEs and how to execute regulations in different industries. In 1994, a policy named '*zhua da fang xiao*' (restructuring the big and relaxing control over small ones) was implemented by taking three steps: transforming small SOEs at the county level to non State-owned ownership; laying off SOE workers at the city level; and merging, grouping and corporatizing large SOEs.[70] Take China's petrol industry as an example. In 1998, the State Council made the decision that State-owned oil enterprises would be merged into two divisions. The first division is called the China National Petroleum Corporation ('CNPC'), which monopolizes production and downstream refining and retailing of petrol in 12 northern Chinese provinces. The second division is called the China Petroleum & Chemical Corporation ('CPCC'), which monopolizes the petrol market in 19 provinces of southern China.[71] Small and medium-sized private oil companies became bankrupt and were forced to leave the market as a consequence of the monopolization by these two divisions.[72] Similar mergers can also be seen in other industry sectors. The resulting divisions are supported by the government. SOEs often enjoy an incomparable advantage in terms of fiscal support, technology, intellectual capacities in research and development, and market information. Consequently, SOEs obtain noticeable market power in certain industries.

The outcome of this policy is that large SOEs were consolidated into even more powerful groups.[73] In 2000, statistics from the State Economic and Trade

69 J. Wu, 'Looking Back at the Tortuous Path of the Socialist Market Economy Development' (回望社会主义市场经济的曲折路径), *People.com*, 15 July 2006, available at <http://theory.people.com.cn/GB/49154/49155/4594081.html> (in Chinese) accessed 28.03.2014; *see also* M.S. BLODGETT, R.J. HUNTER JR. and R.M. HAYDEN (2009), 'Foreign Direct Investment, Trade and China's Competition Laws', *Denver Journal International Law and Policy*, vol. 37, p. 205.

70 Y. CAO, Y. QIAN and B.R. WEINGAST (1997), 'From Federalism, Chinese Style, to Privatization, Chinese Style', *The William Davidson Institute at the University of Michigan Business School Working Paper No. 126*, p. 2.

71 X. WANG (2008), *supra* n. 12, p. 148; X. WANG (2004), 'Challenges/Obstacles Faced by Competition Authorities in Achieving Greater Economic Development through the Promotion of Competition', Speech at the OECD Global Forum on Competition, Centre for Co-operation with Non-members Directorate for Financial, Fiscal and Enterprise Affairs, 09 January 2004, available at <www.ftc.gov/bc/international/docs/compcomm/2004--Challenges%20Obstacles%20aced%20by%20Competition.pdf>, p. 2.

72 X. WANG (2004), *supra* n. 71, p. 2.

73 W. ZHENG (2010), *supra* n. 29, p. 663.

Commission showed that the profits of the top ten enterprises composed 74.2 percent of the total profits of 520 major enterprises nationwide. The top ten enterprises were China National Petroleum Corporation, China Mobile, China Petrochemical Corporation, China Telecom, China National Offshore Oil Corporation, the State Power Corporation of China, Guangdong Electricity Corporation, Shanghai Automotive Industry Corporation (group), China Unicom and Yuxi Hongta Tobacco (group) Co. Ltd. They are either in State-dominated industries or are a solely State-owned monopolies.[74]

In 2006, Li Rongrong, the Chairman of the State Assets Supervision and Administration Commission ('SASAC'),[75] released the progress of the reform on SOEs in a press conference arranged by the State Council Information Office.[76] Li's report further clarified the goals of the merger policy towards SOEs: it aims to consolidate the large SOEs, and at the same time to strengthen State control of essential industries. According to Li, SOEs in sectors that are essential to the national economy and national security will still be under the direct control of the State. For industries such as oil, petrochemicals and natural gas, and other types of power generation and distribution, as well as telecommunications and armaments, the assets of these enterprises should be solely owned by the State, or a majority share is to be held by the State.[77] For the coal, aviation and shipping industries, the State must hold a controlling stake.[78] Furthermore, central SOEs should have a dominant control over the sectors of machinery, automobiles, IT, construction, iron and steel, as well as non-ferrous metals.[79]

3.2. MERGER POLICY FOR SOEs

SOEs in China were not held to serve an economic function of increasing profits, but were assigned a clear social function, including providing and protecting employment as well as retirement pensions, ensuring health care, and compensating the education expenses for workers' children.[80] Therefore, the primary goal of SOEs is not to maximize profits; instead, it is the social

---

[74]   Y.J. JUNG and Q. HAO (2003), *supra* n. 29, p. 116.

[75]   This bureau and its offices at regional level were established by the central government in 2003. Their responsibility is to supervise SOEs owned by both central and local governments.

[76]   H. ZHAO (2006), 'China Names Key Industries for Absolute State Control', *China Daily*, 19 December 2006, available at <www.chinadaily.com.cn/china/2006–12/19/content_762056. htm> accessed 28.03.2014. *See also* X. LAN, 'State Seeks Control of Critical Industries', *Beijing Review*, 11 January 2007, available at <www.bjreview.com.cn/print/txt/2007–01/09/ content_52480.htm> accessed 28.03.2014.

[77]   H. ZHAO (2006), *supra* n. 76.

[78]   H. ZHAO (2006), *supra* n. 76.

[79]   H. ZHAO (2006), *supra* n. 76.

[80]   C. BAI, J. LU and Z. TAO (2006), 'The Multitask Theory of State Enterprise Reform: Empirical Evidence from China', *The American Economic Review*, vol. 96, no. 2, p. 353.

responsibilities, such as safeguarding employment and supply.[81] According to the data provided by Meng and Dollery, from 1998 to 2003, half of the industrial staff and workers in China were employed by SOEs.[82]

Before the 1978 Market Reform, there was no policy or law which regulates market competition.[83] Profit-oriented competition was condemned 'as a symptom of corrupt capitalist systems', which was not accepted by the communist ideology.[84] During the reform, merger and acquisitions between SOEs are often supervised by state regulators. It was considered that merger policy for SOEs may not be necessary and concentrations between SOEs are often justified for the reason of achieving economies of scale. The consolidation between SOEs, which is led by the State, is also for the purpose of strengthening the State's control in certain industries.[85]

Moreover, the government believed that the ongoing competition between various small and medium-sized enterprises often leads to 'excessive competition', and to mitigate the negative effects the government must intervene. 'Excessive competition' refers to the destructive outcome resulting from the highly intensive competition in some industries.[86] Many policy makers believed that there was 'too much competition' among small business operators.[87] According to Zheng, these industries included cement, building materials, DVD players, electronics, LCD flat panels, dairy products, biomass power, retails, construction, airlines and ocean shipping. Companies in these industries often engage in intense price competition, which has a destructive outcome.[88] Owen, Sun and Zheng's research on press reports concluded that the industries involving in the 'excessive competition' included maritime shipping, dairy products, household appliance industry and the travel agency industry.[89]

Given the widely accepted claims of the 'excessive competition', it was argued by some policy makers in China that the merger policy would not be needed because the primary goal of the economic policy is to consolidate small companies, and to establish more powerful companies which will be able to compete in the global market.[90] This concern not only prolonged the process of

---

[81]   J.R. SAMUELS (2007), *supra* n. 29, p. 176. X. MENG and B. DOLLERY (2005), 'Institutional Constraints and Feasible Reform for State-Owned Enterprises in China', *University of New England, School of Economics Working Paper Series in Economics No. 2005–17*, p. 8.

[82]   X. MENG and B. DOLLERY (2005), *supra* n. 81, p. 8.

[83]   S.K. MEHRA and Y. MENG (2009), *supra* n. 36, p. 386.

[84]   B.M. OWEN, S. SUN and W. ZHENG (2005), *supra* n. 13, p. 127.

[85]   W. ZHENG (2010), *supra* n. 29, pp. 664–666.

[86]   B.M. OWEN, S. SUN and W. ZHENG (2008), *supra* n. 7, p. 247.

[87]   B.M. OWEN, S. SUN and W. ZHENG (2008), *supra* n. 7, p. 249. Note that it was based on the policy makers' belief that the competition in some industries was perceived as being 'excessive'; however, it was unclear which competition theory this belief is rooted in.

[88]   W. ZHENG (2010), *supra* n. 29, pp. 682–683.

[89]   B.M. OWEN, S. SUN and W. ZHENG (2008), *supra* n. 7, p. 247.

[90]   B.M. OWEN, S. SUN and W. ZHENG (2008), *supra* n. 7, p. 249.

implementing the AML, but has also been clearly incorporated in Article 5 of the AML, which states that concentrations for the reason of 'expanding business scopes' should be allowed.[91]

With respect to the discussion of adopting a competition law, the Chinese policy makers were aware that legal rules should be established to prohibit monopoly conduct. The Price Law of 1997 and the Countering Unfair Competition Law of 1993 both have included articles to prohibit anticompetitive conduct, as well as anticompetitive behavior such as price restriction agreements between private market players. It was also prohibited for SOEs or public administrations to abuse their monopoly power.[92] Articles 4 and 5 of the Countering Unfair Competition Law identify the type of anticompetitive behavior which will be sanctioned by law. Article 14 of the Price Law provides details of what counts as anticompetitive behavior with respect to price control.

However, it was a challenging task for policy makers in China to enact a comprehensive competition law during the transition, due to the fact that the government played two roles simultaneously – it was both the owner of the SOEs and the regulator of the market.[93] As a market player, the government has to ensure that SOEs maintain a dominant role in key industries.[94] Meanwhile, as a market regulator, the government needs to implement rules to establish a competitive and well-functioning market. The conflict between these goals, and the question of how to retain direct control of SOEs in certain industries in particular, remained a highly challenging and controversial issue for policy makers in China, and this issue prolonged the drafting process of the AML.[95]

4. MERGER AND ACQUISITION BY FOREIGN INVESTORS

4.1. FOREIGN DIRECT INVESTMENT

The 1978 Market Reform brought China into the international market and provided opportunities for China to participate in global capital investment. From the beginning of the reform in 1978 until the end of 1995, the FDI that China has received reached USD 128.1 billion in total.[96] By 1992, almost a

---

[91] B.M. Owen, S. Sun and W. Zheng (2008), *supra* n. 7, p. 249.
[92] M.S. Blodgett, R.J. Hunter Jr. and R.M. Hayden (2009), *supra* n. 69, p. 205.
[93] B.M. Owen, S. Sun and W. Zheng (2008), *supra* n. 7, p. 240.
[94] B.M. Owen, S. Sun and W. Zheng (2008), *supra* n. 7, p. 244.
[95] B.M. Owen, S. Sun and W. Zheng (2008), *supra* n. 7, pp. 243–244.
[96] H.G. Broadman and X. Sun (1997), 'The Distribution of Foreign Direct Investment in China', *Policy Research Working Paper*, The World Bank, China and Mongolia Department Country Operations Division in February 1997, p. 1.

quarter of total FDI inflows to developing countries were received by China and this share has increased to 40 percent by 1997.[97] From 1990 to 2000, the average annual inward FDI flows in China was around USD 30 billion.[98] In 2002, China was the largest recipient of FDI in the world.[99] In 2006, the annual inward FDI flows increased to USD 72 billion and this number reached USD 108 billion in 2008.[100] To the end of 2010, the estimated stock of FDI reached USD 574.3 billion.[101]

FDI is transferred to the host country in two ways: one way is through greenfield investment, and the other way is through mergers and acquisitions. According to the report published by the UNTCAD, developing economies often host more greenfield investment than M&As. For example, by the end of 2011, developing and transition economies hosted more than two thirds of the total value of the greenfield investment around the globe, and only 25 percent of cross-border M&As were undertaken in these economies.[102] In most developed economies, however, cross-border M&As are often the largest components of the FDI.[103] In China, the greenfield investment is also playing a dominant role. Equity joint venture ('EJV'), contractual joint venture ('CJV') and wholly foreign-owned enterprises ('WFOE') are the three main types of enterprises that can be established by receiving greenfield investment in China. In addition, foreign invested joint-stock companies ('FIJSC') can be also established according to the Chinese company law and other specific regulations.

The first wave of FDI in China started in the 1980s and at that time most foreign investors chose to establish EJVs and CJVs.[104] During the 1990s, the second wave of FDI in China mostly took the form of WFOEs.[105] From 1989 to 1995, compared with EJVs and CJVs, the number of newly established WFOEs has mostly increased.[106] From the late 1990s, an increasing number of foreign

---

[97]   H.G. BROADMAN and X. SUN (1997), *supra* n. 96, p. 3.

[98]   M. WILLIAMS (2009), 'Foreign Investment in China: Will the Anti-Monopoly Law be a Barrier or a Facilitator?', *Texas International Law Journal*, vol. 45, no. 1, p. 130.

[99]   OECD (2003), 'Trends and Recent Developments in Foreign Direct Investment', *Directorate for Financial, Fiscal and Enterprise Affairs*, available at <www.oecd.org/dataoecd/52/11/2958722.pdf>, p. 4.

[100] M. WILLIAMS (2009), *supra* n. 98, p. 130.

[101] Z. LIU and Y. QIAO (2012), *supra* n. 48, p. 101.

[102] UNCTAD (United Nations Conference on Trade and Development) (2011), 'World Investment Report 2011, Non-equity Modes of International Production and Development', United Nations: New York and Geneva, p. 10, available at <http://unctad.org/en/docs/wir2011_embargoed_en.pdf >.

[103] OECD (2003), *supra* n. 99, p. 7.

[104] M.W. PENG (2006), 'Making M&A Fly in China', *Harvard Business Review*, p. 1; H. HUANG (2007), 'China's New Regulation on Foreign M&A: Green Light or Red Flag?', *University of New South Wales Law Journal*, vol. 30, no. 3, p. 804.

[105] M.W. PENG (2006), *supra* n. 104, p. 1; H. HUANG (2007), *supra* n. 104, p. 804.

[106] H.G. BROADMAN and X. SUN (1997), *supra* n. 96, p. 4.

investors have chosen to merge with Chinese enterprises.[107] Mergers and acquisitions accounted for 11 percent of all FDI flows in 2004.[108] This number continued to increase in 2005, when it accounted for nearly 14 percent of total foreign investment.[109] According to the annual report by the Zero2IPO Research Institution, by the end of 2010 there were 521 domestic M&A cases in China, and the total amount reached USD 19.39 billion. 57 of these cases were outbound M&As, with a total value of USD 13.20 billion. 44 of these cases were inbound M&As, with a total value of USD 2.22 billion.[110] One of the most significant change in the global mergers today is that the formerly regulated State-owned monopolies in public utilities and telecommunications, as well as the transportation industry, have now experienced cross-border M&As.[111]

This increase, specifically in China, may have been influenced by the developments in policy and law. During the first few years after the 1978 Reform, foreign investors were only allowed to establish enterprises in some industries and collaboration with SOEs was also under restrictions. After 22 years of development of the market economy, M&As by foreign investors were accepted in the 10th National Five-Year Plan in 2001,[112] and several administrative provisions were enforced during these five years. Among them, the most important provision, the Interim Provisions on Mergers and Acquisitions of Domestic Enterprises for Foreign Investors, which was enacted by four state administrations[113] in 2003, has four articles explicitly covering merger control issues. Besides the internal political and legal support, M&As were highly accelerated by China's entry into the World Trade Organization ('WTO') in late 2001, which made it possible for Chinese enterprises to compete in the global

---

[107] P. LIN and J. ZHAO (2012), 'Merger Control Policy Under China's Anti-Monopoly Law', *Review of Industrial Organization*, vol. 41, p. 110.

[108] UNCTAD (United Nations Conference on Trade and Development) (2006), 'World Investment Report 2006: FDI from Developing and Transition Economies: Implications for Development', United Nations: New York and Geneva, available at <http://unctad.org/en/docs/wir2006_en.pdf>.

[109] H. ZOU and P. SIMPSON (2008), 'Cross-border Mergers and Acquisitions in China: An Industry Panel Study: 1991–2005', *Asia Pacific Business Review*, vol. 14, no. 4, pp. 491–512.

[110] Data available on Zero2IPO website <www.zero2ipogroup.com/en/research/reportdetails.aspx?r=23ef4658-e96b-4b24-9774-540ce1062101>.

[111] M.S. JACOBS (2001), 'Mergers and Acquisitions in a Global Economy: Perspectives from Law, Politics and Business', *Depaul Business Law Journal*, vol. 13, no. 1, p. 4.

[112] In the 10th Five-Year Plan (2001–2005) for National Economy and Social Development, M&As by foreign investors and restructuring SOEs by using foreign investments were both encouraged. *See* Guomin Jingji He Shehui Fazhan Dishige Wunianjihua Gangyao (国民经济和社会发展第十个五年计划纲要) [The Tenth Five Year Plan for National Economic and Social Development] (approved by the Fourth Session of the Ninth National People's Congress on 15 March 2001), available at <www.people.com.cn/GB/shizheng/16/20010318/419582.html> (in Chinese) accessed 04.04.2014.

[113] These four state administrations are the Ministry of Foreign Trade and Economic Cooperation (MOFTEC), the State Administration of Taxation (SAT), the State Administration for Industry and Commerce (SAIC), and the State Administration of Foreign Exchange (SAFE).

---

market, and at the same time pressures on Chinese policy makers were imposed to further open the market for foreign investors.

4.2. ENTRY INTO THE WTO

China's acceptance as an integral part of the WTO in September 2001 is another important external factor for the enactment of competition and merger polices in China.[114] The WTO recognized China as an emerging market economy,[115] and at the same time the entry to the WTO also became the catalyst to the maturation of the market mechanism in China.[116] Chinese leaders took the opportunity of being a member of the WTO not only to expand the scope of international trade, but more importantly to use China's membership as an external pressure to better tackle the difficulties that it faces during its economic reform.[117]

The WTO has clearly indicated its members' obligation to the reduce trade barriers, as well as their responsibilities to ensure fair market competition.[118] Seeing that most of the developed countries have enacted a competition law in order to establish a fair competition environment, legislators in China were aware that a competition law could contribute to creating a legal framework for economic development.[119] By September 2002, over 2,300 government regulations which would be considered inconsistent with the WTO requirements were reviewed, amended, or repealed.[120] In March 2001, the Standing Committee of China's National People's Congress ('NPC') stated that a draft comprehensive antitrust law would soon be issued, which would specifically deal with the difficulties in establishing a real competitive market in China.[121] The motivation of the Chinese officials to enact a competition law, according to Gerber, might be understood as signalling its willingness to perform its role in

---

[114]   The World Trade Organization concluded negotiations on China's terms of membership of the WTO on 17 September 2001. The agreement was adopted formally at the WTO Ministerial Conference in Doha, Qatar in November 2001. *See* WTO News: 2001 Press Releases: WTO successfully concludes negotiations on China's entry, 17 September 2001, available at <www.wto.org/english/news_e/pres01_e/pr243_e.htm> accessed 20.03.2014.

[115]   B. WILLIAMS (2001), 'The Influence and Lack of Influence of Principles in the Negotiation for China's Accession to the World Trade Organization', *George Washington International Law Review*, vol. 33, p. 791.

[116]   X. WANG (2004), *supra* n. 71.

[117]   D.C. CLARKE (2003), 'China's Legal System and the WTO: Prospects for Compliance', *Washington University Global Studies Law Review*, vol. 2, p. 98.

[118]   WTO News, '2001 Press Releases: WTO successfully concludes negotiations on China's entry', *supra* n. 114.

[119]   Y.J. JUNG and Q. HAO (2003), *supra* n. 29, p. 122.

[120]   M.S. BLODGETT, R.J. HUNTER JR. and R.M. HAYDEN (2009), *supra* n. 69, p. 210; Asian Development Bank, 'Private Sector Assessment, People's Republic of China', November 2003, Publication Stock No. 091003, available at <www.adb.org/sites/default/files/pub/2003/PRC_PSA.pdf>, p. 17.

[121]   M.S. BLODGETT, R.J. HUNTER JR. and R.M. HAYDEN (2009), *supra* n. 69, p. 210.

the international system, and this signal would be important to obtain support from the international community in the WTO.[122]

4.3. MERGER POLICY FOR FOREIGN INVESTORS

Entry into the WTO provided the opportunity for China to participate in international competition. However, legislators in China were concerned that Chinese enterprises were still small and were vulnerable to competition on the global market.[123] Foreign investors often have superior knowledge, technology, capital and management skills. On the other hand, they may easily squeeze the marketplace for domestic companies.[124] After the entry into the WTO, the increase of market power by foreign companies has attracted public attention. Seeing these, several regulations have been implemented for the specific purpose of regulating foreign M&As. In 2003, the Ministry of Foreign Trade and Economic Cooperation (including Former Ministry of Foreign Economy and Trade), the State Administration of Taxation, the State Administration for Industry and Commerce, the State Administration of Foreign Exchange, jointly issued the Interim Provisions on Acquisition of Domestic Enterprises by Foreign Investors.[125] This provision was further amended in 2006 and in 2009. Article 21 of the 2003 Provision states that under five circumstances, the merging parties must notify to the Ministry of Foreign Economy and Trade, and the State Administration of Industry and Commerce,[126] and a decision will be made by these two administrative agencies after assessing whether the merger will increase market concentration, impede competition, or harm consumers.

Meanwhile, Article 22 of this Provision listed four circumstances in which the merging party can apply for exemptions. First, the merger will improve the market condition for fair competition; second, the merger will restructure the

---

[122]   D.J. GERBER (2008), *supra* n. 7, p. 281.
[123]   Y.J. JUNG and Q. HAO (2003), *supra* n. 29, p. 120.
[124]   Y.J. JUNG and Q. HAO (2003), *supra* n. 29, p. 122.
[125]   Waiguo Touzizhe Binggou Jingnei Qiye Zanxing Guiding (外国投资者并购境内企业暂行规定) [Interim Provisions for Foreign Investors to Merge Domestic Enterprises] (promulgated by the Ministry of Foreign Trade and Economic Cooperation, the State Administration of Taxation, the State Administration for Industry and Commerce, the State Administration of Foreign Exchange, issued on 7 March 2003, effective on 12 April 2003), available at <http://en.pkulaw.cn/display.aspx?cgid=44880&lib=law> (in English), and <www.sasac.gov.cn/n1180/n2385773/n2386215/2537266.html> (in Chinese) accessed 04.04.2014.
[126]   (1) The foreign merging party's assets in China is more than RMB 3 billion; (2) the foreign merging party's turnover in Chinese market in the current year is more than RMB 1.5 billion; (3) the foreign merging party with its associated companies have more than a 20 percent market share in Chinese market; (4) after the merger, the foreign merging party with its associated companies have more than a 25 percent market share in China; (5) after the merger, the foreign merging party's related industry has more than 15 foreign invested companies.

loss-making company, which will guarantee employment; third, the merger will bring personnel who have expertise in technologies and management, and the merger will increase the competitiveness of the company in the global market; and fourth, the merger will improve the environment. The amendment in 2006 kept the compulsory notification procedure unchanged. On 8 March 2007, the Guide for the Anti-Monopoly Declaration by a Foreign Investor in the Merger or Acquisition of a Domestic Enterprise[127] was enacted. In the 2009 amendment,[128] after the promulgation of the AML, the notification procedure stated in this provision has been deleted, because the notification requirements have been clarified in the AML as well as in the notification provisions issued by the State Council after the promulgation of the AML.

The central message of this 2003 Provision, as well as its 2006 and 2009 amendments, is that mergers which will increase market concentration levels must be notified to the authority and must wait for an investigation of the anticompetitive effects. However, it is not clear whether this investigation is based on economic theory and, if so, which economic criterion will be applied. Moreover, the authority has not explained how the thresholds stated in the notification requirements are calculated.

After a closer look at these provisions, a question might arise as to whether these merger provisions are issued particularly for the purpose of enhancing market competition. Article 1 of the 2003 Provision summarizes that this Provision is issued with the following purposes: encouraging and regulating foreign investors to invest in China; bringing advanced technologies and management experiences to China; using foreign investment to improve allocation of resources; ensuring employment, enhancing fair competition and national economic security. Importantly, this Article 1 remains the same in the 2006 and 2009 amendments. It might send a signal that merger policy in China is not only for the goal of improving efficiency, or consumer welfare. The multiple goals stated in Article 1 reflect the concerns of social welfare, and more generally, the balance between utilizing foreign investments and improving the domestic economy. Moreover, this provision as well as its amendments seems to be more

---

[127] Waiguo Touzizhe Binggou Jingnei Qiye Fanlongduan Shenbao Zhinan (外国投资者并购境内企业反垄断申报指南) [Guide for the Anti-Monopoly Declaration by a Foreign Investor in the Merger or Acquisition of a Domestic Enterprise] (promulgated by the Ministry of Commerce on 8 March 2007, effective on 8 March 2007), available at <www.lawinfochina.com/display.aspx?lib=law&id=6267> (in English and Chinese) accessed 01.04.2014.

[128] Shangwubu Guanyu Waiguo Touzizhe Binggou Jingnei Qiye De Guiding (商务部关于外国投资者并购境内企业的规定) [Ministry of Commerce PRC on Promulgation of the Provisions on M&A of a Domestic Enterprise by Foreign Investors] (promulgated by the Ministry of Commerce on 22 June 2009, effective on 22 June 2009), available at <www.gov.cn/flfg/2009-07/24/content_1373405.htm> (in Chinese) and <www.lawinfochina.com/display.aspx?id=9547&lib=law&SearchKeyword=&SearchCKeyword=%b9%d8%d3%da%cd%e2%b9%fa%cd%b6%d7%ca%d5%df%b2%a2%b9%ba%be%b3%c4%da%c6%f3%d2%b5%b5%c4%b9%e6%b6%a8> (in English) accessed 01.04.2014.

relevant if it is considered as an industrial policy instead of a competition policy. For example, Article 12 of the 2006 amendment states that the concentration which will control 'well-known or traditional trademarks or brand names in China' has to be reported to the MOFCOM.[129]

It worth mentioning that 'industrial policy' is also a new concept in China. Industrial policy appeared for the first time in China in the 7th Five-Year Plan of National Economic and Development in 1986.[130] On 25 March 1994, the 16th executive meeting of the State Council approved the Outline of State Industry Policies for the 1990s.[131] In 1995, the Ministry of Civil Affairs, the State Development and Reform Commission, and the State Economic and Trade Commission issued the Provisional Regulations on Direction Guide to Foreign Investment.[132] In 1997, the Ministry of Foreign Trade and Economic Cooperation, the State Development and Reform Commission, and the State Economic and Trade Commission issued the Category of Industries Guiding Foreign Investments.[133] Under these provisions, the treatment of foreign investment was categorized as 'prohibited', 'restricted', 'accepted' and 'encouraged'.[134] One of the senior officials has explained that the role of the industrial policy in China is to increase the competitiveness of the firms by encouraging mergers and restructuring, to promote economies of scale, to

---

[129]   P. LIN and J. ZHAO (2012), *supra* n. 107, p. 111.

[130]   Guomin Jingji He Shehui Fazhan Diqige Wunianjihua (1986–1990) (国民经济和社会发展第七个五年计划) [The Seventh Five Year Plan for National Economic and Social Development] (approved by the Fourth Session of the Sixth National People's Congress on 12 April 1986), available at <http://news.xinhuanet.com/ziliao/2005–02/06/content_2554021.htm> (in Chinese), accessed 01.04.2014; G. ZHANG (2008), 'Controls on the Admission of Customs and Anti-monopoly of Foreign Mergers and Acquisitions of Domestic Enterprises: A Review of the Regulations Governing Mergers and Acquisitions of Domestic Enterprises by Foreign Investors' (外资并购的准入管制和反垄断管制 — 评《关于外国投资者并购境内企业的规定》), *Journal of Nanjing Normal University* (南京师大学报), November 2008, no. 6, p. 21.

[131]   Jiushi Niandai Guojia Chanye Zhengce Gangyao (90年代国家产业政策纲要) [Outline of State Industry Policies for the 1990s] (promulgated by the State Council on 25 March 1994, effective 25 March 1994), available at <http://en.pkulaw.cn/display.aspx?cgid=9530&lib=law> (in English and Chinese) accessed 02.04.2014.

[132]   Zhidao Waishang Touzi Fangxiang Zanxing Guiding (指导外商投资方向暂行规定) [Provisional Regulations on Direction Guide to Foreign Investment] (promulgated by the Ministry of Civil Affairs, the State Development and Reform Commission, the State Economic and Trade Commission on 20 June 1995, effective 28 June 1995), available at <http://en.pkulaw.cn/display.aspx?cgid=12656&lib=law> (in English and Chinese) accessed 02.04.2014.

[133]   Waishang Touzi Chanye Zhidao Mulu (外商投资产业指导目录) [Category of Industries Guiding Foreign Investments] (promulgated by the Ministry of Foreign Trade and Economic Cooperation, the State Development and Reform Commission, the State Economic and Trade Commission, 31 December 1997, effective on 1 January 1998), available at <http://en.pkulaw.cn/display.aspx?id=71&lib=law&SearchKeyword=catalogue for industries&SearchCKeyword=K46kIOgCppmDRNKvAC1F9gJlSfN4JEFzmc%2frPBmvuUE%3d> (in English and Chinese) accessed 03.04.2014. This category was updated in 2002, 2004, 2007 and 2011.

[134]   G. ZHANG (2008), *supra* n. 130, p. 21.

---

increase economic efficiency, to enhance the capacities of innovation, and to develop the competitiveness of the economy.[135]

In addition to the industrial policy considerations, the merger policy of 2003, as well as its amendments in 2006 and 2009, implicitly signalled that one of the goals of the merger policy is to regulate foreign investments.[136] It is worth noting that since the mid-2000s, there has been a growing concern among the public and the policy makers that foreign enterprises hold a dominant position in several industries. Therefore, it is more likely that they will engage in anticompetitive conduct.[137] This concern is called 'economic patriotism' by Lin and Zhao.[138] It was reported by the domestic media that foreign companies held a dominant position in industries producing computers, cables, sedan cars, rubber, switchboards, beer, paper, and elevators.[139] A survey in 2005 indicated that Microsoft held 95 percent of the market share of computer operating systems, Kodak held at least 60 percent in the photosensitive material market, Michelin held 70 percent of the radial ply tyre market, and Sony held about 18 percent of the camera market.[140] In 2006, the Development Research Center under the State Council released a report stating that the assets of 21 out of 28 major industrial sectors were controlled by foreign investors.[141] In particular, mergers by foreign companies will significantly increase their market share and will strengthen their dominant position. It was reported that after Kodak's acquisition of Lucky Film in China, the market share that Kodak held in the Chinese film products market increased to 70 percent.[142]

The concerns directed at foreign companies engaged in anticompetitive conduct by obtaining a dominant position were so widespread throughout the country that they became one of the major driving forces for the enactment of the AML.[143] The goal of preventing foreign M&As from affecting national

---

[135] *See* Z. Liu and Y. Qiao (2012), *supra* n. 48, p. 103; X. Zhao (2008), 'The Nature, Characteristics, and Institutional Concepts of the Anti-Monopoly Law' (反垄断法的性质、地位、特征及其主要制度理念), 29 August 2008, available at <http://jjs.ndrc.gov.cn/gzdt/200808/t20080829_233729.html> (in Chinese) accessed 03.04.2014.

[136] B.M. Owen, S. Sun and W. Zheng (2008), *supra* n. 7, p. 253.

[137] P. Lin and J. Zhao (2012), *supra* n. 107, p. 111; H. Liu (1998), 'Law Regulating Foreign M&As in China' (略论外资并购中国企业的法律规制途径), *Modern Law Science* (现代法学), vol. 2, p. 77.

[138] P. Lin and J. Zhao (2012), *supra* n. 107, p. 111.

[139] Y.J. Jung and Q. Hao (2003), *supra* n. 29, p. 122.

[140] Zhang summarized a survey by the Anti-Monopoly Bureau of the State Administration of Industry and Commerce (SAIC). *See* M. Zhang (2005), 'The Target of the AML' ('反垄断' 剑指何处), *Foreign Investment in China* (中国外资), 2005 no. 1, p. 47.

[141] H. Huang (2007), *supra* n. 104, p. 810, *see also* Q. Wu (2006), 'China Regulates Foreign Mergers for More Investment', 11 September 2006, *Embassy of the PRC in the USA*, available at <www.china-embassy.org/eng/gyzg/t271391.htm> accessed 20.03.2014.

[142] M. Williams, *Competition Policy and Law in China, Hong Kong and Taiwan*, Cambridge University Press 2005, p. 213.

[143] P. Lin and J. Zhao (2012), *supra* n. 107, p. 112.

economic security was clearly mentioned by the Judicial Committee of the NPC when it reviewed the draft of the AML in 2007.[144] It was also widely reported by various media in China that the AML would be implemented to mitigate the anticompetitive effects of foreign enterprises operating in China.[145] For this reason, an integration of two goals in the implementation of the merger policy in China can be observed: on the side of industrial policy considerations, the merger policy tends to protect domestic enterprises or national brands;[146] while on the side of preventing 'hostile foreign acquisitions',[147] the merger policy tends to put emphasis on the effects of mergers on national economic security. The interaction between two major political goals can be observed from the merger cases which were published by the MOFCOM after the promulgation of the AML, and the fifth chapter of this book will discuss these cases in detail.

5. AN OVERVIEW OF THE ANTI-MONOPOLY LAW AND THE MERGER POLICY

5.1. COMPETITION POLICY BEFORE THE AML

The earliest competition policies in China are the Provisional Rules on the Development and Protection of Socialist Competition, an administrative regulation which was adopted by the State Council on 17 October 1980.[148] This regulation for the first time acknowledged that the pricing system under the planned economy should be adjusted to stimulate competition, under the condition that prices of key products must remain stable. It was also acknowledged that technology exchange and development should be encouraged.[149] Seven years later, a more detailed administrative regulation on price control was adopted by the Chinese State Council.[150]

---

[144] P. LIN and J. ZHAO (2012), *supra* n. 107, p. 112.

[145] P. LIN and J. ZHAO (2012), *supra* n. 107, p. 112.

[146] C. PAN (2008), 'The Loss of State Assets in Foreign M&As' (论外资并购中国有资产流失问题及法律规制), *Journal of Sichuan Economic Management Institute* (四川经济管理学院学报), vol. 65, no. 3, p. 24.

[147] An official from the State Council used this phrase to explain that the AML is against foreign M&As which would affect national economic security. *See* P. LIN and J. ZHAO (2012), *supra* n. 107, p. 112.

[148] Guanyu Kaizhan He Baohu Shehuizhuyi Jingzheng De Zanxing Guiding (关于开展和保护社会主义竞争的暂行规定) [Provisional Rules on the Development and Protection of Socialist Competition] (promulgated by the State Council on 17 October 1980, effective on 17 October 1980, and repealed on 6 October 2001), available at <http://finance.sina.com.cn/g/20050418/12411526820.shtml> (in Chinese) accessed 04.04.2014.

[149] Y.J. JUNG and Q. HAO (2003), *supra* n. 29, p. 127.

[150] Zhonghua Renmin Gongheguo Jiage Guanli Tiaoli (中华人民共和国价格管理条例) [Regulations of the People's Republic of China on Price Control] (promulgated by the State

Since the early 1990s, several laws and administrative regulations which aimed at preventing anticompetitive practices were implemented in China. The Law of the People's Republic of China for Countering Unfair Competition[151] was promulgated in 1993. It sketches the basic framework for competition policy before the AML. It prohibits predatory pricing which will restrict competition (Article 11), or forced tying and bundling (Article 12), and this law prohibits public utilities or other enterprises holding monopoly positions that restrict competition by forcing others to purchase specific commodities (Article 6). Article 7 of this law also deals with administrative monopoly. It states that government organs should not abuse administrative power to restrict competition by forcing others to purchase products.[152]

The other issues that this law addresses, such as bribery, false advertisement, prohibition of fraudulent practices, and coercive sales, made some commentators believe that this law is more like a consumer protection law, not an antitrust law.[153] This law is by no means a comprehensive competition law, as it did not cover the broad competition issues and did not provide competition rules for mergers.[154]

It should be highlighted that the enforcement agency for the Law of Countering Unfair Competition is the State Administration for Industry and Commerce (SAIC) with its local branches (AIC).[155] In 1994, both the SAIC and the AIC set up their offices, being especially responsible for fair trade affairs.[156] After the enactment of the AML, the function of dealing with anti-monopoly practices was formally regulated by the State Council and the SAIC became one of the enforcement agencies.[157]

After the SAIC was empowered with antitrust duties by the Law of Countering Unfair Competition, in December 1993, the SAIC promulgated the Certain Regulations on Prohibiting Anti-competitive Practices of Public

---

Council on 11 September 1987, effective on 11 September 1987), available at <http://en.pkulaw.cn/display.aspx?cgid=3479&lib=law> (in English and Chinese) accessed 04.04.2014.

[151] Zhonghua Renmin Gongheguo Fanbuzhengdangjingzheng Fa (中华人民共和国反不正当竞争法) [Anti-Unfair Competition Law of the People's Republic of China] (promulgated by the Standing Committee of the National People's Congress on 2 September 1993, effective on 2 September 1993), available at <http://tfs.mofcom.gov.cn/aarticle/date/i/s/200503/20050300027909.html> (in Chinese) and <http://en.pkulaw.cn/display.aspx?cgid=6359&lib=law> (in English), accessed 04.04.2014.

[152] Anti-Unfair Competition Law of the People's Republic of China, translation is based on <http://en.pkulaw.cn/display.aspx?cgid=6359&lib=law>.

[153] B.M. OWEN, S. SUN and W. ZHENG (2008), *supra* n. 7, p. 233.

[154] B.M. OWEN, S. SUN and W. ZHENG (2005), *supra* n. 13, p. 139.

[155] Y.J. JUNG and Q. HAO (2003), *supra* n. 29, p. 129.

[156] S. K. MEHRA and Y. MENG (2009), *supra* n. 36, p. 403.

[157] Guowuyuan Bangongting Guanyu Yinfa Guojia Gongshang Xingzheng Guanli Zongju Zhuyao Zhize Neishe Jigou He Renyuan Bianzhi Guiding De Tongzhi (国务院办公厅关于印发国家工商行政管理总局主要职责内设机构和人员编制规定的通知) [The State Council Notice on Major Duties, Internal Organization and Administration of the SAIC] (issued on 11 July 2008), available at <www.jetro.go.jp/world/asia/cn/ip/law/pdf/origin/2008080758891502.pdf> (in Chinese) accessed 03.04.2014.

Enterprises.[158] This regulation focuses on the abuse of market position of public utility companies. In addition, this administrative provision emphasizes the problem of administrative monopoly.[159] The earliest rule on administrative monopoly was promulgated by the State Council in November 1990,[160] named as the Notice Concerning the Breaking of Local Market Blockades and Further Encouraging Commodity Circulation. It targets on breaking down trade barriers established by the local governments. In April 2001, after the SAIC was upgraded to a ministerial level,[161] the State Council enacted the Provisions of the State Council on Prohibiting Regional Blockade in Market Economic Activities.[162] This provision specifically focuses on the problem of regional protectionism. In the same month, the State Council enacted another decision on rectifying and standardizing the order in the market economy.[163] Administrative monopoly and local protectionism are both prohibited under Article 11 of this decision. It is worth mentioning that in addition to the anti-monopoly regulations, administrative monopoly is also addressed by the Administrative Reconsideration Law[164] and by the Administrative Procedure Law.[165]

---

158 Guanyu Jinzhi Gongyong Qiye Xianzhi Jingzheng Xingwei De Ruogan Guiding (关于禁止公用企业限制竞争行为的若干规定) [Certain Regulations on Prohibiting Anti-competitive Practices of Public Enterprises] (promulgated by the State Administration for Industry and Commerce, 24 December 1993, effective on 24 December 1993), available at <http://en.pkulaw.cn/display.aspx?cgid=8847&lib=law> (in English and Chinese) accessed 04.04.2014.

159 Administrative monopoly refers to monopolistic behavior that is supported by government and regulatory agencies at both central and regional levels. The central government protects specific sectors or departments through exercising administrative authority, thus impeding competition in those sectors. Local governments exert administrative power over enterprises within the region and protect the profits of these enterprises by creating market barriers, restricting the flow of products. This can be aptly characterized as local protectionism. *See* Y. GUO and A. HU (2004), 'The Administrative Monopoly in China's Economic Transition', *Communist and Post-Communist Studies*, vol. 37, no. 2, p. 273. Local protectionism has been widely seen in many regions in China. A detailed discussion on administrative monopoly is beyond the scope of this research.

160 S.K. MEHRA and Y. MENG (2009), *supra* n. 36, pp. 388, 401.

161 S.K. MEHRA and Y. MENG (2009), *supra* n. 36, p. 401.

162 Guowuyuan Guanyu Jinzhi Zai Shichang Jingji Huodong Zhong Shixing Diqu Fengsuo De Guiding (国务院关于禁止在市场经济活动中实行地区封锁的规定) [Provisions of the State Council on Prohibiting Regional Blockade in Market Economic Activities] (promulgated by the State Council on 21 April 2001, effective on 21 April 2001), available at <http://en.pkulaw.cn/display.aspx?cgid=35595&lib=law> (in English and Chinese) accessed 03.04.2014.

163 Guowuyuan Guanyu Zhengdun He Guifan Shichang Jingji Zhixu De Jueding (国务院关于整顿和规范市场经济秩序的决定) [Decisions of the State Council on Rectifying and Standardizing the Order in the Market Economy] (promulgated by the State Council on 27 April 2001, effective on 27 April 2001), available at <http://en.pkulaw.cn/display.aspx?cgid=35594&lib=law> (in English and Chinese) accessed 03.04.2014.

164 Zhonghua Renmin Gongheguo Xingzheng Fuyi Fa (中华人民共和国行政复议法) [Administrative Reconsideration Law of the People's Republic of China] (promulgated by the National People's Congress, 29 April 1999, effective on 1 October 1999, revised on 27 August 2009), available at <http://en.pkulaw.cn/display.aspx?cgid=22100&lib=law> (in English and Chinese) accessed 03.04.2014.

165 Zhonghua Renmin Gongheguo Xingzheng Susong Fa (中华人民共和国行政诉讼法) [Administrative Procedure Law of the People's Republic of China] (promulgated by the

In June 2003, the National Development and Reform Commission ('NDRC'), which became another enforcement agency of the AML in later years, issued the Interim Provisions on Preventing the Acts of Price Monopoly.[166] This regulation is in accordance with the 1997 Price Law. Article 3 of this regulation states that market dominance should be determined by three elements: the market share in the relevant market, the substitutability and the difficulty of market entry. This regulation also mentions the prohibition of abuse of market dominance, price coordination and the government agencies' illegal price intervention.[167] It indicates that the NDRC starts to share the responsibility of the enforcement of combating monopolistic practices, with a focus on the conduct of pricing.[168]

The Ministry of Commerce established their antitrust office in 2004, showing their interest in investigating antitrust cases and in drafting legislation, especially in the field of merger and acquisitions. The office was named as the Ministry of Commerce Anti-Monopoly Bureau ('MOFCOM'). This office is responsible for the implementation of the Interim Provisions for Foreign Investors to Merge Domestic Enterprises, an administrative regulation on merger and acquisitions issued in March 2003.[169] This provision has explicitly mentioned the premerger notification requirements in its chapter 5, and the notification should be submitted both to the MOFCOM and the SAIC. During 2007, the MOFCOM has conducted over 220 reviews on merger cases.[170] These practices made the MOFCOM more experienced in investigating antitrust cases and implementing other merger control guidelines after the enactment of the AML.

Besides, there are several other governmental agencies which also play a role in antitrust decisions.[171] Anti-monopoly policies have also been reflected in other laws such as the Law on Protection of Consumer Rights and Interests of

---

National People's Congress, 4 April 1989, effective on 1 October 1990), available at <http://en.pkulaw.cn/display.aspx?cgid=4274&lib=law> (in English and Chinese) accessed 03.04.2014.

[166] Zhizhi Jiage Longduan Xingwei Zanxing Guiding (制止价格垄断行为暂行规定) [Interim Provisions on Preventing the Acts of Price Monopoly] (promulgated by the State Development and Reform Commission, 18 June 2003, effective on 1 November 2003), available at <http://en.pkulaw.cn/display.aspx?cgid=47253&lib=law> (in English and Chinese) accessed 03.04.2014.

[167] Interim Provisions on Preventing the Acts of Price Monopoly, *supra* n. 166.

[168] S.K. MEHRA and Y. MENG (2009), *supra* n. 36, p. 404.

[169] Interim Provisions for Foreign Investors to Merge Domestic Enterprises (外国投资者并购境内企业暂行规定), *supra* n. 125.

[170] Z. WU (2008), *supra* n. 40, p. 115.

[171] Z. WU (2008), *supra* n. 40, pp. 115–116; *see also* X. WANG (2006), 'The Relationship between Antitrust Enforcement Agencies and Industry Regulators' (论反垄断法执法机构与行业监管机构的关系), 23 September 2006, 中国民商法律网 (civillaw.com.cn), available at <www.civillaw.com.cn/article/default.asp?id=28604> (in Chinese) accessed 04.04.2014.

1993,[172] the Foreign Trade Law of 1994,[173] the Law on Commercial Banks of 1995,[174] the Price Law of 1997,[175] and the Bidding Law of 1999.[176]

5.2.   THE DRAFTING PROCESS OF THE AML

In 1987, an Antitrust Law drafting team was established under the Legislative Affairs Office of the State Council.[177] The task of drafting the AML was allocated to a group in 1994, whose members were selected from the SAIC and the State Economic and Trade Commission ('SETC').[178] This group drafted the competition law for China by examining antitrust laws in other jurisdictions, including the antitrust laws in the United States, Germany, Japan, Australia, and South Korea.[179]

---

[172]   Zhonghua Renmin Gongheguo Xiaofeizhe Quanyi Baohu Fa (中华人民共和国消费者权益保护法) [Law of the People's Republic of China on Protection of Consumer Rights and Interests] (promulgated by the Standing Committee of the National People's Congress on 31 October 1993, effective on 1 January 1994, revised on 27 August 2009), available at <http://en.pkulaw.cn/display.aspx?cgid=6384&lib=law> (in English and Chinese) accessed 03.04.2014.

[173]   Zhonghua Renmin Gongheguo Duiwai Maoyi Fa (中华人民共和国对外贸易法) [Foreign Trade Law of the People's Republic of China] (promulgated by the Standing Committee of the National People's Congress on 12 May 1994, effective on 1 July 1994, revised on 6 April 2004), available at <http://en.pkulaw.cn/display.aspx?cgid=52228&lib=law> (in English and Chinese) accessed 03.04.2014.

[174]   Zhonghua Renmin Gongheguo Shangye Yinhang Fa (中华人民共和国商业银行法) [Law of the People's Republic of China on Commercial Banks] (promulgated by the Standing Committee of the National People's Congress, 10 May 1995, effective on 1 July 1995, amended on 27 December 2003), available at <www.pkulaw.cn/fulltext_form.aspx?Gid=11600> (in English and Chinese) accessed 03.04.2014; see Article 9 of Chapter 1, 'Commercial banks should follow the principle of fair competition in their business and should not be engaged in unfair competition.'

[175]   Zhonghua Renmin Gongheguo Jiage Fa (中华人民共和国价格法) [Price Law of the People's Republic of China] (promulgated by the Standing Committee of the National People's Congress, 29 December 1997, effective on 1 May 1998), available at <http://en.pkulaw.cn/display.aspx?cgid=19158&lib=law> (in English and Chinese) accessed 03.04.2014. This law was enforced by the National Development and Reform Commission (NDRC), and local price administration agencies. Article 14 of Chapter 1 of this law prohibits price fixing, dumping sales at below cost prices, and price discrimination.

[176]   Zhonghua Renmin Gongheguo Zhaobiao Toubiao Fa (中华人民共和国招标投标法) [The Bidding Law of the People's Republic of China] (promulgated by the Standing Committee of the National People's Congress on 30 August 1999, effective on 1 January 2000), available at <http://en.pkulaw.cn/display.aspx?cgid=23176&lib=law> (in English and Chinese) accessed 03.04. 2014. See Article 32 in Chapter 3: 'Tenderers shall not collude with each other in setting bidding prices, nor shall they exclude other tenderers from fair competition and harm the lawful rights and interests of the tendee and other tenderers. Tenderers shall not collude with the tendee in injuring the interests of the state, general public and other people. Tenderers shall be forbidden to win any bid by offering any bribe to the tendee or any member of the bid-evaluation committee.'

[177]   P. NEUMANN (2003), 'The Slow Boat to Antitrust Law in China', Faegre Baker Daniels, 23 December 2003, available at <www.faegrebd.com/4709> accessed 24.03.2014.

[178]   Y. HUANG (2008), supra n. 3, p. 118.

[179]   C.W. HITTINGER and J.D. HUH (2007), 'The People's Republic of China Enacts its First Comprehensive Antitrust Law: Trying to Predict the Unpredictable', New York University Journal of Law and Business, vol. 4, p. 249.

After the SETC was abolished during the government agency reform in 2003, MOFCOM took its place.[180] The standing committee of the National People's Congress included the 'Anti-Trust Law' in the eighth (in 1994), the ninth (in 1998) and the tenth (in 2003) legislative schedule. The drafting process, however, took nearly a decade. The first finished draft was distributed among business professionals and legal scholars in 2002. During the drafting process, foreign experts and officials from the competition authorities in the US, Germany, Japan, Australia, and Korea, as well as officials from international organizations were consulted.[181] The draft law was reviewed by experts from both public and private sectors in the EU, Japan, and Korea.[182] In October 2004, another draft was submitted by the MOFCOM to the Legislative Affairs Office of the State Council.[183] In June 2006, the Legislative Affairs Office of the State Council submitted the finished draft to the Standing Committee of the National People's Congress ('NPC'). When Mr Cao Kangtai, the Director of the Legislative Office under the State Council, submitted this draft to the NPC for the legislative review, he mentioned three reasons why this AML should be enacted:[184] first, monopolistic agreements should be prohibited for the reason that both consumers and other competitors will be harmed; monopolistic agreements will also be obstacles to establishing an integrated national market; second, a law has to be established to mitigate the negative effects created by mergers and concentrations; third, a competition framework needs to be established in China, which will form an open and transparent legal environment for business.

In June 2006, Premier Minister Wen Jiabao chaired the State Council executive meeting, during which the Chinese Anti-Monopoly Law (draft) was discussed and passed. The draft was revised and further reviewed by the Standing Committee of the National People's Congress in June 2007.[185] On 30 August 2007, the 29th session of the Tenth National People's Congress passed the People's Republic of China Anti-Monopoly Law and this law took effect on 1 August 2008.

---

[180] M. SHANG (2005), 'The Development and Legislation of Competition Policy in China' (发展中的中国竞争政策与立法), MOFCOM website, 27 April 2005, available at <http://tfs. mofcom.gov.cn/aarticle/dzgg/f/200504/20050400081489.html> accessed 28.03.2014; *see also* B.M. OWEN, S. SUN and W. ZHENG (2008), *supra* n. 7, p. 236.

[181] T.R. HOWELL, A.W. WOLFF, R. HOWE and D. OH (2009), 'China's New Anti-Monopoly Law: A Perspective from the United States', *Pacific Rim Law and Policy Journal*, vol. 18, no. 1, p. 56; D.J. GERBER (2008), *supra* n. 7, p. 284.

[182] T.R. HOWELL, A.W. WOLFF, R. HOWE and D. OH (2009), *supra* n. 181, p. 56.

[183] J.A. BERRY (2005), *supra* n. 42, p. 140; *see also* Y. ZHANG (2004), 'The Submitted Version of the Anti-Monopoly Law Has been Formed' (我国《反垄断法》送审稿已形成), *Xinhua Net*, 27 October 2004, available at <http://news.xinhuanet.com/legal/2004–10/27/content_2146394.htm> accessed 23.03.2014.

[184] Y. HUANG (2008), *supra* n. 3, p. 119.

[185] B.M. OWEN, S. SUN and W. ZHENG (2008), *supra* n. 7, p. 236.

5.3. AN OVERVIEW OF THE AML

The Anti-Monopoly Law is composed of 57 articles in 8 chapters. Chapter 1 provides general provisions. Chapter 2 (Articles 13–16) deals with monopoly agreements,[186] including the prohibited horizontal monopoly agreements (Article 13), the prohibited vertical monopoly agreements (Article 14) and a list of exemptions that may be granted (Article 15). The prohibited monopoly agreements include fixing or changing prices of commodities; restricting the level of output or sales; dividing the market of sales or raw material procurement; limiting the purchase of new technology or new facilities; involvement in boycott transactions; fixing the price of commodities for resale to a third party; and restricting the minimum price for resale to a third party. Article 15 provides seven circumstances that can be exempted from these prohibitions, including monopoly agreements that for the purpose of improving technologies, developing new products, improving product quality, enhancing efficiency and public interest, promoting competition for small and medium-sized businesses, or mitigating sales loss in economic recessions, preserve justifiable interests engaging in international trade and cooperation.[187]

Chapter 3 (Articles 17–19) covers the abuse of a dominant market position.[188] Article 17 first lists the behaviors that should be considered as abuse of a dominant position. These acts are selling or buying products at unfairly high or low prices, and, without justification, selling products at prices below cost, refusing to trade, exclusive dealing, tying, or applying dissimilar prices or terms.[189] Article 18 specifies the determining variables for defining dominant market status, including the market share in the relevant market, the competitiveness of the relevant market, the capacity of controlling the sales or raw material procurement market, the undertaking's financial and technical condition, and the difficulty of market entry.[190] Article 19 further clarifies the criteria for calculating market dominance. A business operator will be considered to hold a dominant market position when its market share in the relevant market is at least 50 percent; or two undertakings' joint market share accounts for two thirds of the relevant market; or three undertakings' joint market share is three quarters or above. Specifically, in the latter two circumstances, the business operator with a market share of less than ten percent should not be taken into account.[191]

Chapter 4 (Articles 20–31) of the AML is focused on concentrations.[192] This chapter lays the legal foundation for the merger control policy, followed by

---

[186]   AML Chapter 2, Arts. 13–16.
[187]   AML Chapter 2.
[188]   AML Chapter 3, Arts. 17–19.
[189]   AML, Art. 17.
[190]   AML, Art. 18.
[191]   AML, Art. 19.
[192]   AML Chapter 4, Arts. 20–31.

several administrative rules enacted after the AML. This chapter includes the definition of concentration, the circumstances under which a concentration may not be declared to the anti-monopoly authority under the State Council, the documents to be submitted for a declaration of a concentration, the procedure of declared concentration review, the relevant elements that shall be considered in concentration examination, the exemptions of prohibition regarding public interests, restrictive conditions, publication of decisions and considerations of national security.

The last four chapters of the AML deal with the issues of 'restrictions on administrative monopoly',[193] 'investigation into the suspicious monopolistic conduct',[194] 'legal liabilities'[195] and 'supplementary provisions'.[196]

5.4. ENFORCEMENT OF THE AML

5.4.1. *Three Enforcement Agencies*

The drafting process of the AML took nearly 14 years. One of the major obstacles to the enactment of the AML was the power struggle between three regulatory agencies – the MOFCOM, the NDRC and the SAIC. All of them were eager to take the lead in the drafting and the enforcement of the AML.[197] The tension between them was not solved when the AML was enacted;[198] therefore, the enforcement power of the AML was divided between these three regulatory agencies and the Anti-Monopoly Commission only plays an advisory role.[199]

According to Articles 9–10 of the AML, the competence for drafting competition policies is granted to the Anti-Monopoly Commission (AMC), a central antitrust authority subordinated to the State Council.[200] This Commission

---

[193]   AML Chapter 5, Arts. 32–37.

[194]   AML Chapter 6, Arts. 38–45.

[195]   AML Chapter 7, Arts. 46–54.

[196]   AML Chapter 8, Arts. 55–57.

[197]   N. Bush (2005), 'Chinese Competition Policy: It Takes More Than a Law', *China Business Review*, vol. 32, no. 3, p. 34.

[198]   L. Zhang (2005), 'Three Ministries Fight The Enforcement Competence of the AML' (三部委争立反垄断法, 主管者缺位致今年出台无望), *Beijing Morning Post*, 11 January 2005, available at <http://finance.sina.com.cn/roll/20050111/06181283920.shtml> (in Chinese) accessed 22.03.2014.

[199]   G. Li and A. Young (2008), 'Competition Laws and Policies in China and Hong Kong: A Tale of Two Regulatory Journeys', *Journal of International Trade Law and Policy*, vol. 7, no. 2, p. 188.

[200]   According to Article 9 of the AML, the five functions that this commission plays are (English translation adopted from people.com): '(1) studying and drafting related competition policies; (2) organizing the investigation and assessment of overall competition situations in the market, and issuing assessment reports; (3) constituting and issuing anti-monopoly guidelines; (4) coordinating anti-monopoly administrative law enforcement; (5) other functions as assigned by the State Council.' Article 10 of the AML: 'The anti-monopoly

is responsible for policy formulation and co-ordination. The AMC may authorize local governments in provinces, autonomous regions and municipalities to take responsibility for enforcement. On 28 July 2008, the General Office of the State Council published the Notice of the General Office of the State Council on the Main Functions and Members of the Anti-Monopoly Commission of the State Council[201] and stated that the main functions of the AMC include researching and drafting competition policies, providing guidelines, issuing reports on the competition status of the market, coordinating and assisting the enforcement. The enforcement functions, however, were not explicitly mentioned in this announcement. The AMC office consists of one director, Wang Qishan, who is the Vice Premier of the State Council, four vice-directors and 14 commissioners.[202]

Two months after the promulgation of the AML, in October 2008, the Ministry of Commerce released a report which assigns responsibility for the enforcement of the AML to three administrative authorities. First, the NDRC is responsible for enforcing the rules of the AML on anticompetitive agreements and abuse of dominance that are price-related. Second, the SAIC is responsible for investigating non-price-related anticompetitive behavior, including monopolistic agreements, abuse of dominant position and abuse of administrative power to restrict competition. Third, the Anti-Monopoly Bureau of the Ministry of Commerce (MOFCOM), established in August 2008, deals with pre-merger and acquisition notifications, investigations and assessments, as well as competition issues in international trade. The SAIC, the NDRC and the Ministry of Commerce are three State-level authorities under the direct supervision of the State Council. The SAIC and the NDRC have government departments at provincial levels. The Chinese antitrust law authorizes the SAIC, the NDRC, and the MOFCOM, these three ministerial level departments the power of antitrust enforcement and these new antitrust responsibilities have to be combined with other existing administrative duties, such as drafting industrial and commercial policies, formulating national plans for industry, and facilitating domestic and international trade.

---

authority designated by the State Council (hereinafter referred to as the Anti-Monopoly Authority under the State Council) shall be in charge of anti-monopoly law enforcement in accordance with this Law. The Anti-monopoly Authority under the State Council may, when needed, authorize the corresponding authorities in the people's governments of the provinces, autonomous regions and municipalities directly under the Central Government to take charge of anti-monopoly law enforcement in accordance with this Law.'

[201] Guowuyuan Bangongting Guanyu Guowuyuan Fanlongduan Weiyuanhui Zhuyao Zhize He Zucheng Renyuan De Tongzhi (国务院办公厅关于国务院反垄断委员会主要职责和组成人员的通知) [Notice of the General Office of the State Council on the Main Functions and Members of the Anti-Monopoly Commission of the State Council] (issued by the General Office of the State Council, 28 July 2008, effective on 28 July 2008), available at <www.lawinfochina.com/display.aspx?lib=law&id=7190>(in English and Chinese) accessed 03.04.2014.

[202] Notice of the General Office of the State Council on the Main Functions and Members of the Anti-Monopoly Commission of the State Council, *supra* n. 201.

In addition to the division of work between the NDRC, the SAIC and the MOFCOM, several vital industries, such as telecommunications, postal services, railways, electricity and banking, remain under the direct supervision of sector-specific administrative authorities. For example, the sector of telecommunications falls under the control of the Ministry of Information and Industry ('MII').[203]

5.4.2. MOFCOM: the Merger Enforcement Agency

On 17 June 2011, MOFCOM announced the formal establishment of an AMC office, which will operate within MOFCOM.[204] This office undertakes nine major responsibilities:[205] (1) drafting regulations, provisions and documents of concentrations of undertakings; (2) reviewing, investigating and assessing concentrations; receiving concentration applications and notifications; taking related hearings and investigations; (3) investigating other concentration cases reported by antitrust enforcement agencies; (4) investigating monopolistic conduct in foreign trade, and take actions to mitigate negative effects; (5) guiding domestic enterprises overseas in antitrust litigations; (6) organizing negotiations on competition clauses in multilateral and bilateral agreements; (7) facilitating international cooperation on multilateral and bilateral competition policy; (8) other work assigned by the Anti-Monopoly Committee of the State Council; (9) other work assigned by the leaders.

Articles 20–31 of the AML formulate the competition rules for mergers and acquisitions. Following these rules, in 2009, the MOFCOM implemented several guidelines which provided a few details in the enforcement of the merger control policy.[206] According to Articles 25 and 26 of the AML, after receiving the application submitted by the merging enterprises, the MOFCOM should make a decision within 30 days. The concentration should not be conducted before this decision is made. The second phase of examination takes 90 days. The MOFCOM can approve the concentration, prohibit the concentration, or approve the

---

[203] X. ZHANG and V.Y. ZHANG (2007), *supra* n. 2, p. 190.

[204] S. NING and R. YIN, 'Formal Establishment of Anti-Monopoly Commission Office within MOFCOM Approved', 17 June 2011, *King & Wood Mallesons, China Law Insight*, available at <www.chinalawinsight.com/2011/06/articles/corporate/antitrust-competition/formal-establishment-of-antimonopoly-commission-office-within-mofcom-approved/> accessed 22.03.2014.

[205] MOFCOM, 'The Responsibilities of the MOFCOM', 13 June 2011, MOFCOM website, available at <http://fldj.mofcom.gov.cn/article/gywm/200809/20080905756026.shtml> (in Chinese) and <http://english.mofcom.gov.cn/departments/fldj2/> (in English) accessed 03.04.2014.

[206] Two guidelines were published by the MOFCOM right after the enactment of the AML: on 03 August 2008, the MOFCOM issued the Thresholds for Prior Notification of Concentrations of Undertakings, and the Guide of the Anti-Monopoly Committee of the State Council for the Definition of the Relevant Market, which was published on MOFCOM website on 24 May 2009.

concentration with conditions. In certain circumstances, this procedure can be extended to no longer than 60 days.

5.5. MERGER GUIDELINES AFTER THE AML

The notification provision is issued by the State Council. Several guidelines have been issued to follow this provision. It is the same for the market definition provision. These guidelines, although were drafted by the MOFCOM, have to be approved and issued by the Anti-Monopoly Commission. This is to confirm that the standards stated in the guidelines, such as the market definition, are to be applied in all fields of the antitrust investigations by all enforcement authorities.[207]

5.5.1. Notification Guidelines

On 3 August 2008, the State Council released the Provisions of the State Council on Thresholds for Prior Notification of Concentrations of Undertakings.[208] The guidelines have five articles and especially specify the thresholds for the declaration of concentrations, and state that even if the enterprises do not reach this standard, they may also have to be examined if anticompetitive effects are expected to occur. Article 3 of this Provision lists two thresholds and when a concentration reaches this threshold, a prior notification should be filed. The first circumstance is when the participating undertaking' combined worldwide turnover is more than RMB 10 billion in the previous accounting year, and at least two participating undertaking's turnover within China are both more than RMB 400 million in the previous accounting year. The second circumstance is when the participating undertakings' combined turnover within China is more than 2 billion yuan in the previous accounting year, and at least two participating undertakings' turnover in China is more than RMB 400 million in the previous accounting year.[209] According to Article 4 of this Provision, concentrations

---

[207] A. EMCH (2011), 'Antitrust in China – the Brighter Spots', *European Competition Law Review*, vol. 3, p. 133.

[208] Guowuyuan Guanyu Jingyingzhe Jizhong Shenbao Biaozhun De Guiding (国务院关于经营者集中申报标准的规定) [Provisions of the State Council on Thresholds for Prior Notification of Concentrations of Undertakings] (adopted at the 20th Executive Meeting of the State Council on 1 August 2008, effective on 3 August 2008), available at <www.gov.cn/zwgk/2008–08/04/content_1063769.htm> (in Chinese) and <http://fldj.mofcom.gov.cn/aarticle/c/200903/20090306071501.html> (in English) accessed 05.04.2014. On 6 June 2012, the MOFCOM published a revised form for pre-merger notifications and the instructions for completing this form and submitting the supporting documents. From 7 July 2012, this new form should replace the current one which was issued on 5 January 2009. To read the form, see <http://fldj.mofcom.gov.cn/aarticle/zcfb/201206/20120608166903.html> (in Chinese).

[209] Provisions of the State Council on Thresholds for Prior Notification of Concentrations of Undertakings, *supra* n. 208, Article 3.

below this threshold may also be subject to an anti-monopoly investigation, when this concentration may have anticompetitive effects.

Following this provision issued by the State Council, several guidelines were implemented which further clarify the information to be submitted and the procedure to be followed. On 5 January 2009, the MOFCOM issued the Guiding Opinions of the Anti-Monopoly Bureau of the Ministry of Commerce on the Declaration Documents and materials of the Concentration of Undertakings.[210] On 15 July 2009, the Measures for calculating the Turnover for the Declaration of Business Concentration in the Financial Industry[211] was issued by the China Banking Regulatory Commission, China Insurance Regulatory Commission, the China Securities Regulatory Commission, the Ministry of Commerce and the People's Bank of China. This provision provides guidance on the calculation of turnover for financial institutions. On 21 November 2009, the MOFCOM issued the Measures for the Undertaking Concentration Declaration.[212] On 30 December 2011 the MOFCOM issued the Interim Measures for Investigating and Handling Failure to Legally Declare the Concentration of Business Operators.[213]

5.5.2. Assessment Guidelines

According to Articles 25 and 26 of the AML, after the notification is accepted, the authority (specifically MOFCOM) has to conduct a preliminary review of the proposed concentration and issue a written decision within 30 days. If the

---

[210] Shangwubu Fanlongduanju Guanyu Jingyingzhe Jizhong Shenbao Wenjian Ziliao De Zhidao Yijian (商务部反垄断局关于经营者集中申报文件资料的指导意见) [Guiding Opinions of the Anti-Monopoly Bureau of the Ministry of Commerce on the Declaration Documents and Materials of the Concentration of Business Operators] (issued by the Ministry of Commerce, 5 January 2009, effective on 5 January 2009), available at <http://en.pkulaw.cn/display.aspx?cgid=122866&lib=law> (in English and Chinese) accessed 05.04.2014.

[211] Jinrongye Jingyingzhe Jizhong Shenbao Yingye'e Jisuan Banfa (金融业经营者集中申报营业额计算办法) [Measures for Calculating the Turnover for the Declaration of Business Concentration in the Financial Industry] (issued by the China Banking Regulatory Commission, the China Insurance Regulatory Commission, the China Securities Regulatory Commission, the Ministry of Commerce, and People's Bank of China, on 15 July 2009, effective on 15 August 2009), available at <http://fldj.mofcom.gov.cn/aarticle/c/200907/20090706411691.html> (in Chinese), and <http://en.pkulaw.cn/display.aspx?cgid=119448&lib=law> (in English) accessed 05.04.2014.

[212] Jingyingzhe Jizhong Shenbao Banfa (经营者集中申报办法) [Measure for the Undertaking Concentration Declaration] (promulgated by the Ministry of Commerce on 21 November 2009, effective on 1 January 2010), available at <www.lawinfochina.com/display.aspx?lib=law&id=8183&CGid> (in English and Chinese) accessed 05.04.2014.

[213] Wei Yifa Shenbao Jingyingzhe Jizhong Diaocha Chuli Zanxing Banfa (未依法申报经营者集中调查处理暂行办法) [Interim Measures for Investigating and Handling Failure to Legally Declare the Concentration of Business Operators] (issued by the Ministry of Commerce, 30 December 2011, effective on 1 February 2012), available at <http://en.pkulaw.cn/display.aspx?cgid=164975&lib=law> (in English) and <http://fldj.mofcom.gov.cn/aarticle/zcfb/201201/20120107921682.html> (in Chinese) accessed 05.04.2014.

MOFCOM decides to conduct an in-depth review, this process takes 90 days, and can be extended to no more than 150 days. After the review, a written decision should be issued and notified to the business operators.

There are three categories of guidelines have been issued and implemented to assess merger effects after the AML came into force. The first category is guidelines that are applied to define the relevant market. In 2009, the Guidelines for Defining the Relevant Market, was issued by the Anti-Monopoly Commission. However, this guideline does not have binding force. On 24 May 2009, the State Council issued the Guide of the Anti-Monopoly Committee of the State Council for the Definition of the Relevant Market.[214]

The second category of guidelines refers to the guidelines that are applied to assess competitive effects. Article 27 of the AML lists six elements that the authority will consider during the investigation of anticompetitive effects: (1) the participating undertakings' market share in the relevant market, and the controlling power in that market; (2) the level of concentration in the relevant market; (3) the concentration's technological impact; (4) the concentrations' effects on consumers and other business operators; (5) the concentration's effects on national economic development; (6) other elements considered by the authority. On 29 August 2009, the MOFCOM issued the Interim Provisions on the Assessment of Competitive Effects of Concentrations of Undertakings.[215] On 24 November 2009, the MOFCOM issued the Measures for the Undertaking Concentration Examination.[216] On 11 March 2010, the MOFCOM issued the Working Guidelines of the Anti-Monopoly Bureau of the Ministry of Commerce on Concentrations of Undertakings[217] and in 2011 the MOFCOM issued the Interim Rules on the Assessment of Competitive Impacts of Concentrations of Undertakings.

---

[214] Guowuyuan Fanlongduan Weiyuanhui Guanyu Xiangguan Shichang Jieding De Zhinan (国务院反垄断委员会关于相关市场界定的指南) [Guide of the Anti-Monopoly Committee of the State Council for the Definition of the Relevant Market] (issued by the Anti-Monopoly Committee of the State Council on 24 May 2009), available at <http://fldj.mofcom.gov.cn/ aarticle/j/200907/ 20090706384131.html> (in Chinese) accessed 05.04.2014.

[215] Shangwubu Guanyu Pinggu Jingyingzhe Jizhong Jingzheng Yingxiang De Zanxing Guiding (商务部关于评估经营者集中竞争影响的暂行规定) [Interim Provisions on Assessing the Impact of Concentration of Business Operators on Competition] (issued by the Anti-Monopoly Committee of the State Council on 29 August 2011, effective on 5 September 2011), available at http://en.pkulaw.cn/display.aspx?cgid=157952&lib=law> (in English and Chinese) accessed 05.04.2014.

[216] Jingyingzhe Jizhong Shencha Banfa (经营者集中审查办法) [Measure for the Undertaking Concentration Examination] (issued by the Ministry of Commerce 24 November 2009, effective on 1 January 2010), available at <www.lawinfochina.com/display.aspx?lib=law&id= 8184&CGid=> (in English and Chinese) accessed 05.04.2014.

[217] Jingyingzhe Jizhong Fanlongduan Shencha Banshi Zhinan (经营者集中反垄断审查办事指南) [Working Guidelines of the Anti-Monopoly Bureau of the Ministry of Commerce on Concentrations of Undertakings] (issued by the Ministry of Commerce on 11 March 2010), available at <http://fldj.mofcom.gov.cn/article/xgxz/200902/20090206034057.shtml> (in Chinese) accessed 05.04.2014.

The third category of guidelines in merger analysis is the application of remedies. Article 29 of the AML formulates the basic rules for merger remedies. On 5 July 2010, the MOFCOM issued the Interim Provisions on the Divestiture of Assets or Business in the Concentration of Business Operators.[218] In August 2010, the MOFCOM issued the Provisional Rules on the Implementation of Business Divestiture in Concentrations between Undertakings.

6.   NON-ECONOMIC GOALS IN THE AML AND MERGER POLICY

As discussed in the previous sections, the drafting process of the AML was to a large extent influenced by the specific competition goals in China. Although the AML followed the structure of the competition law and policy in the EU which deals with monopoly agreements, abuse of dominant position, and concentrations, a particular aspect that makes the AML distinct from the competition policy in both the US and the EU is that it incorporates various non-economic goals.[219] The Anti-Monopoly Law in China contains several articles which indicate that the competition policy in China does not solely focus on economic goals. Article 1 of the AML states that this law is enacted for five objectives, including restraining monopolistic behavior, protecting competition, promoting efficiency, protecting the interest of consumers and the public, and contributing to the development of the socialist market economy. This article indicates that the Anti-Monopoly Law pursues various economic and non-economic goals, including the consumer welfare standard, the total welfare standard, and public interest concerns.[220] Following Article 1, the AML contains several articles that address the goal of contributing to a socialist market economy and the goal of promoting public interest. Moreover, these two goals have also been extended to the concerns of protecting SOEs and regulating mergers that involve foreign investors. These concerns will be explained in the following sections.

---

[218] Shangwubu Guanyu Shishi Jingyingzhe Jizhong Zichan Huo Yewu Boli De Zanxing Guiding (商务部关于实施经营者集中资产或业务剥离的暂行规定) [Interim Provisions on the Divestiture of Assets or Business in the Concentration of Business Operators] (issued by the Ministry of Commerce on 5 July 2010, effective on 5 July 2010), available at <http://en.pkulaw.cn/display.aspx?cgid=134980&lib=law> (in English and Chinese) accessed 05.04.2014.

[219] S.B. FARMER (2013), *supra* n. 13, p. 22.

[220] P. SHAN, G. TAN, S.J. WILKIE and M.A. WILLIAMS (2011), 'China's Anti-Monopoly Law, What is the Welfare Standard', *University of South California (USC) Center in Law, Economics and Organization Research Paper No. C11–18*, and *USC Legal Studies Research Paper No. 11–25*, p. 7.

6.1. THE DEVELOPMENT OF A SOCIALIST MARKET ECONOMY

Article 4 of the AML states that competition rules will be applied in a way which fits into the socialist market economy. The implementation of these rules must contribute to the establishment of a 'unified', 'open', 'competitive and orderly' market system. This article signals that the role of the AML is to achieve the broader goals of establishing a well-functioning market system with a specific characteristic of 'socialist market economy'.

6.2. CONCERNS OF PROTECTING SOEs

To provide further explanations of the multiple goals of the AML, there are several articles that clarify the application of the AML to certain industries, as well as the situations to grant exemptions. Under the section on 'monopoly agreement', Article 7 of the AML pays attention to the State-owned economy. This article states that for State-controlled industries, industries which are crucial for the national economy and national security, as well as industries operating 'exclusive operations and sales', their lawful business will be protected by the State. Moreover, their business operations, as well as the prices of their products and services, will be 'regulated and controlled' by the State, for the purpose of safeguarding 'consumer interests' and 'promoting technical progresses'. This article also states that the business operators in these industries should conduct 'self-discipline' and should not damage consumer interests by abusing their 'dominant' or 'exclusive' positions.

6.3. PROMOTING PUBLIC INTEREST

Article 15 of the AML provides the circumstances for granting exemptions for business operators who are involved in monopoly agreements. There are seven circumstances where exemptions can be applied. The first situation is when the agreement is for the purpose of promoting research and development for new products. The second circumstance is when the agreement is for the purpose of improving product quality, increasing efficiency, unifying product standards, and upgrading product specialization. The third situation is when the agreement is for the purpose of increasing efficiency for small and medium-sized operators and improving their competitiveness. The fourth circumstance is when the agreement is for the purpose of protecting the environment, saving energy, helping victims after the natural disasters, and other social public interests. The fifth circumstance is when the agreement is signed during economic recessions and for the purpose of mitigating the loss because of sales decreasing or excessive production. The sixth circumstance is when the agreement is for the justifiable interests in international trade and international economic cooperation. The seventh is other circumstances that are justified by laws and stipulated by the State Council.

When a monopoly agreement falls under one of the first five circumstances, to receive an exemption from Articles 13 and 14, the business operator has to prove that this agreement ensures consumers will share the benefits generated by this agreement. Moreover, this agreement will not severely restrict competition in the relevant market.

The seven circumstances listed in this article indicate several different goals that the competition rules in China can take into account. For example, the goal of promoting 'technological improvement' mentioned in first circumstance, the concerns of protecting 'small and medium-sized operators' under the third circumstance, and the emphasis on the 'social public interest' in the fourth circumstance. The sixth circumstance particularly focuses on the lawful interest of domestic firms in international trade.

Under the section on 'concentrations', Article 28[221] states two situations when a concentration can be exempted from a prohibition. The first situation is when the concentration can prove that the potential positive effects will be larger than the negative effects that it has on competition. The second situation is when the concentration pursues public interests. This article emphasizes the importance of 'public interest' again.

Moreover, Article 27 of this AML lists six factors that the antitrust authority should consider in the assessment of concentrations. The third factor is the effects of concentrations on technological progress. The fifth factor is the impact of the concentrations on national economic development. On 25 May 2010, the SAIC issued Regulations on the Prohibition of the Abuse of Dominant Market Positions, and Article 8 of this regulation listed the factors which will be included to assess competitive effects. One important factor is the effects on 'social public interests and economic development'.

The Interim Provisions on the Assessment of Competitive Effects of Concentrations of Undertakings issued on 5 September 2011 states that the 'market share' and the 'market concentration levels' are the 'evidence of adverse effects'. However, the question of how to define and to assess the 'adverse effect' and the 'public interest' remains unanswered.

---

[221] Article 28, AML: 'Where a concentration has or may have effect of eliminating or restricting competition, the Anti-monopoly Authority under the State Council shall make a decision to prohibit the concentration. However, if the business operators concerned can prove that the concentration will bring more positive impact than negative impact on competition, or the concentration is pursuant to public interests, the Anti-monopoly Authority under the State Council may decide not to prohibit the concentration.'

6.4. NATIONAL SECURITY REVIEW

Besides the considerations of the 'public interest' and the 'national economic development', a concentration including foreign investors should also go through a 'national security test'. Article 31 of the AML states that when a foreign investor participates in the concentration, besides the examination of competition effects, an additional examination on national security might also be applied, which is conducted under other relevant state provisions.

On 25 August 2011, the MOFCOM published the Regulation on the Implementation of the Security Review System for Mergers and Acquisitions of Domestic Enterprises by Foreign Investors[222] to implement a previous circular Notice on Establishing a Security Review System for Mergers and Acquisitions of Domestic Enterprises by Foreign Investors,[223] issued by the State Council on 3 February 2011. This regulation once again draws attention to the issue of national security and imposes challenges on future antitrust decisions regarding the question of how to make a wise tradeoff between other industrial policies and competition policies.

7. INTERPRETING THE MULTIPLE GOALS OF THE CHINESE ANTI-MONOPOLY LAW

In the previous section, it was made clear that both the AML and merger policy in China have been formulated in a way of incorporating various policy goals. In this section, the issue of competition goals in China will be addressed from a normative perspective. The question will be how scholars, legislators and policy makers in China interpret the goals of the AML, as well as, in their opinions, which goal the AML should prioritize. This normative study may enhance the understanding of how competition policy in China was formulated to satisfy the social, political and economic preferences.

---

[222] Shangwubu Shishi Waiguo Touzizhe Binggou Jingnei Qiye Anquan Shencha Zhidu Youguan Shixiang De Zanxing Guiding (商务部实施外国投资者并购境内企业安全审查制度有关事项的暂行规定) [The Interim Measures on Relevant Matters Concerning the Implementation of Security Review of Mergers and Acquisitions of Domestic Enterprises by Foreign Investors] (issued by the Ministry of Commerce on 4 March 2011, effective on 5 March 2011), available at <http://wzs.mofcom.gov.cn/article/n/201103/20110307432685.shtml> (in Chinese) accessed 05.04.2014.

[223] Guowuyuan Bangongting Guanyu Jianli Waiguo Touzizhe Binggou Jingnei Qiye Anquan Shencha Zhidu De Tongzhi (国务院办公厅关于建立外国投资者并购境内企业安全审查制度的通知) [Notice of the General Office of the State Council on the Establishment of the Security Review System for Mergers and Acquisitions of Domestic Enterprises by Foreign Investors] (issued by the General Office of the State Council on 3 February 2011, effective on 3 March 2011), available at <http://en.pkulaw.cn/display.aspx?cgid=145049&lib=law> (in English and Chinese) accessed 05.04.2014.

7.1. ACADEMIC SCHOLARS

7.1.1. Non-Economic Goals versus Economic Goals

Most scholars in China agree that the goal of the Anti-Monopoly Law should include economic goals, in particular the goal of promoting efficiency.[224] The reason is that although China has experienced a rapid economic development in recent years, it is still on its way to becoming a high-income country. Therefore, the goals of promoting economic growth, as well as enhancing efficiency, should be included in the Anti-Monopoly Law.

Although some scholars in China argue that efficiency should be the primary goal, most scholars argue that the efficiency goal needs to be balanced with the goal of promoting fairness.[225] With respect to the hierarchy between these different goals, Ding argued that the goal of 'protecting fair competition' under Article 1, serves as a functional goal, which laid the basis for the competition policy in China. The other three goals – improving efficiency, protecting consumer welfare and social interests – are the results that the AML is expected to achieve. Because the AML is enacted to achieve these three results, the fundamental functions of the law are the production function and the distribution function, with the production function superior to the distribution function.[226]

By contrast, Lv and Tao argue that maximizing consumer welfare should be the ultimate goal of the competition law in China. The reason is that economic growth should benefit the majority of the society. The goal of promoting competition and efficiency, are only two most useful instruments to serve the goal of maximizing consumer welfare.[227] Wu and Wei argued that when the goals of competition law conflict with each other, which goal should be taken as the superior goal should be decided according to the economic, social and political situation in the country as well as the international environment.[228]

---

[224] H. GAO and X. DONG (2008), 'The Goal and the Values of the AML' (论我国反垄断法的价值目标及其实现), *Socialism Studies* (社会主义研究), serial no. 180, no. 4, p. 97; M. DING (2011), 'On the Functions and its Optimization of Antitrust Law' (反垄断法的目标选择及其功能优化刍议), *Journal of Tianjin University of Finance and Economics* (天津财经大学学报), issue 8, p. 128; Z. LV and W. TAO (2008), 'The Ultimate Goal of the AML' (浅谈我国反垄断法的终极目标), *Study on China Administration for Industry & Commerce* (中国工商管理研究), no. 4, p. 27.

[225] H. GAO and X. DONG (2008), *supra* n. 224, p. 97.

[226] M. DING (2011), *supra* n. 224, p. 128.

[227] Z. LV and W. TAO (2008), *supra* n. 224, p. 27.

[228] H. WU and W. WEI (2005), 'The Goals of the AML' (论反垄断法的价值目标), *The Jurist* (法学家), no. 3, p. 98.

7.1.2.   *The Development of a Socialist Market Economy*

According to Professor Gerber, the AML in China has been influenced by the incentive structures, due to the important role that the central government has played in the economic development in China.[229] The incentives to take actions are motivated by specific ideological goals, such as pursuing social equality, which are announced by the government or other institutions.[230]

After the 1978 Market Reform, the main feature of the political reform is that the Chinese Communist Party ('CCP') moved from the 'dogmatic approach of the Maoist version of the Marxism-Leninism' to a 'pragmatic, market oriented approach'. During the development of economic policy, the ideology of socialism has been reflected by the term of 'socialist market economy'.[231] Wu and Wei argued that the goal of the economic reform in China is to establish a socialist market economy, which promotes both economic efficiency and social fairness. Therefore, it is necessary to balance the efficiency goal and the fairness goal in antitrust enforcement, if the ultimate goal is to ensure a healthy development of the socialist market economy, and to establish a socialist harmonious society.[232] Hamp-Lyons argued that the goal of establishing a 'socialist market economy' indicates China's strong interest in sustaining 'social stability'. Therefore, the goals of competition policy in China will be different from those of the United States or the European Union.[233]

Montinola *et al.* and Wang accepted that the term 'socialist market economy' reflects the ideology of socialism.[234] Shan *et al.* argued that the goal of 'promoting the healthy development of the socialist market economy' mentioned in Article 1 of the AML may give preference to the gains to the SOEs, or it could be understood as protecting the interests of specific producers.[235] According to Hamp-Lyons, when a merger forces an inefficient competitor to close down, the Chinese government might prohibit this merger and choose to protect the inefficient local firms, because closing a firm will result in workers losing their jobs. In this way, when the goal of 'efficiency' and the 'socialist goal' conflict with each other, the 'social stability' goal might have a higher weight.[236] Fox argued that it is reasonable for the Chinese government to take employment into

---

[229]   D.J. GERBER (2008), *supra* n. 3, p. 277.

[230]   D.J. GERBER (2008), *supra* n. 3, p. 277.

[231]   G. MONTINOLA, Y. QIAN and B.R. WEINGAST (1995), 'Federalism, Chinese Style: The Political Basis for Success in China', *World Politics*, vol. 48, no. 1, p. 52; X. WANG (2008), *supra* n. 12, p. 133.

[232]   H. WU and W. WEI (2005), *supra* n. 228, p. 98.

[233]   C. HAMP-LYONS (2009), 'The Dragon in the Room: China's Anti-Monopoly Law and International Merger Review', *Vanderbilt Law Review*, vol. 62, no. 5, p. 1580.

[234]   G. MONTINOLA, Y. QIAN and B.R. WEINGAST (1995), *supra* n. 231, p. 52; X. WANG (2008), *supra* n. 12, p. 133.

[235]   P. SHAN, G. TAN, S. J. WILKIE and M. A. WILLIAMS (2011), *supra* n. 220, p. 6.

[236]   C. HAMP-LYONS (2009), *supra* n. 233, p. 1580, footnote 15.

account, as stability is a clear social goal. She proposed that Chinese antitrust authorities should prohibit the mergers which will create no clear harm or benefit for consumers, but which will lead to the bankruptcy of local firms.[237]

7.1.3. Competition Policy versus Industrial Policy

International scholars have given interpretations for the articles in the AML mentioning the non-economic goals. For example, Article 5 of the AML reads: 'Business operators may, through fair competition, voluntary alliance, concentrate themselves according to law, expand the scope of business operations, and enhance competitiveness.'[238] Fels argued that this article can be taken as a signal that merger rules will not be enforced strictly towards domestic transactions, especially those initiated by national champions.[239] Howell *et al.* argued that the exemptions provided by Article 15 of the AML might indicate that the AML will be enforced to protect some competitors against others for industrial policy purposes.[240]

Another example is Article 7 of the AML: 'With respect to the industries controlled by the State-owned economy and concerning the lifeline of national economy and national security or the industries implementing exclusive operation and sales according to law, the state protects the lawful business operations conducted by the business operators therein. The State also lawfully regulates and controls their business operations and the prices of their commodities and services so as to safeguard the interests of consumers and promote technical progresses. The business operators as mentioned above shall lawfully operate, be honest and faithful, be strictly self-disciplined, accept social supervision, shall not damage the interests of consumers by virtue of their dominant or exclusive positions.'[241]

Article 7 leaves room for future interpretation, and adds uncertainties in antitrust enforcement concerning the tradeoff between the interests of industries that are controlled by the State and the welfare gains of consumers. Liu and Qiao argued that this article puts particular weight on the protection of 'industries that are controlled by the State-owned economy and that are critical to the well being of the national economy'.[242] Similarly, in the context of abuse of dominant position, the AML has stated several rules with the statement of 'without

---

[237] E.M. Fox (2007), 'Economic Development, Poverty, and Antitrust: The Other Path', *Southwestern Journal of Law and Trade in the Americas*, vol. 13, pp. 211, 228, 229.

[238] Art. 5 AML, English translation is based on <http://english.peopledaily.com.cn/90001/ 90776/90785/6466798.html>.

[239] A. Fels (2012), 'China's Antimonopoly Law 2008: An Overview', *Review of Industrial Organization*, vol. 41, p. 14.

[240] T.R. Howell, A.W. Wolff, R. Howe and D. Oh (2009), *supra* n. 181, p. 60.

[241] Art. 7, AML, English translation is based on <http://english.peopledaily.com.cn/90001/ 90776/90785/6466798.html>.

[242] Z. Liu and Y. Qiao (2012), *supra* n. 48, p. 103.

justification'. The question of how to interpret these rules has to be answered by the enforcement agency, and how these rules will be balanced with the industrial policy, is still uncertain.[243] Williams pointed out that it is doubtful whether SOEs will be granted special protection and whether domestic and foreign enterprises will be equally treated.[244] Fox argued that this article indicates that SOEs are 'regulated and controlled' by the State. Moreover, the State, not the enforcement agency of the AML, is empowered to make a decision on their anti-competitive conduct.[245]

Fels saw this article as a compromise between the competition policy and the industrial policy in China. According to Fels, this article can be interpreted in three ways: the SOEs are completely exempted, or not exempted at all, or an intermediate position that in most cases the AML is also applied to SOEs; however, in situations where SOEs are undertaking activities that are required by the State, they will be protected by the AML.[246] Lin proposed a 'competition-neutral principle', to deal with the relationship between the industrial policy and the competition policy.[247] This principle is that industrial policy should only be considered in the situation where a transaction has neither anti-competitive nor pro-competitive effects. To be more precise, industrial policy should not be taken as the critical factor to determine competitive effects.[248] This principle proposed by Lin indicates that when the competition policy is conflicting with the industrial policy, the criteria to be used to decide the case should be the competitive effects of the merger. In any situation, an anticompetitive merger should not be allowed and a procompetitive merger should not be banned.[249] The ultimate goal of a competition law should be promoting competition.[250] According to Lin, this principle not only can be applied to concentrations, but also to other domains of competition law, such as cases related to abuse of dominant position and monopolistic agreements.

7.1.4.   The Considerations of Public Interests

According to Wei, the compromise between competition policy and industrial policy is covered under the 'public interest' defense in the AML. Wei argued that it is common for many emerging countries to include public interest

---

[243] Z. Liu and Y. Qiao (2012), *supra* n. 48, p. 104.
[244] M. Williams (2009), *supra* n. 98, p. 137.
[245] E.M. Fox (2008) 'An Anti-Monopoly Law for China – Scaling the Walls of Government Restraints', *Antitrust Law Journal*, vol. 75, p. 178.
[246] A. Fels (2012), *supra* n. 239, p. 15.
[247] P. Lin (2009), 'Balancing Competition Policy and Industrial Policy under China's AML', presentation at the 5th summer workshop on industrial organization and management strategy, Tsinghua University, Beijing; P. Lin and J. Zhao (2012), *supra* n. 107, p. 129.
[248] P. Lin and J. Zhao (2012), *supra* n. 107, p. 129.
[249] P. Lin and J. Zhao (2012), *supra* n. 107, p. 129.
[250] P. Lin and J. Zhao (2012), *supra* n. 107, p. 129.

concerns in their antitrust laws. The goals of antitrust law are affected by the process of market liberalization as well as by the process of economic development.[251] In the case of China, Berry argued that economic development is facilitated through the tradeoffs between liberalizing the market and retaining the 'centralized, communist political system',[252] as any increase in economic freedom requires the reduction of the control from the central government.[253]

In fact, the process of drafting the AML reflects the evolution of this tradeoff. The promulgation of the AML itself shows the success of transforming the country from a centrally planned economy to a socialist market economy. According to Professor Wang Xiaoye, a main drafter of the AML, the enactment of the AML is an 'achievement of Chinese economic reform'.[254] According to Professor Huang Yong, an advisory expert of the drafting of the AML, the most challenging task of enacting an antitrust law during this transition is to strike a balance between promoting competition and maintaining the dominant control of the SOEs in strategic industries.[255]

This difficult tradeoff makes the concept of 'public interest' controversial: it is not clear whether the interest of 'the universal good of the Chinese people' also includes the interest of 'certain business operators'.[256] For example, according to Articles 15 and 28 of the AML, monopoly agreements will be granted an exemption if they are for the benefit of 'public interest'.[257] To explain this, Wu and Jin argued that the choice of the competition policy goal is affected by national industrial policy, trade and economic policy.[258] Granting exemptions may leave room for future interpretations, and a decision will be made by the authority to strike a balance between the goals of competition law and the goals of other social and economic policies.[259]

Another way to compromise between the competition policy and other social economic policies in the enforcement of the antitrust law in China might be interpreting the concepts in a broader way. Berry argued that the extent to which the AML can achieve its goals is dependent on precisely how the policy makers define and interpret the key terms stated in the law and in the provisions, for example, the definition of the 'relevant market' and the 'monopoly market

---

[251] D. Wei (2013), *supra* n. 31, p. 126.
[252] J.A. Berry (2005), *supra* n. 42, p. 143.
[253] J.A. Berry (2005), *supra* n. 42, p. 143.
[254] X. Wang (2008), *supra* n. 12, p. 134.
[255] Y. Huang (2008), *supra* n. 3, p. 119.
[256] X. Wang (2008), *supra* n. 12, p. 142.
[257] X. Wang (2008), *supra* n. 12, p. 143.
[258] H. Wu and S. Jin (2009), 'The Social Goals of the AML' (论《反垄断法》的社会公共目标 — 以《反垄断法》的实施为契机), *Journal of Capital Normal University* (首都师范大学学报), vol. 188, no. 3, p. 44.
[259] H. Wu and S. Jin (2009), *supra* n. 258, p. 44.

share'.[260] In addition, the enforcement agencies will have to work together to ensure the consistent application of the AML.[261]

7.1.5.   Considerations of National Security

Delury argued that the definition of 'national security' used by Chinese regulators is broader than that is used in the context of Western laws.[262] It not only refers to the national defense security, but also covers three other areas, namely, 'national economic stability', the 'basic societal order', and the 'research and development capacity for key technologies related to national security.'[263] According to Huang, the 'national security' in Article 31 of the AML refers to the economic interest. Since the Market Reform started thirty years ago, it has been a growing concern that foreign investment in certain industries might endanger the domestic economy.[264] Specific merger rules should be implemented to block the unwelcomed deals by applying a national security justification.[265] In the notice issued by the State Council, the security review procedure will be applied in two situations. The first is when the acquisition targets industries or supports activities that are related to national defense security. The second situation is when the acquisition targets industries that are related to national economic security, such as important sectors in agricultural production, energy resources, infrastructure, transportation services, technology and major equipment manufacturing.[266]

7.1.6.   Efficiency and Welfare Standards

Lin and Zhao argued that although the MOFCOM did not officially announce how efficiencies were treated, it is no doubt that efficiencies are one of the 'countervailing factors' in merger decisions.[267] Article 28 of the AML indicates

---

[260]   J.A. BERRY (2005), *supra* n. 42, p. 148.

[261]   J.A. BERRY (2005), *supra* n. 42, p. 149.

[262]   J. DELURY (2008), 'Harmonious' in China, *Policy Review*, vol. 148, p. 35.

[263]   K.B. GOLDSTEIN (2011), 'Reviewing Cross-border Mergers and Acquisitions for Competition and National Security: A Comparative Look at How the United States, Europe, and China Separate Security Concerns from Competition Concerns in Reviewing Acquisitions by Foreign Entities', *Tsinghua China Law Review*, vol. 3, no. 2, p. 31.

[264]   Y. HUANG (2008), *supra* n. 3, p. 129.

[265]   Y. HUANG (2008), *supra* n. 3, p. 129.

[266]   P. LIN and J. ZHAO (2012), *supra* n. 107, p. 117.

[267]   P. LIN and J. ZHAO (2012), *supra* n. 107, p. 125 (the second author of this paper confirmed this by her personal experience of being commissioned to draft the merger guidelines). Lin and Zhao mentioned that Articles 9 and 12 of the Interim Regulation on the Assessment of the Competitive Effects of Concentrations of Undertakings published by the MOFCOM, 'efficiency' may be taken as a 'countervailing factor'. 2009 Horizontal Merger Guidelines Conditions for the Recognition of Efficiencies, MOFCOM, Guidelines on the Review of Unilateral Effects and Coordinated Effects in Horizontal Concentrations between Undertakings (Consultation Opinion).

that efficiencies might be taken into account after deciding whether a merger is anticompetitive or not.[268] In this way, efficiency considerations, such as the effects of cost savings and economies of scale, can only serve as 'offset factors' in the anticompetitive mergers, not as factors to decide whether a merger is competitive or anticompetitive.[269] This article is also more in line with the total welfare standard than a consumer welfare standard.[270]

With respect to the welfare standard applied in the merger policy in China, Shan *et al.* argued that Article 1 of the AML includes both a consumer welfare standard and a total welfare standard. In addition, public interest concerns, environmental and national securities issues also have to be integrated in antitrust decisions.[271] In particular, the goal of 'promoting economic development' seems to be more consistent with the total welfare standard.[272] Nevertheless, their examination of the published merger case lead to the conclusion that the MOFCOM tends to apply a consumer welfare standard.[273] However, to Berry, this argument could be troublesome, as he argued that consumer interests played a very limited role during the development of the AML and the merger policy.[274] According to Berry, consumers in China may benefit from the increased efficiency of the society, however, it is unconvincing that policy makers in China are incentivized to consider the welfare of consumers at the first stage of their decisions.

From a normative view, Lin and Zhao argued that under the total welfare standard, efficiencies should be taken into account to decide the competitive nature of a merger. Moreover, from a normative view, the total welfare standard is more likely to be the welfare standard that the AML strives to follow. The reason is that the AML has put considerable emphasis on the industrial policy considerations, which indicates that the producer surplus should not be ignored.[275] Hence, for Lin and Zhao, it is more practical to follow the total welfare standard than a consumer welfare standard.[276]

According to Ding, the language of the AML tends to indicate a message of a total welfare standard.[277] For example, Article 15 of the AML provides seven circumstances in which the exemptions can be granted.[278] It seems that these

---

268   P. LIN and J. ZHAO (2012), *supra* n. 107, p. 127.

269   P. LIN and J. ZHAO (2012), *supra* n. 107, p. 127.

270   P. SHAN, G. TAN, S.J. WILKIE and M.A. WILLIAMS (2011), *supra* n. 220, p. 7.

271   P. SHAN, G. TAN, S.J. WILKIE and M.A. WILLIAMS (2011), *supra* n. 220, p. 7.

272   P. SHAN, G. TAN, S.J. WILKIE and M.A. WILLIAMS (2011), *supra* n. 220, p. 8.

273   P. SHAN, G. TAN, S.J. WILKIE and M.A. WILLIAMS (2011), *supra* n. 220, p. 26.

274   J.A. BERRY (2005), *supra* n. 42, p. 150.

275   P. LIN and J. ZHAO (2012), *supra* n. 107, p. 127.

276   P. LIN and J. ZHAO (2012), *supra* n. 107, p. 127.

277   M. DING (2011), *supra* n. 224, p. 128.

278   Article 15, AML: 'An agreement among business operators shall be exempted from application of articles 13 and 14 if it can be proven to be in any of the following circumstances: (1) for the purpose of improving technologies, researching and developing new products; (2) for the purpose of upgrading product quality, reducing cost, improving efficiency, unifying

exemptions can show the process of negotiating between different interests. Granting exemptions for a monopolistic agreement for the reasons of 'improving technologies', 'upgrading product quality', 'enhancing operational efficiency', or 'mitigating decreases in sales', may show a clear preference towards the productive function of the AML, instead of the distributive function.[279] The primary concern of this law is more likely to maximize the 'economic cake' and how to fairly distribute the welfare between consumers and producers are only the secondary concerns.[280]

Ding's argument was supported by Yu Donghua.[281] According to Yu, only a total welfare standard can explain factors (3) (the positive effects of a merger on technological development), (5) (the merger effects on national economic development) and (6) (other elements) listed under Article 27 of the AML.[282] The second reason is that under Article 28 of the AML, the concentration will not be prohibited if it has positive effects on public interest. This also proved that an efficiency defence can only be used under a total welfare standard. The third reason listed by Yu is that an efficiency defense can be applied during the notification procedure. Only under the total welfare standard can efficiency defense be applied.

---

product specifications or standards, or carrying out professional labor division; (3) for the purpose of enhancing operational efficiency and reinforcing the competitiveness of small and medium-sized business operators; (4) for the purpose of achieving public interests such as conserving energy, protecting the environment and relieving the victims of a disaster and so on; (5) for the purpose of mitigating serious decrease in sales volume or obviously excessive production during economic recessions; (6) for the purpose of safeguarding the justifiable interests in the foreign trade or foreign economic cooperation; or (7) other circumstances as stipulated by laws and the State Council. Where a monopoly agreement is in any of the circumstances stipulated in Items 1 through 5 and is exempt from Articles 13 and 14 of this Law, the business operators must additionally prove that the agreement can enable consumers to share the interests derived from the agreement, and will not severely restrict competition in relevant market.'

[279] M. DING (2011), *supra* n. 224, p. 128.

[280] M. DING (2011), *supra* n. 224, p. 128.

[281] D. YU (2012), 'A Study on the Choose of Welfare Standards in Merger Antitrust Control' (横向并购反垄断控制的福利标准选择研究), *Fudan Journal* (复旦学报), no. 6, p. 103.

[282] Article 27 AML: 'In the case of the examination on the concentration of business operators, it shall consider the relevant elements as follows: (1) the market share of the business operators involved in the relevant market and the controlling power thereof over that market, (2) the degree of market concentration in the relevant market, (3) the influence of the concentration of business operators on the market access and technological progress, (4) the influence of the concentration of business operators on the consumers and other business operators, (5) the influence of the concentration of business operators on the national economic development, and (6) other elements that may have an effect on the market competition and shall be taken into account as regarded by the Anti-monopoly Authority under the State Council.'

7.2.   THE LEGISLATIVE DEBATE

The legislative process of the AML took more than a decade. It has been widely argued that an antitrust law may not be necessary for China at that time.[283] The legislators in China were concerned that the Chinese enterprises might not be capable to compete with multinational firms in global markets.[284] Concentrations in certain industries between Chinese enterprises should be tolerated, as they were not comparable with enterprises in developed economies.[285]

During the drafting process of the AML, representatives from various groups have been debated on the goal of the AML.[286] For example, in June 2006, during the 22nd meeting of the 10th Standing Committee of the National People's Congress, representatives from Guangdong, Beijing and Shanghai proposed to delete the goal of 'promoting economic efficiency', and representatives from Guangdong, Guangxi and Anhui proposed to delete the goal of 'maintaining the legitimate rights and interests of producers'.[287] Representatives from Guangxi and China University of Political Science and Law proposed to delete the goal of 'protecting consumers' interest.' Representatives from Beijing and National Lawyers Association proposed to add the goal of 'protecting national interest'.[288] In June 2007, during the 28th meeting of the 10th Standing Committee of the National People's Congress, representative Nan Zhenzhong proposed to add the goal of 'protecting the legitimate interests of producers',[289] and representative Chen Shu proposed to delete the goal of 'promoting efficiency'.[290]

7.3.   POLICY MAKERS

Policy makers and officials from the three competition authorities – the SAIC, the NDRC and the MOFCOM – had reached some general consensus on the functions, as well as the objectives of this AML. First of all, many of the officials have stated that the drafting process of the AML kept pace with the development of the market reform in China. A well-functioning market system would require

---

283   Y. HUANG (2008), *supra* n. 3, p. 118; International scholars have also argued that competition policy may not be served as a precondition for the development of the Chinese economy. *See for example*, T.S. ULEN (2011), 'The Uneasy Case for Competition Law and Regulation as Decisive Factors in Development: Some Lessons for China', in M. FAURE and X. ZHANG (eds.), *Competition Policy and Regulation, Recent Developments in China, the US and Europe*, Edward Elgar 2011, pp. 13–44.
284   Y. HUANG (2008), *supra* n. 3, p. 118.
285   Y. HUANG (2008), *supra* n. 3, p. 118.
286   M. DING(2011), *supra* n. 224, p. 128.
287   M. DING (2011), *supra* n. 224, p. 128.
288   M. DING (2011), *supra* n. 224, p. 128.
289   M. DING (2011), *supra* n. 224, p. 128.
290   M. DING (2011), *supra* n. 224, p. 128.

a comprehensive and effective competition law. For example, Cao Kangtai, the Director of the Legislative Office of the State Council, explained the draft of the AML in 2007 that '[t]he adoption of the AML as the "economic constitution" will be crucial to deepening reform in China, and promoting its international trade and economic cooperation'.[291] Shang Ming, the first director of the antitrust bureau of the MOFCOM, has acknowledged that the success of the economic development in China for the last 30 years shows that a 'free and fair market competition order' is 'necessary' to ensure the market economy is developed healthily, efficiently and in an orderly way.[292]

In addition, the market system in China has to be established under the socialist political system; therefore, the role of the AML has to be aligned with the requirements of a socialist market economy. In July 2005, the Minister of the National Development and Reform Commission ('NDRC'), Ma Kai, said in a forum in Beijing that by the end of 2004, China has 'basically completed' the procedure of transforming the highly centralized economy to a socialist market economy. The socialist market economic system is characterized as public ownership playing the major role, with the coexistence of other types of ownerships.[293] Shang Ming perceived that the Anti-Monopoly Law is a 'significant landmark' in the development of the 'socialist market economy' system within the 'socialist legal system with Chinese characteristics'.[294] The special characteristics of China's economic and political structure make that the AML does not follow the patterns of competition laws in other jurisdictions, and there are a few implications that the officials have generally agreed on.

The first implication is that the AML targets various economic and non-economic goals, and does not restrict itself to the economic goal of promoting efficiency. After publishing the new Judicial Interpretation in June 2012, a spokesperson of the Intellectual Property Tribunal of the Supreme People's Court highlighted the multiple goals that China's Anti-Monopoly Law is trying to achieve,[295] including the maintenance of the market order, the protection of consumers and undertakings, promotion of the public interest, enhancing competitiveness and economic security, and the promotion of a healthy development of the socialist market economy. More importantly, these goals correspond to the objectives of the National Economic and Social Development

---

[291]   Y. TANG, 'Interview: Director Cao Kangtai', *Outlook Weekly* no. 50 2007, available at <http://lw.xinhuanet.com/htm/content_2362.htm> accessed 28.03.2014; *see also* X. GUO (2007), 'Economic Constitution Prohibiting Monopolistic Conduct', *Legal Daily* 26 August 2007, available at <www.npc.gov.cn/npc/oldarchives/cwh/common/zw.jsp@hyid=0210029_____&label=wxzlk&id=370729&pdmc=flzt.htm> accessed 28.03.2014.

[292]   M. SHANG (2009), *supra* n. 51, p. 4.

[293]   PEOPLE'S DAILY, 'China has Socialist Market Economy in Place', *People's Daily Online*, 13 July 2005 available at <http://english.people.com.cn/200507/13/eng20050713_195876.html> (in English) accessed 05.04.2014.

[294]   M. SHANG (2009), *supra* n. 51, p. 4.

[295]   S.B. FARMER (2013), *supra* n. 13, p. 15.

12th Five-Year Plan, passed by the National People's Congress in March 2011.[296] Zhao Xiaoguang, the Director of the Department of Industry, Communications and Commerce at the Legal Affairs Office of the State Council, argued that the ultimate goal of the competition law is to maximize the total benefit to the society.[297] The focus of this law should be the entire society, not any individuals in any specific market. To implement the competition law in China, Zhao argued, it is important to consider the specific social and political characteristics in China in its transition from a planned economy to a socialist market economy.[298] Competition law can be enforced differently in different countries, and in different time periods. Zhao argued that this difference lies in the fact that countries are at different stages of economic development. As a result, the enforcement of the AML has to be in accordance with the specific social, political and economic characteristics of China.[299]

The second implication is that the treatment of foreign investors has to be aligned with the goal of protecting national security. On the one hand, the positive effects of the foreign investments have been widely acknowledged. The MOFCOM recognized that foreign investments have made an important contribution to the economic development in China. In a research paper published by the Research Institute of the MOFCOM, it was clarified that foreign investments have not 'threatened the economic safety', or 'controlled the technology market or any sensitive business sector'. Given the positive influences of the foreign companies, the officials confirmed that the AML will be equally applied to both domestic and foreign enterprises.[300] During an interview in December 2004, Director Shang Ming confirmed that there is no clause in the draft of the Anti-Monopoly Law targeting multinational companies. The AML will be applied to domestic and foreign enterprises with all types of ownerships.[301] Wu Zhenguo, the Deputy Director General of the Department of Law and Treaties and the Anti-Monopoly Investigation Office of the MOFCOM, confirmed this standpoint and argued that the AML is enforced to guarantee all enterprises to compete at the same stage.[302] Zhang Qiong, the associate director of the Legislative Affairs Office of the State Council, confirmed in an interview that this

296   Guomin Jingji He Shehui Fazhan Di Shierge Wunian Jihua Gangyao (国民经济和社会发展第十二个五年计划纲要) [The Twelfth Five-Year Plan for National Economic and Social Development] (approved by the Fourth Session of the Eleventh National People's Congress on 16 March 2011), available at <http://news.xinhuanet.com/politics/2011–03/16/c_121193916.htm> (in Chinese) accessed 04.04.2014; S.B. FARMER (2013), *supra* n. 13, p. 15.

297   X. ZHAO (2008), *supra* n. 135.

298   X. ZHAO (2008), *supra* n. 135.

299   X. ZHAO (2008), *supra* n. 135.

300   T.R. HOWELL, A.W. WOLFF, R. HOWE and D. OH (2009), *supra* n. 181, pp. 53–96.

301   X. WANG (2004), 'Interview: Shang Ming: Anti-Monopoly Law is not only for Multinational Companies', *Xinhua Net*, 23 December 2004, available at <http://expo2010.china.com.cn/news/txt/2004–12/23/content_5736697.htm> accessed 05.04.2014.

302   Z. WU (2008), *supra* n. 40, p. 100.

AML will be equally applied to foreign and domestic enterprises.[303] The AML does not specifically target mergers by multinationals. On the other hand, to mitigate the negative effects of foreign investments is a clear goal of the AML and its merger policies. Zhang emphasizes that mergers which will affect national economic security will be prohibited.[304]

The third implication is that given the special features of the AML and its role of contributing to a socialist market economy, the enforcement system of the AML in China might be different from other jurisdictions. An officer from the SAIC stated that the SAIC has been fully aware that the experiences of antitrust enforcement in western countries had shown the antitrust authority should be maintained professional, independent and non-political.[305] In particular, the goal of protecting employment, or promoting economic growth, should not override the goal of competition.[306] However, this officer mentioned that China faces challenges to establish an independent competition authority, given that its political system requires the officials to follow the leadership from the authority at the higher level.[307] The authority at higher level might prioritize other values than competition, and in this situation antitrust law in China might not be properly enforced.[308]

7.4. CONCLUSION

By taking a normative view, this section discusses how legislators, Chinese and international scholars and policy makers approach the question of how the goals of the AML and merger policies in China should be. The legislative debate in China could show that there was no consensus on what the goals of the AML should include. The discussion among scholars focus on the issue of economic goals versus non-economic goals, how to incorporate the goal of contributing to a socialist market economy, the application of the AML towards domestic and international enterprises, the concerns of public interest as well as national security, and lastly, the choice of welfare standards under the efficiency goal.

The officials from the competition authorities have reached some general conclusions on the function of the AML and its merger policies. The primary concern of this law is to contribute to the establishment of a socialist market economy. This function gives the AML special characteristics and it will not fully follow the patterns of competition laws in other countries. First of all, the

---

[303] XINHUA NEWS, 'AML's Equal Treatment of Domestic and Foreign Mergers' (国务院法制办: 《反垄断法》不影响企业正当并购), *Xinhua Net*, 10 September 2007, available at <http://news.xinhuanet.com/newscenter/2007–09/10/content_6699043.htm> accessed 21.01.2014.
[304] XINHUA NEWS, 'AML's Equal Treatment of Domestic and Foreign Mergers', *supra* n. 303.
[305] X. WANG (2004), *supra* n. 71, p. 3.
[306] X. WANG (2004), *supra* n. 71, p. 3.
[307] X. WANG (2004), *supra* n. 71, p. 3.
[308] X. WANG (2004), *supra* n. 71, p. 3.

AML embodies various economic and non-economic goals and the goal of promoting economic efficiency is not the superior goal. The second characteristic is the treatment of foreign investors. As a general rule, foreign enterprises will be treated equally with domestic enterprises. However, it is a clear goal of the merger policy to mitigate the negative effects of foreign investments. For this reason, foreign companies have to be examined if they affect national economic security. The third characteristic is the enforcement system of the AML. The political system might make it challenging for China to establish fully independent antitrust agencies. The current three-agency model might weaken the enforcement power of the AML.

8.   CONCLUSION

The drafting process of the AML took more than a decade. It took a remarkably long time because of the challenge of establishing a legal framework for a competitive market under a socialist regime. The major difficulty that legislators in China faced was how to strike a balance between different goals that this AML strives to achieve. To find a solution, the AML has included a multitude of policy goals, which are stated in Article 1. However, the definition of these goals is far from clear, which gives rise to controversies in its implementation. This chapter summarizes the background of the 1978 Market Reform and presents the reasons for including multiple goals in the AML. There are several findings that this chapter can draw together.

First, the AML and merger policy in China target various economic and non-economic goals. Besides economic efficiency, the AML also includes broader goals such as protecting consumer welfare, protecting the public interest, and contributing to a socialist market economy. Second, the drafting process of the AML was prolonged by the nationwide debate over what role the AML will play during the transition from a centrally planned economy towards a socialist market economy. This chapter takes merger control policy as an example and shows that mergers between SOEs and mergers by foreign investors have been treated in accordance with different preferences. These different considerations and preferences of policy goals have been reflected in several articles within the context of the AML. Under Article 5 of the AML, SOEs are encouraged to become more powerful, and mergers between SOEs may be exempted for the reason of promoting economies of scale. In addition, SOEs in industries that are crucial for national economy are also well protected by Article 7 of the AML. For foreign investors, besides Article 31, other detailed guidelines have also been implemented for a clearer examination of the effects of mergers which would have a negative effect on national security.

Third, from a normative perspective, scholars and policy makers in China generally agree that one of the major concerns of the competition law in China is to contribute to the establishment of a socialist market economy. This function gives the AML a specific characteristic and it does not fully follow the patterns of competition laws in other countries. In this respect, the goals of competition law in a jurisdiction not only have to be aligned with its economic and regulatory system, but also depend on how the role of this law is to be understood, given the political and cultural background of that country.[309] The competition law in China was drafted in a way which can fit into its cultural, social and economic preferences.[310] The drafting process of the AML corresponded to the development of the openness of the market. The concerns of establishing a legal framework for transactions between domestic enterprises as well as between foreign investors became the driving forces for enacting this law. As the circumstances of the economic developments in China change, these preferences may also evolve, which will in turn affect the political choices on the goals of the merger control policy. These changes will be observed by following how this AML will be implemented, as well as how merger cases will be decided in years to come.

---

[309] B.M. OWEN, S. SUN and W. ZHENG (2005), *supra* n. 13, p. 126.
[310] J.R. SAMUELS (2007), *supra* n. 29, p. 201.

CHAPTER 3

GOALS OF COMPETITION
POLICY IN THE US AND THE EU:
A LAW AND ECONOMICS
PERSPECTIVE

1. INTRODUCTION

'Antitrust Policy cannot be made rational until we are able to give a firm answer to
one question: what is the point of the law – what are its goals? Everything else follows
from the answer we give.'
    R.H. Bork[311]

The previous chapter argued that competition policy in China has to a large extent
been influenced by its policy goals. The positive analysis shows that the formulation
of the AML and its merger policy was driven by two opposite goals: the push power
from the side of preventing foreign investors from abusing dominant positions and
from affecting national security; on the other hand, the pull power of resisting to
apply the AML to SOEs and to domestic firms. This finding indicates that to
enhance the understanding of the competition policy in one jurisdiction, the first
task to be taken is to define the goals of the competition law.

This chapter explores the evolutions of the understanding on the antitrust
goals both in the US and the EU from a law and economics perspective. Before
analyzing the evolutions of merger rules, it is necessary to use this chapter to
investigate goals of antitrust law from a broader perspective. The reason is that
the goals of merger rules are to a large extent influenced by the goals of
competition policy. The debate on the goal of the Sherman Act is highly relevant
for the discussion of the goals of the Clayton Act and its amendment, the Celler-
Kefauver Act.[312] Moreover, both economic and legal theories of competition law
and policy could also be applied to the implementation of merger rules.
Therefore, this chapter discusses the goals of competition policy in general, and

---

311   R.H. Bork (1978), *supra* n. 19, p. 50.
312   M.N. Berry (1996),'Efficiencies and Horizontal Mergers: In Search of a Defense', *San Diego
       Law Review,* vol. 33, p. 531.

the next chapter will focus on how the evolution of antitrust goals affects the implementation of merger rules in the US and the EU.

The reason for choosing the antitrust system in the US and the EU is straightforward: both of these two antitrust regimes have experienced a long history of antitrust enforcement, and both have been served as important examples for the legislators in China when the AML was drafted.[313] The experiences of enforcing antitrust law in the US and the EU show that the goal of antitrust law is a highly debated issue. It is an evolution driven by various schools of thought regarding the function and role of an antitrust law in one jurisdiction, and the hierarchy of the goals is also affected by the particular historical, cultural, and political background of that country.

In this chapter, the evolution of antitrust goals is investigated from both a positive and a normative perspective. To start the discussion, each part of this chapter first examines the debate between academic scholars on the normative issue of which goal an antitrust law should pursue. In law and economics literature, the prominent schools of antitrust thought in the US include the Harvard School, the Chicago School, and scholars in the Post-Chicago School Era. In Europe, the competition law was heavily influenced by Ordoliberal scholars. The second part of the study will explore in practice what are the goals that antitrust authorities and courts have paid attention to in their decisions. Given the fact that the Sherman Act did not explicitly define the antitrust's goals in the US,[314] the first question to be answered in the positive study is to what extent these schools of thought have indeed affected the enforcement of the antitrust law. In addition, another question may arise whether the legislators, scholars and politicians have different interpretations for the goal that the antitrust law has prioritized. In general, the study in this chapter shows that a consensus on which welfare standard the competition law should pursue still has not been reached among US scholars.[315] This chapter tends to prove that the difficulties of reaching such a consensus lie in the fact that the choice of the antitrust goals is often affected by various factors, and the priorities of goals may evolve over time. Moreover, different understandings of the goals of the antitrust law may lead to different results in the implementation of the competition law and policy.

The structure of this chapter is as follows. After the introduction, the second section of this chapter presents the debate on the goals of antitrust law in the US. This debate is discussed in a chronological order. The influence of populism, the Harvard School and the Chicago School on the understanding of antitrust goals will be discussed respectively. The end of this section deals with the current

---

[313] D.J. GERBER (2008), *supra* n. 7, p. 285.
[314] Sherman Antitrust Act, 15 U.S.C. §§1–7.
[315] J.B. BAKER (2013), 'Economics and Politics: Perspectives on the Goals and Future of Antitrust', *Fordham Law Review*, vol. 81, p. 2180.

debate on welfare standards. This study could show that as time goes by, the understanding of the goals of antitrust law in the US tends to focus more on economic goals. However, it is still not clear whether the economic goal should be pursued under the total welfare standard, or under a consumer welfare standard.[316] For example, Chicago School scholar Robert Bork tended to prove by reading the legislative history of the Sherman Act that the efficiency goal should be pursued according to a total welfare standard.[317] A post-Chicago School scholar, Robert Lande, who insisted applying a consumer welfare standard, attempted to provide counter-arguments to Bork by explaining the legislative intent.[318]

Parallel with the structure in this section, the third section of this chapter will be organized to discuss the development of EU competition policy. It first discusses the Ordoliberalism thinking, which influenced the formulation of EU competition policy in the 1950s. Following the theoretical foundation, this section also presents the goals of competition law mentioned in the treaties, and how these goals were interpreted by the Competition Commissioners. The last section concludes.

2. GOALS OF ANTITRUST LAW IN THE US

2.1. INTRODUCTION

The starting point to discuss the goals of antitrust law in the US is the legislative intent of the Sherman Act. From a positive view, the language used by the Sherman Act is broad and is subject to further judicial interpretations.[319] Meanwhile, during the last one hundred years, federal

---

[316] J.B. BAKER (2013), *supra* n. 315, p. 2176.

[317] Although he named it as consumer welfare standard, *see* discussions in section 2.4.1.3. *See generally* R.H. BORK (1966), 'Legislative Intent and the Policy of the Sherman Act', *Journal of Law and Economics*, vol. 9, pp. 7–48; R.H. BORK (1967), *supra* n. 20, pp. 242–253; R.H. BORK (1978), *supra* n. 19.

[318] *See generally* R.H. LANDE (1982), 'Wealth Transfers as the Original and Primary Concern of Antitrust: The Efficiency Interpretation Challenged', *Hastings Law Journal*, vol. 34, pp. 65–152; R.H. LANDE (1988), 'The Rise and (coming) Fall of Efficiency as the Ruler of Antitrust', *The Antitrust Bulletin*, vol. 33, pp. 429–465; R.H. LANDE (1989), 'Chicago's False Foundation: Wealth Transfers (Not Just Efficiency) Should Guide Antitrust', *Antitrust Law Journal*, vol. 58, pp. 631–644; R.H. LANDE (2013), 'A Traditional and Textualist Analysis of the Goals of Antitrust: Efficiency, Preventing Theft from Consumers, and Consumer Choice', *Fordham Law Review*, vol. 81, pp. 2349–2403.

[319] It is commonly agreed that the language used by the Sherman Act is broad and is subject to further judicial interpretations. This could be seen as the specific feature of the antitrust law in the US. *See e.g.* W.E. KOVACIC and C. SHAPIRO (1999), 'Antitrust Policy: A Century of Economic and Legal Thinking', *University of California Working Paper No. CPC 99–09*, p. 18 ('No other country has adopted an antitrust statute that contains equally broad substantive provisions and relies so heavily on a common law method of judicial interpretation to

---

courts in the US did not clarify one definition or statement concerning the values of this antitrust law which will guide the enforcement of this law.[320] There are different views on the principles that Congress had in mind when the Sherman Act was adopted in 1890. For example, according to May and Fox, Congress did not perceive tensions between different goals, and it was believed that the goal of efficiency does not conflict the wider considerations of other social goals, such as protecting the small and medium-sized firms.[321] Fox argues that members from both Congress and the Supreme Court perceived that different antitrust's goals complemented each other.[322] By contrast, based on his study on the Congressional Record, Bork argues that the only goal that Congress intended to implement was the value of consumer welfare.[323]

The debate on which goal the antitrust law in the US should pursue continues until today. It can be held that since the 1980s, economic analysis has played a more important role in the US antitrust enforcement. The original concerns of protecting the small business, promoting fairness and other non-economic goals gradually faded away.[324] For example, Kirkwood argued that since the article by Robert Lande in 1982, the debate on the goals of the antitrust law in the US has switched from non-economic goals (populism) versus economic goals to the discussion within the scope of economic goals, in particular between the consumer welfare standard and the total welfare standard. The shift to economic goals, in particular, the consumer welfare goal, can be proved by a survey that he

---

implement them'). *See also* J.B. BAKER (2002), 'A Preface to Post-Chicago Antitrust', in A. CUCINOTTA, R. PARDOLESI and R. VAN DEN BERGH (eds.) *Post-Chicago Developments in Antitrust Analysis*, Edward Elgar, p. 60 ('The primary antitrust statutes provide little guidance to firms trying to comply with them or to courts attempting to interpret them ... In consequence, these statutes sometimes appear to resemble a social Rorschach test, on which courts and commentators can project a variety of perspectives and goals'). The best explanation is given by Senator Sherman: 'It is difficult to define in legal language the precise line between lawful and unlawful combinations. This must be left for the courts to determine in each particular case. All that we, as lawmakers, can do is to declare general principles, and we can be assured that the courts will apply them as to carry out the meaning of the law, as the courts of England and the United States have done for centuries.' (1890) *Cong. Rec.* vol. 21, 2460, cited by E.T. SULLIVAN and J.L. HARRISON, *Understanding Antitrust and Its Economic Implications*, 4th ed., LexisNexis 2003, p. 6.

[320]   R.H. BORK (1966), *supra* n. 317, p. 7.

[321]   J. MAY (1989), 'Antitrust in the Formative Era: Political and Economic Theory in Constitutional and Antitrust Analysis, 1880–1919', *Ohio State Law Journal*, vol. 50, pp. 257–396; *see also* E.M. FOX (1981), 'The Modernization of Antitrust: A New Equilibrium', *Cornell Law Review*, vol. 66, p. 1142.

[322]   E.M. FOX (1981), *supra* n. 321, p. 1142.

[323]   R.H. BORK (1966), *supra* n. 317, p. 7.

[324]   *See* J.F. BRODLEY (1987), 'The Economic Goals of Antitrust: Efficiency, Consumer Welfare and Technological Progress', *New York University Law Review*, vol. 62, p. 1021 ('The operational difference between the antitrust enforcement views of the Reagan Administration and those of previous administrations centers not on the political and social purposes of the law, but on the meaning of the economic goal itself').

conducted together with Robert Lande on the judicial decisions issued from 1993 to 2008.[325] Baker and Blumenthal argued that since the implementation of the 1982 Horizontal Merger Guidelines, economic goals have obtained the primacy in merger policy.[326] The social and political concerns of antitrust law are 'intellectually passé', and 'the relic of another era'.[327] However, the confusion of the antitrust policy goals does not come from the tension between economic goals and non-economic goals.[328] The real tension exists in the tradeoff between preserving efficiency and guaranteeing a fair share of efficiency gains to consumers.[329] The issue whether from a normative perspective the consumer welfare or the total welfare should be the goal that the US antitrust law should pursue remains a question unsolved by US scholars,[330] as well as by the US judges from the Supreme Court.[331]

This section will present the debate on antitrust goals in the US by following a chronological order. After the introduction, the second section will first discuss Populism approach towards antitrust law, which focuses on social and political goals of antitrust. This section will also discuss its influence in the courts, as well as the criticism from academic scholars. The third section will focus on the Harvard School's views on competition goals, as well as to what extent these views have been influenced in the courts. Following the same structure, the fourth session gives attention to the views on competition goals by the Chicago School. The fifth section will present the debate on antitrust goals in the post-Chicago era. Particular attention will be paid to the academic debate on the consumer welfare standard and the total welfare standard. The last section will conclude.

2.2. SOCIAL AND POLITICAL GOALS OF ANTITRUST

2.2.1. Populism

When the Sherman Act was enacted, the term 'competition' was not understood as an economic notion, and economic goals of the antitrust law were not formally

---

325 J.B. KIRKWOOD (2013), 'The Essence of Antitrust: Protecting Consumers and Small Suppliers from Anticompetitive Conduct', *Fordham Law Review*, vol. 81, p. 2440; R.H. LANDE (1982), *supra* n. 318, p. 65; J.B. KIRKWOOD and R.H. LANDE (2008), 'The Fundamental Goal of Antitrust: Protecting Consumers, Not Increasing Efficiency', *Notre Dame Law Review*, vol. 84, p. 191, 211–236.

326 D.I. BAKER and W. BLUMENTHAL (1983), 'The 1982 Guidelines and Preexisting Law', *California Law Review*, vol. 71, no. 2, p. 317.

327 D.I. BAKER and W. BLUMENTHAL (1983), *supra* n. 326, p. 318.

328 E.M. FOX (1981), *supra* n. 321, p. 1186.

329 E.M. FOX (1981), *supra* n. 321, p. 1186.

330 J.B. BAKER (2013), *supra* n. 315, p. 2180.

331 R.D. BLAIR and D.D. SOKOL (2012), 'The Rule of Reason and the Goals of Antitrust: An Economic Approach', *Antitrust Law Journal*, vol. 78, p. 480.

applied or treated as the main goal in early years of antitrust decisions.[332] According to Fox, the term 'antitrust' contains a message that this law was against the concentrated economic power. The linkage between 'antitrust' and 'competition' is rooted in the belief that business in small unites are better to engage in an effective competition. The belief of 'distrusting the big' may come from other resources than economic theories. For example, it was the argument of the People's Party, which was formed in 1891, who argued that power should be decentralized to the people, and should not concentrated in big business or in big governments. This idea is referred to as populism.[333] The policy implication of populism was that the US antitrust law was against the concentration of economic power, and that small firms should be protected because they are in a relatively weaker position.[334]

2.2.2. Influence of Populism in Court

The four most prominent judges who supported the idea of populism were Judge Learned Hand, Chief Justice Warren, Justice Hugo Black and Justice William Douglas.[335] In *United States v. Aluminum Co. of America*,[336] Judge Learned Hand showed his concern that the creation of big firms would put the small business in a 'helpless position'.[337] Judge Learned Hand expressed his preference of establishing a legal system for small firms to compete in the market. The danger of the 'big' business was not the accumulation of wealth, but restraining business opportunities for small firms. He argued that the antitrust law should not merely deal with economic motives, but also consider social and moral values. Judge Learned Hand stated: 'It is possible, because of its indirect social or moral effect, to prefer a system of small producers, each dependent for his

---

[332] *See e.g.* W.H. PAGE, (2008), 'The Ideological Origins and Evolution of U.S Antitrust Law', in W.D. COLLINS and J. ANGLAND (eds.), *Issues in Competition Law and Policy*, American Bar Association Section of Antitrust Law, volume 1, p. 1.

[333] E.M. FOX (1981), *supra* n. 321, p. 1144, footnote 12. *See also* W.L. LETWIN (1956), 'Congress and the Sherman Antitrust Law:1887–1890', *University of Chicago Law Review*, vol. 23, no. 2, pp. 221, 232, 233.

[334] H. HOVENKAMP (1989), 'Antitrust's Protected Classes', *Michigan Law Review*, vol. 88, no. 1, pp. 28–29.

[335] E.M. FOX (1981), *supra* n. 321, pp. 1142–1143.

[336] *United States v. Aluminum Co. of America*, 148 F. 2d 416, 428, 429 (2d Cir. 1945).

[337] *United States v. Aluminum Co. of America*, 148 F. 2d 416,428 (2d Cir. 1945) Judge Learned Hand said: 'We have been speaking only of the economic reasons which forbid monopoly; but there are others, based upon the belief that great industrial consolidations are inherently undesirable, regardless of their economic results. In the debates in Congress Senator Sherman himself ... showed that among the purposes of Congress in 1890 was a desire to put an end to great aggregations of capital because of the helplessness of the individual before them.' Judge Hand cited Senator Sherman and Senator George to support his argument. R.H. BORK (1966), *supra* n. 317, p. 8.

success upon his own skill and character, to one in which the great mass of those engaged must accept the direction of a few.'[338]

Chief Justice Warren held a similar understanding in *Brown Shoe Co. v. United States*.[339] Chief Justice Warren claimed that the antitrust law should reach the goal of deconcentration at all costs.[340] Justice Warren held that 'It is competition, not competitors, which the Act protects. But we cannot fail to recognize Congress's desire to promote competition through the promotion of viable, small, locally owned business. Congress appreciated that occasional higher costs and prices might result from the maintenance of fragmented industries and markets. It resolved these competing considerations in favor of decentralization.'[341] The justification for prohibiting this merger was the 'trend toward vertical integration', which might be explained by the fact that the Supreme Court put emphasis on the number of competing small firms.

In the 1960s, Justice Hugo Black's view on the active use of the antitrust law for the market intervention gained the support from the majority of the Supreme Court.[342] Justice Black shared a populist view and focused on giving 'freedom' and 'opportunity' for small businesses.[343] For example, in *United States v. Von's Grocery Co.*,[344] Justice Black quoted the words of Judge Learned Hand in *United States v. Aluminum Co. of America*: 'Throughout the history of these statutes it has been constantly assumed that one of their purposes was to perpetuate and preserve, for its own sake and in spite of possible cost, an organization of industry in small unites which can effectively compete with each other.'[345]

Justice Douglas showed the preference to small business, and emphasized the spirit of individualism.[346] Supreme Court Justice William O. Douglas stated in the decision *United States v. Columbia Steel Co.*:[347] 'Size can become a menace both industrial and social. It can be an industrial menace because it creates gross inequalities against existing or putative competitors. Industrial power should be decentralized. It should be scattered into many hands so that the fortunes of the people will not be dependent on the whim or caprice, the political prejudices, and emotional stability of a few self-appointed men. The fact that they are not

---

[338] Cited by R.H. BORK and W.S. BOWMAN, JR (1965), 'The Crisis in Antitrust', *Columbia Law Review*, vol. 65, no. 3, p. 370.

[339] *Brown Shoe Co., Inc. v. United States*, 370 U.S. 294, 344 (1962).

[340] E.M. Fox (1981), *supra* n. 321, p. 1143, footnote 8.

[341] Cited by E.M. Fox (1981), *supra* n. 321, p. 1143.

[342] W.H. PAGE (2008), *supra* n. 332, p. 9.

[343] For example, in *Fortner Enterprises, Inc. v. United States Steel Corp.*, 394 U.S. 495 (1969); *United States v. Von's Grocery Co.*, 384 U.S. 270 (1966); cited by Fox, E.M. (1981), *supra* n. 321, pp. 1142, 1143 footnote 8.

[344] *United States v. Von's Grocery Co.*, 384 U.S. 270, 274, 275, n. 7 (1966).

[345] 148 F 2d at 429, cited by R.H. BORK (1966), *supra* n. 317, p. 9.

[346] For example, *United States v. Falstaff Brewing Corp.*, 410 U.S. 526, 543 (1973), cited by E.M. Fox (1981), *supra* n. 321, p. 1143, footnote 8.

[347] *United States v. Columbia Steel Co.*, 334 U.S. 495, 534 (1948), cited by T.R. HOWELL, A.W. WOLFF, R. HOWE and D. OH (2009), *supra* n. 181.

vicious men but respectable and social minded is irrelevant. That is the philosophy and the command of the Sherman Act'.[348]

Notably, the influence of populism on judiciary started to decline in the mid-1960s. This trend was driven by the academic debate on the increasing role of the economic analysis of antitrust.[349] Between the mid-1960s and the mid-1970s, the populist judges at the Supreme Court, Chief Justice Warren, Justice Black and Justice Douglas, retired. To take their positions, several non-populist judges were appointed by the President Nixon and the President Ford.[350] After the development of case law during last five decades, according to Baker and Blumenthal, populists' view in the Warren Court era has little influence today and the social and political views on antitrust policy have been limited to a 'minority status'.[351]

2.2.3. Criticism from Academic Scholars

In the late 1970s, the attitude of protecting the 'small' from the 'big' was criticized by the Chicago school scholars, who claimed that when a firm expands its market power through internal cooperation can only show that it is more efficient and more capable to generate social wealth. Easterbrook rejected to apply the 'small is beautiful' argument to explain the legislative intent of the Sherman Act.[352] Bork argued that giving superior values to small business was 'dubious' and 'radical'.[353] According to Bork, putting small business to a favorable position, however, cannot be justified by economic theories. He criticized that the populist approach was 'protecting competitors' instead of 'protecting competition', or, it was to achieve the goal of protecting the 'small business welfare'.[354]

In addition to the criticism that has been given by the Chicagoans, DeBow provided a third argument which implies that the populist approach may encourage rent-seeking behavior.[355] DeBow explained that under the 'small is beautiful' criterion, a firm which is willing to develop its productive capacity would be challenged, and in this situation the defendant firm may have to bear rent-protecting costs.[356] The populist theory of antitrust would encourage governments to expand the objectives of the antitrust enforcement, and the

---

[348] Cited by T.R. HOWELL, A.W. WOLFF, R. HOWE and D. OH (2009), *supra* n. 181.

[349] D.I. BAKER and W. BLUMENTHAL (1983), *supra* n. 326, p. 318.

[350] E.M. FOX (1981), *supra* n. 321, p. 1143.

[351] D.I. BAKER and W. BLUMENTHAL (1983), *supra* n. 326, p. 320.

[352] *See e.g.* F.H. EASTERBROOK (1986), 'Workable Antitrust Policy', *Michigan Law Review*, vol. 84, p. 1703 ('The few references in the legislative history to "small dealers" are a sideshow').

[353] R.H. BORK and W.S. BOWMAN, JR. (1965), *supra* n. 338, p. 370.

[354] R.H. BORK (1967), *supra* n. 20, p. 242.

[355] M.E. DEBOW (1991), 'The Social Costs of Populist Antitrust: A Public Choice Perspective', *Harvard Journal of Law and Public Policy*, vol. 14, p. 212.

[356] M.E. DEBOW (1991), *supra* n. 355, p. 219.

government intervention may lead to greater social costs, including deadweight losses and rent-seeking costs.[357] Therefore, a careful cost-benefit analysis should be conducted before the proposal of an extensive use of antitrust law.[358]

Baker and Blumenthal argued that since the 1970s, the populist values of antitrust have lost support from scholars, policy makers, as well as from judges in the US.[359] The major drawback of social and political values is that they are 'vague' and 'unquantifiable'.[360] These general principles developed by sociology and political science are difficult to be calculated in antitrust enforcement whereas economic analysis often provides clearer results.[361]

2.3. HARVARD SCHOOL

2.3.1. *The Structure-Conduct-Performance Paradigm*

In the 1930s, a group of scholars from the University of Harvard[362] developed the 'Structure-Conduct-Performance' ('SCP') paradigm, which paved the way for the economic analysis of competition policy. The SCP framework indicates that the market performance is determined by the conduct used by the participants in the market and that the conduct is further decided by the market structure. Market structure, conduct and performance can all be affected by competition policy and government regulations.

The measurements of these three variables are calculated as follows. Performance can be assessed by the level of profit margins, rates of return, product quality and quantities, the progress of technology.[363] Conduct can be assessed by the proxies of research and development, tactics and strategy, choices on product and price, and by investigating whether firms engage in collusion with competitors.[364] The proxies that can be used to measure structure include the number of buyers and sellers, vertical integration, barriers to entry, and product differentiation. The two most important factors that influence the market structure include the number of suppliers and their market shares.[365] The general condition of the market structure depends on both the supply and

---

[357] M.E. DeBow (1991), *supra* n. 355, p. 220.

[358] M.E. DeBow (1991), *supra* n. 355, p. 222.

[359] D. I. Baker and W. Blumenthal (1983), *supra* n. 326, p. 319.

[360] D. I. Baker and W. Blumenthal (1983), *supra* n. 326, p. 319.

[361] D. I. Baker and W. Blumenthal (1983), *supra* n. 326, p. 319.

[362] J.S. Bain, *Barriers to New Competition*, Harvard University Press 1956; E.S. Mason (1939),'Price and Production Policies of the Large-Scale Enterprise', *American Economic Review*, vol. 29, pp. 61–74.

[363] S. Voigt and A. Schmidt, *Making European Merger Policy More Predictable*, Springer 2005, p. 14.

[364] S. Voigt and A. Schmidt (2005), *supra* n. 363, p. 14.

[365] S. Voigt and A. Schmidt (2005), *supra* n. 363, p. 14.

demand sides, including the elasticity of demand and supply, the supply of raw materials, the growth rate, and the substitutes of products.

Harvard School scholars emphasize the importance of structure. They argue that a concentrated market structure will lead to a substantial increase of market power; therefore, market concentration should be prohibited by competition policy. Competition law should be enforced to ensure that the market structure is always maintained at a certain level and to keep market power below the suitable threshold. Therefore, government intervention is necessary to keep the market structure at an appropriate level. In particular, antitrust policy is applied to ensure market power is below a certain threshold, and to reach this goal, structural remedies are preferable to behavioral remedies.[366] According to Harvard School scholars, two forms of state intervention can be justified: if the concentration level is too high, divestiture remedies should be given. By contrast, if the concentration level is low and the supply of firms is large, the government should provide supporting instruments in research and development ('R&D'), in order to strengthen the technological progress.[367]

2.3.2.   Harvard School's View on the Goals of Antitrust Law

The Harvard School advocated the economic goals of antitrust law, but does not agree that economic goals are the only objective. As a simplified division, Harvard approach to antitrust can be put in the middle between the Columbia School and the Chicago School.[368] The Chicago School holds a strong confidence in the robustness of the market and takes efficiency as the sole aim of antitrust. On the left side, the Columbia School scholars, represented by Louis Schwartz, argued that antitrust law is used for non-economic goals.[369] The Harvard School stands in between. Like the Chicago School's view on economic goals, Harvard School scholars prioritize economic goals,[370] and they agree that antitrust policy is used to promote a desirable economic performance, which can be best measured by the impact on economic efficiency and progress.[371] Unlike Chicagoans' rigid claim of seeing efficiency as the *exclusive*

---

[366]   The differences between structural and behavioral remedies, see discussion Chapter 5, section 3.2.7.

[367]   S. VOIGT and A. SCHMIDT (2005), *supra* n. 363, p. 16.

[368]   H. HOVENKAMP (1996), 'The Areeda – Turner Treatise in Antitrust Analysis', *The Antitrust Bulletin*, vol. 41, p. 822.

[369]   According to Hovenkamp, Louis Schwartz is the representative of the Columbia School. Columbia School scholars emphasize non-economic goals of the antitrust law. H. HOVENKAMP (1996), *supra* n. 368, p. 823, L.B. SCHWARTZ (1979), '"Justice" and Other Non-Economic Goals of Antitrust', *University of Pennsylvania Law Review*, vol. 127, no. 4, pp. 1076–1081.

[370]   D.F. TURNER (1987), 'The Durability, Relevance, and Future of American Antitrust Policy', *California Law Review*, vol. 75, no. 3, p. 798.

[371]   C. KAYSEN and D. TURNER, *Antitrust Policy: An Economic and Legal Analysis*, Harvard University Press 1959, p. 11.

aim, Harvard School scholars accept various ultimate goals for antitrust policy. They propose a hierarchy of antitrust aims and the primary goal is to limit undue market power in order to promote a desirable economic performance.[372] To Harvard scholars, it is necessary to regulate business conduct on the ground of 'fair dealing'.[373] Moreover, efficiency and progress[374] are the still the central concerns of the antitrust law, although social goals such as the fairness concern between big and small business also take a position in this hierarchy. According to Areeda, social and political goals, such as providing equal opportunity, promoting fairness, safeguarding equal income distribution, can be achieved through an effective competition which aims at maximizing consumer welfare.[375] For example, based on the theory of productive and allocative efficiency, price-fixing cartels should be prohibited. This decision could well serve all other social and political goals as well.[376] Areeda argues that in most cases, political and social values are consistent with economic goals, and in the situation when they encounter conflicts, it should be a primary concern to fulfill the interest of customers.[377]

2.3.3.   Influence of the Harvard School in Court

Between the 1940s and the mid-1970s, the Harvard theory of 'Structure-Conduct-Performance' ('SCP') implied a structural approach of antitrust enforcement in the US.[378] By putting emphasis on the market structure, it is more likely that horizontal mergers are perceived as harmful, and an example would be *United States v. Von's Grocery Co.*[379] The Harvard approach, which supports a strong government intervention, coincided with the active enforcement of antitrust policy in the 1930s and 1940s, when Thurman Arnold served as the Assistant Attorney General at the Antitrust Division of the DOJ and several pro-interventionist judges were appointed by President Roosevelt.[380]

---

[372]   C. KAYSEN and D. TURNER (1959), *supra* n. 371, p. 44.

[373]   C. KAYSEN and D. TURNER (1959), *supra* n. 371, p. 45.

[374]   'Progress' here refers to growth and innovation in new production methods and new products. C. KAYSEN and D. TURNER (1959), p. 11.

[375]   P. AREEDA (1983), 'Introduction to Antitrust Economics', *Antitrust Law Journal*, vol. 52, p. 534.

[376]   P. AREEDA (1983), *supra* n. 375, p. 534.

[377]   P. AREEDA (1983), *supra* n. 375, p.534.

[378]   J.B. BAKER (2013), *supra* n. 315, p. 2184.

[379]   J.B. BAKER (2013), *supra* n. 315, p. 2184; Baker gave this example. *United States v. Von's Grocery Co.*, 384 U.S. 270 (1966).

[380]   For example, Justices William Douglas (*United States v. Columbia Steel Co.*, 334 U.S. 495 (1948)) and Justice Hugo Black (*Ford Motor Co. v. United States*, 335 U.S. 303 (1948)) *See* W.H. PAGE (2008), *supra* n. 332, p. 8.

By the 1960s, the SCP structural approach dominated the antitrust policy debate in the US, and its popularity can be explained by two reasons.[381] First of all, it provided a practical tool for the bureaucrats, legislators and judges to assess the anticompetitive conduct. The focus on market concentration could give a clear identification for the potential antitrust violation.[382] In the 1960s, the populist judges at the Supreme Court to a large extent relied on the SCP framework in their merger decisions.[383] The second reason is that this framework reconfirmed the populist view on the role of the antitrust law. It provided the economic justification for the preferences of a market with small businesses, and with deconcentrated market power.[384] This 'anti-bigness' goal has been politically supported by Democrats, such as Philip Hart, Emmanuel Celler, and Wright Patman.[385]

2.4. CHICAGO SCHOOL

In the mid-1970s, a group of economists and lawyers associated with the University of Chicago led a revolution in antitrust thinking.[386] The prominent representatives, among many others, include Robert Bork, Frank Easterbrook, Richard Posner[387] and George Stigler.[388] Although Chicago School scholars were not the pioneers who 'discovered' economic analysis of antitrust law, they were the first to argue antitrust should *only* achieve economic goals.[389] In this way, Chicagoans are often regarded as the ones who led the revolution towards an 'economic approach' of antitrust law.[390] After the 1970s the efficiency approach

---

[381] M.A. EISNER and K.T. MEIER (1990), 'Presidential Control versus Bureaucratic Power: Explaining the Reagan Revolution in Antitrust', *American Journal of Political Science*, vol. 34, no. 1, p. 272.

[382] M.A. EISNER and K.T. MEIER (1990), *supra* n. 381, p. 272.

[383] W.H. PAGE (2008), *supra* n. 332, p. 9.

[384] M.A. EISNER and K.T. MEIER (1990), *supra* n. 381, p. 272.

[385] M.A. EISNER and K.T. MEIER (1990), *supra* n. 381, p. 272.

[386] J.B. BAKER (2002), *supra* n. 319, p. 11.

[387] R.A. POSNER (1979) 'The Chicago School of Antitrust Analysis', *University of Pennsylvania Law Review*, vol. 127, no. 4, p. 925.

[388] J.B. BAKER (2002), *supra* n. 319, p. 11. It has been acknowledged that Chicago approach to antitrust law was developed by Prof. Aaron Director at the University of Chicago Law School. But Prof. Aaron Director was not the first scholar from the University of Chicago who had influenced antitrust policy. For example, Henry Simon, who was strongly against central planning and argued for decentralization was influential in the 1930s. Prof. Aaron Director played a role of bridging the old Chicago School to the new Chicago School, who are famous for their efficiency arguments. W.E. KOVACIC and C. SHAPIRO (1999), *supra* n. 319, p. 13. *See also* E.W. KITCH (1983), 'The Fire of Truth: A Remembrance of Law and Economics at Chicago, 1932–1979', *Journal of Law and Economics*, vol. 26, no. 1, pp. 163–234.

[389] H. HOVENKAMP (1985), 'Antitrust Policy after Chicago', *Michigan Law Review*, vol. 84, no. 2, p. 223; H. HOVENKAMP (2001), 'Post-Chicago Antitrust: A Review and Critique', *Columbia Business Law Review*, p. 265.

[390] The rise of 'economic approach', represented by the Chicago School, refers to 'an approach concerned exclusively with efficiency.' *See* H. HOVENKAMP (1985), *supra* n. 389, p. 223.

became the most influential school of thought in antitrust policy, and the influence of political and social goals diminished.[391]

The Chicago School applied the developments of neoclassical economics, and views that market competition is a dynamic, evolutionary process.[392] Rationally behaving firms are motivated to engage in competition to maximize their profits. Therefore, profit maximizing behavior, such as merger between firms, even when it may lead to an increase of the market power, should be justified by competition law, because the increased market concentration implies that the firm has achieved efficiency.[393] During the dynamic process of market competition, more efficient competitors will drive out less efficient ones. If a firm can hold a monopoly position, this can be regarded as an indicator that this firm is the most efficient one, according to the idea of 'the survival of the fittest'.[394] More importantly, the increased profits will benefit consumers in the end, and will also contribute to an efficient allocation of resources.

Chicago School scholars argue that competition policy should pay attention to the improvement of efficiency and to the elimination of barriers to entry, and should not focus on the level of market concentration. It is for the reason that firms are rational profit maximizers, and allocative efficiency will be achieved during the competition between firms in the market. They distrust the capacity of governments; therefore, governmental regulations and competition laws should intervene at a minimum level.

2.4.1.   Chicago School's View on the Goals of Antitrust Law

2.4.1.1.   Efficiency as the Sole Aim

Robert Bork argues that the *only* and *ultimate* goal of antitrust policy is to improve allocative efficiency, to the extent that productive efficiency will not be impaired to produce neither gain nor loss in consumer welfare.[395] Bork elaborated the importance of allocative efficiency by reviewing the legislative

---

[391]   For example, Baxter argues that 'where there is a conflict, social and political goals should yield to economic considerations primarily for two reasons: first, the statutes themselves focus on efficiency; and second, non-efficiency goals are too intractable to be used as enforcement standards.' Judge Posner argues that 'Almost everyone professionally involved in antitrust today – whether as litigator, prosecutor, judge, academic, or informed observer – not only agrees that the only goal of the antitrust laws should be to promote economic welfare, but also agrees on the essential tenets of economic theory that should be used to determine the consistency of specific business practices with that goal.' R.A. POSNER, *Antitrust Law*, 2nd ed., University of Chicago Press 2001, p. ix.

[392]   W.H. PAGE (2008), *supra* n. 332, p. 10.

[393]   M.A. EISNER and K.T. MEIER (1990), *supra* n. 381, p. 273.

[394]   S. VOIGT and A. SCHMIDT (2005), *supra* n. 363, p. 14.

[395]   'The whole task of antitrust can be summed up as the effort to improve allocative efficiency without impairing productive efficiency so greatly as to produce either no gain or a net loss in consumer welfare.' R.H. BORK (1978), *supra* n. 19. Bork has been harshly criticized the social

debates in 1890 and concluded that consumer welfare was the only concern when the Sherman Act was adopted by the US Congress.[396] Bork criticized the 'populist' approach in antitrust thinking, and argued that antitrust law should not focus on any political or social goals.[397]

2.4.1.2. Rejecting the Goal of 'Maximizing Competition'

In his earlier work, Bork criticized that the goal of 'maximizing competition' is not 'conceivable' at all because it will destroy social wealth.[398] In his influential book *Antitrust Paradox* in 1978, Bork rejected protecting competition as the goal of antitrust, although he acknowledged 'the preservation of competition' was the right word to translate the statutory language of antitrust laws since the Sherman Act.[399] Bork criticized the ambiguity of this word as a goal of antitrust,[400] and he proposed that the goal should be clarified to 'consumer welfare'. Interestingly, antitrust history shows that consumer welfare as an antitrust policy goal provokes even more confusion and ambiguity in later years.[401]

Bork's disagreement with the goal of 'maximizing competition' was also supported by Easterbrook, another representative from the Chicago School. He explains that the view on competition should not be maximizing the number of

---

and moral goals to be considered by antitrust policy. *See e.g.* R.H. Bork and W.S. Bowman, Jr. (1965), *supra* n. 338, p. 370.

[396] *See generally* R.H. Bork (1966), *supra* n. 317, pp. 7–48. Bork was the first scholar who elaborated in detail how allocative efficiency could be achieved through competition. *See e.g.* R.H. Bork and W.S. Bowman, Jr. (1965), *supra* n. 338, p. 365 ('Why should we want to preserve competition anyway? The answer is simply that competition provides society with the maximum output that can be achieved at any given time with the resources at its command. Under a competitive regime, productive resources are combined and separated, shuffled and reshuffled in search for greater profits through greater efficiency ... Output is maximized because there is no possible rearrangement of resources that could increase the value to consumers of total output.').

[397] R.A. Skitol (1999), *supra* n. 25, p. 248.

[398] *See* R.H. Bork (1967), *supra* n. 20, p. 252 ('It is a prescription for the annihilation of our society and most of the individuals in it. Even a policy of pushing to a condition that a majority of economists would agree constituted pure competition would involve a vast destruction of the wealth of our society'). Bork also rejected the standard of 'workable competition' (for details of the concept of 'workable competition' *see* J.M. Clark (1940), 'Toward a Concept of Workable Competition', *The American Economic Review*, vol. 30, no. 2, pp. 241–256).

[399] R.H. Bork and W.S. Bowman, Jr. (1965), *supra* n. 338, p. 370.

[400] R.H. Bork (1978), *supra* n. 19, p. 58 ('[p]art of the confusion about goals arises from the ambiguity of the word "competition"').

[401] 'Since *Reiter*, "consumer welfare" is the stated goal of the U.S. competition laws. What it means we do not know', B. Orbach (2013), p. 2275. '"Competition" is not more confusing or abstract than "consumer welfare", which has no particular meaning in antitrust.' B. Orbach (2013), 'How Antitrust Lost Its Goal', *Fordham Law Review*, vol. 81, p. 2277. For the controversy of consumer welfare goal, *see generally* B. Orbach (2011), 'The Antitrust Consumer Welfare Paradox', *Journal of Competition Law and Economics*, vol. 7, p. 133 More detailed discussion in sections 2.4.1.3 and 2.5.

rivals, because every firm or individual has to be involved in a certain type of coordination and compete in other domains.[402] For Easterbrook, cooperation is a way to generate efficiencies; hence, to maximize competition by destroying all forms of cooperation would destroy all the engines of efficiency.[403]

Following Easterbrook's argument, even if competition is the goal, it should be first discussed how to measure the level of competition,[404] and which instrument could fulfill this goal, because before reaching a conclusion, both the competitive and anticompetitive effects must be carefully analyzed. Judging whether the market is 'competitive' enough from counting the number of rivals would be regarded a very dogmatic, structural approach, and only based on one threshold to put per se bans on certain conduct will impose distortions.

It should be emphasized that both Bork and Easterbrook's view on competition goals reflect their general understanding of dynamic efficiency. Although most economists agree that competition should be understood as a dynamic process,[405] it has been debated whether this process should be protected, therefore, as a justification for intervention. Chicago School scholars do not agree with including 'progressiveness' as a criterion to make a judgment on antitrust cases,[406] because they believe dynamic efficiency will be achieved through the interaction within a free market, and antitrust intervention would only impose distortion.[407] For the Chicagoans, competition is a dynamic process and only the fittest will survive through this process. However, antitrust policy

---

[402]   F.H. EASTERBROOK (1984), 'The Limits of Antitrust', *Texas Law Review*, vol. 63, no. 1, p. 1.

[403]   F.H. EASTERBROOK (1984), *supra* n. 402, p. 4 ('Cooperation is the source of monopoly, yet it is also the engine of efficiency').

[404]   The question remains, if it is not 'maximum competition', will it be 'optimal competition'? But what happens if this 'optimal level' cannot be known – as Easterbrook put it: 'Antitrust is an imperfect tool for the regulation of competition. Imperfect because we rarely know the right amount of competition there should be.' (F.H. EASTERBROOK (1984), *supra* n. 402, p. 39). *See also* F.H. EASTERBROOK (1986), *supra* n. 352, p. 1700 ('No antitrust policy should be based on a belief that atomistic competition is better than some blend of cooperation and competition. The right blend varies from market to market.' Nevertheless, Easterbrook expressed the very 'Chicago School' view.).

[405]   Bork perceives competition as a dynamic, evolutionary process: *see* R.H. BORK and W.S. BOWMAN, JR. (1965), *supra* n. 338, p. 375. Schumpeter argues that competition is a dynamic, technological progress of 'creative destruction', which involves innovation and imitation between competing firms: *see* J.A. SCHUMPETER, *Capitalism, Socialism and Democracy*, Harper Perennial Modern Thought 2008, pp. 81–86. Hayek views competition as a 'discovery procedure'. He claims that all individuals and firms only have a limited knowledge beforehand and market competition is an experiment to determine the best products which satisfy consumers' preferences the most. Therefore, competition is a 'trial and error' process to solve the knowledge problem: *see* F.A. v. HAYEK (1948), 'The Meaning of Competition', in *Individualism and Economic Order*, University of Chicago Press, pp. 92–106, and F. A. v. HAYEK (1978), 'Competition as a Discovery Procedure', in *New Studies in Philosophy, Politics, Economics and the History of Ideas*, University of Chicago Press, pp. 179–190.

[406]   Bork rejected the goal of 'protecting competitive progress', regardless of whether it was interpreted as 'preserving competitors' or 'maximizing competition'. *See* R.H. BORK (1967), *supra* n. 20, p. 252.

[407]   E.M. FOX (1986), 'Consumer Beware Chicago', *Michigan Law Review*, vol. 84, p. 1717.

should not intervene to preserve dynamic effects, because the competitive process will protect itself. Chicago scholars believe that letting firms choose what to do will lead to dynamic efficiency. They trust private power and do not believe in government intervention. In general, Chicago scholars claim that antitrust policy only serves as a filter[408] to provide a check in a static manner and let the efficient firms go; whereas other scholars may argue that it is necessary to provide conditions and preserve the freedom to compete in order to achieve dynamic efficiency.[409]

2.4.1.3. Bork's Use of 'Consumer Welfare'

The 'consumer welfare' used by Bork, however, does not refer to the concept of consumer surplus. Instead, it means the 'maximization of wealth or consumer want satisfaction' and 'the aggregate efficiency of our economy',[410] 'to make us as wealthy as possible'.[411] Bork has explicitly linked the goal of promoting efficiency with the goal of increasing the wealth,[412] and the distributive effects or other non-economic goals should not be taken into account by antitrust law. In today's view, what Bork meant by using the term 'consumer welfare' is closer to a total welfare principle.[413]

However, it is doubtful whether Bork misused the words 'consumer welfare' intentionally, as Lande said, 'Bork's deceptive use of the term "consumer welfare" instead of the more honest term "total welfare," was a brilliant way to market the efficiency objective.'[414] Bork argued that for firms sell products to serve the needs of consumers, they should be judged under antitrust law according to the criterion of which operate more efficiently. The reason is that if a firm operates efficiently, it will increase welfare and this welfare will be transferred to consumers. For firms which do not merely operate to serve consumers, such as farm and labor organizations, the criterion of efficiency might not be applicable.[415]

---

[408] For a detailed description of how to use the filter, *see* F.H. EASTERBROOK (1984), *supra* n. 402. Laying confidence on the function of the market might also be the reason that Chicagoans believe the use of antitrust law should remain modest, for example, they reject the view of applying efficiency defense in merger cases.

[409] *See* E.M. Fox (1986), *supra* n. 407, p. 1718; see discussions in section 2.4.3.3.

[410] R. BORK (1978), *supra* n. 19.

[411] R. BORK (1978), *supra* n. 19.

[412] *See* R.H. BORK and W.S. BOWMAN, JR. (1965), *supra* n. 338, p. 374 ('Any law that makes the creation of efficiency the touchstone of illegality can only tend to impoverish us as a nation.').

[413] B.Y. ORBACH (2011), *supra* n. 401, p. 137, pp. 143–144 ('[t]he facts that Bork presented had little to do with conventional definitions of consumer welfare. When Bork wrote "consumer welfare", he had in mind "allocative efficiency" and other concepts ... Put simply, the Borkean consumer welfare was related to "efficiency" and "social wealth"').

[414] R.H. LANDE (2013), *supra* n. 318, p. 2360, footnote 54.

[415] *See* R.H. BORK (1966), *supra* n. 317, p. 12; R.H. BORK (1967), *supra* n. 20, p. 251 ('I take "efficiency" to be defined in terms of meeting consumer desires.').

Bork's understanding of seeing efficiency as the end result, which can be visualized by the outcome of social wealth, is different from the 'consumer welfare' goal as understood today. Under the consumer welfare standard, the wealth of consumers is taken as the end result, and consumers must get a fair share of the social wealth. An important difference between the consumer welfare and the total welfare standard lies in the question of whether the short-run harm on consumers could be tolerated. For example, when promoting productive efficiency has an immediate effect on consumers, such as through increased prices, this conduct would be allowed under a total welfare standard, because the benefits of promoting productive efficiency will be transferred to consumers in the long run.[416] However, scholars who support a consumer welfare standard would argue against this conduct, because consumers suffer the harm caused by the increase in prices.

Another complication of the understanding of the consumer welfare goal lies in the difficulty of defining the 'consumer'. Intuitively, the consumer welfare goal would require a consistent requirement for antitrust implementation and the suffering of consumers should not be tolerated at any time. However, there might be a conflict between the welfare of consumers in the short run, or in the long run; as well as between the gains to consumers in different markets, and between consumers who enter the market at different time. Prohibiting a merger which creates efficiency and raises prices at the same time, will be beneficial for consumers in the market today, but will reduce welfare for the consumers in the future.[417]

2.4.2. Influence of the Chicago School in Court

The Chicago School's view on antitrust law has played a more important role since the 1970s. In the academic community, the Chicago's view was supported by the development of neo-classical microeconomic theory.[418] With the development of economic theories, the influence of the structural approach started to decline. At the political level, the Chicagoans who argued for a limited state intervention were welcomed by the Reagan administration.[419]

During the Reagan administration in the 1980s, Chicago school scholars were appointed both to the enforcement agencies, and to the Supreme Court as

---

[416] See BRODLEY (1987), *supra* n. 324, p. 1042. It is even justified to let the consumers suffer a short-term pain in exchange for efficiency gains. *See* BRODLEY (1987), *supra* n. 324, p. 1046 ('The efficiencies justification is an application of the principle developed earlier that under certain circumstances antitrust should temporarily subordinate the immediate consumer interest in order to achieve a durable gain in production or innovation efficiency and thereby enhance total social welfare.').

[417] See A.J. MEESE (2013), 'Reframing the (false?) Choice between Purchaser Welfare and Total Welfare', *Fordham Law Review*, vol. 81, p. 2251.

[418] M.A. EISNER and K.T. MEIER (1990), *supra* n. 381, p. 273.

[419] M.A. EISNER and K.T. MEIER (1990), *supra* n. 381, p. 273.

well as the lower federal courts.[420] William Baxter, the Assistant Attorney General ('AAG') of the DOJ once said: 'Economic efficiency provides the only workable standard from which to derive operational rules and by which the effectiveness of such rules can be judged.'[421] Under the influence of William Baxter, the 1982 Merger Guidelines incorporated various factors in the assessment of the competitive effects.[422]

Starting from the Burger Court, by moving away from the focus on market concentration, the Supreme Court has paid more attention to the market impact and to the potential efficiency gains.[423] The Supreme Court clearly stated that efficiency is the primary goal of antitrust in *Continental T.V., Inc. v. GTE Sylvania, Inc.,*[424] and *Brunswick Corp. v. Pueblo Bowl-O-Mat, Inc.*[425] In 1979, the Supreme Court quoted Bork's argument in the decision of *Reiter v. Sonotone Corp.,*[426] and stated that 'Congress designed the Sherman Act as a "consumer welfare prescription"'. The Supreme Court took a stand towards economic goals and it seems that the influence of political and social goals of the previous years has been gradually mitigated. For example, in *Redwood Theatres, Inc. v. Festival Enterprises, Inc.,*[427] the Supreme Court held that 'the debate over the purposes of the antitrust laws has generally acknowledged a balance of economic, social and political goals'. In *Cieri v. Leticia Query Realty, Inc.,*[428] the Supreme Court of Hawaii held that 'There is little if anything in the cases that suggests the courts have in fact been willing to pursue populist goals at the expense of competition and efficiency … If anything, they support the priority of competition and its efficiency goals.'

Meanwhile, in the late 1970s, along with some important changes of the seats in the Senate,[429] an explicit change in judicial appointments could be observed.

420 R.A. SKITOL (1999), *supra* n. 25, p. 250.
421 W. BAXTER (1985), 'Responding to the Reaction: The Draftsman's View', in E.M. FOX and J.T. HALVERSON (eds.), *Antitrust Policy in Transition: The Convergence of Law and Economics*, American Bar Association, p. 308, quoted by M.A. EISNER and K.T. MEIER (1990), *supra* n. 381, p. 273.
422 J.B. BAKER (2002), *supra* n. 319, p. 13.
423 E.M. FOX (1981), *supra* n. 321, p. 1152 ('Whereas the word "power" dominated Warren Court antitrust opinions, the words "efficiency" and "market impact" have prominence in Burger Court antitrust opinions.').
424 *Continental T.V., Inc. v. GTE Sylvania, Inc.,* 433 U.S. 36 (1977).
425 *Brunswick Corp. v. Pueblo Bowl-O-Mat, Inc.,* 429 U.S. 477 (1977).
426 *Reiter v. Sonotone Corp.,* 442 U.S. 330, 343 (1979).
427 *Redwood Theatres, Inc. v. Festival Enterprises, Inc.,* 200 Cal. App. 3d 687, 709, n. 11 (Ct. App. 1988).
428 *Cieri v. Leticia Query Realty, Inc.,* 905 P. 2d 29, 35 (Haw. 1995).
429 In 1976, Richard Lugar, Malcolm Wallop, Orrin Hatch and S.I. Hayakawa, who had narrower preferences to antitrust policy, took the seats of Vance Hartke, Gale McGee, Frank Moss and John Tunney. *See* W.E. KOVACIC (1990), '*The Antitrust Paradox* Revisited: Robert Bork and the Transformation of Modern Antitrust Policy', *The Wayne Law Review*, vol. 36, pp. 1422–1423 ('While it is questionable whether Congress would have enacted deconcentration legislation later in the 1970s even if Hart, Mansfield, McGee, Moss, and other liberal

Many of the appointees by Richard Nixon to the Supreme Court as well as the lower courts were less keen on government intervention in antitrust issues.[430] The Supreme Court's position in supporting the economic goals has a substantial influence on urging the antitrust agencies to apply economic analysis in their decisions.[431]

An important issue concerning the Chicago's influence on the court decisions is that it remained unclear whether courts have interpreted consumer welfare the same way as what the Chicagoans argued. The 'consumer welfare' goal mentioned by Bork in fact refers to 'total welfare'. When courts today quoted 'consumer welfare' from Bork, it remains unclear whether this term refers to its true meaning (consumer welfare), or to the meaning that was applied by Bork (total welfare).[432] According to the research by Blair and Sokol, the words of Bork have been cited in more than 100 court cases, including Supreme Court cases and lower court cases, in order to prove that 'consumer welfare' was the antitrust goal. It is questionable whether these courts referred to the meaning of 'consumer welfare' (which is what Bork states) or 'total welfare' (what Bork truly means).[433] Although Blair and Harrison argued that it seems that the Supreme Court has misused the words by Bork, and it was consumer welfare that the Supreme Court referred to, it is highly difficult to prove what the Supreme Court had in mind when they referred to 'consumer welfare' in their decisions.[434]

2.4.3. Criticism from Academic Scholars

2.4.3.1. Interpreting Legislative Intent

The first criticism of making efficiency the sole aim of antitrust is that the evidence of proving that the Congress took efficiency as the reason for the

---

legislators had not left the Senate, their departure marked a change in congressional preferences that virtually foreclosed favorable consideration of the types of bills to which *The Antitrust Paradox* referred.').

[430] W.E. Kovacic and C. Shapiro (1999), *supra* n. 319, p. 13.

[431] *See* D.A. Hyman and W.E. Kovacic (2013), 'Institutional Design, Agency Life Cycle, and the Goals of Competition Law', *Fordham Law Review*, vol. 81, p. 2170 ('No matter how determined an antitrust agency is to advance a legal argument, when the Supreme Court slaps it down hard, it is sensible for the agency to reexamine its position, and make a different argument the next time around.'). As Bork said, 'the prestige of the Court is so high that by taking the lead in formulating new policy, it may make further legislative change in the same direction much easier.' *See* R.H. Bork and W.S. Bowman, Jr. (1965), *supra* n. 338, p. 370; *see also* R.H. Bork (1967), *supra* n. 20, p. 242 ('Antitrust policy is determined, far more than most people realize, by the Supreme Court.').

[432] 'A Westlaw search in the "ALLFEDS" and "SCT" databases finds that there are 18 Supreme Court cases and 180 total federal court cases that cited to Bork's Antitrust Paradox. Most of these cases, however, do not seem to appreciate the context in which Bork wrote.' R.D. Blair and D.D. Sokol (2012), *supra* n. 331, pp. 473, 476, footnote 23.

[433] R.D. Blair and D.D. Sokol (2012), *supra* n. 331, p. 476.

[434] R.D. Blair and D.D. Sokol (2012), *supra* n. 331, p. 480.

enactment of the Sherman Act and the Clayton Act is not robust. Lande argued that the economic theory of allocative efficiency, marked by the well-known deadweight loss triangle, was not born until 1938.[435] For Lande, productive efficiency was not the goal to be achieved, as it is hard to understand why a law of 'antitrust' was enacted when the 'trusts' at that time were operating highly efficiently.[436] Easterbrook confirmed that monopoly and oligopoly theory in general was only developed in 1930s, which was mainly contributed by Joan Robinson and Edward Chamberlin.[437] Hovenkamp argued that in the 1890s, economists were not able to provide sufficient explanations for high fixed costs by using marginalist models.[438] The theory of efficiency and allocative efficiency is associated with a field of economic theory called welfare economics, which was developed dramatically in the twentieth century. For example, after Pareto and Barone, Kaldor, Hicks and Hotelling are named as new welfare economists. Bergson and Samuelson developed the social welfare function.[439] Historian Richard Hofstadter also confirmed that it was the central fear of the concentration of power that raised anxiety, and the early cases against business operators were not from an economic concern.[440]

2.4.3.2. The Concerns of Distributive Effects

The second criticism is that it is difficult to justify the Sherman Act from a pure efficiency standpoint of view because at that time the monopolist profits through supracompetitive pricing were perceived as 'robbery', and such pricing effects should be restrained. The idea of productive efficiency, although indeed were mentioned when the Sherman Act, the FTC Act, the Clayton Act and the Celler-

---

435   Lande argues that Hotelling was the first economist who developed the theory of allocative efficiency in 1938. *See* H. HOTELLING (1938), 'The General Welfare in Relation to Problems of Taxation and of Railway and Utility Rates', *Econometrica* vol. 6, no. 3, pp. 242–269. Lande claims this triangle did not appear in Alfred Marshall's *Principles of Economics* in 1890. R.H. LANDE (2013), *supra* n. 318, p. 2384, footnotes 169–170.

436   As Lande put in a vivid way: 'If efficiency had been Congress's overriding concern, it would have enacted a "protrust law" not an "antitrust law."' *See* R.H. LANDE (2013), *supra* n. 318, p. 2369 ('The antitrust statutes focus instead on more general principles. Section 1 of the Sherman Act is concerned with arrangements in "restraint of trade", not arrangements that "lead to higher prices".').

437   F.H. EASTERBROOK (1986), *supra* n. 352, p. 1702.

438   *See* H. HOVENKAMP (2001), *supra* n. 389, p. 259.

439   T. SCITOVSKY (1951), 'The State of Welfare Economics', *The American Economic Review*, vol. 41, no. 3, p. 307.

440   Richard Hofstadter: 'The progressive case against business organizations was not confined to economic considerations. At bottom, the central fear was fear of power and the greater the strength of an organized interest the greater the anxiety it aroused. Hence it was the trusts, the investment banking houses, the interlocking directorates, the swollen private fortunes that were most criticized.' R. HOFSTADTER (1955), *The Age of Reform, from Bryan to F. D. R.*, Knopf, p. 225, p. 239, cited by BAKER and BLUMENTHAL (1983), *supra* n. 326, p. 318.

Kefauver Act were enacted,[441] efficiency gains were not justified if it was kept in the pockets of the producers.[442] In this aspect the legislative intent would be consistent with the Chicago arguments, since the core idea of efficiency is that firms that operate more efficiently should be allowed to keep their profits. The justification behind this is that firms are engaged in a competition to achieve efficiency and to increase profits, through which process social welfare is maximized. The efficiency criterion does not look at the internal wealth distribution between consumers and producers; instead, it only gives attention to the total welfare of the society.

Fox argues that the legislators of the Celler-Kefauver Amendment were hostile towards concentrations and did not believe consumers could benefit from efficiency gains.[443] This hostile attitude towards trusts was not based on economic empirical evidence; instead, it mainly came from a political consensus that high concentration would lessen competition.[444] Lande argues that in the late nineteen century it was understood that wealth transfer was the major effect generated by monopolization.[445] It should be clarified that the 'wealth transfer' mentioned here does not mean that antitrust law will take the profit from the rich to compensate the poor, as the consumers were not necessarily poorer than producers. It refers to the monopolistic profits being illegal because they are taken from the hands of consumers through *supra* competitive pricing.[446]

In this sense, according to today's understanding of economic theory, the consumer welfare goal with a strong focus on the distribution of wealth might be more relevant to explain the main theme through the legislative history.[447] 'Efficiency' is not the right answer to the question of why antitrust law exists in the US.[448]

---

[441]   R.H. LANDE (2013), *supra* n. 318, p. 2359, for example, the statement of Sen. Robinson when the FTC Act was enacted: 'Nearly all normal business men can distinguish between "fair competition" and "unfair competition." Efficiency is generally regarded as the fundamental principle of the former – efficiency in producing and in selling' (51 *Cong. Rec.* 11, 231 (1914)). R.H. LANDE (2013), *supra* n. 318, p. 2359, footnote 48.

[442]   As Senator Sherman put it: '[a]mong them all none is more threatening than the inequality of condition, of wealth, and opportunity that has grown within a single generation out of the concentration of capital into vast combinations. The saving of cost goes to the pockets of the producers' (21 *Cong. Rec.* 2460 (1890)).

[443]   See E.M. FOX (1981), *supra* n. 321, p. 1150; E.M. FOX and L.A. SULLIVAN (1987), 'Antitrust – Retrospective and Prospective: Where are We Coming From? Where are We Going?', *New York University Law Review*, vol. 62, p. 940.

[444]   See E.M. FOX and L.A. SULLIVAN (1987), *supra* n. 443, p. 942.

[445]   R.H. LANDE (2013), *supra* n. 318, pp. 2371–2373.

[446]   E.M. FOX (1981), *supra* n. 321, p. 1144, footnote 12. See also *Standard Oil Co. v. United States*, 221 U.S. 1 (1911).

[447]   Lande equates 'price standard' with 'wealth transfer concern', and the price standard is 'consistent with the definitions of "restraint of trade"' ('a "restraint of trade" usually means a practice that restricts output and therefore raises prices': R.H. LANDE (2013), *supra* n. 318, p. 2372).

[448]   See e.g. E.M. FOX (1981), *supra* n. 321, p. 1154 ('The claim that efficiency has been *the* goal and *the* fulcrum of antitrust is weak at best'). See also E.M. FOX (1981), *supra* n. 321, p. 1152, quoted F.S. MCCHESNEY (1980), 'On the Economics of Antitrust Enforcement', *Georgetown*

2.4.3.3. Protecting Competition as the Goal

The third criticism is that efficiency may not be considered as the only antitrust goal. According to Fox, neither the statutory language nor the legislative history could indicate efficiency was the only objective of the antitrust law in the US.[449] Fox argued that if the Chicago school scholars take efficiency as the only antitrust goal, it will be necessary to discuss why all other dominant values which the statutes may imply should be rejected.[450] Fox argued that the *true* reason of why antitrust system exists in the US was to achieve goal of 'competition', in other words, 'freedom', but not 'efficiency'.[451] Based on Fox's study, from the 1950s to early 1970s, the primary concern of the antitrust law in the US was the dispersion of power, not efficiency. Freedom to compete will be created when the concentrated power is constrained. Consumers' interests could be relevant only because they were the victims of concentrated economic power.[452] Meanwhile, the legislative history of merger laws[453] has also shown that when the economic power was decentralized, the number of competitors could increase and in this way individual freedom would be better protected.[454] The Supreme Court made a direct link between competition and decentralization.[455] Competition is lessened when there are fewer participants in the market. The number of competitors as well as the extent to which business is concentrated became the criterion to decide merger cases.[456]

Law Journal, vol. 68, pp. 1103–1104 ('society that values efficiency will not necessarily demand an antitrust system.').

[449] E.M. Fox (1981), *supra* n. 321, p. 1146.

[450] E.M. Fox (1981), *supra* n. 321, p. 1146.

[451] *See generally,* H. THORELLI, *The Federal Antitrust Policy: Origination of an American Tradition,* Johns Hopkins Press, 1955. *See also,* E.M. Fox (1981), *supra* n. 321, p. 1153 ('Rather than standing for efficiency, the American antitrust laws stand against private power. Distrust of power is the one central and common ground that over time has unified support for antitrust statutes. Interests of consumers have been a recurrent concern because consumers have been perceived as victims of the abuse of too much power. Interests of entrepreneurs and small business have been a recurrent concern because independent entrepreneurs have been seen as the heart and lifeblood of American free enterprise, and freedom of economic activity and opportunity has been thought central to the preservation of the American free enterprise system'); E.M. Fox and L.A. SULLIVAN (1987), *supra* n. 443, p. 936 ('Unlike some commentators and a few judges who seek to remake the antitrust law, most courts that apply the antitrust laws have not forgotten what the body of law is about. Antitrust is rooted in a preference for pluralism, freedom of trade, access to markets and freedom of choice.').

[452] E.M. Fox (1981), *supra* n. 321, pp. 1150–1151.

[453] *See* discussions by Fox about the legislative history of the Clayton Act in 1914 and its Celler-Kefauver Amendment in 1950. E.M. Fox (1981), *supra* n. 321, pp. 1150–1151.

[454] E.M. Fox (1981), *supra* n. 321, p. 1151.

[455] E.M. Fox (1981), *supra* n. 321, p. 1151.

[456] For example, *Ford Motor Co. v. United States,* 335 U.S. 303 (1948); *FTC v. Procter & Gamble Co.,* 386 U.S. 568 (1967); *United States v. Von's Grocery Co.,* 384 U.S. 270 (1966); *Brown Shoe Co., Inc. v. United States,* 370 U.S. 294 (1962) *see* E.M. Fox (1981), *supra* n. 321, p. 1151, footnote 57.

Baker argued that the original legislative intent of the Sherman Act was not for the purpose of achieving efficiency, as Robert Bork advocated, nor the goal of consumer welfare, as Robert Lande claimed. The Sherman Act was to prevent private actors from interfering with the competitive process, and to protect individuals' economic liberty.[457] Baker's argument might be agreed by Senator Sherman. Senator John Sherman, under whose name the Sherman Act was enacted, once described this act in 1890 as 'a bill of rights, a charter of liberty'.[458] Pitofsky argued that the Congress expressed a clear concern on concentrated economic power when the Clayton Act was amended in 1950. This concern is rooted in the US tradition of preferring a system with checks and balances to prevent abuse of concentrated power by the State.[459]

When the Sherman Act was enacted in 1890, to the law makers the danger of 'trusts' was the 'restraints of trade'. The concept of 'protecting competition' was not explicitly mentioned in the text; however, to some scholars, this competition goal has been implicitly referred to by using the words 'restraints of trade'.[460] Orbach illustrated the term 'restraint of trade' by the goal of 'protecting competition' in modern antitrust concept, because the status of 'competition' could be achieved when there is no 'restraint of trade'. For example, in *Chicago Board of Trade v. United States*, the US Supreme Court emphasized the competition goal.[461] In *FTC v. Procter & Gamble Co.*,[462] the reasoning of 'impairing competitive conditions' was used by the FTC as an important justification for the merger decision. The FTC focused on the effects on barriers to new entry after the merger, and put the protection of competition as the ultimate goal of antitrust, not the instrument to achieve efficiency.[463]

---

[457]   J.B. BAKER (2013), *supra* n. 315, p. 2177.

[458]   21 *Cong. Rec.* 2461 (1890), cited by R.H. BORK and W.S. BOWMAN (1965), *supra* n. 338, p. 363.

[459]   R. PITOFSKY (1979), 'The Political Content of Antitrust', *University of Pennsylvania Law Review*, vol. 127, no. 4, p. 1054.

[460]   *See e.g.* B. ORBACH (2013), *supra* n. 401, pp. 2253–2277; H. HOVENKAMP (1989), 'The Sherman Act and the Classical Theory of Competition', *Iowa Law Review*, vol. 74, pp. 1019. In particular, Orbach cited the words by Senator George Hoar, one of the main drafters of the Sherman Act: 'The great thing that this bill does, except affording remedy, is to extend the common-law principles, which protected fair competition in trade in old times in England, to international and interstate commerce.' B. ORBACH (2013), p. 2262 and 21 *Cong. Rec.* 3152 (8 April 1890).

[461]   *Chicago Board of Trade v. United States,* 246 U.S. 231, 238 (1918), ('The true test of legality is whether the restraint imposed is such as merely regulates and perhaps thereby promotes competition or whether it is such as may suppress or even destroy competition'), cited by B. ORBACH (2013), *supra* n. 401, p. 2270.

[462]   *Proctor & Gamble Co.*, 386 U.S. 568 (1967).

[463]   The FTC's statement has also shown that when the goal of protecting competition conflicts with the goal of achieving efficiency, the competition goal prevails, because 'efficiency' can also be categorized as 'anticompetitive'. *See* R.H. BORK and W.S. BOWMAN, JR. (1965), *supra* n. 338, p. 374.

The concept of protecting competition has also been interpreted as the goal of 'protecting freedom', as the famous claim that the 'Sherman Act is the "Magna Carta of free enterprise"' in *United States v. Topco Assocs., Inc.*,[464] and 'Sherman Act as a "charter of freedom"' in *Appalachian Coals, Inc. v. United States*.[465] Minda argued that the antitrust has a particular American tradition and is historically 'as American as "apple pie" and the "fourth of July"'. Preventing power concentration has a long history in American culture.[466] However, the 'freedom' goal does not mean that firms are allowed to choose what they want to do. Freedom of the individual market participant will be impeded when economic power is concentrated by a few firms. It is necessary to rely on a legal system which could safeguard this freedom by granting all market participants an equal opportunity to compete.[467]

2.5. THE DEBATE ON WELFARE STANDARDS IN THE POST-CHICAGO ERA

The current debate on competition policy goals focuses on the choice between the consumer welfare standard and the total welfare standard.[468] It seems that this debate takes a normative perspective, that is, which standard should be applied in the antitrust enforcement in the US, although scholars may seek evidence by conducting a positive study on legislation and judicial decisions throughout antitrust history. However, a consensus concerning the interpretation of the term of consumer welfare has not been achieved among lawyers and economists.[469] The confusion may come from the misuse of the term 'consumer welfare' by Bork, as what he meant was in fact 'total welfare'. The most important difference between these two standards lies in the fact that the total welfare standard does not take distributive effects into account. Under the total welfare standard, it is socially desirable that resources are allocated efficiently, and it does not make a value judgment between one additional value in the hands of consumers or producers. The representatives of the total welfare

---

[464] *United States v. Topco Assocs., Inc.*, 405 U.S. 596, 610 (1972).

[465] *Appalachian Coals, Inc. v. United States*, 288 U.S. 344, 359 (1933).

[466] G. MINDA (1995), 'Antitrust at Century's End', *Southern Methodist University Law Review*, vol. 48, p. 1757.

[467] This reflects a political concern of setting fair rules for the game. Protecting equal opportunity can be seen as a political goal. E.M. Fox and L.A. SULLIVAN (1987), *supra* n. 443, p. 944.

[468] *See e.g.* R.D. BLAIR and D.D. SOKOL (2012), *supra* n. 331, p. 475: 'In order to implement the rule of reason, however, it is necessary to know what 'value' or 'values' the antitrust laws should promote. Although some support can be found for other values, the most prominent are consumer welfare and total welfare.'

[469] As Brodley claimed, 'Consumer welfare is the most abused term in modern antitrust analysis'. J.F. BRODLEY (1987), *supra* n. 324, p. 1032.

standard are Robert Bork, Richard Posner and Frank Easterbrook. These scholars do not perceive that the efficiency goal conflicts with the consumer welfare goal.[470] For example, Easterbrook argues that since consumers benefit the most from the antitrust policy promoting allocative and productive efficiency, the efficiency goal and the consumer welfare goal are not very different.[471] Therefore, they agreed that there is only one, consistent goal that Congress had in mind, which passed this message on to judges and juries.[472]

By contrast, for scholars who advocate a consumer welfare standard, equalizing efficiency and the consumer welfare goal might be misleading, as the efficiency goal gives an equal treatment to consumer and producers. In contrast, the consumer welfare goal does not give the same value of additional one euro increase to consumers and to producers. The argument by Easterbrook refers to the situation where the efficiency goal increases consumer welfare. However, there are other situations where promoting the efficiency goal requires a sacrifice of the consumer welfare in the short run, or in the long run. Moreover, the efficiency goal accepts the Kaldor-Hicks requirement but the consumer welfare goal does not. The differences between these two goals cannot be ignored.

Scholars who advocate the consumer welfare goal, such as Robert Lande, argue that consumer welfare, not efficiency, is the real purpose of antitrust in the US.[473] By applying a consumer welfare standard, scholars will only focus on the welfare effects of consumers, and will not look at welfare effects on producers, or on the whole society. In this perspective, a wealth transfer from consumers to producers should be prohibited. Representatives of the consumer welfare standard are Robert Lande, John Kirkwood, Steven Salop, and Robert Pitofsky.

However, it remains highly controversial to interpret 'consumer welfare' from both legal and economic perspectives. The debate lies in three aspects: 'consumer', 'welfare', and 'consumer welfare'. It remains unclear whether 'consumer' refers to the end-use customer, or also includes retailers from the distribution chain,[474] and whether 'consumer welfare' could be measured by 'consumer surplus'.[475] The interpretation of 'consumer welfare' adds the additional difficulty of setting clear thresholds and criteria in antitrust practice.

This section summarizes the debate on welfare goals among US scholars. The first section focuses on consumer welfare. The first part discusses how 'consumer'

---

[470] See e.g. F.H. EASTERBROOK (1986), supra n. 352, p. 1703 ('However you slide the legislative history, the dominant theme is the protection of consumers from overcharges. This turns out to be the same program as one based on "Efficiency"').

[471] See F.H. EASTERBROOK (1986), supra n. 352, p. 1703.

[472] See F.H. EASTERBROOK (1986), supra n. 352, p. 1703.

[473] R.H. LANDE (1982), supra n. 318, pp. 65–152; R.H. LANDE (1988), supra n. 318, pp. 429–465; R.H. LANDE (1989), supra n. 318, pp. 631–644.

[474] See discussion in section 2.5.1.1.

[475] See discussion in section 2.5.1.3.

in the antitrust context has been interpreted. The second part discusses the definition of consumer welfare. The third issue is whether consumer welfare can be economically assessed by its proxy 'consumer surplus'. The fourth part discusses that the standard of 'consumer welfare' does not aim at 'maximizing consumer welfare', because the desired level of well-being of consumers is not to 'maximize' it. The last part discusses the extension of the consumer welfare standard. It is called the 'consumer choice' standard by Lande. The second section of this chapter addresses the debate between the consumer welfare and the total welfare standard. There are two issues that will be discussed: firstly the distributive issue, and the second is the implementation issue. Consumer welfare is argued to have an advantage in practice because it is easier to implement. However, the criticism of this standard is its distributive nature, as some economists argue that wealth transfer should not be the target of competition policy.

2.5.1.   Consumer Welfare Standard

2.5.1.1.   Who is the Consumer?

Kirkwood and Lande claimed that the consumer welfare goal has been accepted and is fully applied 'at all levels of the federal courts' for the last twenty years.[476] Throughout the judicial decisions that they have investigated, it was concluded that the consumer protection goal, not economic efficiency, always prevailed.[477] Lande argued that when the Sherman Act was enacted, Congress' original concerns for 'consumers' should be interpreted as 'any direct purchasers' in the market. It is not necessary to distinguish between direct and indirect consumers, or consumers purchasing different products.[478] With respect to the antitrust administrative work today, Lande and Kirkwood suggested that 'consumers' can be defined as the direct purchasers in the relevant market. There is no need to trace the effects through the distribution chain and to distinguish between immediate and final consumers.[479] Moreover, Kirkwood has been aware of the situation where the buyers have superior power, and he specifically defines the consumer who should be protected as the buyer in the 'sell-side case' and the supplier in the 'buy-side case'.[480] This clarification gives a reply to the criticism that the consumer welfare (surplus) standard would encourage the buying

---

[476]   J.B. KIRKWOOD (2013), *supra* n. 325, p. 2443.

[477]   J.B. KIRKWOOD (2013), *supra* n. 325, p. 2443.

[478]   *See* R.H. LANDE (2013), *supra* n. 318, p. 2358, footnote 45: 'While Congress frequently referred to "consumers", it did not appear to care only about ultimate consumers. Rather, Congress wanted to protect all who were overcharged.'

[479]   They argue that direct purchasers always pass on 'at least part of' the price effects to final consumers; therefore, direct purchasers are 'a reasonable proxy for impact on ultimate consumers'. J.B. KIRKWOOD and R.H. LANDE (2008), *supra* n. 325, p. 203; J.B. KIRKWOOD (2013), *supra* n. 325, p. 2450, footnotes 107, 108.

[480]   J.B. KIRKWOOD (2013), *supra* n. 325, p. 2432.

cartel.[481] The explanations provided by Kirkwood and Lande tend to include the welfare of both 'final consumers' and other buyers in the distribution chain in the definition of 'consumer welfare'.

2.5.1.2. What is Consumer Welfare?

The definition of 'consumers' is also an important issue to discuss the differences between the total welfare and the consumer welfare goal. Promoting efficiency to maximize social welfare does not have a different meaning as maximizing consumer welfare if it is believed that 'all of us are consumers'.[482] Following this logic, Bork argued that the efficiency goal will not conflict with the consumer welfare goal. As discussed in previous sections, this view suffers from the bias that efficiency and consumer welfare will be achieved at the same time. In most cases, a part of the gains to consumers has to be given off in order to maximize social welfare. Another issue that should not be ignored is, in the situation where everyone is a consumer, there is a conflict between the welfare gains among consumers. Maximizing social welfare does not necessarily mean maximizing every individual consumer's welfare.[483] There is still a distributive concern regarding which consumer is entitled to be made better off, if it will require a welfare loss from another consumer. In practice, when the courts referred to the concept of 'consumer welfare', they tend to give a superior treatment to a part of individuals and allow them to enjoy welfare gains at the cost of the others.[484] This could show that the goal of promoting consumer welfare does not refer to promoting the welfare of every individual in the society. Since the consumer welfare goal provides a clear focus to distributive concerns, the definition of 'consumer' would be of vital importance.

---

[481]   *See generally*, D.W. CARLTON (2007), 'Does Antitrust Need to Be Modernized?', *Journal of Economic Perspectives*, vol. 21, no. 3, p. 158; R.W. PITTMAN (2007) 'Consumer Surplus as the Appropriate Standard for Antitrust Enforcement', *Competition Policy International*, vol. 3, no. 2, p. 211 (arguing buying cartels should not be allowed by antitrust policy because when monopsonist has market power, the inputs will be paid at the low monopsony price, which will lead to the output reduction and welfare loss on the downstream as well as the final consumers. When a monopsonist does not have market power, the upstream customers, instead of the downstream customers, suffer a welfare loss). George Stigler defines 'monopsony' as the situation when the buyer has power in the market. As there is only one buyer in the market, the buyer can exercise monopsony power to reduce the purchase price and quantity. For a detailed discussion on monopsony and antitrust policy *see* R.D. BLAIR and J.L. HARRISON (1991), 'Antitrust Policy and Monopsony', *Cornell Law Review*, vol. 76, pp. 297–340; G.J. STIGLER, *The Theory of Price*, Macmillan 1987.

[482]   H. HOVENKAMP (1982), 'Distributive Justice and the Antitrust Laws', *George Washington Law Review*, vol. 51, p. 5 ('The answer, of course, is that all of us are consumers at one time or another.').

[483]   H. HOVENKAMP (1982), *supra* n. 482, p. 6.

[484]   H. HOVENKAMP (1982), *supra* n. 482, p. 6 Hovenkamp gave the example of *United States v. Von's Grocery Co.* 384 U.S. 270 (1966) and *Times-Picayune Pub. Co. v. United States*, 345 U.S. 594 (1953).

2.5.1.3. Consumer Welfare or Consumer Surplus?

One common way of measuring consumer welfare is to use its proxy consumer surplus,[485] which is economically defined as the difference between the market price and the consumers' willingness to pay. Consumer surplus of the market as a whole is estimated by adding up the value of each individual consumer surplus. The sum of the consumer surplus and the producer surplus equals the total surplus. The economic justification of using the consumer surplus to measure the consumer welfare is the neoclassical price-theory. Marshall explains that when the market price is increased, assuming the income level keeps constant, the individual consumer's utility will be reduced when the consumption level is decreased.

The use of consumer surplus as the proxy of consumer welfare raises controversies from both economic and legal perspectives. From an economic perspective, interpreting consumer welfare as the maximization of consumer surplus and the reduction of prices, however, does not satisfy the Pareto criterion, or the Kaldor-Hicks criterion.[486] Pareto optimality will not be satisfied, as the price reduction is often at the expense of the profits earned by the firms. Nor does it satisfy the Kaldor-Hicks criterion, because consumers must be made better off before being compensated by the producers.[487]

From a legal perspective, the consumer surplus standard in economic terms can hardly capture the real meaning of 'consumer welfare'. In their book *Fairness versus Welfare*[488] Kaplow and Shavell argued that only a welfare-based normative approach should be employed in the evaluation of legal rules. The reason is that any government decision which is not based on individual welfare will, in some circumstances, violate the Pareto Principle. Non-welfare goals, such as notions of fairness or corrective justice should not play a role. The concept of the 'welfare standard' they use, however, is broader than in the conventional economic approach, that is, the maximization of wealth. They argue that the concept of 'welfare' should include all aspects of an individual's well-being. As Stucke pointed out, the definition of the consumer welfare goal contains broad social, political, economic and moral values.[489] A decision based on estimating the

---

485   J.F. Brodley (1987), *supra* n. 324, p. 1033. It has been commonly acknowledged that consumer surplus principle was first defined by Alfred Marshall in his book Principles of Economics in 1890. *See* A. Marshall, *Principles of Economics*, Macmillan and Co. 1891 *see also* J.M. Currie, J.A. Murphy and A. Schmitz (1971), 'The Concept of Economic Surplus and Its Use in Economic Analysis', *The Economic Journal*, vol. 81, no. 324, pp. 741–799.

486   R. Van den Bergh (2007), 'The "More Economic Approach" and the Pluralist Tradition of European Competition Law (comment)' in D. Schmidtchen, M. Albert and S. Voigt (eds.), *The More Economic Approach to European Competition Law*, Mohr Siebeck 2007, p. 29.

487   R. Van den Bergh (2007), *supra* n. 486, p. 29.

488   L. Kaplow and S. Shavell, *Fairness versus Welfare*, Harvard University Press 2002, p. 3.

489   Stucke quoted the words by Hayek, 'the welfare of a people cannot be adequately expressed as a single end, but only as a hierarchy of ends, a comprehensive scale of values in which every

change of price and quality will not fully satisfy the consumer welfare goal, as other factors which may affect the gains to consumers, such as variety and innovation, should also be incorporated.[490] The broad and undetermined definition of consumer and consumer welfare leads to a gap between the policy statement and what has been applied in practice.[491]

2.5.1.4. Consumer Welfare Maximization

In the modern debate on the consumer welfare goal, it was argued that consumer welfare is not to be 'maximized'.[492] Orbach claimed that in some circumstances consumers will be harmed by simply applying the conventional consumer welfare or the total welfare standard. Welfare differs from surplus because welfare refers to the effects on individual's well-being as a result of the activity. For example, the negative effects on health must be taken into account when a consumer purchases cigarettes. If the goal of an antitrust law is to protect 'consumer surplus', it is equivalent to the goal of 'protecting low prices'.[493] Therefore, the definition of welfare should also be extended to the evaluation of well-being, even to the individual's subjective assessment of satisfaction.[494]

Orbach pointed out that consumers cannot benefit from price reduction in all situations, because the increased consumption of some products will harm consumers and will result in an undesirable outcome. These products are known as 'bads', and the examples are tobacco, alcohol, abortions, firearms, gambling, pornography, junk food, guns and sex services.[495] Moreover, consumer preferences are not always elastic to prices. Consumers have personalized preferences to the special features of products, such as the age of wine, which is the exclusivity of status goods.[496] Low price does not necessarily change consumers' tastes. Another important limitation of the conventional consumer welfare goal is that it underestimates how intensive legal regimes affect

---

need of every person is given its place.' F.A. HAYEK, *The Road to Serfdom: Text and Documents*, edited by B. CALDWELL, University of Chicago Press 2007, p. 101; M.E. STUCKE (2012) 'Reconsidering Antitrust Goals', *Boston College Law Review*, vol. 53, p. 572.

490   M.E. STUCKE (2012), *supra* n. 489, p. 576.

491   M.E. STUCKE (2012), *supra* n. 489, p. 577.

492   E.M. Fox (2013), 'Against Goals', *Fordham Law Review*, vol. 81, p. 2159.

493   B. ORBACH (2013), 'Foreword: Antitrust' Pursuit of Purpose', *Fordham Law Review*, vol. 81, p. 2155.

494   For example, to what extent people feel happy. *See e.g.,* M.E. STUCKE (2013), 'Should Competition Policy Promote Happiness?', *Fordham Law Review*, vol. 81, p. 2585. Note that the definition of consumer welfare by the OECD: 'Consumer welfare refers to the individual benefits derived from the consumption of goods and services. In theory, individual welfare is defined by an individual's own assessment of his/her satisfaction, given prices and income', OECD Glossary of Industrial Organization Economics and Competition Law 29, available at <www.oecd.org/dataoecd/8/61/2376087.pdf>, cited by STUCKE (2013), p. 2585, footnote 50.

495   B.Y. ORBACH (2011), *supra* n. 401, p. 152.

496   B.Y. ORBACH (2011), *supra* n. 401, p. 158.

innovation. Consumers today are more willing to upgrade their products and this decision is more affected by companies' strategic decisions.[497]

2.5.1.5. Consumer Choice

Lande argued that the price standard which is used to measure consumer welfare should be extended to a choice standard. The ultimate goal of an antitrust law should be protecting consumer choices.[498] This standard is particularly useful for three categories of cases: when the market has little price competition, when consumers' search costs are high and when firms compete through other variables instead of price, such as quality, variety and creativity of the product.[499] Lande illustrated the importance of consumer choice by giving an example of a merger between media companies. After the merger, the supply of different views and opinions for consumers will be reduced, and such supply cannot be easily restored as the supply of cookies.[500] Another drawback of limiting the focus on current market price is, especially in high-tech markets, that it ignores the impact of innovation and the development of new ideas in the future.[501] This argument seems to indicate that the current consumer welfare standard cannot accurately deal with competitive effects in a dynamic market.

Lande's argument on consumer choice is to a large extent based on his judgment that some factors of the product, such as quality, variety, product safety, convenience and product innovation, cannot be reflected by price.[502] Based on the recent development of modern industrial organization, however, this assumption does not hold. There are two areas of research in industrial economics that have to be investigated before applying this consumer choice standard. One area is the economic methods of adjusting non-price factors;[503] the other area is how economic literature addresses the long-term effects generated from innovation and the issue of dynamic efficiency.[504] Nevertheless, it seems that Lande could be comforted by the recent development in the 2010

---

[497] B.Y. ORBACH (2011), *supra* n. 401, p. 158.

[498] R.H. LANDE (2001), 'Consumer Choice as the Ultimate Goal of Antitrust', *University of Pittsburgh Law Review,* vol. 62, p. 50;.

[499] R. H. LANDE (2013), *supra* n. 318, p. 2396.

[500] R.H. LANDE (2013), *supra* n. 318, p. 2396.

[501] R. H. LANDE (2013), *supra* n. 318, p. 2397.

[502] R. H. LANDE (2001), *supra* n. 498, p. 515; N.W. AVERITT and R.H. LANDE (2007), 'Using the "Consumer Choice" Approach to Antitrust Law', *Antitrust Law Journal,* vol. 74, no. 1, p. 184.

[503] Wright and Ginsburg put a long list of economic literature to illustrate how quality-adjusted prices are used in antitrust analysis. He argued that the discussion on quality-adjusted prices dated back to early 1900s. J.D. WRIGHT and D.H. GINSBURG (2013), 'The Goals of Antitrust: Welfare Trumps Choice', *Fordham Law Review,* vol. 81, p. 2410.

[504] *See e.g.* GINSBURG and J.D. WRIGHT (2012), 'Dynamic Analysis and the Limits of Antitrust Institutions', *Antitrust Law Journal,* vol. 78, no. 1, pp. 1–21; J.G. SIDAK and D.J. TEECE (2009), 'Dynamic Competition in Antitrust Law', *Journal of Competition Law and Economics,* vol. 5, no. 4, pp. 581–631.

Merger Guidelines in the US, which do indeed put emphasis on non-price factors, such as quality, service and new products.[505]

2.5.2. Consumer Welfare versus Total Welfare

2.5.2.1. Distributive Issues

One important factor that distinguishes between the consumer welfare and the total welfare standards is whether distributive effects should be taken into account. While some legal scholars advocate the consumer welfare goal perceive the wealth transfer from consumers to producers is *per se* harmful, and this transfer should be prohibited,[506] economists generally agree that distributive issues should be dealt *separately* from the welfare considerations.[507] For example, Motta[508] argues that the welfare standard is a measure to assess 'how efficient' an industry is, and the concept of welfare does not address the issue of how income should be distributed among market players. Kaplow[509] has emphasized the difficulty of achieving distributive objectives through a competition law. Distributive goals, he argued, should be targeted by the tax and transfer system. Under the tax and transfer system, the payments are directly related to income, age, disability, family configurations and other factors. By contrast, under competition law, there are only two categories –the consumer and the producer. Most competition law cases deal with intermediate goods, such as computer chips, which are used by both consumers and other producers. The harmed party for one unit of price increase on computer chips is more difficult to examine.[510]

Salop argued that the consumer welfare standard adopted by the antitrust policy does not mean that the goal of an antitrust law is to redistribute wealth. It only provides a threshold to safeguard the property rights of the consumers by blocking the conduct that is going to take wealth away from consumers.[511]

---

[505] Merger Guidelines 2010 §10, 'A primary benefit of mergers to the economy is their potential to generate significant efficiencies and thus enhance the merged firm's ability and incentive to compete, which may result in lower prices, improved quality, enhanced service, or new products.' Some economists have expressed their doubt on how to assess this 'improved quality, enhanced service, or new products', *see e.g.* R.D. BLAIR and J.S. HAYNES (2011), 'The Efficiencies Defense in the 2010 Horizontal Merger Guidelines', *Review of Industrial Organization*, vol. 39, pp. 63–67.

[506] 'The transfer is exploitative: like robbery, it is a form of coerced taking', J.B. KIRKWOOD (2013), *supra* n. 325, p. 2453.

[507] M. MOTTA, *Competition Policy Theory and Practice*, Cambridge University Press 2004, p. 18.

[508] M. MOTTA (2004), *supra* n. 507, p. 18.

[509] L. KAPLOW (2011), 'On the Choice of Welfare Standards in Competition Law', *Harvard John M. Olin Center for Law, Economics and Business Discussion Paper No. 693, 2011/5*, p. 2.

[510] L. KAPLOW (2011), *supra* n. 509, p. 5.

[511] S.C. SALOP (2010), 'Question: What is the Real and Proper Antitrust Welfare Standard? Answer: The *True* Consumer Welfare Standard', *Loyola Consumer Law Review*, vol. 22, no. 3,

Moreover, a merger policy that adopts the consumer welfare goal would be more effective in protecting consumers' wealth than other mechanisms, such as transferring the wealth back to consumers through an inefficient tax system.[512]

2.5.2.2. Implementation Issues

Economists and lawyers both agree that setting clear, predictable rules is important for implementing antitrust laws,[513] although they might have different opinions on how to secure legal certainty as they have distinct preferences to the goals of antitrust. Kirkwood and Lande claimed that the consumer welfare standard is more workable than the efficiency goal.[514] Focusing on the consumer welfare goal, only the loss to consumers has to be assessed; by contrast, under the total welfare standard, the loss to consumers must be compared with the gains to producers, and this process brings additional complexity and difficulty for antitrust administrators.[515] The total welfare standard, according to Kirkwood and Lande, embraces all the problems and difficulties that the consumer welfare goal has, such as the question of how to measure the long-term impact. The tradeoff between consumer loss and producer gains only makes the total welfare standard harder to administer.[516] This argument has been supported by some economists. For example, it was argued that the consumer welfare standard may 'simplify' merger analysis.[517] In merger cases, a total welfare standard requires a difficult calculation between the increases in profits and the consumer welfare losses. A consumer welfare standard would simply the analysis by limiting the calculation to the price effects.[518] Moreover, Carlton argues that relying on a short-term consumer surplus standard is easier for antitrust decision makers to monitor.[519]

However, there are also a few limitations on implementing antitrust policy based on the consumer welfare standard. The first difficulty is the ambiguous meaning of 'consumer welfare'. Given the broad interpretation of consumer welfare, to give an answer to the question of how to quantify consumer welfare is

---

p. 350.

512 S.C. Salop (2010), *supra* n. 511, p. 351.

513 *See e.g.* J.F. Brodley (1987), *supra* n. 324, p. 1042 ('The substantive and procedural rules of antitrust should be stable and predictable so that businesses can undertake transactions with maximum certainty and security'). E.M. Fox (1981), *supra* n. 321, p. 1140 ('stability and continuity in the antitrust rule of law provides for greater certainty and therefore more effective deterrence').

514 R.H. Lande (1988), *supra* n. 318, pp. 436–437, 452; A. Fisher, F. Johnson and R. Lande (1985), 'Mergers, Market Power and Property Rights: When Will Efficiencies Prevent Price Increases?', unpublished manuscript, *FTC Working Paper No. 130.*

515 J.B. Kirkwood (2013), *supra* n. 325, p. 2449.

516 J.B. Kirkwood (2013), *supra* n. 325, p. 2451.

517 M. Motta (2004), *supra* n. 507, p. 21.

518 M. Motta (2004), *supra* n. 507, p. 21.

519 D.W. Carlton (2007), *supra* n. 481, p. 159.

a challenging task. In a survey conducted by the International Competition Network ('ICN'), 28 percent of respondents replied that it is 'not possible' to quantify consumer harm.[520] Second, the consumer welfare standard does not consider the gains of firms. When firms lose profits, they will have less incentive to innovate and to produce new products, and at the same time distribute fewer dividends, which often in turn leads to a loss of consumer welfare.[521]

To apply the economic model to real life antitrust cases, another fundamental question is whether the economic solution could provide a clear and definite standard. If the model is uncertain regarding whether a business conduct is likely to generate efficiency or not, using this ambiguous welfare analysis might be endangered by lobbying from powerful groups.[522] The original models developed by the Chicago School and the Harvard School based on neoclassical price theory, have been made much more complex and sophisticated by economists in the post-Chicago era.[523] Modern industrial organization theories on the strategic interaction between oligopolists made the effects of economies of scale more difficult to predict.[524]

2.6. CONCLUSION

For over a century, thanks to the efforts of numerous lawyers, economists, psychologists, philosophers, mathematicians, the understanding of 'competition' in the US has been enriched, refined, and thoroughly developed. The debate on the goals of antitrust law in the US does not result in a brutal fight between different groups of thinkers; rather, it is a bright picture with beautiful colors, which contains dedications from different schools of thought over decades.

The US antitrust system relies on the common goal of guaranteeing a robust market.[525] Neither public nor private power is allowed to restrain competition in the market. Economic analysis of the effects of competition and monopolistic conduct provides better understanding of how to safeguard this market. In particular, modern industrial organization theory gives better explanations on the reasons and effects of interactions between firms in the market. The comparative advantage in speaking the language used in the business world gives economists a prioritized seat among all the participating painters.

---

520   M.E. STUCKE (2012), *supra* n. 489, p. 574; International Competition Network (2011), *Competition Enforcement and Consumer Welfare – Setting the Agenda*, p. 14.
521   M. MOTTA (2004), *supra* n. 507, p. 21.
522   H. HOVENKAMP (1985), *supra* n. 389, p. 224.
523   H. HOVENKAMP (1985), *supra* n. 389, p. 224.
524   H. HOVENKAMP (1985), *supra* n. 389, p. 224. Contestable market, game theory and transaction costs are three major development of industrial organization in the 'post-Chicago' era. *See* R. VAN DEN BERGH and P. CAMESASCA (2006), *supra* n. 18.
525   E.M. FOX (2013), *supra* n. 492.

Nevertheless, although the efficiency argument gives judges a neutral and practical tool to make difficult assessments, it does not solve the puzzle of how efficiency gains could eventually be transferred to consumers. The discussion of the goals of the US antitrust law focuses on the choice between the total welfare goal and the consumer welfare goal. In addition, the difficulty of defining 'consumer' and 'consumer welfare' adds complexity to the question of the welfare goals from both legal and economic perspectives, and this debate still continues today.

3. GOALS OF COMPETITION LAW IN THE EU

3.1. INTRODUCTION

Far beyond the focus of the consumer welfare goal and the total welfare goal in the US, competition law and policy in Europe embraces a much longer list of policy goals.[526] The reason for this difference is that competition policy in Europe is not as an end in itself; instead, it is often regarded as an instrument to achieve broader goals for the European Union.[527] Starting from the Rome Treaty, the fundamental role of the EU competition policy is to achieve an integrated common market, and this goal might come at the cost of sacrificing efficiency. Therefore, promoting efficiency to maximize economic welfare is not the primary concern for the legislators of the EU competition law. Moreover, for European legislators, one euro flowing to consumers does not contain the same value as one euro to the producers. Consumer welfare often receives more attention from the public policy makers in Europe and this goal is treated more from a political standpoint, not purely based on an economic analysis. In recent years, in addition to the goals of protecting consumer welfare, total welfare, and the protection of the freedom to compete, the Commission has added other social, political, even environmental goals to the competition policy, hoping this combination could result in a more integrated European market.

The goals of competition policy in Europe are different from the objectives of the US antitrust law primarily in two respects. Firstly, the EU competition policy is utilized as an instrument to achieve broader goals of the European Union, and the most important concern is to establish a common market among all Member States. In this aspect, competition is not an end in itself. Ever since the European Coal and Steel Community ('ECSC') was founded in 1951, it has been made clear that competition policy is considered as a crucial instrument to facilitate the market integration between Member States. The second aspect is that for

---

[526] R.J. VAN DEN BERGH and P.D. CAMESASCA (2006), *supra* n. 18, p. 1.
[527] L. MCGOWAN and S. WILKS (1995), 'The First Supranational Policy in the European Union: Competition Policy', *European Journal of Political Research*, vol. 28, p. 141.

European policy makers, economic goals are not the only concern. It has been a long tradition in Europe to emphasize the 'social objectives' of the economic policy.[528] Therefore, allocative efficiency, as advocated by the Chicago School in the US, is not the only goal that the EU competition law strives to achieve.

Although the goals of EU competition law have not been described precisely in any political documents or decisions,[529] the European scholars generally agree on four prominent goals including both economic and political concerns for competition and market integration.[530] These four goals for competition law and policy in the EU are: (1) promoting market integration; (2) enhancing consumer welfare; (3) increasing total welfare; and (4) protecting the 'freedom to compete', which follows the German Ordoliberal approach. The following sections will discuss these four goals in detail.

3.2. THE MARKET INTEGRATION GOAL

The primary concern of EU competition policy is the political goal of promoting market integration. It refers to the goal of eliminating the trade barriers between Member States and to create a uniform common market. The market integration goal has two dimensions. The first aspect is that to establish a common market, the trade barriers set up by the private powers against the free flow of persons, goods, services and capital must be prohibited. Neither the public power at the Member States level, nor private enterprises are allowed to undertake practices that will conflict with the unification of the common market, which safeguards the free movement of goods, services, persons, and capital within the European Union.[531]

The second dimension of the market integration goal is that EU competition policy is not considered as an end in itself; instead, it functions as an instrument to contribute to the wider goals of the European Union, which include other industrial, environmental, social and regional concerns.[532] For example, Article 2 of the Treaty on the European Communities ('TEC Treaty') stated that the ultimate goals of the European Community include a 'harmonious, balanced

---

[528] D.J. GERBER, *Law and Competition in Twentieth Century Europe: Protecting Prometheus*, Clarendon Press 1998, pp. 73–83.

[529] C. AHLBORN and J. PADILLA (2007), 'From Fairness to Welfare: Implications for the Assessment of Unilateral Conduct under EC Competition Law', in C.D. EHLERMANN and M. MARQUIS (eds.), *European Competition Law Annual 2007: A Reformed Approach to Article 82 EC*, Hart Publishing, p. 40.

[530] *See* C. KIRCHNER (1998), 'Future Competition Law', in C.D. EHLERMANN and L.L. LAUDATI (eds.), *The Objectives of Competition Policy, European Competition Law Annual 1997*, Oxford, pp. 513–523.

[531] R. VAN DEN BERGH and P.D. CAMESASCA (2006), *supra* n. 18, p. 2.

[532] A. SCHMIDT (2001), 'Non-Competition Factors in the European Competition Policy: The Necessity of Institutional Reforms', Center for Globalization and Europeanization of the Economy, *Georg-August-Universitaet Goettingen, Discussion Paper No. 13*, p. 4; C. AHLBORN and J. PADILLA (2007), *supra* n. 529, p. 40.

and sustainable development of economic activities, a high level of employment and of social protection, and a high degree of competitiveness and convergence of economic performance'. Article 3 of the TEC Treaty describes the means of achieving these goals, including establishing a system ensuring that competition in the internal market is not distorted, strengthening the competitiveness of the Community industry, the promotion of research and technological development. Article 3(1)(g) of the TEC Treaty held that the ultimate goal of the European Union is to 'establish a system ensuring that competition in the internal market is not distorted.'[533] In the situation where the goal of competition policy conflicts with other policies, this article has frequently been referred by the European Court of Justice ('ECJ'), as this article indicates the fundamental role of the competition policy to achieve the objectives of the Community.[534] Although there are also other principles that will be taken into account by the competition authority, such as consumer welfare, the freedom to compete, the protection of equal opportunities for small and medium-sized enterprises and industrial policy, in practice the competition goals may have been restrained by the political goal of the European Union.[535]

3.3.   THE CONSUMER PROTECTION GOAL

3.3.1.   *Consumer Welfare versus Total Welfare*

Under EU competition law, the goal of consumer welfare focuses on the gain of consumers and pays attention to the transfer between consumer surplus and producer surplus. In Europe, the loss of consumer surplus cannot be counterbalanced by the efficiency gains of producer surplus.[536] This concern contradicts with the goal of total welfare. A total welfare goal disregards the distributional effects and does not accept the difference between one euro in the hand of consumers or in the hand of producers. It is also called 'the constant dollar (or euro)' philosophy.[537] The consideration of consumer welfare has been clearly stated in Article 101(3) TFEU and Article 2(1)(b) of the Merger Regulation.[538]

---

[533]   Cited by I. LIANOS (2013), 'Some Reflections on the Question of the Goals of EU Competition Law', *CLES Working Paper Series 3/2013*, p. 37.

[534]   *See e.g.* Case C-67/96, *Albany International BV v. Stichting Bedrijfspensioenfonds Textielindustrie* [1999] ECR I-5751; Case C-309/99, *J.C.J. Wouters, J.W. Savelbergh and Price Waterhouse Belastingadviseurs BV v. Algemene Raad van de Nederlandse Orde van Advocaten* [2002] ECR I-1577; Case C-289/04 P, *Showa Denko KK v. Commission* [2006] ECR I-5859, para. 55, cited by I. LIANOS (2013), *supra* n. 533, p. 38.

[535]   A. SCHMIDT (2001), *supra* n. 532, p. 5.

[536]   R. VAN DEN BERGH and P.D. CAMESASCA (2006), *supra* n. 18, p. 3.

[537]   A. JONES and B. SUFRIN (2004), *supra* n. 26, p. 13.

[538]   R. VAN DEN BERGH and P.D. CAMESASCA (2006), *supra* n. 18, p. 3.

According to the Guidelines on the Application of Article 81(3) of the Treaty, consumers, including all direct and indirect product users, must receive a 'fair share' of the potential efficiency gains,[539] and it would not be accepted to use the efficiency gains to compensate consumers if consumers are affected by increased prices, or lower quality.[540] Therefore, EU competition law does not allow the Kaldor-Hicks efficiency criterion, referring to the situation when the winner (producer) could potentially compensate the loser (consumers) with a positive total net gain. Article 101(3) TFEU clearly states the consumers must be effectively and fully compensated.[541] It shows that EU competition law emphasizes the consumer welfare goal with a clear distributive concern.[542]

3.3.2. Defining 'Consumer Welfare'

In *Post Danmark A/S v. Konkurrencerådet*,[543] the ECJ claimed that the primary goal of EU competition law is to 'prevent consumer harm'. However, under EU competition law, 'consumer harm', and 'consumer' are both broad concepts. For example, in the Guidance on the Commission's Enforcement Priorities in Applying Article 82 of the EC Treaty to Abusive Exclusionary Conduct by Dominant Undertakings,[544] consumers will be 'harmed' when the restriction of competition results in increased prices, lower innovation, or lower consumer choice.[545] In *Konkurrensverket v. TeliaSonera Sverige AB*, the ECJ explained that

---

[539]   Communication from the Commission: *Guidelines on the application of Article 81(3) of the Treaty* [2004] OJ C101/97, paras 85–86 (para 85: 'The concept of "*fair share*" implies that the *pass-on of benefits* must at least compensate consumers for any actual or likely negative impact caused to them by the restriction of competition found under Article 81(1) (Article 101(1) TFEU). In line with the overall objective of Article 81 (Article 101 TFEU) to prevent anti-competitive agreements, the net effect of the agreement must at least be neutral from the point of view of those consumers directly or likely affected by the agreement. If such consumers are worse off following the agreement, the second condition of Article 81(3) is not fulfilled. The positive effects of an agreement must be balanced against and compensate for its negative effects on consumers'; para 86: 'It is not required that consumers receive a share of each and every efficiency gain identified under the first condition. It suffices that sufficient benefits are passed on to compensate for the negative effects of the restrictive agreement. In that case consumers obtain a fair share of the overall benefits. If a restrictive agreement is likely to lead to higher prices, consumers must be fully compensated through increased quality or other benefits. If not, the second condition of Article 81(3) (Article 101(3) TFEU) is not fulfilled.') Cited by I. LIANOS (2013), *supra* n. 533, p. 21.

[540]   I. LIANOS (2013), *supra* n. 533, p. 8.

[541]   I. LIANOS (2013), *supra* n. 533, p. 21.

[542]   I. LIANOS (2013), *supra* n. 533, p. 8.

[543]   Case C-209/10, *Post Danmark A/S v. Konkurrencerådet* [2012] ECR I-0000, para 20, cited by I. LIANOS (2013), *supra* n. 533, p. 15.

[544]   Communication from the Commission: *Guidance on the Commission's Enforcement Priorities in Applying Article 82 of the EC Treaty to Abusive Exclusionary Conduct by Dominant Undertakings* [2009] OJ C45/7.

[545]   Communication from the Commission: *Guidance on the Commission's Enforcement Priorities in Applying Article 82 of the EC Treaty to Abusive Exclusionary Conduct by Dominant Undertakings* [2009] OJ C45/7, para 19: 'The aim of the Commission's enforcement activity in

consumers can be harmed both directly and indirectly: 'Accordingly, Article 101 TFEU must be interpreted as referring not only to practices which may cause damage to consumers directly, but also to those which are detrimental to them through their impact on competition.'[546] In the Guidelines on the Application of Article 81(3) of the Treaty, 'consumer' refers to both direct and indirect users of products, wholesalers, retailers and final consumers.[547] The same explanation has also been provided in the Guidelines on the Assessment of Horizontal Mergers under the Council Regulation on the Control of Concentrations between Undertakings,[548] and the Guidance on the Commission's Enforcement Priorities in Applying Article 82 Treaty to Abusive Exclusionary Conduct by Dominant Undertakings.[549] However, in *Österreichische Postsparkasse AG and Bank für Arbeit und Wirtschaft AG v Commission*, the General Court held that the European competition policy has an 'undeniable impact' on the final consumers.[550] In general, the Court of Justice of the EU has not clarified the definition of 'consumer' or 'consumer welfare'.[551] According to Lianos, it is not clear neither from the Commission's guidelines, nor from the court decisions, what the distinction between consumer welfare, consumer surplus and consumer choice is.[552]

---

relation to exclusionary conduct is to ensure that dominant undertakings do not impair effective competition by foreclosing their competitors in an anti-competitive way, thus having an adverse impact on consumer welfare, whether in the form of higher price levels than would have otherwise prevailed or in some other form such as limiting quality or reducing consumer choice.' Cited by I. LIANOS (2013), *supra* n. 533, p. 16.

[546]   Case C-52/09, *Konkurrensverket v. TeliaSonera Sverige AB* [2011] ECR I-527, paras 21–24, cited by I. LIANOS (2013), *supra* n. 533, p. 35.

[547]   Communication from the Commission: *Guidelines on the Application of Article 81(3) of the Treaty* [2004] OJ C101/97, paras 13, 84 (para 13: 'The objective of Article 81 (Article 101 TFEU) is to protect competition on the market as a means of enhancing consumer welfare and of ensuring an efficient allocation of resources. Competition and market integration serve these ends since the creation and preservation of an open single market promotes an efficient allocation of resources throughout the Community for the benefit of consumers.'); see also para 84: 'The concept of *"consumers"* encompasses *all direct or indirect users of the products* covered by the agreement, including producers that use the products as an input, wholesalers, retailers and final consumers, i.e. natural persons who are acting for purposes which can be regarded as outside their trade or profession.'); quoted by P. AKMAN (2010), '"Consumer" versus "Customer": The Devil in the Detail', *Journal of Law and Society*, vol. 37, no. 2, p. 317.

[548]   Guidelines on the Assessment of Horizontal Mergers under the Council Regulation on the Control of Concentrations between Undertakings [2004] OJ C 31/03.

[549]   Communication from the Commission: *Guidance on the Commission's Enforcement Priorities in Applying Article 82 of the EC Treaty to Abusive Exclusionary Conduct by Dominant Undertakings* [2009] OJ C45/7, *supra* n. 544.

[550]   Joined Cases T-213/01 and T-214/01, *Österreichische Postsparkasse AG and Bank für Arbeit und Wirtschaft AG v. Commission* [2006] ECR II-1601, para 115: 'The ultimate purpose of the rules that seek to ensure that competition is not distorted in the internal market is to increase the well-being of consumers … Competition law and competition policy therefore have an undeniable impact on the specific economic interests of final customers who purchase goods or services.'). Cited by I. LIANOS (2013), *supra* n. 533, p. 36.

[551]   I. LIANOS (2013), *supra* n. 533, p. 16.

[552]   I. LIANOS (2013), *supra* n. 533, p. 16.

However, under EU consumer protection policy, 'consumer' only refers to the 'end-users'.[553] From a normative point of view, it is confusing if EU consumer protection law and EU competition law protect different 'consumers'.[554] In fact, the differences in the interpretation of 'consumer' under consumer protection law and under competition law is called the 'Chicago trap', which refers to the misuse of 'consumer welfare' by the Chicago School scholars, when what they really meant was 'total welfare'.[555]

3.4.   THE TOTAL WELFARE GOAL AND INDUSTRIAL POLICY

The relationship between the competition policy and the industrial policy in the EU can be investigated from two angles. The first aspect is how competition policy values small business. During the early years after the Rome Treaty was enacted, the Commission believed that cooperation between small and medium-sized enterprises ('SMEs') should be encouraged, in order to compete with their rivals in the United States.[556] The Commission took the view that compared with large firms, SMEs are more innovative, dynamic and more likely to provide employment.[557] The Commission often issued a pass for the agreements between SMEs to save energy for the investigations in agreements between big firms.[558] In the 1968 Commission Notice, the Commission perceived competition policy as an active motor to encourage the cooperation between SMEs because such cooperation enables them to compete in larger markets.[559]

The second aspect is how competition policy deals with 'national champions'. In Europe, national government may give favorable treatment to domestic firms against foreign competitors. In merger cases, Member State governments often impose political pressure on the transaction for the interest of national industry. The EU Commission used to take Article 21 of the 1989 EC Merger Regulation to

---

[553]   Council Directive 93/13/EEC of 5 April 1993 on Unfair Terms in Consumer Contracts [1993] OJ L 95/29, Article 2(b); Directive 2005/29/EC of the European Parliament and of the Council of 11 May 2005 concerning Unfair Commercial Practices Directive [2005] OJ L 149/22, Article 2(a); quoted by P. AKMAN, (2010), *supra* n. 547, p. 317.

[554]   P. AKMAN (2010), *supra* n. 547, p. 322.

[555]   P. AKMAN (2010), *supra* n. 547, p. 322; K.J. CSERES, *Competition Law and Consumer Protection*, Kluwer Law International 2005, p. 331.

[556]   D.J. GERBER (1994a), 'The Transformation of European Community Competition Law?', *Harvard International Law Journal*, vol. 35, no. 1, p. 112.

[557]   M. MOTTA (2004), *supra* n. 507, p. 22.

[558]   D.J. GERBER (1994a), *supra* n. 556, p. 112.

[559]   Commission Notice of 3 July 1968 [1965–1969 Transfer Binder], CCH Comm. Mkt. Rep. §9248, at 8517 ('The Commission welcomes cooperation among small and medium-sized enterprises where such cooperation enables them to work more economically and increase their productivity and competitiveness on a larger market.') B.E. HAWK (1972), 'Antitrust in the EEC – the First Decade', *Fordham Law Review*, vol. 41, p. 234.

intervene the transaction from a broader public interest concern at the EU level.[560] Article 21 holds that 'Member States may take appropriate measures to protect legitimate interests other than those taken into considerations by this Regulation and compatible with general principles and other provisions of Community law.' According to this article, the concerns of 'public security', 'plurality of the media' and 'prudential rules' are all included as 'legitimate interests'.[561] Because it supported the national automobile industry, the *Volvo/Scania*[562] merger received a lot of support from the Swedish government.[563] Similarly, the French President Jacques Chirac and Prime Minister Laurent Fabius personally defended the *Schneider/Legrand* merger.[564] The Greek government supported the *Olympic/Aeagean Airlines* merger.[565] However, all these mergers were prohibited by the Commission for fear of creating a dominant position in the relevant market.[566]

It was argued that competition policy in Europe used to be strongly related to its industrial policy.[567] The discussion on the role of the industrial policy has been restarted in 2002 by the Commission.[568] Remarkably, in April 2004, the Communication on Industrial Policy for an Enlarged Europe[569] was adopted at the same day as the Communication on a pro-active European Competition Policy.[570] It is a clear sign that the Commission considers that competition policy does not contradict industrial policy. Instead, both polices could be integrated as

---

[560] Geradin and Girgenson gave three examples: *Unicredito/HVB* (Case No COMP/M.3894) Commission Decision 18 October 2005; *Abertis/Autostrade* (Case No COMP/M 4249) Commission Decision of 22 September 2006 and *E.ON/Endesa* (Case No COMP/M4110) Commission Decision of 25 April 2006. See D. GERADIN and I. GIRGENSON (2011), 'Industrial Policy and European Merger Control – A Reassessment', in Fordham Competition Law Institute, *International Antitrust Law and Policy*, Chapter 14, p. 363.

[561] D. GERADIN and I. GIRGENSON (2011), *supra* n. 560, p. 362.

[562] *Volvo/Scania* (Case No COMP/M.1672) Commission Decision 14 March 2000.

[563] D. GERADIN and I. GIRGENSON (2011), *supra* n. 560, p. 365.

[564] D. GERADIN and I. GIRGENSON (2011), *supra* n. 560, p. 365. *Schneider/Legrand* (Case No COMP/M.2283) Commission Decision of 30 January 2002.

[565] D. GERADIN and I. GIRGENSON (2011), *supra* n. 560, p. 366. *Olympic/Aegean Airlines* (Case No COMP/M 5830) Commission Decision of 26 January 2011.

[566] D. GERADIN and I. GIRGENSON (2011), *supra* n. 560, p. 365. By studying a net sample of 96 merger decisions issued by the European Commission under the Merger Regulation before September 2002, Bergman, Jakobsson and Razo concluded that political influence, in particular the nationality of the merging firms, does not affect the results of the decisions. See M.A. BERGMAN, M. JAKOBSSON and C. RAZO (2005), 'An Econometric Analysis of the European Commission's Merger Decisions', *International Journal of Industrial Organization*, pp. 717–737.

[567] J. GALLOWAY (2007) 'The Pursuit of National Champions: The Intersection of Competition Law and Industrial Policy', *European Competition Law Review*, vol. 3 p. 172.

[568] Commission Communication of 11 December 2002, *Industrial Policy in an Enlarged Europe* [COM (2002) 714 final].

[569] Commission Communication of 20 April 2004, *Fostering Structural Change: an Industrial Policy for an Enlarged Europe* [COM (2004) 274 final].

[570] Commission Communication of 20 April 2004, *A Pro-active Competition Policy for a Competitive Europe* [COM (2004) 293 final].

they both promote innovation and the economic growth.[571] These objectives are the common goals included in the agenda of the European Union.[572] However, the Commission did not address the issue of the potential conflicts between these two polices, and the question of how to deal with the potential tension between different goals remains unanswered, as economic theory shows that industrial policy is not always consistent with the goal of allocative efficiency.[573]

3.5. THE INFLUENCE OF ORDOLIBERALISM

To analyze the influence of Ordoliberlism on the development of competition law and policy in Europe, it is important to understand the long tradition of incorporating social goals in the competition policy. In Europe, the view on the social objectives of the competition law and policy in is rooted in the historical debate on the relationship between the State and economy. In history, the rise and fall of liberalism and nationalism has given competition law a different focus on its objectives.[574] In Europe, Germany is the country that has the longest experience with implementing competition law.[575] However, the roots of liberalism, which is the driving force for promoting the values of competition, has been relatively weak in Germany, for the reason that Germany has a long tradition of bureaucratic control, and economic activities were mainly directed by government bureaucracies. The German idea of 'freedom' is often placed under the discussion of the relationship between the individual and the State or the Community (*Gemeinschaft*). In the eighteenth century, before studying the 'classical economics' imported from England, the German 'Cameralism' scholars studied economic activities from the perspective of assessing their value to the State. In the late nineteen century, the historical school of economics (historicism) dominated the economics profession in Germany. The historical school argued that economic conduct should be understood from the

---

[571]   This point is illustrated by Commissioner Kroes: 'Competition policy – which above all else is designed to ensure the maintenance of competitive markets – is therefore central to an industrial policy aimed at enhancing the competitiveness of industry.' N. KROES (2008), 'Exclusionary Abuses of Dominance – the European Commission's Enforcement Priorities', speech at the Fordham University Symposium, New York, 25 September 2008, available at <http://europa.eu/rapid/press-release_SPEECH-08–457_en.htm?locale=en> accessed 05.04.2014.

[572]   *See e.g.* Commission Communication to the Council and the European Parliament of 21 November 2003 "Some Key Issues in Europe's Competitiveness – Towards an Integrated Approach" [COM (2003) 704 final]; *see also* N. KROES (2007), 'Foreword', in *Report on Competition Policy 2007,* published by the European Commission, COM (2008) 368 final, p. 3, available at <http://ec.europa.eu/competition/publications/annual_report/2007/en.pdf>.

[573]   R. VAN DEN BERGH and P.D. CAMESASCA (2006), *supra* n. 18.

[574]   The analysis in this section is based on D.J. GERBER (1998), *supra* n. 528, pp. 73, 76, 78, 81, 83, 239.

[575]   Gesetz gegen Wettbewerbsbeschränkungen (GWB).

specific historical context, and the theory of economic behavior such as 'invisible hand' would be of little use. After the Second World War, Ordoliberalism was considered the most influential school of thought on competition in Germany, which perceived the goals of competition law from the perspective of humanist values. For Ordoliberals, the ultimate goal of a competition policy is to establish a society which can protect 'human dignity' and 'personal freedom'.[576]

3.5.1.   Ordoliberalism

The key ideas of Ordoliberlism were developed by a group of scholars from the University of Freiburg in West Germany in the 1930s. The Freiburg School representatives include the economist Walter Eucken, and two lawyers Franz Boehm and Hans Grossmann-Doerth. Together with other intellectuals who were not associated with Freiburg,[577] they developed the 'Ordoliberal' school of thought, which laid the theoretical foundations for the German competition law in the post-war era.[578]

Having experienced the economic and social crisis in the early 1930s in Germany, Freiburg School scholars believed that abuse of private economic power must be prevented through a well-functioning legal system. Competition among private sectors is important for the economic prosperity in the society. More importantly, economic freedom is essential for the protection of political freedom.[579] Economic freedom can be impeded by two sources, one is by the political power, and the other is by the economic power. Both of these two sources of power must be restrained in order to protect individual freedom. Therefore, neither government intervention nor the market power can be fully trusted. Ordoliberal thinking provides a 'third way' solution between the central planning and a *laissez-faire* liberal market, and this solution is that law should be formulated and enforced to safeguard individual's freedom, and to restrain concentrations of private economic power.

The goals of competition law are perceived by Ordoliberal scholars from both an economic and a political perspective,[580] and the primary policy goals of a competition law are to preserve the 'freedom to compete (*Wettbewerbsfreiheit*)'

---

[576]   D.J. GERBER (1998), *supra* n. 528, pp. 239, 240.

[577]   According to Ahlborn and Grave, the scholars who contributed to the Ordoliberlaism thinking include Leonhard Miksch, Wilhelm Roepke, and Alexander Ruestow. C. AHLBORN and C. GRAVE (2006), 'Walter Eucken and Ordoliberalism: An Introduction from a Consumer Welfare Perspective', *Competition Policy International*, vol. 2, no. 2, p. 198;.

[578]   D.J. GERBER (1998), *supra* n. 528, p. 236.

[579]   D.J. GERBER (1994b), 'Constitutionalizing the Economy: German Neo-Liberalism, Competition Law and the "New Europe"', *American Journal of Comparative Law*, vol. 42, p. 36.

[580]   C. AHLBORN and C. GRAVE (2006), *supra* n. 577, p. 210.

and to pursue a 'complete competition (*vollstandiger Wettbewerb*)'.[581] From the economic perspective, competition is essential for an efficient use of resources, and for the well functioning of the economic system, whereas from the political perspective, the increased private decision making in economic activities would contribute to the reduction of the state power, through which individual freedom will be protected.[582] Ordoliberal scholars do not acknowledge the potential conflicts between pursuing a political and an economic goal, because both goals will lead to the same direction: a desirable economic outcome will ultimately be achieved by pursuing political goals.[583] More importantly, for Ordoliberals, economic prosperity does not refer to a constant economic growth, but to 'improving economic performance (*Leistungssteigerung*)', which makes the creation of an 'economic order' necessary.[584] Therefore, it is important to fulfill social and political goals at various dimensions, such as to encourage competition, to provide equal opportunities, and to ensure a fair distribution of wealth,[585] in order to construct the legal foundations for the success in economic performance.

According to Walker Eucken, a desirable market competition is in the form of 'complete competition', where no firm has the power to impose pressure on the other firm, and price can only be 'taken' from the market.[586] The concept of 'complete competition' was not developed by economic models; instead, it exhibits a more political concern of the dispersion of power.[587] Ordoliberals' view on the objective of competition is close to the economic definition of 'perfect competition', not 'workable competition'. When monopolists exist and the market is not perfect, Ordoliberals argue that the State has to intervene to maintain 'ordered regulated competition'.[588]

Another key concept that was developed by Ordoliberals is the 'economic order' (*Ordnungen*). Ordoliberals argue that individual freedom should be protected, as well as be restricted to the extent of the freedom of others. Therefore,

---

[581] V.J. Vanberg (2009), 'Consumer Welfare, Total Welfare and Economic Freedom – on the normative foundations of competition policy', *Freiburg Discussion Paper on Constitutional Economics No. 09/3*, p. 9 Erich Hoppmann argues that the freedom to compete is 'Ein Ziel in sich selbst, weil sich in ihm wirtschaftliche Freiheit manifestiert.' (Vanberg translates: 'The freedom to compete must, as a manifestation of individual economic freedom, be regarded as a "goal in itself"'): see E. Hoppmann (1967), 'Wettbewerb als Norm der Wettbewerbspolitik', in *ORDO-Jahrbuch für die Ordnung von Wirtschaft und Gesellschaft* 18, p. 79. E. Hoppmann (1988), *Wirtschaftsordnung und Wettbewerb*, Nomos.

[582] D.J. Gerber (2008), *supra* n. 7, p. 240.

[583] C. Ahlborn and C. Grave (2006), *supra* n. 577, p. 210.

[584] D.J. Gerber (1994b), *supra* n. 579, p. 38.

[585] D.J. Gerber (1994b), *supra* n. 579, p. 38.

[586] C. Ahlborn and C. Grave (2006), *supra* n. 577, p. 200.

[587] Ahlborn and Grave translated the words by Eucken: 'Competition is by no means only an incentive mechanism but, first of all an instrument for the deprivation of power (*Entmachtungsinstrument*) ... the most magnificent and most ingenious instrument of deprivation of power in history.' C. Ahlborn and C. Grave (2006), *supra* n. 577, p. 200.

[588] P. Akman (2009), 'Searching for the Long-Lost Soul of Article 82 EC', *Oxford Journal of Legal Studies*, vol. 29, no. 2, p. 275.

a legal framework must be established to protect a 'competitive order', and to ensure that this order functions properly and efficiently.[589] Only under this system market competition can generate a desirable outcome for the society.[590] Moreover, this order (*Ordnungspolitik*) should be established within a law-based state,[591] and should be constructed through 'judicially enforceable rules'.[592] As a result, this legal framework also functions as an 'economic constitution (*Wirtschaftsverfassung*)', and courts become the 'organs of national economic policy'.[593] In this way, market competition is considered a dynamic process that results within this order, and is regarded as the 'twin sister' of the legal society.[594]

To fulfill the requirements of this order, Ordoliberals argue that new entrants, including small and medium-sized firms, should all be protected when entering the market to compete. Abuse of dominant position by large firms must be prohibited.[595] According to Eucken, monopolies must be regulated by an independent Monopoly Office, which functions as the competition authority.[596]

Ordoliberalism had a profound impact on competition law and policy in Germany after the Second World War. In particular, Ludwig Erhard, the first Minister of Economics for the Federal Republic of Germany, accepted many Ordoliberal ideas.[597] The reason why Ordoliberal thoughts gained popularity at that time could be explained by their strong promise that an economic order based on competition would contribute to a dramatic economic development and a sustained economic success.[598] Influenced by Ordoliberal thoughts, German competition law emphasizes market structure and the degree of dominance.[599] It is distinctly different from US antitrust law in that German competition law sets a clear threshold for intervention.[600]

3.5.2. The Influence of Ordoliberalism on EU Competition Law

When the competition policy at the EU level was drafted in the 1950s, German competition law with a close tie to the Ordoliberal tradition attracted the most

---

589   C. AHLBORN and C. GRAVE (2006), *supra* n. 577, p. 201.
590   C. AHLBORN and C. GRAVE (2006), *supra* n. 577, p. 198.
591   C. AHLBORN and C. GRAVE (2006), *supra* n. 577, p. 201.
592   I. LIANOS (2013), *supra* n. 533, p. 28.
593   W. RÖPKE (1942), *The Social Crisis of Our Times*, Transaction Publishers, Part 2, Chapter 2, p. 193.
594   V.J. VANBERG (2009), *supra* n. 581, p. 8.
595   R.C. SINGLETON (1997), 'Competition Policy For Developing Countries, A Long-run, Entry-based Approach', *Contemporary Economic Policy*, vol. 15, no. 2, p. 3.
596   C. AHLBORN and C. GRAVE (2006), *supra* n. 577, p. 204.
597   C. AHLBORN and C. GRAVE (2006), *supra* n. 577, p. 198.
598   D.J. GERBER (2008), *supra* n. 7, p. 241.
599   C. AHLBORN and C. GRAVE (2006), *supra* n. 577, p. 207.
600   For example, according to section 19(3), Act against Restraint of Competition, a company 'is presumed to be dominant if it has a market share of at least one third.' Cited and translated by C. AHLBORN and C. GRAVE (2006), *supra* n. 577, p. 207.

attention.[601] One important reason was that at that time Germany was the European country with the longest experience in antitrust law, and it provided a better source than US antitrust law for other European countries, given the similarities in culture political and economic background.[602] Another feature that made the German competition law system attractive was the successful economic performance of Germany in the 1950s to 1960s. As the Ordoliberal thinking is highly relevant to contributing to economic development, it became an important intellectual source for other countries in Europe which were striving to establish an effective economic system.[603]

The influence of Ordoliberalism on EU competition law can be analyzed in three aspects. The first aspect is the structural approach adopted by EU competition law. Based on the Ordoliberal view, competition law is formulated for the purpose of protecting individual freedom to take part in the competition in the market.[604] It is the competitive process, not any individual group that is considered as the main focus of the competition policy.[605] The competition provisions provided under Article 85 and 86 of the Rome Treaty to a large extent reflected this Ordoliberal thinking, and a particular attention was paid to the notion of 'abuse of dominant position'.[606] Notably, the concept of 'dominant position' was considered as a clear German Ordoliberal thought.[607] More importantly, Ordoliberal ideas have also been accepted by many competition policy makers in the EU.[608] For example, Walter Hallstein, an advocator of Ordoliberal ideas, represented Germany during the negotiation of the Rome Treaty, and himself became the first president of the European Commission.[609] Hans von der Groeben was another supporter of the Ordoliberal School, who served as the first Competition Policy Commissioner at the European Commission. In 1965, he claimed that one of the fundamental goals of competition policy in Europe is 'to establish an effective and workable competitive system'.[610] Lianos's research has shown that even in recent years Ordoliberal thinking still plays a role in the decisions made by the Commission. For example, in *British Airways*,[611] Advocate General Kokott confirmed that Article 102 TFEU indeed indicated the Ordoliberal approach of pursuing the

---

[601]   D.J. GERBER (2008), *supra* n. 7, p. 332.

[602]   D.J. GERBER (2008), *supra* n. 7, p. 332.

[603]   D.J. GERBER (2008), *supra* n. 7, p. 332.

[604]   I. LIANOS (2013), *supra* n. 533, p. 24.

[605]   I. LIANOS (2013), *supra* n. 533, p. 25.

[606]   D.J. GERBER (2008), *supra* n. 7, p. 264.

[607]   D.J. GERBER (2008), *supra* n. 7, p. 264.

[608]   D.J. GERBER (2008), *supra* n. 7, p. 264.

[609]   D.J. GERBER (2008), *supra* n. 7, p. 340.

[610]   T. BASKOY (2005), 'Effective Competition and EU Competition Law', *Review of European and Russian Affairs*, vol. 1, no. 1, p. 2; CEC (1996), *Ninth General Report on the Activities of the Community*, The Publications Department of European Communities, p. 59.

[611]   Opinion AG J. Kokott, Case C-95/04 *British Airways plc. v. Commission* [2007] ECR I-2331, para 68, cited by I. LIANOS (2013), *supra* n. 533, p. 33.

competition goal of freedom to compete.[612] In addition, the argument of 'protecting the structure of the market' as the goal of Article 81 EC can also be found in *T-Mobile Netherlands BV et al. v. NMa*,[613] and in *GlaxoSmithKline Services Unlimited v. Commission*.[614]

The second aspect of the influence of Ordoliberal thinking lies in the fact that competition policy in Europe pursues broader social goals. The Ordoliberal thinking emphasizes that the role of competition law is to establish the 'rule of the game'[615] and to form an 'economic order', within which the individual's freedom to compete will be safeguarded. Therefore, competition policy is not an end in itself; instead, it is considered to be a means to achieve broader social goals of the society.[616] The Ordoliberal tradition gives competition law and policy in Europe a broader coverage on the social goals.[617]

The third aspect of the influence of Ordoliberal thinking is the argument of enforcing competition law through judicial power. Besides the Ordoliberal

---

[612] *See* opinion AG J. Kokott, Case C-95/04 P, *British Airways plc. v. Commission* [2007] ECR I-2331, para 68: 'Article 102 TFEU forms part of a system designed to protect competition within the internal market from distortions (Article 3(1)(g) EC). Accordingly, Article 82 EC, like the other competition rules of the Treaty, is not designed only or primarily to protect the immediate interests of individual competitors or consumers, but to protect the structure of the market and thus competition as such (as an institution), which has already been weakened by the presence of the dominant undertaking on the market. In this way, consumers are also indirectly protected. Because where competition as such is damaged, disadvantages for consumers are also to be feared.' Cited by I. LIANOS (2013), *supra* n. 533, p. 33.

[613] Case C-8/08, *T-Mobile Netherlands BV and Others v. Raad van bestuur van de Nederlandse Mededingingsautoriteit* 2009 [ECR] I-4529, para 38 ('Article 81 EC, like the other competition rules of the Treaty, is designed to protect not only the immediate interests of individual competitors or consumers but also to protect the structure of the market and thus competition as such.').

[614] Case T-168/01, *GlaxoSmithKline Services Unlimited v. Commission* [2009] ECR I-9291, para 63 ('Secondly, it must be borne in mind that the Court has held that, like other competition rules laid down in the Treaty, Article 81 EC aims to protect not only the interests of competitors or of consumers, but also the structure of the market and, in so doing, competition as such.'). Cited by I. Lianos (2013), *supra* n. 533, p. 34.

[615] L. ERHARD (1958), *Prosperity through Competition*, p. 102 (original in German: *Wohlstand für Alle*, Düsseldorf 1957). Cited by N. GOLDSCHMIDT (2012), 'Alfred Müller-Armack and Ludwig Erhard: Social Market Liberalism', *Freiburg Discussion Papers on Constitutional Economics No. 04/12*, p. 14.

[616] 'All we are asking for is the creation of an economic and social order which equally guarantees economic activity and humane living conditions. We call for competition because it can be utilized to reach this goal – in fact, the goal cannot be reached without it. It is a means, not an end in itself.' The first volume of the ORDO year book, edited by Walter Eucken and Franz Böhm, preface in ORDO 1 (1948), p. XI, translated by N. GOLDSCHMIDT (2012), *supra* n. 615, p. 15.

[617] Freiburg school scholars specifically pay attention to the 'social question', as Walter Eucken said 'everything is socially important'. W. EUCKEN, *Grundsätze der Wirtschaftspolitik*, 6th ed., Tübingen 1990, p. 313, translated and cited by N. GOLDSCHMIDT (2012), *supra* n. 615, p. 15. The founding father of the 'social market economy', Prof. Müller-Armack shares the same view on the objective of economic policy is to safeguard social benefits. N. GOLDSCHMIDT (2012), *supra* n. 615, p. 18.

approach, another pattern for framing a competition law that has been discussed in the postwar years in Europe is the administrative control model. In the 1940s and 1950s, many countries in Europe enacted their competition law, holding the belief that competition law would generate potential benefits such as stimulating economic growth and combating inflation.[618] According to Gerber, most of these countries were influenced by the discussion of competition law in the 1920s, and different from Germany, their competition laws followed the administrative control model.[619] In these countries, competition law is treated under the domain of public law, or administrative law. The norms that are adopted to describe anticompetitive conduct are general, vague and conveyed little information.[620] Government officials are authorized to play the central role of applying and enforcing these norms with a high level of discretion.[621] The basic criterion for administrators to control conduct is the harmful effects, not the characteristics or the forms of the conduct.[622] Under the administrative control model, the enforcement of competition law is 'soft' and primarily aims at achieving compliance.[623] Competition policy is operated as a form of economic policy, in the same institutional pattern as industrial policies or price controls.[624] Treating competition law the same way as administrative regulation makes the goals of competition law to a large extent vague and uncertain.[625] The definition of notions such as 'public interest' or 'abuse of economic power' is far from clear and the specific sanctions for the anticompetitive conduct are largely lacking.[626] During the negotiation in the 1950s when the Rome Treaty was drafted, it was debated among Member States concerning the enforcement pattern of the competition law. Strongly influenced by the Ordoliberalism, the German delegates perceived that the competition law system created under the Rome Treaty was judicial, and should be enforced through impartial judicial procedures.[627] For the French delegates, however, competition law at the EU level should be treated more as an administrative policy.[628] They argued that decisions on competition issues should be made by an official, in accordance with the specific needs of the Community and the Member States.[629] According to Gerber, the early development of the

---

618   D.J. Gerber (1998), *supra* n. 528, p. 171.
619   D.J. Gerber (1998), *supra* n. 528, pp. 171, 173. These countries include: Austria, Belgium, Denmark, Finland, France, the Netherlands, Norway, Sweden and the United Kingdom.
620   D.J. Gerber (1998), *supra* n. 528, p. 174.
621   A separate administrative office is usually established to enforce competition law. A special commission or court is often created to receive appeals of these administrative decisions. D.J. Gerber (1998), *supra* n. 528, pp. 173, 175.
622   D.J. Gerber (1998), *supra* n. 528, p. 174.
623   D.J. Gerber (1998), *supra* n. 528, p. 175.
624   D.J. Gerber (1998), *supra* n. 528, p. 228.
625   D.J. Gerber (1998), *supra* n. 528, p. 228.
626   D.J. Gerber (1998), *supra* n. 528, p. 228.
627   D.J. Gerber (1994a), *supra* n. 556, p. 104.
628   D.J. Gerber (1998), *supra* n. 528, p. 343.
629   D.J. Gerber (1994a), *supra* n. 556, p. 104.

competition system in Europe nevertheless showed a strong preference for the judicial pattern.[630] Nevertheless, the visions of EU competition policy from a judicial or an administrative perspective have competed for decades and the role of EU competition law continues to be debated today.[631]

3.6.   THE EVOLUTION OF LEGAL DOCTRINE

3.6.1.   Historical Backgrounds

The process of European integration was first initiated by the Treaty of Paris in 1951, which established the European Coal and Steel Community ('ECSC'). The six founding countries of the European Economic Community are France, Germany, Italy, Belgium, the Netherlands, and Luxembourg. Competition provisions were found under Article 65 and 66 of this Treaty, with a clear goal of contributing to the integration of the Community.[632] Article 65 prohibits agreements between private firms which may directly or indirectly impede competition within the Common Market.[633] Article 65 provided the basis for the Article 81 of the Treaty of Rome, which was later renumbered as Article 85 in the Treaty of Amsterdam.[634] Article 66(7) of the Treaty of Paris dealing with the issue of the abuse of dominant position later corresponded to Article 82 of the Treaty of Rome, and was renumbered as Article 86 under the Treaty of Amsterdam.[635] The enforcement of these provisions, however, was rather limited.[636]

From the late 1940s to the early 1950s, there was an intense debate at the policy level in Europe regarding the unification of Europe. As other plans, such as establishing a European Political Community, or a European Defense Community, all failed, uniting Europe through economic functions was seen as the last option to strengthen the economic cooperation between countries and to stimulate economic growth in Europe.[637] Therefore, in 1955, the plan of creating a common market in Europe gained political support during the conference in

---

[630]   One example could be between 1958 and 1962, Arvid Deringer, a German attorney chaired a committee of the European Parliament to draft the Regulation 17, which provided the institutional framework for enforcing the competition provisions of the Treaty of Rome. Regulation 17 reflected the German view on the judicial nature of the competition law. D.J. GERBER (1998), *supra* n. 528, p. 349.

[631]   D.J. GERBER (1998), *supra* n. 528, p. 347.

[632]   D.J. GERBER (1998), *supra* n. 528, p. 337.

[633]   M. MOTTA (2004), *supra* n. 507, p. 13.

[634]   M. MOTTA (2004), *supra* n. 507, p. 13.

[635]   M. MOTTA (2004), *supra* n. 507, p. 13.

[636]   D.J. GERBER (1998), *supra* n. 528, p. 342.

[637]   D.J. GERBER (1994a), *supra* n. 556, pp. 101, 102.

Messina.[638] In 1956, the Foreign Ministers of the six founding states of the ECSC had a meeting in Brussels. In the same year, the 'Spaak Report' was drafted by the Heads of Delegations to the Foreign Ministers,[639] which laid the foundations for the Treaty of Rome in 1958.

According to this report, the process of European integration had two important goals.[640] As a political goal, it was believed that the unification of Europe will resolve the potential conflicts and wars between countries. As an economic goal, the increased cooperation between Member States will contribute to the economic prosperity in Europe.[641] The economic goals of an integrated market include 'to compete with the US and the USSR',[642] to 'ensure the most rational distribution of activities', and as to achieve an 'optimum rate of economic expansion'.[643]

3.6.2.   The Market Integration Goal of the EEC

The competition policy in the European Union was first adopted by Article 85 and Article 86 of the Treaty of Rome on 25 March 1957, based on which the European Economic Community ('EEC') was established.[644] The Rome Treaty formulated a list of principles to be achieved by the European Union. The primary goal of this treaty is to establish a common market, where neither public nor private powers could impose restrictions on the free movement of goods, services, capital and persons. To achieve this goal, competition policy was considered as a vital tool to break down the trade barriers between Member States and to promote the free flow of goods, services, capital and persons. Article 85 of this Treaty prohibits monopolistic agreements and Article 86 prohibits the abuse of dominant position.

It was the goal of economic integration that dominated the construction of the competition system under the Treaty of Rome.[645] After the plans for establishing a European Defense Community and a European Political Community were both rejected, the economic cooperation had a strong responsibility in building a 'new Europe'.[646] Although the economic benefits of

---

[638]   D.J. GERBER (1998), *supra* n. 528, p. 343.

[639]   Report of the Heads of Delegation to the Ministers of Foreign Affairs (the 'Spaak Report'),
(original in French: Rapport des chefs de delegation aux Ministres des Affaires Etrangeres),
Intergovernmental Committee on European Integration, 21 April 1956, available at
<http://aei.pitt.edu/996/1/Spaak_report_french.pdf>; P. Akman (2009), *supra* n. 588, p. 278.

[640]   D.J. GERBER (1998), *supra* n. 528, p. 343.

[641]   D.J. GERBER (1998), *supra* n. 528, p. 343.

[642]   'No country in Europe was able to compete on its own'. P. AKMAN (2009), *supra* n. 588, p. 278.

[643]   P. AKMAN (2009), *supra* n. 588, p. 279.

[644]   Treaty Establishing the European Economic Community, 25 March 1957, 298 UNTS 3 (EEC
Treaty or Treaty of Rome).

[645]   D.J. GERBER (1998), *supra* n. 528, p. 347.

[646]   D.J. GERBER (1998), *supra* n. 528, p. 347.

competition, such as price reduction, were acknowledged, it was believed by the Commission and the Court that these benefits were subordinated to the goal of economic integration and the economic goal of promoting competition was considered to reinforce the political goal of promoting market integration.[647] In 1972, in the first annual report on competition policy, the Commission clearly stated that the primary goal is to protect market integration by eliminating private restrictive conduct.[648] Meanwhile, the Court of Justice also prioritized the goal of market integration in competition cases, and actively played its role by cooperating with the Commission.[649]

3.6.3. The Extension of the Policy Goal of the TEU

Between late 1980s and early 1990s, dramatic economic changes were undertaken in Europe to accelerate the progress of market integration.[650] In December 1991, the European Union was established by the Treaty on European Union ('TEU'), which raised more ambitious goals on economic and monetary integration.[651] Besides the integration goal, the TEU extended the goals of competition policy to other social values, in particular, the industrial policy goal, the environmental goal and social goals. Article 3(3) TEU states that the goal of the Union is to establish 'a highly competitive social market economy' in the common market, and to ensure 'full employment and social progress'.[652] Article 13 of the TEU emphasized the goal of 'improving the competitiveness of the Community's industry' and 'encouraging an environment favorable to cooperation between enterprises'.[653] The concern of improving the 'competitiveness' of the European industries was also included in 1997 when the Treaty of Amsterdam was adopted.[654]

3.6.4. The Social Goals of the TFEU

The Treaty of Lisbon even further extended the social goals of competition policy in the EU. Since the adoption of the Lisbon Treaty, the goal of an 'open market economy with free competition' under Article 4(1) TEC[655] has been changed to

---

647   D.J. Gerber (1998), *supra* n. 528, p. 347.
648   'Concerning the competition applicable to enterprises, Community policy in the first place must prevent the substitution of state restrictions and obstacles to trade which have been abolished, by private measures with similar consequences.' Premier rapport sur la politique de concurrence (1972), at 13. The Report was originally written in French. The quoted text was translated by Hawk. See B.E. Hawk (1972), *supra* n. 559, p. 231.
649   D.J. Gerber (1994a), *supra* n. 556, p. 108.
650   D.J. Gerber (1998), *supra* n. 528, p. 369.
651   D.J. Gerber (1998), *supra* n. 528, p. 370.
652   I. Lianos (2013), *supra* n. 533, p. 40.
653   D.J. Gerber (1998), *supra* n. 528, p. 371.
654   I. Lianos (2013), *supra* n. 533, p. 38.
655   I. Lianos (2013), *supra* n. 533, p. 40.

achieve the goal of a 'highly competitive social market economy'.[656] To achieve this goal, a general principle was set under Article 7 TFEU for all policies and activities in the EU, 'The Union shall ensure consistency between its policies and activities, taking all of its objectives into account and in accordance with the principle of conferral of powers.'[657] In the following Articles 8–13 of the TFEU, these objectives were listed, including: the equality between men and women,[658] the promotion of employment, social protection, the promotion of education and against social exclusion, the protection of human health,[659] against discrimination,[660] protecting the environment and promoting sustainable development,[661] and consumer protection.[662] Animal welfare has also been included in Article 13 of the TFEU. As competition policy is also subject to Article 7, it is highly debatable how it can be implemented to create a balance between all these broad goals, in particular, how a tradeoff can be made between efficiency, consumer welfare and animal rights.

How to strike a balance between other goals within competition policy and goals of the common market also remains an open question. For example, to safeguard the 'social market economy', it is necessary to promote employment.[663] Through which mechanism can competition policy be applied together with employment policy to achieve one common goal, is highly uncertain. In March 2000, the Lisbon Agenda stated that by 2010 Europe would be 'the most competitive and the most dynamic knowledge-based economy in the world.'[664] It was criticized that the new 'Europe 2020' goal which encourages industrial policy at the EU level to deal with economic crisis and globalization is far beyond the domain of competition law.[665]

---

[656]   Art. 3(3) TFEU: 'the sustainable development of Europe based on balanced economic growth and price stability, a highly competitive social market economy, aiming at full employment and social progress.'

[657]   Art. 7 TFEU, cited by A. JONES and B. SUFRIN (2010), *supra* n. 26, p. 52.

[658]   Art. 8 TFEU.

[659]   Art. 9 TFEU.

[660]   Art. 10 TFEU.

[661]   Art. 11 TFEU.

[662]   Art. 12 TFEU.

[663]   *See* Article 9 TFEU: 'In defining and implementing its politics and activities, the Union shall take into account requirements linked to the promotion of a high level of employment, the guarantee of adequate social protection, the fight against social exclusion, and a high level of education, training and protection of human health.' According to Lianos, Lisbon Treaty has led the enforcement of other competition rules also take into account of the broad social and political goals of the Treaty: I. LIANOS (2013), *supra* n. 533, p. 45.

[664]   D. GERADIN and I. GIRGENSON (2011), *supra* n. 560, p. 372. Presidency Conclusions, Lisbon European Council, 23–24 March 2000 available at <www.europarl.europa.eu/summits/lis1_en.htm#a>.

[665]   D. GERADIN and I. GIRGENSON (2011), *supra* n. 560, p. 373. Commission Communication: 'An Integrated Industrial Policy for the Globalisation Era Putting Competitiveness and Sustainability at Centre Stage' [COM (2010) 614]; Commission Communication: 'Europe 2020 A Strategy for Smart, Sustainable and Inclusive Growth' [COM (2010) 2020 final].

3.7. A VIEWPOINT FROM THE COMPETITION COMMISSIONERS

3.7.1. Commissioner Karel Van Miert (1993–1999)

From 1993 to 1999, Karel Van Miert served as the EU Competition Commissioner.[666] In 1993, Commissioner Van Miert stated that: 'The aims of European Community's competition policy are economic, political, and social. The policy is concerned not only with promoting efficient production but also achieving the aims of the European treaties.' In the documents that are published in the following years, the goals of EU competition policy have indeed been extended to a broad coverage. For example, in 1995, the environmental goals were emphasized in the 25th Annual Report on Competition Policy.[667] In 1999, in the Communication on the Strategy for Europe's Internal Market,[668] the goal of competition law was clarified as 'maintenance of competitive markets' and 'the creation of a single common market'. In the White Paper on Modernisation of Rules Implementing Article 85 and 86 of the EC Treaty,[669] published in 1999, the competition goal was to 'ensuring effective competition'. In the Commission Notice on the Guidelines on Vertical Restraints,[670] published in 2000, it was stated that market integration enhances competition in the Community, and market integration was considered as an additional goal of EC competition policy.

3.7.2. Commissioner Mario Monti (1999–2004)

Mario Monti served as the Competition Commissioner from September 1999 to November 2004.[671] Unlike Commissioner Van Miert, during several of his public speeches Commissioner Monti focused on the ultimate goal of protecting consumer welfare. For example, in 2000 he stated that the primary goal is to protect competition, as it enhances consumer welfare and creates an efficient

---

666 K. Van Miert, 'Frontier-Free Europea', 5 May 1993. A. Bagchi (2005) 'The Political Economy of Merger Regulation', *American Journal of Comparative Law*, vol. 53, p. 8.

667 XXVth Report on Competition Policy 1995, European Commission, para 85. Cited by H. Schweitzer (2007), 'Competition Law and Public Policy: Reconsidering an Uneasy Relationship. The Example of Article 81', *European University Institute (EUI) Working Papers, Law 2007/30*, p. 6, footnote 19.

668 Communication from the Commission to the European Parliament and the Council: *The Strategy for Europe's Internal Market* [COM (99) 624 final].

669 White Paper on Modernisation of the Rules Implementing Articles 85 and 86 of the EC Treaty [1999] OJ C 132/1, Executive Summary part 8. 'The Commission has now come to concentrate more on ensuring effective competition by detecting and stopping cross-border cartels and maintaining competitive structures.'

670 Commission Notice: *Guidelines on Vertical Restraints* [2000] OJ C 291/1, para 7.

671 N. Levy (2005), 'Mario Monti's Legacy in EC Merger Control', *Competition Policy International*, vol. 1, no. 1, p. 99.

allocation of resources.[672] In 2001, he stated that the goal of EU competition law is to protect consumer welfare by maintaining a high degree of competition in the common market.[673] In 2002, he stated that '[o]ne of the main purposes of European competition policy is to promote the interests of consumers, that is, to ensure that consumers benefit from the wealth generated by the European economy'.[674] Commissioner Monti also published in *The Economist* in 2002, emphasizing the consumer protection goal of the EU competition policy.[675] In the 2004 Guidelines on the Application of Article 101(3), it was mentioned that 'protect competition' was an instrument to 'enhancing consumer welfare' and to 'ensuring an efficient allocation of resources'.[676] In October 2004, Commissioner Monti stated that 'consumer interest is the main goal and competition policy becomes a tool for structural reform'.[677]

3.7.3. Commissioner Neelie Kroes (2004–2010)

From 2005, Neelie Kroes became the Competition Commissioner and she continued to keep the focus on the goal of consumer welfare. However, unlike Commissioner Monti, Commissioner Kroes also gave attention to the competitiveness of the European industries. In Commissioner Kroes's speeches, a swing between the consumer protection goal and the goal of promoting competitiveness can be observed. For example, in February 2005, Commissioner Kroes stated that 'competition policy is a key element to foster the competitiveness of Europe's industries and to attain the goals of the Lisbon strategy'.[678] In her

---

[672] M. MONTI (2000), 'European Competition Policy for the 21st Century', speech at the Twenty-eighth Annual Conference on International Antitrust Law and Policy, The Fordham Corporate Law Institute, New York, 20 October 2000, available at <http://europa.eu/rapid/press-release_SPEECH-00-389_en.htm?locale=en>.

[673] 'The goal of competition policy, in all its aspects, is to protect consumer welfare by maintaining a high degree of competition in the common market.' M. MONTI, 'The Future for Competition Policy in the European Union', speech at Merchant Taylor's Hall, 9 July 2001, available at <http://europa.eu/rapid/press-release_SPEECH-01-340_en.htm>; *see also*, M. MONTI, (2001), 'Foreword', *XXXth Report on Competition Policy*, European Commission 2001.

[674] M. MONTI (2002), 'Foreword', in *XXXIInd Report on Competition Policy 2002, European Commission*.

[675] 'Preserving competition is not, however, an end in itself. The ultimate policy goal is the protection of consumer welfare. Europe's consumers have been the principal beneficiaries of the Commission's enforcement of the regulation, enjoying lower prices and a wider choice of products and services as a result.' M. MONTI, 'Europe's Merger Monitor', *The Economist*, 7 November 2002, available at <www.economist.com/node/1429439> accessed 05.04.2014; Cited by N. LEVY (2005), *supra* n. 671.

[676] [2004] OJ C 101/97, published as part of the package of Notices accompanying Regulation 1/2003.

[677] M. MONTI (2004), 'A Reformed Competition Policy: Achievements and Challenges for the Future', speech at the Center for European Reform in Brussels, 28 October 2004, available at <http://europa.eu/rapid/press-release_SPEECH-04-477_en.htm?locale=en>.

[678] Communication of the Commission to the Spring European Council, *Working Together for Growth and Jobs: A New Start for the Lisbon Strategy*, [COM (2005) 24], 2 February 2005.

September 2005 speech, Commissioner Kroes stated that 'Our aim is simple, to protect competition as a means of enhancing consumer welfare and ensuring an efficient allocation of resources.'[679] In December 2005, Kroes emphasized that the goal of the EU competition policy was 'to protect consumer welfare',[680] whereas in September 2006, Commissioner Kroes said that the goal was 'to support the competitive process in the internal market'[681] and in November 2006, she put the focus back on consumers: 'The consumer is at the heart of competition enforcement' and 'the potential harm to consumers is at the heart of what we do'.[682]

In 2007, Commissioner Kroes stated that interpreting industrial policy as 'protectionism' is 'old-fashioned'.[683] She claimed that it is time to develop a modern industrial policy which aims at strengthening the competitiveness of the European Union, as well as at increasing the capability of European industries to compete in global markets. Therefore, a properly defined industrial policy will guarantee the conditions for European firms to benefit from the competition in the global economy, from which citizens will also get a fruitful reward. In this aspect, industrial policy does not conflict with competition policy, as both of these two economic policies are used as instruments[684] to achieve the goal of Europe set by the Lisbon Treaty: to promote long-term economic growth, to ensure employment, and to strengthen the competitiveness of the European economy.[685] Moreover, both of these two policies work together under the

---

679   N. KROES (2005), 'Delivering Better Markets and Better Choices', speech at the European Consumer and Competition Day, 15 September 2005, available at < http://europa.eu/rapid/press-release_SPEECH-05-512_en.htm> ('consumer welfare is now well established as the standard the Commission applies when assessing mergers and infringements of the Treaty rules on cartels and monopolies. Our aim is simple: to protect competition in the market as a mean of enhancing consumer welfare and ensuring an efficient allocation of resources.'). In another speech in September 2005, Commissioner Kroes emphasized the goal of Article 82 is to enhance consumer welfare and to promote allocative efficiency, see N. KROES (2005), 'Preliminary Thoughts on Policy Review of Article 82', speech at the Fordham Corporate Law Institute, 23 September 2005, available at <http://europa.eu/rapid/press-release_SPEECH-05-537_en.htm>.

680   DG Competition, Discussion Paper on the Application of Article 82 of the Treaty to Exclusionary Abuses, December 2005, para 4.

681   N. KROES (2006), 'Industrial policy and competition law & policy', speech at Fordham University School of Law, 14 September 2006, available at <http://europa.eu/rapid/press-release_SPEECH-06-499_en.htm?locale=en>.

682   N. KROES (2006), 'Competition Policy and Consumers', speech at the General Assembly of Bureau Européen des Unionsde Consommateurs (BEUC), 16 November 2006, available at <http://europa.eu/rapid/press-release_SPEECH-06-691_en.htm?locale=en>.

683   N. KROES (2007), 'Speech: Industrial Policy and Competition Law and Policy', *Fordham International Law Journal*, vol. 30, p. 1406 ('Ladies and gentlemen, it is time to put old-fashioned industrial protectionism to bed and, instead, to develop a modern, proactive industrial policy which embraces change and paves the way for our future competitiveness.').

684   Kroes emphasized that 'competition' is not a goal but an instrument to reach a broader goal: 'Competition policy is not an end to itself, not even for a Competition Commissioner. It is a means to reach a goal.' N. KROES (2007), *supra* n. 683, p. 1412.

685   N. KROES (2007), *supra* n. 683, p. 1406. Lisbon European Council, Presidency Conclusions, 23–24 March 2000, available at <http://ue.eu.int/ueDocs/cms_Data/docs/pressData/en/ec/00100-rl.en0.htm>.

common goal of promoting competitiveness: competition policy designs and maintains a competitive market, and lays the structural foundations for promoting the competitiveness of industries.[686] However, in April 2008, Kroes once again returned to the goal of consumer welfare as she claimed that 'defending consumers' interests is at the heart of the Commission's competition policy'.[687]

3.8. CONCLUSION

Competition policy in Europe is different from antitrust law in the US in two perspectives. The first one is the different views on the relationship between the State and the market. Unlike the free market economists in the Chicago School, European scholars have less confidence in the function of the market. To Ordoliberal scholars, the market itself does not generate a desirable outcome.[688] Competition law, either enforced by the judicial power or by the administrative power, plays a role of correcting market failures. Ordoliberal scholars believe that the function of competition law is to protect individual's freedom to participate in competition, and to avoid both market failure and government failure. The goal of competition law is not to protect the outcome of the market, but to protect the process, to safeguard the environment for competition. In the Ordoliberal's language, competition law is to form a legal order within which the individuals' rights to compete are protected.

The second perspective is that the role of competition policy in Europe is to achieve broader political goals of the European Union. The goals of competition law should be consistent with the goals of the European Union. The fundamental

---

[686] N. Kroes (2007), *supra* n. 683, p. 1408.

[687] N. Kroes (2008), 'Consumers at the Heart of EU Competition Policy', speech at the BEUC, 22 April 2008, available at <http://europa.eu/rapid/press-release_SPEECH-08-212_en.htm?locale=en>.

[688] As the founding father of Ordoliberalism, Walter Eucken said: 'The problem will not solve itself simply by our letting economic systems grow up spontaneously. The history of the century has shown this plainly enough. The economic system has to be consciously shaped.' W. Eucken (1950), *The Foundations of Economic History and Theory of Economic Reality*, William Hodge & Company, p. 314 (original in German: *Die Grundlagen der Nationalökonomie*, Jena 1940), cited by N. Goldschmidt, *supra* n. 615, p. 1. *See also* K. Aiginger, M. McCabe, D.C. Mueller and C. Weiss (2001), 'Do American and European Industrial Organization Economists Differ?', *Review of Industrial Organization*, vol. 19, p. 383 ('One of the differences between Americans and Europeans that is most noticeable – at least to an economist – concerns attitudes toward government and government intervention in market processes. As a broad generalization, Europeans are more likely to favor state ownership of enterprise, subsidies for enterprise, government regulations of competition including price ceilings and floors, vertical restrictions on trade and even cartel agreements as ways for solving 'market failures' and improving social welfare. These differences are evident in both the rhetoric and ideologies of Europeans and European politics, and in the policies in place.').

goal formulated by the Rome Treaty is to break down trade barriers between Member States and to establish a common market. Competition law is regarded as a crucial instrument to achieve this goal. Therefore, competition policy in Europe is not an end of itself, nor is it a purely independent policy. It is highly interrelated with other economic policies and to a large extent interfered with by political concerns. Therefore, unlike the US antitrust law, which has narrowed down the focus on welfare standards, the European competition law is left with various policy goals and a consensus has not yet achieved. Parallel with the discussion on competition goals, the goals of the European Union have also been modified during the last several decades. On top of the goal of establishing a common market, the goals of promoting employment, increasing consumer welfare, strengthening competitiveness of the European firms, achieving efficiency have also been emphasized. Moreover, environmental, political and social goals are also the concern of the commissioners and the judges in Europe.

4. CONCLUSION

Looking back the discussion for the last one hundred years, a question arises again: do antitrust goals really matter? There are several quick answers. For example, to set a clear hierarchy on competition goals will ensure the enforcement of the competition law to be consistent, therefore to strengthen legal certainty.[689] Second, economic theories often show that achieving one goal is often at the cost of another; achieving all the goals is simply impossible. Third, economic analysis often starts from the assumption of a desired welfare outcome, total welfare, consumer welfare, or distributive effects. Only under this assumption can economic modeling or data analysis follow.[690] In some cases the choice of assumption does not matter in the sense that different models lead to the same result. In other cases it does matter because the results lead to completely different directions.

However, economists are only economists. Economists are not anthropologists. The results provided from modeling and data analysis can hardly capture all factors that affect competition in the real world. Nor will any single discipline do. The real world is far more complex, dynamic and uncertain.

---

[689] One of the major criticisms on the broad goals under the EU competition law is that it creates uncertainties. By contrast, the major advantage of the uniformed efficiency goal advocated by the Chicago School is that it results in certainty. O. ODUDU (2010), 'The Wider Concerns of Competition Law', *Oxford Journal of Legal Studies*, vol. 30, p. 600.

[690] As Stigler put it: 'The apparatus of economics is very flexible: without breaking the rules of the profession – by being illogical or even by denying the validity of the traditional theory – a sufficiently clever person can reach *any* conclusion he wishes on any *real* problem (in contrast to formal problems).' G.J. STIGLER (1965), *Essays in the History of Economics*, University of Chicago Press, p. 63.

The same concept might have distinct interpretations in different time periods, or from different angles. The picture becomes more blurred when the goal of competition law is heavily influenced by other political goals. Politicians often sketch a goal of a country for the next five years during his election campaign; however, it is highly doubtful whether this goal will have the same meaning after he wins the election. Meanwhile, if the politician decides to move to a more lenient or tougher enforcement of antitrust laws, it seems there is always a good argument that can be found from the goal perspective, as it provides so many choices by interpreting them![691]

To give a word a precise meaning is a highly demanding philosophical task. It requires decades of desperate thinking and years of scientific training. To train antitrust enforcers this skill will certainly impose an extra burden on tax payers. In the real world, the decision is often made by applying a proxy, such as looking at the 'level of concentration', 'price increase', or 'market share'. The quality of the proxy has been improved dramatically when modern economic techniques such as merger simulation have been developed in recent years. They become more practical and useful to estimate the function of the market. However, the development of proxies only helps antitrust enforcers speed up their daily work and provide more robust economic evidence for their decisions. It does not solve the philosophical question of how to choose, and implement antitrust goals in the particular case.[692] Moreover, the proxy that has been used in the past may not be attractive anymore today. For example, economic wealth used to be good proxy to measure the well-being of human life. Competition policy gains public support when it targets on maximizing social wealth. This proxy might be outdated today as well-being can be better assessed through other principles, such as 'welfare', or more directly 'happiness'.[693] Under this new proxy, the way that competition policy is implemented will have to be modified. This complexity means the question of the goals of antitrust law is unsolved and this debate among economists and lawyers still continues.

---

[691] As illustrated by Ernst-Joachim Mestmäcker, 'Politicians and legislators love the ambivalence of final purposes, leaving their determination to the ensuing political or legal process.' E.J. MESTMÄCKER (2011), 'The Development of German and European Competition Law with Special Reference to the EU Commission's Article 82 Guidance of 2008', in L.F. PACE (ed.), *European Competition Law: The Impact of the Commission's Guidance on Article 102*, Edward Elgar, p. 25.

[692] There is a private interest concern here: the antitrust lawyers and practitioners care more about how to win the antitrust case by applying the techniques, methods or arguments which are the most favorable for them. Antitrust enforcers, administrators and judges study the goal of antitrust law in order to use it as a practical tool in their daily work. Therefore, discussions on practical proxies and economic techniques always attract more audience. After all, to fully understand the philosophy of antitrust goal is often unnecessary as it does not generate private benefit.

[693] M.E. STUCKE (2013), *supra* n. 494, pp. 2575–2645.

CHAPTER 4

INTEGRATING THE EFFICIENCY GOAL IN MERGER CONTROL POLICY: A COMPARATIVE PERSPECTIVE

1. INTRODUCTION

The discussion in the previous chapter shows that the goals of competition policy in the US and the EU have been influenced by multiple factors, and the choices on the goals may evolve over time. This chapter focuses on how this evolution will affect the implementation of merger rules in the US and the EU. The central research question in this chapter is: in line with the development of economic theory, to what extent the goal of promoting efficiency has been incorporated in the merger policy in the US and the EU.

In the US, the goals of merger rules are to a large extent consistent with the development of economic theories on competition. Under section 7 of the Clayton Act, a merger will be considered unlawful when it 'may substantially lessen competition', or 'tend to create a monopoly'.[694] To examine the merger effects, the primary concern is centered at the market structure before and after the merger.[695] In the 1960s, after section 7 of the Clayton Act was amended,[696] the Supreme Court followed the enforcement pattern of per se rules, and an efficiency defense was generally rejected.[697] The strong structural approach taken by the Supreme Court imposes a clear presumption on the anticompetitive harm of a merger based on the criterion of market concentration.[698] This approach was clarified by the Supreme Court in *United States v. Philadelphia National Bank* in 1963: it 'lightens the burden of proving illegality only with respect to mergers whose size makes them inherently suspect.'[699] The attitude of heavily relying on the market concentration, and at the same time rejecting the

---

[694] Clayton Act §7, 15 U.S.C §18.
[695] R.D. BLAIR and J.S. HAYNES (2011), *supra* n. 505, p. 67.
[696] Celler-Kefauver Act of 1950.
[697] W. KOLASKY and A. DICK (2003), 'The Merger of Guidelines and the Integration of Efficiencies into Antitrust Review of Horizontal Mergers', *Antitrust Law Journal*, vol. 71, no. 1, p. 210.
[698] J.B. BAKER and C. SHAPIRO (2007), 'Reinvigorating Horizontal Merger Enforcement', *Reg-Markets Center Working Paper No. 07–12*, p. 1–2.
[699] *United States v. Philadelphia National Bank,* 374 U.S. 321, 363 (1963), cited by J.B. BAKER and C. SHAPIRO (2007), *supra* n. 698, p. 2.

efficiency claims was supported by the 'Structure-Conduct-Performance' ('SCP') paradigm developed by the Harvard School scholars.[700] This SCP approach indicates that market power is best examined through the level of market concentration, and when firms in the highly concentrated industries charge monopolistic prices, economic performance will be negatively affected.[701]

In the 1970s, Chicago School scholars started to argue that efficiency should be the goal of the antitrust law in the US. Between the 1960s and the 1970s, although Chicago School scholars strongly advocated that efficiency should be the ultimate goal of antitrust, they generally rejected to apply efficiency gains to counterbalance market power, for the simple reason that efficiencies are difficult to measure. They argued that due to the predictability problem, efficiency gains of a merger should not be assessed on a case-by-case basis and therefore an efficiency defense should not be allowed; instead, it is necessary to increase the thresholds for the merger to be challenged.[702] As Richard Posner said, measuring efficiency would be 'an intractable subject for litigation',[703] or, as Robert Bork said, 'measuring efficiencies are beyond the capacities of the law'.[704] The policy implication of their efficiency arguments is restricted to increasing the thresholds of the market concentration level for the merger to be examined.

The landmark of shifting the balance towards the efficiency goal is the famous tradeoff model presented by Professor Oliver E. Williamson in 1968, which illustrates how efficiency gains can be applied to counterbalance the anticompetitive harms generated by a merger. This diagram shows that merger decisions should focus on the competitive effects, not only on the level of market concentration. Williamson's research was supported and accepted by Donald Turner,[705] the Assistant Attorney General ('AAG') of the Department of Justice, who hired Oliver E. Williamson as his Special Economic Assistant and applied Williamson's finding to the 1968 Merger Guidelines.[706] Both the methodology and the conclusions of Williamson's work have been extensively debated.[707] The consensus reached among economists and legal scholars in the US is that efficiencies are counted as the benefits of a merger, and should be taken into account to counterbalance the potential anticompetitive harm caused by the increase of the market power.[708] Nevertheless, the process of adopting an efficiency defense in merger enforcement has been slow.[709]

---

[700] J.S. Bain (1956), *supra* n. 362; Baker and Shapiro (2007), *supra* n. 698, p. 3.

[701] D.B. Audretsch, W.J. Baumol and A.E. Burke (2001), 'Competition Policy in Dynamic Markets', *International Journal of Industrial Organization*, vol. 19, p. 615.

[702] *See* W. Kolasky and A. Dick (2003), *supra* n. 697, p. 213.

[703] R.A. Posner (1976), *Antitrust Law: An Economic Perspective*, University of Chicago Press, p. 112.

[704] R. H. Bork (1978), *supra* n. 19 cited by W. Kolasky and A. Dick (2003), *supra* n. 697, p. 217.

[705] 'Donald Turner selected Williamson as his special economic assistant.' *See* W. Kolasky and A. Dick (2003), *supra* n. 697, p. 209.

[706] W. Kolasky and A. Dick (2003), *supra* n. 697, pp. 209, 212.

[707] A.A. Fisher and R.H. Lande (1983), 'Efficiency Considerations in Merger Enforcement', *California Law Review*, vol. 71, No. 6, p. 1583.

[708] A.A. Fisher and R.H. Lande (1983), *supra* n. 707, p. 1583.

[709] M.N. Berry (1996), *supra* n. 312, p. 516.

Under the 1968 Horizontal Merger Guidelines, the analysis of merger cases followed a highly structural approach and efficiencies were only considered in 'exceptional cases'.[710] Efficiency gains only became a major concern in the 1982 Horizontal Merger Guidelines,[711] during the time when the conservative attorney William Baxter served as the Assistant Attorney General of the DOJ, and the conservative economist James Miller chaired the FTC. The 1982 Merger Guidelines incorporated the Chicago School ideas and increased the thresholds for the merger to be challenged.

The 1984 Horizontal Merger Guidelines[712] made an important step to place efficiencies as a crucial factor in the decision of mergers. These Guidelines made the efficiency defense a formal doctrine,[713] which is comparable to the failing company doctrine. This change indicates that efficiency has been incorporated as an essential part of the merger assessment.[714] The new section on efficiency written by J. Paul McGrath further incorporated the tools to measure and to evaluate efficiency gains.[715] This section remained the same in the 1997 Merger Guidelines. The evolution of merger policy in the US could show a clear trend of shifting from the focus on market concentration to the analysis of competitive effects. In the US, although market concentration is still an important parameter to serve as the starting point of the merger analysis, an increasing attention has been given to the competitive effects, in which efficiency is considered as one of the important factors.[716]

It is also a slow process to integrate efficiency considerations into merger analysis in the EU.[717] In Europe, the merger policy at the EU level was developed in the late 1980s. Similar to the situation in the US, the original language of the 1989 Merger Regulation was not clear with respect to how efficiency claims will be taken into account in merger assessment.[718] In the 1990s, the Commission showed a hostile attitude towards efficiency claims and refused to take efficiency arguments into account to offset the adverse competitive effects. Under the 1989

---

[710] US Department of Justice, 1968 Merger Guidelines.

[711] US Department of Justice, 1982 Merger Guidelines.

[712] US Department of Justice, 1984 Merger Guidelines.

[713] When DOJ was headed by J. Paul McGrath, and this efficiency section mostly remained until 1997 Merger Guidelines. W. KOLASKY and A. DICK (2003), *supra* n. 697, p. 209.

[714] In 1984 Merger Guidelines, efficiencies section was moved to 'competitive effects' section, and according to J. Paul McGrath, this change aims at not to 'balance expected efficiencies against expected anticompetitive consequences', but to 'look at efficiencies in determining whether the merger was anticompetitive at all'. *See* R.A. POGUE, H.M. REASONER, J.H. SHENEFIELD and R.A. WHITING (1985), '60 Minutes with J. Paul McGrath – interview', *Antitrust Law Journal*, vol. 54, pp. 131, 141, cited by W. KOLASKY and A. DICK (2003), *supra* n. 697, p. 220.

[715] W. KOLASKY and A. DICK (2003), *supra* n. 697, p. 209.

[716] J.B. BAKER and C. SHAPRIO (2007), *supra* n. 698, p. 1.

[717] R. PITOFSKY (2007), 'Efficiency Consideration and Merger Enforcement: Comparison of US and EU Approaches', *Fordham International Law Journal*, vol. 30, p. 1414.

[718] R. PITOFSKY (2007), *supra* n. 717, p. 1414.

EC Merger Regulation, concentrations were assessed by the 'Dominant Test'[719] and a merger would not be permitted if it created or strengthened the dominant position. The negative view on efficiencies gradually changed after the Merger Regulation was revised in 2004. Merger-specific efficiencies were accepted by the Commission as a positive factor. Efficiency gains will be taken into account if the benefits can be 'passed-through' to consumers. In recent years, several press releases have shown that some cases were terminated during the investigation due to the possible efficiency gains,[720] one example is the *Korsnas/AD Cartonboard* case in 2006.[721]

The structure of this chapter is as follows. After the introduction, the second section summarizes the economic theories of efficiency. The first part introduces the economic theories on efficiency, including production efficiency, dynamic efficiency and allocative efficiency. In particular, this part discusses the conflicts between these three types of efficiencies. Theory and practice generally show that it is impossible to achieve these efficiencies at the same time. However, the development of the concept of 'innovation' makes the tradeoff between dynamic efficiency and productive efficiency more complex. The third section focuses on the economic analysis of merger effects, and the Williamson tradeoff model will be particularly discussed. The fourth section discusses how the efficiency goal has been integrated in the US merger control policy. The first part presents the academic debate on the efficiency goal in the US, and the next part discusses how the efficiency goal has been incorporated in the Horizontal Merger Guidelines, and the last part presents how the efficiency arguments were treated by the courts. The fifth section of this chapter presents the evolution of incorporating the efficiency goal in the EU merger control policy, in particular, how the goal of efficiency has been integrated in the Merger Regulation and how it has been evaluated by the courts. The last section of this chapter concludes.

2. ECONOMIC THEORIES OF EFFICIENCY

Efficiency is the situation where the total output is maximized. In economic theory, the concept of efficiency that is used for antitrust issues can be divided into three types: productive efficiency, allocative efficiency and dynamic

---

[719] The Dominance Test ('DT') was formulated under Article 2(3) of the 1989 ECMR: 'A concentration which creates or strengthens a dominant position as a result of which effective competition would be significantly impeded in the common market or in a substantial part of it shall be declared incompatible with the common market'.

[720] R. Pitofsky (2007), *supra* n. 717, p. 1423.

[721] European Commission Press Release IP/06/610: 'Mergers: Commission approves acquisition of AD Cartonboard by Korsnäs', 12 May 2006, available at <http://europa.eu/rapid/press-release_IP-06-610_en.htm> ('The transaction is likely to create synergies which would appear likely to be at least partly passed on to consumers').

efficiency.[722] Productive efficiency is achieved when products are produced at the lowest cost. Productive efficiency and allocative efficiency are both in static models under the presumption of perfect competition. Dynamic efficiency describes innovation and the development process aiming at improving social welfare.

2.1. PRODUCTIVE EFFICIENCY

Productive efficiency refers to the situation where a firm can produce at the lowest cost. A merger will achieve productive efficiency if the combined two firms will be able to reduce costs more effectively than when any of them produces alone.[723] Productive efficiency can be achieved when the concentration facilitates economies of scale, and it will be decreased when the X-inefficiency occurs.[724] When a firm is holding a monopoly position in the market, it will lose the motivation and pressure to compete with his competitors as in the perfectly competitive market. This is named as the 'X-inefficiency'.[725] X-inefficiency on the one hand reveals the internal efficiency loss due to the increasing costs of production and operation; on the other hand it describes the misallocation of resources by keeping the excessive capacity.

2.2. ALLOCATIVE EFFICIENCY

The Chicago School views competition as a struggle for survival, and less efficient firms are hence driven out of the market by a 'natural selection'. The survival firms are regarded as the fittest, even resulting in a market structure with dominant firms.[726] The outcome of the market competition is to achieve allocative efficiency, where resources are allocated to those who value them the most.

Allocative efficiency means that through a well-functioning price system, resources and the production output are allocated to the consumers who value them the most. It refers to the result of a perfectly competitive market equilibrium, where the suppliers will produce to the point when the market price equals the marginal cost, and when the buyers who have the willingness and

---

[722] This division is according to Brodley, although he named 'dynamic efficiency' 'innovation efficiency'. J.F. BRODLEY (1987), *supra* n. 324, p. 1025.

[723] M.N. BERRY (1996), *supra* n. 312, p. 533.

[724] W. KERBER, 'Should Competition Law Promote Efficiency? – Some Reflections of an Economist on the Normative Foundations of Competition Law', in J. DREXL, L. IDOT and J. MONEGER (eds.), *Economic Theory and Competition Law*, Edward Elgar 2009, p. 97.

[725] H. LEIBENSTEIN (1966), 'Allocative Efficiency vs. "X-Efficiency"', *American Economic Review*, vol. 56, no. 3, pp. 392–415; *see also* J.R. HICKS (1935), 'Annual Survey of Economic Theory: The Theory of Monopoly', *Econometrica*, vol. 3, no. 1, p. 8.

[726] R.C. SINGLETON (1997), *supra* n. 595, p. 2.

capacity of purchasing the product at this price will be able to do so.[727] Allocative efficiency is achieved when there is Pareto optimality in the society – a situation that cannot be improved by increasing at least one person's welfare without decreasing the welfare of another person.[728] As the Pareto optimality can rarely be achieved, the Chicago School advocates that the Kaldor-Hicks efficiency can be taken as an alternative solution. That is the situation where the welfare gains of the winner are sufficiently larger than the losses from the loser. It is defined as a potential Pareto optimality because the Pareto efficiency will be achieved when the winner compensate the loser.[729] Without considering the distributive effects, both the Pareto efficiency and the Kaldor-Hicks efficiency make the whole society better off.

2.3.   DYNAMIC EFFICIENCY

The concept of dynamic efficiency incorporates the economic theory of innovation. It has been advocated by economists that innovation is the driving force of economic growth,[730] and competition is regarded as a process which generates innovation. The classic debate on the topic of competition versus innovation is held between Joseph Schumpeter and Kenneth Arrow.[731] Arrow advocates that competition will promote innovation, whereas Schumpeter argues innovation is better achieved by monopolists.[732] Schumpeter's logic is that monopolists are better incentivized to finance R&D when the benefit of an innovation is returned to the firm itself.[733] Compared with competitive firms, monopolists are more likely to implement the innovation plans because of their superior experience and the control of financial resources.[734] For Arrow, this

---

[727]   A. JONES and B. SUFRIN (2004), *supra* n. 26, p. 8.

[728]   R. VAN DEN BERGH and P.D. CAMESASCA (2006), *supra* n. 18, p. 64.

[729]   R. VAN DEN BERGH (2006), *supra* n. 18, p. 82.

[730]   Brodley claimed that '[i]nnovation efficiency or technological progress is the single most important factor in the growth of real output in the United States and the rest of the industrialized world.' *See* J.F. BRODLEY (1987), *supra* n. 324, p. 1026, *See also*, R.M. SOLOW (1957), 'Technical Change and the Aggregate Production Function', *Review of Economics and Statistics*, vol. 39, p. 312; J.G. SIDAK and D.J. TEECE (2009), *supra* n. 504, p. 581.

[731]   J.B. BAKER (2007), 'Beyond Schumpeter vs. Arrow: How Antitrust Fosters Innovation', *Antitrust Law Journal*, vol. 74, p. 575.

[732]   J. SCHUMPETER (2008), *supra* n. 405.

[733]   J. SCHUMPETER (2008), *supra* n. 405; J.B. BAKER (2007), *supra* n. 731, p. 578.

[734]   J. SCHUMPETER (2008), *supra* n. 405; M.A. CARRIER (2008), 'Two Puzzles Resolved: Of the Schumpeter-Arrow Stalemate and Pharmaceutical Innovation Markets', *Iowa Law Review*, vol. 93, p. 403. Schumpeter perceives monopolists are superior to competitors because they have a higher control of methods and resources. Joseph Schumpeter, *Capitalism, Socialism and Democracy*, *supra* n. 405, p. 100 ('There are superior methods available to the monopolist which either are not available at all to a crowd of competitors or are not available to them so readily.'), cited by H. HOVENKAMP (2012), 'Competition for Innovation', available at <http://papers.ssrn.com/sol3/papers.cfm?abstract_id=2008953>, p. 6.

incentive is not obvious because there is no 'additional business' that the monopolist can get from the market. If a monopolist invests in new technology, it will lose the flow of profits generated by the old technology; therefore the monopolist bears an opportunity cost of continuing earning monopoly profits when they innovate.[735] However, for the competitors who do not hold monopolistic positions, they can 'take business away' from the monopolists. Therefore, they are more incentivized to invest in R&D to make improvements. This is named as the 'Arrow Effect' or the 'Replacement Effect'.[736]

There is a very large number of empirical studies focusing on the relationship between competition and innovation. Aghion and Tirole call the empirical test between industry concentration and R&D the 'second most tested hypothesis in industrial organization'.[737] The most important finding of empirical tests is that the relationship between competition and innovation follows a pattern of an 'inverted-U', that is, competition will accelerate innovation up to a certain level, and after this turning point innovation will decrease. Innovation reaches the highest level in industries with a oligopolistic market structure.[738] The 'inverted-U' relationship was initially observed by Scherer[739] and was proved by Levin *et al.*, who found that the 'turning point' is when the four-firm Concentration Ratio (C4)[740] equals 52, and at this point the R&D intensity is maximized.[741] Recently, this finding was confirmed by Aghion *et.al* in their study on the relationship between innovation and product market competition. In their model, competition may encourage innovation by increasing the incremental profits; this is named as 'escape-competition effect', which is demonstrated by the first part of the 'inverted-U'. The decreasing part of the 'inverted-U' model explains the 'Schumpeterian effect', which refers to the

---

735   R.J. GILBERT (2006), 'Looking for Mr. Schumpeter: Where are we in the Competition-Innovation Debate', in A.B. JAFFE, J. LERNER and S. STERN (eds.), *Innovation Policy and the Economy*, vol. 6, p. 165; J.B. BAKER (2007), *supra* n. 731, p. 578.

736   J.B. BAKER (2007), *supra* n. 731, p. 578; K.J. ARROW (1962), 'Economic Welfare and the Allocation of Resources for Innovation', in R.R. NELSON (eds.), *The Rate and Direction of Economic Activity*, Princeton University Press.

737   The first most tested hypothesis is the relationship between firm size and profits. In most of the empirical studies, 'R&D expenditures' or 'patent counts' are often taken as the proxy of 'innovation', and 'industry concentration' is used for measuring the level of 'competition'. *See* R.J. GILBERT (2006), *supra* n. 735, pp. 187,191–193; P. AGHION and J. TIROLE (1994), 'The Management of Innovation', *Quarterly Journal of Economics*, vol. 109, pp. 1185–1209.

738   J.B. BAKER (2007), *supra* n. 731, p. 583.

739   F.M. SCHERER (1967), 'Market Structure and the Employment of Scientists and Engineers', *American Economic Review*, vol. 57, pp. 524–531; F.M. SCHERER (1967), 'Research and Development Resource Allocation under Rivalry', *Quarterly Journal of Economics*, vol. 81, p. 359. For an overview of the empirical evidence, *see* R.J. GILBERT (2006), *supra* n. 735, pp. 188–189.

740   Four-firm Concentration Ratio (C4) standard is defined as the market concentration level can be determined by the first four firms with the largest market shares in the market.

741   R.C. LEVIN, W.M. COHEN and D.C. MOWERY (1985), 'R&D Appropriability, Opportunity, and Market Structure: New Evidence on Some Schumpeterian Hypotheses', *American Economic Review*, vol. 75, pp. 20–24.

situation where competition reduces the incentives for innovation by reducing the monopoly rents.[742]

However, this finding can by no means be taken as a definite truth. Studies by some other scholars did not show that the relationship between competition and innovation follows such an 'inverted-U' non-linear pattern. For example, Nickel and Blundell found that it is a positive linear relationship,[743] whereas Salop, Dixit and Stiglitz argued that it is a negative relationship because competition will discourage innovation by reducing postentry rents.[744] With respect to the study on monopoly, a recent paper by Evans and Hylton proved the positive relationship between monopoly and innovation.[745] This finding reflects the Greenstein and Ramey's theoretical model ten years earlier, which concluded that monopolists profit more from innovation.[746]

The ambiguity of the economic evidence lies in the simple fact that empirical studies on competition and innovation often focus on a particular industry and rely on the particular characteristics of the market and the technological conditions.[747] For example, Gilbert argued, Schumpeter's view could be justified when the intellectual property rights are nonexclusive, in which case competition in R&D will reduce the value of innovation. However, even if Arrow's conclusion could be applied to the situation where intellectual property rights are exclusive, his arguments should be treated with caution for product innovation, in particular when products are differentiated and when product innovation will change the ability to discriminate among consumers. The reason is that the 'replacement effects' for product innovation are less obvious than for process innovation.[748] In recent years, a new methodology called experimental

---

[742] See P. AGHION, N. BLOOM, R. BLUNDELL, R. GRIFFITH and P. HOWITT (2005), 'Competition and Innovation: An Inverted-U Relationship', *Quarterly Journal of Economics*, vol. 120, no. 2, p. 720.

[743] For example, S. NICKELL (1996), 'Competition and Corporate Performance', *Journal of Political Economy*, pp. 724–746; R. BLUNDELL, R. GRIFFITH and J. VAN REENEN (1999), 'Market Share, Market Value and Innovation in a Panel of British Manufacturing Firms', *Review of Economic Studies*, pp. 529–554; cited by P. AGHION *et al.* (2005), *supra* n. 742, p. 703.

[744] S. SALOP (1977), 'The Noisy Monopolist: Imperfect Information, Price Dispersion, and Price Discrimination', *Review of Economic Studies*, vol. 44, no. 3, pp. 393–406; A. DIXIT and J. STIGLITZ (1977), 'Monopolistic Competition and Optimum Product Diversity', *American Economic Review*, vol. 67, no. 3, pp. 297–308, cited by P. AGHION *et al.* (2005), *supra* n. 742, p. 711.

[745] D.S. EVANS and K.N. HYLTON (2008), 'The Lawful Acquisition and Exercise of Monopoly Power and Its Implications for the Objectives of Antitrust', *Competition Policy International*, vol. 4, no. 2, pp. 203–241.

[746] S. GREENSTEIN and G. RAMEY (1998), 'Market Structure, Innovation and Vertical Product Differentiation', *International Journal of Industrial Organization*, vol. 16, pp. 285–311.

[747] The indeterminacy problem of economic evidence, however, should be dealt with carefully. The contradicting results from empirical tests does not lead to a conclusion of economic analysis is of little use – as Gilbert said: 'It is not that we don't have a model of market structure and R &D, but rather that we have many models and it is important to know which model is appropriate for each market context.' R.J. GILBERT (2006), *supra* n. 735, p. 165.

[748] R.J. GILBERT (2006), *supra* n. 735, p. 162, p. 167.

economics has been applied in order to assess the impact of innovation on competition in a direct manner.[749]

In merger enforcement, innovation effects have been incorporated as an important factor when the merger decisions are issued. For example, in the US, between 1990 and 1994, among the total 135 mergers challenged by the DOJ and the FTC, only 4 cases were considered to concern 'innovation effects', accounting for 3 percent. This number increased between 1995 and 1999, when the cases challenged for the reason of 'innovation effects' represented 18 percent of the total merger cases.[750] From 2000 to 2003, this number increased to 38 percent.[751] In Europe, Magdalena Laskowska's research shows that among the 155 merger decisions taken by the European Commission from 1989 to 2008, during the phase-II in-depth investigation, innovation played a relatively important role in 23 decisions, and in 29 decisions the Commission briefly mentioned innovation when assessing the competitive effects.[752]

Although there is no doubt that innovation should be considered as a factor in the merger assessment, it is still not clear how antitrust law should be adjusted according to the economic effects on innovation. The first unsolved issue is whether antitrust law should be modified to have innovation as a goal because, as Markham put it, '[e]ven if all could agree with this general conclusion, however, it is not clear that this would argue for a significant reorientation of antitrust policy goals or modification of the present standards for attaining them.'[753] The second issue is whether the view that monopolists are more incentivized to innovate would justify a lenient enforcement of antitrust laws, as the conduct of charging monopoly prices might be justified by the arguments of 'taking risks to produce innovation and other efficiencies'.[754] By contrast, a more

---

[749]   S.E. ØSTBYE and M.R. ROELOFS (2013), 'The Competition-Innovation Debate: Is R&D Cooperation the Answer?', *Economics of Innovation and New Technology*, vol. 22, no. 2, pp. 153–176; Østbye and Roelofs list literature on experimental economics which examine the relationship between competition and innovation. For example, D. DARAI, D. SACCO and SCHMUTZLER (2010), 'Competition and Innovation: An Experimental Investigation', *Experimental Economics*, vol. 13, pp. 439–460; D. SACCO and A. SCHMUTZLER (2011), 'Is There a U-Shaped Relation between Competition and Investment?', *International Journal of Industrial Organization*, vol. 29, pp. 65–73; F. SØRENSEN, J. MATTSSON and J. SUNDBO (2010), 'Experimental Methods in Innovation Research', *Research Policy*, vol. 39, pp. 313–322.
[750]   R.J. GILBERT (2006), 'Competition and Innovation', in W.D. COLLINS (ed.) *Issues in Competition Law and Policy*, American Bar Association Antitrust Section, Chapter 26, p. 2.
[751]   R.J. GILBERT (2006), *supra* n. 735, p. 160.
[752]   M. LASKOWSKA (2010), 'Dynamic Efficiencies and Technological Progress in EC Merger Control', available at <http://works.bepress.com/magdalena_laskowska/1> and <http://papers.ssrn.com/sol3/papers.cfm?abstract_id=2336956>, p. 3.
[753]   J.W. MARKHAM (1974), 'Concentration: A Stimulus or Retardant to Innovation?' in H.J. GOLDSCHMID and H.M. MANN (eds.), *Industrial Concentration: The New Learning*, Little Brown & Co., p. 268, cited by D.H. GINSBURG (1979), 'Antitrust, Uncertainty and Technological Innovation', *The Antitrust Bulletin*, vol. 24, p. 661.
[754]   This argument was made by Thomas Barnett, the Assistant Attorney General at the Department of Justice Antitrust Division in 2008. T.O. BARNETT (2008), 'Maximizing

active enforcement of antitrust law would be conducted if economic theories show the opposite, as Arrow proves that innovation may come from the smaller firms. In this case, it is more likely that small firms would cooperate in innovating new technologies whereas monopolists often act unilaterally.[755]

2.4. CONFLICTS BETWEEN ALLOCATIVE, DYNAMIC AND PRODUCTIVE EFFICIENCIES

Although the goals of promoting allocative efficiency, productive efficiency and dynamic efficiency are interconnected,[756] the conflicts between these goals should not be underestimated. To begin with, the goal of achieving allocative efficiency and productive efficiency are not always consistent. The first tension between these two goals is that in contrast to allocative efficiency, productive efficiency does not meet the Pareto Improvement, because less efficient firms are driven out of business by more efficient firms, being that can produce at a lower cost.[757] Therefore, the less efficient suppliers are made worse off. The second tension is demonstrated by the Williamson tradeoff.[758] The Williamson tradeoff diagram shows that the increase of productive efficiency through mergers is at the cost of allocative inefficiency, in the form of a 'deadweight loss'.[759] When two companies merge to achieve economies of scale, productive efficiency will be satisfied, but might result in the situation where the price is above competitive levels, resulting in an allocative inefficiency.[760]

The conflict between the view of dynamic efficiency and allocative efficiency not only refers to the process of innovation but is also applied to other general concepts, such as 'consumer preference', the meaning of which can be changed over time.[761] The tradeoff between the short-term effects on allocative efficiency, for example, the reduction of price, and the long-term dynamic efficiency gains generated by the positive effects on innovation, leads to a more difficult discussion, that is, to what extent competition should be viewed as a 'process' rather than the 'static outcome'.[762] In fact, through dynamic interaction of

---

Welfare through Technological Innovation', *George Mason Law Review*, vol. 15, p. 1191, 1291 However, his argument might be biased. See criticism by J.B. BAKER (2008), '"Dynamic Competition" Does not Excuse Monopolization', <http://papers.ssrn.com/sol3/papers.cfm?abstract_id=1285223>, p. 3.

[755] H. HOVENKAMP (2012), *supra* n. 734, p. 9.
[756] A. LINDSAY, *The EC Merger Regulation: Substantive Issues*, Sweet & Maxwell 2006, p. 9.
[757] R. VAN DEN BERGH (2006), *supra* n. 18, p. 82.
[758] The Williamson Tradeoff will be presented in detail in the next section 3.2.
[759] W. KERBER (2009), *supra* n. 724, p. 97.
[760] R. VAN DEN BERGH and P.D. CAMESASCA (2006), *supra* n. 18, p. 5.
[761] W. KERBER (2009), *supra* n. 724, p. 100.
[762] D. HAY (2011), 'The Assessment: Competition Policy', *Oxford Review of Economic Policy*, vol. 9, no. 2, p. 3.

innovation, new information and opportunities, a market equilibrium is never achieved. Monopoly profits should be regarded as the reward for innovators and can always been taken by new entries. It results in a more general debate on antitrust goals, that is, whether the antitrust law should focus on the static level of efficiency, or should put emphasis on promoting competition.[763] Furthermore, the concept of dynamic efficiency implies that firms are engaged in a competition for developing new technology and innovation, and the losers of this competition are made worse off. Therefore, the achievement of the dynamic efficiency does not meet the Pareto Improvement either. In this point, dynamic efficiency conflicts with the goal of allocative efficiency.[764]

Given the conflicts among allocative, productive and dynamic efficiency, a practical question may arise concerning whether one type of efficiency should be prioritized in antitrust enforcement. From a theoretical perspective, Bork put allocative efficiency as the primary goal of antitrust and Chicago School scholars generally agree with this view. By contrast, Brodley argued that dynamic efficiency should be prioritized as innovation is the driving force to enhance social wealth, from which consumers will ultimately benefit.[765] Brodley's argument converged to the Schumpeterian view concerning the social benefit of innovation, as Schumpeter argued that competition for technology creates more social benefits than price competition.[766] However, in practice, product efficiency is the benchmark most often used to assess the merger effects, which is measured by its proxies such as economies of scale, price reduction, and the level of output.[767] Hovenkamp argued that antitrust law is not the right instrument to deal with the issue of innovation, given its weakness in assessing information, knowledge and preventing interest capture.[768] Interestingly, the difficulty of measuring innovative efficiency has also been acknowledged by Schumpeter himself, who perceived the process of innovation as 'unpredictable'.[769]

For Chicagoans, dynamic efficiency will be achieved automatically through the interactions between market participants, therefore it does not require an active antitrust enforcement to protect dynamic efficiency. Seeing both

---

[763] D. HAY (2011), *supra* n. 762, p. 3. HAY cited the article by S.C. LITFLECHILD, *The Fallacy of the Mixed Economy*, IEA 1986, who advocates the antitrust goal should be promoting competition.

[764] R. VAN DEN BERGH and P.D. CAMESASCA (2006), *supra* n. 18, p. 82.

[765] J.F. BRODLEY (1987), *supra* n. 324.

[766] This is based on his general theory of innovation contributes the most to economic growth. J. SCHUMPETER, *supra* n. 405, Chapters 7 and 8.

[767] For example, the US 1997 Horizontal Merger Guidelines states: 'certain types of efficiencies are more likely to be cognizable and substantial than others ... efficiencies resulting from shifting production among facilities formerly owned separately, which enable the merging firms to reduce the marginal cost of production ... those relating to research and development are potentially substantial but are generally less susceptible to verification and may be the result of anticompetitive output reductions.'

[768] H. HOVENKAMP (2012), *supra* n. 734, p. 1.

[769] J.A. SCHUMPETER, *supra* n. 405, cited by H. HOVENKAMP (2012), *supra* n. 734, p. 4.

theoretical and practical perspectives, the picture of dynamic efficiency becomes a paradox: on the one hand, economic theory has shown that innovation is the engine for social wealth; on the other hand, antitrust law as a legal instrument can hardly perform an active role. Standing between these two sides, empirical studies seems to give mixed evidence on how innovation is influenced by the market structure and the level of competition. It is still not yet clear whether large firms or small firms are the pioneers who will take the lead in the process of developing new products and promoting innovation. Moreover, recent empirical evidence has even showed that it might be impossible to avoid high concentrations.[770] Economists argue that it might be possible that in the situation where there are few firms in one market and no new firm enters this market, these firms may compete against each other in investing R&D to develop new products and to improve the quality of existing products.[771] As Williamson shows efficiencies generated from price reduction could counterbalance the presence of market power. It thus seems logical to allow an 'innovation efficiency defense' as consumers do benefit from new products. However, the evidence to support an 'innovative efficiency defense' is still far from clear.[772]

2.5. UNSOLVED ISSUES

The concept of innovation originally refers to the development of new technologies, which could reduce the production cost and enhance productive efficiency. Innovation on technologies is often driven by investment in R&D and can be assessed by performance, such as the reduction of costs and the

---

[770]   D.W. CARLTON (2004), 'Using Economics to Improve Antitrust Policy', *Columbia Business Law Review*, vol. 2004, p. 302; note that this argument was used by Microsoft in the *Microsoft* case.

[771]   D.W. CARLTON (2004), *supra* n. 770, p. 302.

[772]   D.W. CARLTON (2004), *supra* n. 770, p. 302; *see also* D.W. CARTON and R. GERTNER (2003), 'Intellectual Property, Antitrust and Strategic Behavior', *Innovation Policy and Economics*, vol. 3, p. 29. D.W. CARTON, 'Antitrust Policy Toward Mergers when Firms Innovate: Should Antitrust Recognize the Doctrine of Innovation Markets?' Testimony before the Federal Trade Commission Hearings on Global and Innovative- Based Competition, 25 October 1995, available at <www.ftc.gov/opp/global/carlton.htm>. Carton pointed out that the direction to follow 'innovation markets' might not be a wise idea. The earlier findings on 'innovation markets' suggest that mergers may negatively affect R&D competition; *see e.g.* R.J. GILBERT and S.C. SUNSHINE (1995), 'Incorporating Dynamic Efficiency Concerns in Merger Analysis: The Use of Innovation Markets', *Antitrust Law Journal*, vol. 63, p. 569. Some further discussion on this issue among economists has been triggered by the *Microsoft* case. *See e.g.* F.M. FISHER and D.L. RUBINFELD (2000), 'United States v. Microsoft: An Economic Analysis', in *Did Microsoft Harm Consumers? Two Opposing Views*, AEI-Brookings Joint Center for Regulatory Studies; R.J. GILBERT and M.L. KATZ (2001), 'An Economist's Guide to U.S. v. Microsoft', *Journal of Economic Perspectives*, vol. 15, pp. 25–44; M.D. WHINSTON (2001), 'Exclusivity and Tying in U.S. v. Microsoft: What We Know and Don't Know', *Journal of Economic Perspectives*, vol. 15, pp. 63–80.

improvement of product quality. However, economic analysis becomes complex when the concept of innovation is extended to the creation of new products. Incorporating the factor of product heterogeneity could change many results of the existing models. Although there is no dispute between economists and lawyers that increasing product variety, or, in Lande's words, 'consumer choices', will benefit consumers, it remains a difficult issue to measure it.

Notably, there are four difficult questions that remain unsolved: the first issue is how market structure (or in general 'competition') could affect innovation; the second issue is how to deal with the tradeoff between innovative efficiency and market power (which could be measured by the price increase); the third question is if there is a conflict, whether to prioritize innovative efficiency (such as enhancing product variety), or to prioritize productive efficiency (such as focusing on price reduction), or allocative efficiency; and the fourth question is whether antitrust law can be used as an instrument to specifically promote innovation. As far as the merger enforcement is concerned, the remaining unsolved issue for policy makers and lawyers is whether promoting innovation should be the goal of antitrust policy, and in this respect how the antitrust policy can be applied together with other economic regulations on patents and IP law. For economists, it is still a difficult task to evaluate the R&D efficiencies. When a merger is designed to generate innovation, it is still a challenging issue for economists to seek a solution to evaluate the potential efficiency gain, and to tradeoff the potential benefits generated from innovation with the short-term price increase.[773]

3.   ECONOMIC ANALYSIS OF MERGER EFFECTS

3.1.   ECONOMIC EFFECTS OF MERGERS

Mergers between competing firms will change the market structure by increasing the level of concentrations. The economic effects of mergers can be divided into three scenarios.[774] The first situation is when such increase in concentration is below a certain threshold, and the anticompetitive effects are not great enough to attract the attention of antitrust authorities. In this situation, this concentration does not need to be investigated by the antitrust authorities. This is also defined as the 'safe harbor' under the US Merger Guidelines.

The second situation is when the merger increases market concentration, but the merger-specific efficiencies are sufficient to drive down post-merger prices for consumers; in this case the efficiency gains achieved by the post-merger firms

---

[773]   D.W. CARLTON (2004), *supra* n. 770, p. 302.
[774]   The analysis of these three situations is based on R. D. BLAIR and J.S. HAYNES (2011), *supra* n. 505, pp. 60–63.

can be 'passed-through' to consumers. Under a consumer welfare standard, mergers under this situation should not be prohibited because the increase of market power can be offset by the reduction of prices. The consumers will benefit from the lower price and the increased output. In the 2010 US Merger Guidelines, this 'pass-through' requirement for merger-specific efficiencies has been clearly mentioned under Section 10.

The most difficult scenario is the last one. After the merger, the post-merger price for consumers is increased due to the increase of market concentration; however, the merger reduces the costs for production and distribution, and the merger achieves significant productive efficiencies. In this situation, the antitrust authority has to make a difficult tradeoff to assess the welfare effects on the society between the productive efficiencies and the allocative inefficiencies. This tradeoff is described by Williamson in 1968. Under a consumer welfare standard, this type of merger should be prohibited because consumers will suffer a welfare loss due to the increased prices. The 'pass-through' requirement for merger-specific efficiencies is not met. However, under a total welfare standard, the answer is not straightforward, because the efficiency gain has to be weighed against the welfare loss. If the result of this balance is a surplus, the merger should be allowed.

3.2. THE WILLIAMSON TRADEOFF

In his famous diagram, Oliver Williamson described the third situation in merger assessment. He claimed that decisions on mergers should be based on the tradeoff between the costs and the benefits of a merger.

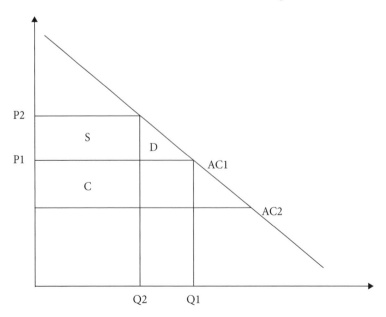

The Williamson tradeoff can be illustrated by the graph above. Before the merger, in a competitive market, the competitive price (P1) equals to the average cost as well as the marginal cost (AC1 = MC1). The corresponding quantity level is Q1. After the merger, the average cost and the marginal cost of the firm are driven down (AC2 = MC2). Given the increased market power, the merged firm is able to lift the price level to P2, resulting in a reduction in output Q2. The effects of the merger can be summarized by three areas showed on the graph: S indicates the wealth transfer from consumers to producers; it shows the distributive effects of the merger. The triangle D shows the deadweight loss caused by the merger, which is defined as allocative inefficiency in economic terms. The rectangle C is the productive efficiency that the merger creates, and it marks the gains to producers due to the cost saving. Williamson argues that when the rectangle C is larger than the triangle D, the net effects of the merger is positive, and the merger should be allowed under the social welfare goal. The economic justification for this judgment is the Kaldor-Hicks efficiency, which describes that the outcome is desirable when the winners (the producer) could potentially compensate the losers (the consumer).[775]

Based on the analysis above, Williamson focuses on the welfare effects of mergers according to a total welfare standard. Williamson separated the welfare effects on consumers to a 'partial equilibrium approach'. Under the partial equilibrium approach, the cost-savings (marked by the rectangle C) indicates the resources that the merged firm can be saved to produce this product, and if these resources are used to produce products in other markets, consumers will benefit from this merger.

3.3. IMPACT ON THE CHOICE OF WELFARE STANDARDS

The Williamson model presents the necessary tradeoff between the costs and the benefits of a merger. This model is the starting point to understand why different policy goals may lead to different decisions on mergers. As Bork put it, '[t]he Williamson tradeoff may be used to illustrate all antitrust issues.' Merger control policy evaluates the effects of a merger and makes a trade-off between the potential market power increase and the efficiency gains. Williamson also admitted that it is not easy to make the tradeoff between the welfare gains of producers and consumers,[776] although he agreed that the goal of antitrust enforcement should be maximizing the overall efficiency.[777]

---

[775] R.D. BLAIR and J.S. HAYNES (2011), *supra* n. 505, p. 62.

[776] '[F]or some products, however, the interests of users might warrant greater weight than those of sellers, for other products, such as products produced by disadvantaged minorities and sold to very rich … a reversal might be indicated', cited by A.A. FISHER and R.H. LANDE (1983), *supra* n. 707, pp. 1594, 1631.

[777] A.A. FISHER and R.H. LANDE (1983), *supra* n. 707, pp. 1594, 1631.

The consumer welfare standard and the total welfare standard are two types of welfare goals. It indicates that a merger will only be prohibited when there is a welfare loss after the merger. The consumer welfare goal only focuses on the welfare on consumers. As discussed in the previous chapter, defining consumers is not an easy task. In practice, two ways of applying the consumer welfare standard in merger cases have been discussed.[778] One way is to examine the merger effects in *each* market which will be potentially affected by the merger. A merger will only be allowed if consumers in *each* market are not made worse off. This is called the 'actual Pareto' principle under the consumer welfare standard.[779] This way treats consumers in each market as a group, and investigates the welfare of these groups in the individual affected market. It does not guarantee that every single consumer is made better off.[780] The other way is to treat all consumers in all markets as one collective group. This approach indicates that even if some consumers suffer a loss in one market, as long as the aggregate consumer welfare in all markets is positive, the merger should be allowed. This approach is called the 'potential Pareto' principle under the consumer welfare standard.[781]

Industrial economics scholars claim that consumer welfare should be preferred in merger assessments, especially in large, complex economies, because firms have a superior information advantage, lobbying advantage and the merger selection advantages.[782] Since firms have superior information, efficiency claims made by the firms might be exaggerated.[783] In addition, the effects of price increase are much more dispersed among consumers than for producers.[784] For one unit price increase, the individual consumer's loss is often not large enough for consumers to gather as a group and use their aggregate power to defend.[785] By contrast, producers often benefit substantially from the price increase, in particular when the number of producers for certain product is limited. Therefore, producers are more incentivized to lobby the government to implement regulations, such as restraining foreign competition, with a result of price increase.[786] For this reason, economists argue that focusing on consumer surplus would balance the lobbying powers between consumers and

---

[778]   K. HEYER (2006), 'Welfare Standards and Merger Analysis: Why not the Best?', *Economic Analysis Group Discussion Paper, EAG 06–8*, p. 2.

[779]   K. HEYER (2006), *supra* n. 778, p. 2.

[780]   K. HEYER (2006), *supra* n. 778, p. 2.

[781]   K. HEYER (2006), *supra* n. 778, p. 2.

[782]   LYONS, B.R. (2004), 'Reform of European Merger Policy', *Review of International Economics*, vol. 12, no. 2, p. 252; B.R. LYONS (2002), 'Could politicians be more right than economists? A theory of merger policy', *Centre for Competition and Regulation, UEA, Working Paper No. 02–01*.

[783]   D. BESANKO and D. SPULBER (1993), 'Contested Mergers and Equilibrium Antitrust Policy', *Journal of Law, Economics and Organization*, vol. 9, no. 1, pp. 1–29.

[784]   M. MOTTA (2004), *supra* n. 507, p. 20.

[785]   M. MOTTA (2004), *supra* n. 507, p. 20.

[786]   M. MOTTA (2004), *supra* n. 507, p. 20.

producers,[787] and in this way it might reduce the cost of lobbying by merged firms.[788] From a legal perspective, a major debate during the revision of the 1997 US Merger Guidelines was the 'pass-on' requirement.[789] Under this requirement, efficiency gains that created by the merger will not be taken into account unless such efficiencies can be 'passed-on' to consumers, for example, through lower prices. The 'pass-on' requirement reflects a clear consumer welfare concern in merger assessment.

4. INTEGRATING EFFICIENCY GOALS IN THE US MERGER CONTROL POLICY

4.1. INTRODUCTION

Merger policy in the US is based on section 7 of the Clayton Act,[790] which was adopted in 1914. The Clayton Act was amended by the Robinson-Patman Act in 1936 (on price discrimination), the Celler-Kefauver Act in 1950[791] (covering asset transactions in cross-ownership merger prohibition), and the Hart-Scott-Rodino Act in 1976 (giving the DOJ and the FTC the authority to review all the mergers above a certain size threshold).[792] Section 7 of the Clayton Act states that the acquisition which 'may be substantially to lessen competition, or to tend to create a monopoly', should not be allowed. This text was formulated in a prophylactic manner which indicates that mergers will be assessed ex ante.[793] The anti-competitive effects can be assessed by comparing the market structure before and after the merger.[794] The US courts followed this basic view of evaluating merger effects by assessing the market structure.

In general, little reference to efficiency arguments can be found in the Congressional debates for the enactment of section 7 of the Clayton Act.[795] The study on the legislative intent of the Clayton Act tends to show that the primary concern of this merger rule is to prevent the concentration of economic power, as well as to deal with the distributive effects between monopolists and consumers.[796] It was a political consensus that concentrated economic power

---

[787] M. MOTTA (2004), *supra* n. 507, p. 20.

[788] D. NEVEN and L.H. ROLLER (2000), 'Consumer surplus versus welfare standard in a political economy model of merger control', *WZB Working Paper FS IV 00–15*.

[789] W. KOLASKY and A. DICK (2003), *supra* n. 697, p. 230.

[790] Clayton Act §7, 15 U.S.C §18.

[791] Celler-Kefauver Act of 1950.

[792] Federal Trade Commission Act, Ch. 311, Article 1, 38 Stat. 717 (1914), codified as amended at 15 U.S.C. §§41–58.

[793] R. D. BLAIR and J.S. HAYNES (2011), *supra* n. 505, p. 59.

[794] R. D. BLAIR and J.S. HAYNES (2011), *supra* n. 505, p. 59.

[795] M.N. BERRY (1996), *supra* n. 312, p. 521.

[796] M.N. BERRY (1996), *supra* n. 312, p. 520.

would impede individual freedom, and might result in totalitarianism which is characterized by a strong government control.[797] Pitofsky argued that Congress saw the merger trend as a dynamic process, which was more likely to create a concentration of power. This trend was inconsistent with the democratic values which were seen as the fundamental political goals.[798] According to Fisher and Lande, the legislators were not aware of the potential conflicts between the goals of protecting consumers and enhancing corporate efficiency.[799] Hence, Congress did not mention the tradeoff between the market power and efficiencies.[800] Moreover, both the legislative history and the language of the statute could provide evidence regarding the issue of allocative inefficiency, which could provide guidance to the judges.[801] As a result, the judicial interpretation on efficiencies has evolved and still continues today.[802]

Between 1968 and 2010, the FTC and the DOJ have issued five versions of Horizontal Merger Guidelines. The first guidelines, which were issued in 1968, acknowledged that mergers would generate efficiency gains. However, under the 1968 Horizontal Merger Guidelines, the application of efficiency arguments in merger assessment was highly restrictive. Efficiency arguments could only be taken into account in 'exceptional' cases,[803] and an efficiency defense was not allowed. After the emergence of the Harvard School and the Chicago School, attention was specially given to the efficiency goals.

The fundamental change on the view of the efficiency goal led to a dramatic revision of the section on efficiency under the merger guidelines. The Assistant Attorney General Paul McGrath completely rewrote the efficiency section and the drafting of the 1984 Horizontal Merger Guidelines was the landmark under which the efficiency claims were taken as an integral part of merger analysis. The structural approach of balancing efficiency gains against anticompetitive harm was replaced by an 'overall assessment' of the merger, through which process efficiency was taken as the decisional power for the judgment. Marked by the introductory paragraph of the 1984 Horizontal Merger Guidelines, the treatment of efficiency was upgraded from 'not a bad thing' to 'the primary benefit of mergers'.[804]

---

[797]   R. PITOFSKY (1979), *supra* n. 459, p. 1064.

[798]   R. PITOFSKY (1979), *supra* n. 459, p. 1071.

[799]   A.A. FISHER and L.H. LANDE (1983), *supra* n. 707, p. 1588.

[800]   A.A. FISHER and L.H. LANDE (1983), *supra* n. 707, p. 1588.

[801]   A.A. FISHER and L.H. LANDE (1983), *supra* n. 707, p. 1589.

[802]   A.A. FISHER and L.H. LANDE (1983), *supra* n. 707, p. 1588.

[803]   Article 10 of this Guideline states that there are three reasons: (1) the Department's adherence to the standards will usually result in no challenge being made to mergers of the kind most likely to involve companies operating significantly below the size necessary to achieve significant economies of scale; (2) where substantial economies are potentially available to a firm, they can normally be realized through internal expansion; and (3) there usually are severe difficulties in accurately establishing the existence and magnitude of economies claim for a merger.

[804]   1984 Horizontal Merger Guidelines §3.5 'The primary benefit of mergers to the economy is their efficiency-enhancing potential, which can increase the competitiveness of firms and result in lower prices to consumers'.

4.2. ACADEMIC DEBATE

4.2.1. Concerns of Legal Uncertainties

When Bork raised the argument of prioritizing efficiency as the antitrust goal, he considered that it would not be necessary to measure efficiency.[805] Bork argued that under the efficiency goal, it could be possible to establish criteria in an 'objective' way, such as setting a level of market share, and estimating which transaction is 'likely' to create efficiency.[806] However, together with other Chicago School scholars, he rejected the application of an efficiency defense in merger decisions for the reason of measurement difficulties.[807] In particular, Bork argued that to quantify efficiencies was 'beyond the capacities of the law',[808] and even though efficiencies can be calculated, it will be 'utterly insolvable' to compare efficiency gains with the potential increase in market power.[809] Similarly, Posner claimed that to measure efficiencies would be 'an intractable subject for litigation'.[810] Bork and Posner both agreed that it remains a difficult task to prove the degree of cost savings generated through a merger.[811] It might also go beyond the capacity of the courts to balance the efficiency gains against the potential anticompetitive harm.[812] For these reasons, Bork and Posner concluded that efficiency defense should not be applied on a case-by-case basis.[813]

Berry listed several measurement problems which can make the efficiency claims highly vulnerable.[814] For example, the source of information with respect to the claimed efficiencies might be controlled by the merging firms. Firms may have superior information with regard to efficiency gains than the antitrust authority.[815] The costs of collecting and transmitting such information must be

---

[805] See R.H. BORK (1965), 'Contrasts in Antitrust Theory: 1', *Columbia Law Review*, vol. 65, no. 3, p. 411 ('Economic analysis does away with the need to measure efficiencies directly. It is enough to know in what sorts of transactions efficiencies are likely to be present and in what sorts anticompetitive effects are likely to be present.').

[806] See R.H. BORK (1965), *supra* n. 805, p. 411 ('The law can then develop objective criteria, such as market shares, to divide transactions likely to be predominantly favorable to consumers through the creation of efficiency from those likely to be predominantly injurious through their suppression of competition.').

[807] M.N. BERRY (1996), *supra* n. 312, p. 542.

[808] R.H. BORK (1978), *supra* n. 19, pp. 126–127, cited by W. KOLASKY and A. DICK (2003), *supra* n. 697, p. 217.

[809] R.H. BORK (1978), *supra* n. 19.

[810] R.A. POSNER (1976), *supra* n. 703, p. 112, cited by M.N. BERRY (1996), *supra* n. 312, p. 542.

[811] J.B. BAKER (2004), 'Efficiencies and High Concentration: Heinz Proposes to Acquire Beech-Nut', in J.E. KWOKA and L.J. WHITE, *The Antitrust Revolution, Economics, Competition and Policy*, 4th ed., Oxford University Press, p. 151.

[812] J.B. BAKER (2004), *supra* n. 811, p. 151.

[813] J.B. BAKER (2004), *supra* n. 811, p. 151.

[814] M.N. BERRY (1996), *supra* n. 312, p. 543.

[815] D. YAO and T.N. DAHDOUH (1993), 'Information Problems in Merger Decision Making and Their Impact on Development of an Efficiencies Defense', *Antitrust Law Journal*, vol. 61, pp. 23–45.

taken into account.[816] Moreover, the efficiency claims are often made before the transaction, and are based on the prediction of future industry performances.[817] Giving weight to the efficiency gains of the mergers and incorporating an efficiency defense in merger control policy may trigger the concern on potential rent-seeking behavior of the firms,[818] which is conceived as a form of social cost. Fisher and Lande defined the costs generated from business uncertainty and excessive litigation as the 'Type 3 error', which will be increased dramatically by applying an efficiency defense.[819] Brodley pointed out the difficulties in measuring efficiency and argued that compared with allocative efficiency and dynamic efficiency, productive efficiencies are the most assessable in antitrust analysis, and it is the reason why in most situations only production-type efficiencies were taken for measuring the competitive effects.[820]

4.2.2. Economic Techniques to Measure Efficiencies

There are certain efficiencies that cannot be generated without a merger, and they are defined as 'merger-specific efficiencies'. Efficiencies created by a merger can be evaluated directly or indirectly. Indirect assessment of merger efficiencies is to estimate how likely a merger will generate efficiencies in the future. The economic techniques that can be applied include the study of the relationship between market structure and the economies of scale and the study of the relationship between the level of market concentration and profitability.[821] Direct assessment of efficiencies refers to the economic techniques which can be applied to quantify the extent to which a merger has indeed generated potential efficiencies.[822] Merging firms will be compared with non-merging firms with respect to their accounting data and the performance of stock market.[823] In recent years, the difficulties of measuring efficiency have been mitigated by the development of new economic techniques, in particular, by applying the method of merger simulation.

Merger simulation refers to an econometrics technique which can precisely predict the price increase after the merger.[824] It takes a direct approach to predict the changes of prices after the merger. Based on this technique, it is possible to

---

[816] J.N.M. Lagerloef and P. Heidhues (2005), 'On the Desirability of an Efficiency Defense in Merger Control', *International Journal of Industrial Organization*, vol. 23, p. 805.
[817] M.N. Berry (1996), *supra* n. 312, p. 543.
[818] F.M. Fisher (1987), 'Horizontal Mergers: triage and treatment', *Journal of Economic Perspectives*, vol. 1, pp. 23–40; p. 39.
[819] A.A. Fisher and R.H. Lande (1983), *supra* n. 707, p. 1586.
[820] Brodley argues that even productive efficiencies can only be measured ex post. None of these three types of efficiencies can be measured ex ante. J.F. Brodley (1987), *supra* n. 324, pp. 1029, 1030.
[821] A.A. Fisher and R.H. Lande (1983), *supra* n. 707, p. 1605.
[822] A.A. Fisher and R.H. Lande (1983), *supra* n. 707, p. 1605.
[823] A.A. Fisher and R.H. Lande (1983), *supra* n. 707, p. 1605.
[824] C.W. Conrath and N.A. Widnell (1999), 'Efficiency Claims in Merger Analysis: Hostility or Humility?', *George Mason Law Review*, vol. 7, no. 3, p. 687.

calculate both the potential efficiency gains as well as the potential harm that a merger will create.[825] Merger simulation provides a practical way to calculate efficiencies, and by applying this technique, the competitive effects of a merger can be measured directly: if the results show that efficiency gain is larger than the harm, the merger should be permitted,[826] and market definition may not matter at all.[827]

The development of merger simulation techniques makes it possible to measure competitive effects in a quantitative manner. In the 1960s, the adverse competitive effects of a merger were determined by calculating the number of firms, as well as their market share.[828] The understanding of the efficiency claims was bounded by the development of economic theories and economic techniques. Courts today are more capable than courts in the 1960s of dealing with the calculation of the benefits and the costs of a merger.[829] Therefore, the academic debate on economic theories and techniques of efficiency may facilitate the process of integrating the efficiency goal in merger assessment.

4.2.3.   Efficiency Defense

In their influential book *Antitrust Law: An Analysis of Antitrust Principles and Their Application*, Areeda and Turner gave a clarification on the meaning of 'efficiency defense'. The terminology does not refer to the fact that efficiencies can be used to defend an illegal merger. Instead, this 'defense' refers to applying efficiency claims as the first order inference and to take efficiency as a portion of evidence in deciding whether a merger is presumed to reduce competition. Therefore, 'efficiency defense' refers to a 'defense to a prima facie case'.[830]

4.3.   MERGER GUIDELINES

4.3.1.   1968 Horizontal Merger Guidelines

Under the 1968 Horizontal Merger Guidelines,[831] the determinant factor to be applied to decide whether a merger should be prohibited was the level of market concentration, which could be measured by the market share.[832] Market power

---

[825]   C.W. Conrath and N.A. Widnell (1999), *supra* n. 824, p. 687.
[826]   C.W. Conrath and N.A. Widnell (1999), *supra* n. 824, p. 687.
[827]   M. Walker (2005), 'The Potential for Significant Inaccuracies in Merger Simulation Models', *Journal of Competition Law and Economics*, vol. 1, no. 3, p. 477.
[828]   C.W. Conrath and N.A. Widnell (1999), *supra* n. 824, p. 693.
[829]   C.W. Conrath and N.A. Widnell (1999), *supra* n. 824, p. 693.
[830]   P.A. Areeda and D.F. Turner, *Antitrust Law: An Analysis of Antitrust Principles and Their Application*, Little Brown 1980, pp. 153–154, cited by W. Kolasky and A. Dick (2003), *supra* n. 697, p. 216.
[831]   US Department of Justice, 1968 Merger Guidelines.
[832]   S.M. Edwards, *et al.* (1981), 'Proposed Revisions of the Justice Department's Merger Guidelines', *Columbia Law Review*, vol. 81, no. 8, p. 1545.

was assessed according to the benchmark of the market structure, with the theoretical justifications provided by the 'Structure-Conduct-Performance' framework developed by the Harvard School.[833] A market is 'highly concentrated' when the market share of the four largest firms is greater than or equal to 75 percent. A market with the four largest firms' market share being less than 75 percent is defined as 'less highly concentrated'.[834] Although efficiencies were accepted as a positive factor, efficiency claims could only be considered in 'exceptional circumstances'.[835] Under the 1968 Horizontal Merger Guidelines, efficiency was put in limited use, and the Department of Justice argued that one of the major difficulties of recognizing efficiency was the measurement problem.[836]

4.3.2.   1982 Horizontal Merger Guidelines

The 1982 Horizontal Merger Guidelines moved forward to incorporate economic analysis in the enforcement of merger policy, and the influence of the populist social and political values on merger analysis has been mitigated.[837] In particular, under the 1982 Guidelines, the economic goals were given priority over other social and political values.[838] The most appealing contribution of the 1982 Guidelines was that efficiency was recognized as an important factor to counterbalance the market concentration. In the 1982 Horizontal Merger Guidelines, market concentration was no longer considered as the only, decisive factor in merger assessment.[839] This guideline states that the harmful anticompetitive effects that were generated through a merger can be balanced with several other factors, including the conditions for future entry, and the market features.[840]

By taking the development of the modern economic theories into account, the 1982 Horizontal Merger Guidelines made a few important changes to the old 1968 Merger Guidelines. Economic tests were widely applied to replace the

---

[833]   US Department of Justice, 1968 Merger Guidelines, para 2: 'Market Structure is the focus of the Department's merger policy chiefly because the conduct of the individual firms in a market tends to be controlled by the structure of that market.'

[834]   US Department of Justice, 1968 Merger Guidelines, paras 5–6.

[835]   US Department of Justice, 1968 Merger Guidelines §10: 'Unless there are exceptional circumstances, the Department will not accept as justification for an acquisition normally subject to challenge under its horizontal merger standards the claim that the merger will produce economies.'

[836]   US Department of Justice, 1968 Merger Guidelines §10: '[a]mong other reasons, (1) The Department's adherence to the standards will usually result in no challenge being made to mergers of the kind most likely to involve companies operating significantly below the size necessary to achieve significant economies of scale; (2) where substantial economies are potentially available to a firm, they can normally be realized through internal expansion; and (3) there usually are severe difficulties in accurately establishing the existence and magnitude of economies claims for a merger.'

[837]   D.I. BAKER and W. BLUMENTHAL (1983), *supra* n. 326, p. 317.

[838]   D.I. BAKER and W. BLUMENTHAL (1983), *supra* n. 326, p. 315; N.B. COHEN and C.A. SULLIVAN (1983), 'The Herfindahl-Hirschman Index and the New Antitrust Merger Guidelines: Concentrating on Concentration', *Texas Law Review*, vol. 62, p. 457.

[839]   J.B. BAKER and C. SHAPIRO (2007), *supra* n. 698, p. 4.

[840]   J.B. BAKER and C. SHAPIRO (2007), *supra* n. 698, p. 4.

subjective judgment.[841] Two major tests were for the first time introduced – one is the Hypothetical Monopolist Test (HMT), which is used for defining the relevant market, and the other is the Herfindahl-Hirschman Index ('HHI')[842] which replaces the old Concentration Ratio ('CR4' or 'CR8') and is used as the thresholds for measuring the market concentration level.[843] In addition, the 1982 Merger Guidelines also incorporated the SSNIP (small but significant and non-transitory increase in price) test for defining the product and the geographic market.

The 1982 Horizontal Guidelines kept most of the efficiency chapter of the 1968 Guidelines unchanged. Efficiency considerations under the 1982 Merger Guidelines include scale economies, integration of production facilities, and multi-plant operations. However, efficiency claims were put in use with cautious. Efficiency arguments can only be applied in 'extraordinary cases', and the efficiency gains of the merger cannot be achieved through other types of merger which would bring less competitive harm, or through internal expansions. Moreover, the cost savings as a result of scale economies must be 'substantial' and the evidence of these savings must be 'clear and convincing'.[844] Kolasky and Dick gave two reasons for the strict application of efficiency claims in the 1982 Guidelines:[845] the first reason was that the thresholds for merger investigations have been set high enough. Therefore, in most cases, firms will be allowed to achieve efficiencies by not having interfered from the DOJ.[846] The second reason was that efficiencies are difficult to prove.[847]

The drafting of the 1982 Horizontal Merger Guidelines was under the leadership of Bill Baxter, and it has reflected the Chicagoan view in the late 1960s to 1970s, which rejected the use of the efficiency claims as a defense due to the difficulties in measurement.[848] As Posner and Bork argued, by taking efficiencies into account, merger rules should be applied to a limited number of transactions,

---

[841] D.I. BAKER and W. BLUMENTHAL (1983), *supra* n. 326, p. 317.
[842] HHI was developed by A.O. Hirschman and O.C. Herfindahl. *See* A.O. HIRSCHMAN, *National Power and the Structure of Foreign Trade*, University of California Press 1945; A.O. HIRSCHMAN (1964), 'The Paternity of an Index', *American Economic Review*, vol. 54, pp. 761–762. *See also* the technical note by S.A. RHOADES (1993), 'The Herfindahl-Hirschman Index', *Federal Reserve Bulletin*, vol. 79, no. 3, pp. 188–189.
[843] According to 1982 Horizontal Merger Guidelines, markets with post-merger HHI below 1000 are defined as 'unconcentrated', markets with post-merger HHI between 1000 and 1800 are defined as 'moderately concentrated', and markets with post-merger HHI over 1800 are defined as 'highly concentrated'. The 'safe harbor' of merger policy is that for mergers will not be likely to be challenged when they increase less than 100 of HHI in the 'unconcentrated' and 'moderately concentrated' markets, as well as increase less than 50 of HHI in the 'highly concentrated' markets. Mergers will not be challenged at all when the post-merger HHI is below 1000. *See* US Department of Justice, 1982 Merger Guidelines Section III(A). *See also* T.E. KAUPER (1983), 'The 1982 Horizontal Merger Guidelines: Of Collusion, Efficiency, and Failure', *California Law Review*, vol. 71, no. 2, p. 510.
[844] US Department of Justice, 1982 Merger Guidelines Section V(A).
[845] W. KOLASKY and A. DICK (2003), *supra* n. 697, p. 218.
[846] W. KOLASKY and A. DICK (2003), *supra* n. 697, p. 218.
[847] W. KOLASKY and A. DICK (2003), *supra* n. 697, p. 218.
[848] US Department of Justice, 1982 Merger Guidelines Section V(1): '[e]ven if the existence of efficiencies were clear, their magnitudes would be extremely difficult to determine'.

with a high level of concentration threshold, but not to apply an efficiency defense.[849] It has been argued that when the threshold of the market share is lifted up, the goal of protecting an efficient market outcome could be equally achieved.[850]

Although the situations of applying efficiency arguments have changed from in the 'exceptional circumstances' to in the 'extraordinary cases', the 1982 Merger Guidelines do not challenge the dominant use of the structural approach in merger analysis.[851] The guidelines states that for mergers in the 'modest concentrated market', it is 'more likely than not' to be challenged; for the mergers in the 'highly concentrated market', it is 'likely to be challenged', and 'except in extraordinary cases'.[852] It implies that under the 1982 Horizontal Merger Guidelines, market concentration is still the starting point and the baseline for merger assessment. Mergers that have met the concentration thresholds are still presumed to be 'anticompetitive'.[853] The primary factor in merger assessment is still the level of market concentration.[854]

4.3.3.   1984 Horizontal Merger Guidelines

The 1984 Horizontal Merger Guidelines accepted efficiencies as a positive factor, and recognized that it can be taken into consideration in the decision of whether a merger should be prohibited. It was acknowledged that the primary contribution of a concentration is the substantial increase in efficiency. A concentration will facilitate economies of scale in production as well as in services, and it will also facilitate the specialization in management, and reduce transportation costs. These will all be considered as benefits of economic efficiencies. The 1984 Guidelines deleted 'more likely than not', and only kept the words of 'likely to challenge mergers in moderate concentrated markets, depending on the analysis of entry and other factors.'[855]

4.3.4.   1992 Horizontal Merger Guidelines

The 1992 Merger Guidelines was the first time that the FTC and the DOJ issued the Horizontal Merger Guidelines jointly. In both the 1982 and 1984 Guidelines, non-structural factors have been recognized as one of the indicators; however, these guidelines did not clarify the extent to which the market characteristics, as well as the competitive effects, can be taken as a component in the merger analysis.[856] The

---

849   R.H. BORK (1978), *supra* n. 19, p. 217; R. POSNER (1976), *supra* n. 703, p. 106; cited by J.B. BAKER and C. SHAPIRO (2007), *supra* n. 698, p. 4.

850   W. KOLASKY and A. DICK (2003), *supra* n. 697, p. 218.

851   N.B. COHEN and C.A. SULLIVAN (1983), *supra* n. 838, p. 468.

852   Cited by C.A. JAMES (1993), 'Overview of the 1992 Horizontal Merger Guidelines', *Antitrust Law Journal*, vol. 61, p. 448.

853   C.A. JAMES (1993), *supra* n. 852, p. 448.

854   C.A. JAMES (1993), *supra* n. 852, p. 448.

855   C.A. JAMES (1993), *supra* n. 852, p. 448.

856   C.A. JAMES (1993), *supra* n. 852, p. 452.

1992 Guidelines further challenged the dominant role of the market concentration in merger analysis. The role of market concentration has been clarified that it serves as one component in the whole analytical framework of deciding the competitive effects of a merger.[857] The 1992 Horizontal Merger Guidelines formulated a complete analytical framework to evaluate the competitive process in the relevant market, and non-structural factors will be fully taken into account during this investigation.[858] The balance of both structural and non-structural factors will show to what extent the merger would be likely to exhibit market power.[859] In particular, efficiency as a major benefit of mergers has been recognized by the change of the opening statement.[860] The requirement of 'established by clear and convincing evidence' was eliminated. It also recognized the benefits of efficiencies that have been stated in the 1984 Horizontal Merger Guidelines.

The 1992 Merger Guidelines specified the productive efficiency in section 4.[861] The cognized efficiencies must be valid, verifiable and merger-specific.[862] In the 1992 Merger Guidelines, a concentration can no longer be considered as anticompetitive, and market concentration does not play the decisive role.[863] However, only merger-specific efficiencies will be taken into account: 'The Agency will reject claims of efficiencies if equivalent or comparable savings can reasonably be achieved by the parties through other means.'[864]

4.3.5.   1997 Horizontal Merger Guidelines

In 1995, the FTC conducted several hearings with regard to the enforcement of the antitrust law, and one of the issues raised was the question of how to integrate efficiencies in antitrust enforcement.[865] In June 1996, the FTC issued a report with the title *Anticipating the 21st Century: Competition Policy in the New High-*

---

[857]   C.A. JAMES (1993), *supra* n. 852, p. 449.

[858]   C.A. JAMES (1993), *supra* n. 852, p. 453.

[859]   C.A. JAMES (1993), *supra* n. 852, p. 453.

[860]   C.W. CONRATH and N.A. WIDNELL (1999), *supra* n. 824, p. 692 ('The primary benefit of mergers to the economy is their efficiency – enhancing potential, which can increase the competitiveness of firms and result in lower prices to consumers. Because the antitrust laws, and thus the standards of the Guidelines are designed to proscribe only mergers that present a significant danger to competition, they do not present an obstacle to most mergers. As a consequence, in the majority of cases, the Guidelines will allow firms to achieve available efficiencies through mergers without interference from the Agency.' U.S. Department of Justice and the Federal Trade Commission, 1992 Horizontal Merger Guidelines §4).

[861]   1992 Merger Guidelines §4: 'Efficiencies resulting from shifting production among facilities formerly owned separately, which enable the merging firms to reduce the marginal cost of production, are more likely to be susceptible to verification, merger-specific, and substantial, and are less likely to result from anticompetitive reductions in output.'

[862]   M.B. COATE (2005), 'Efficiencies in Merger Analysis: An Institutionalist View', *Supreme Court Economic Review*, vol. 13, p. 193.

[863]   C.A. JAMES (1993), *supra* n. 852, p. 449.

[864]   US Department of Justice and Federal Trade Commission 1992 Horizontal Merger Guidelines, §4.

[865]   T.L. GREANEY (2000), 'Not for Import: Why the EU Should not Adopt the American Efficiency Defense for Analyzing Mergers and Joint Ventures', *Saint Louis University Law Journal*, vol. 44, p. 874.

Tech Global Marketplace,[866] which gave a strong support to integrate efficiencies in the merger analysis.[867] Following this FTC Global Report, the role of efficiencies has been expanded in the 1997 Horizontal Merger Guidelines[868] jointly issued by the FTC and the DOJ.[869] A concentration will be permitted if it does not create anticompetitive effects; also efficiencies should be merger-specific and cognizable. Under the 1997 Merger Guidelines, efficiencies are taken as the reverse effort to offset the anticompetitive effects and the scope of efficiencies that could be considered has been extended to improved quality and service, or the development of new products.[870] The 1997 Guidelines recognized that concentrations will generate substantial efficiencies by better utilizing the current resources. There are three preconditions for efficiencies to be 'cognizable': efficiencies must be merger-specific; must be verifiable and must not be taken as the result of the reduction of output through the anticompetitive conduct. Moreover, the 1997 Guidelines adopted a 'sliding scale' approach in calculating the level of efficiency gains, that is, the greater the potential anticompetitive effect will be, the higher level of cognizable efficiency will be required. If the potential anticompetitive effect of a merger is 'large', the required cognizable efficiency has to be 'extraordinary great', in order to offset the potentially adverse competitive effects. One major debate concerning the 1997 Merger Guidelines was whether efficiency gains should have 'passed on' effects on consumers. It was argued that efficiency should only be taken into account when the benefits are 'passed-on' to consumers, for example, by increased output or by reduced prices.[871]

4.3.6. 2010 Horizontal Merger Guidelines

In section 10 of the 2010 Merger Guidelines,[872] the benefits of efficiencies that a merger may create not only include the reduction in price, but also include the 'improved quality, enhanced service, or new products'.[873] To be applied in

---

[866] FTC (1996), 'Anticipating the 21st Century: Competition Policy in the New High-Tech Global Marketplace', Report by Federal Trade Commission Staff, May 1996, available at <www.ftc.gov/system/files/documents/reports/anticipating-21st-century-competition-policy-new-high-tech-global-marketplace/gc_v1.pdf>.

[867] C.S. GOLDMAN, Q.C. *et al.* (2003), 'The Role of Efficiencies in Telecommunications Merger Review', *Federal Communications Law Review*, vol. 56, no. 1, p. 107.

[868] US Department of Justice and the Federal Trade Commission, 1997 Merger Guidelines, available at <www.justice.gov/atr/hmerger/11251.htm>.

[869] FTC, Hearings on Global and Innovation-Based Competition, 12 October 1995, available at <www.ftc.gov/news-events/press-releases/1995/10/federal-trade-commissions-hearings-global-and-innovation-based>.

[870] C.S. GOLDMAN, Q.C. *et al.* (2003), *supra* n. 867, p. 107.

[871] W. KOLASKY and A. DICK (2003) 'The Merger of Guidelines and the Integration of Efficiencies into Antitrust Review of Horizontal Mergers, *Antitrust Law Journal*, vol. 71, no. 1, pp. 207–251, 230.

[872] US Department of Justice and the Federal Trade Commission, 2010 Horizontal Merger Guidelines.

[873] 2010 Merger Guidelines §10: 'a primary benefit of mergers to the economy is their potential to generate significant efficiencies and thus enhance the merged firm's ability and incentive to

---

merger analysis, efficiencies must be 'cognizable' and must be only achieved by merger (merger-specific efficiencies).[874]

In general, the 2010 Merger Guidelines are based on a consumer welfare standard and the goal of protecting consumers has been implicitly mentioned in section 1.[875] Following this standard, efficiencies will be taken into account only when they meet the 'pass-through' requirement, which refers to the situation where efficiency is sufficient to prevent the post-merger price from increasing above the pre-merger level.[876] This 'pass-through' requirement has been mentioned in section 10.[877] In section 10, it is also mentioned that the extent to which efficiencies are taken into account is dependent on the level of the potential anticompetitive harm, which is referred to as the 'sliding scale principle', and if there is substantial anticompetitive harm, the level of cognizable efficiencies must be 'extraordinarily great'.[878]

4.4. JUDICIAL TREATMENT

4.4.1. Hostility toward Efficiency Claims

After the Celler-Kefauver Act, which is the amendment to the Clayton Act, was enacted in the 1960s, the Supreme Court ruled on the anticompetitive effects of a merger based on the level of the market concentration.[879] This structural approach, which puts emphasis on the market concentration and the size of the firm, was supported by the competition theories developed by the Harvard School. In the 1960s, the 'Structure-Conduct-Performance' paradigm was the

---

[874]   compete, which may result in lower prices, improved quality, enhanced service, or new products.' Cited by R.D. BLAIR and J.S. HAYNES (2011), *supra* n. 505, p. 63.

R.D. BLAIR and J.S. HAYNES (2011), *supra* n. 505, p. 59.

[875]   2010 Merger Guidelines §1: 'The unifying theme of these Guidelines is that mergers should not be permitted to create, enhance, or entrench market power or to facilitate its exercise. A merger enhances market power if it is likely to encourage one or more firms to raise price, reduce output, diminish innovation, or otherwise harm customers as a result of diminished competitive constraints or incentives.' Cited by R.D. BLAIR and J.S. HAYNES (2011), *supra* n. 505, p. 59.

[876]   R.D. BLAIR and J.S. HAYNES (2011), *supra* n. 505, p. 59.

[877]   2010 Merger Guidelines §10: 'The Agencies will not challenge a merger if cognizable efficiencies are of a character and magnitude such that the merger is not likely to be anticompetitive in any relevant market. To make the requisite determination, the Agencies consider whether cognizable efficiencies likely would be sufficient to reserve the merger's potential to harm customers in the relevant market, e.g. by preventing price increases in the market.' Cited by R.D. BLAIR and J.S. HAYNES (2011), *supra* n. 505, p. 60.

[878]   2010 Merger Guidelines §10: 'The greater the potential adverse competitive effect, the greater must be the cognizable efficiencies, and the more they must be passed through to customers. When the potential adverse competitive effect of a merger is likely to be particularly substantial, extraordinarily great cognizable efficiencies would be necessary to prevent the merger from being anticompetitive.' Cited by R.D. BLAIR and J.S. HAYNES (2011), *supra* n. 505, p. 60.

[879]   J.B. BAKER and C. SHAPIRO (2007), *supra* n. 698, p. 1.

dominant thinking among economists,[880] and this approach rejected to apply efficiency claims to counterbalance other anticompetitive effects.[881]

In the 1960s, a merger was presumed to be illegal when the combined market share was above 30 percent, in some cases even as low as 10 percent.[882] In *Brown Shoe Co. v. United States*,[883] efficiency arguments were completely rejected because it was understood that the antitrust goal of 'protecting the small business' prevailed any economic goal. Chief Justice Warren held that 'It is competition, not competitors, which the Act protects. But we cannot fail to recognize Congress' desire to promote competition through the protection of viable, small, locally owned businesses. Congress appreciated that occasional higher costs and prices might result from the maintenance of fragmented industries and markets.'[884] Therefore, the justification for prohibiting this merger was 'the trend toward vertical integration', and the Supreme Court focused on the number of competing small firms.

The Supreme Court also rejected the efficiency arguments in *United States v. Philadelphia National Bank*[885] The Supreme Court held that 'a merger the effect of which 'may be substantially to lessen competition' is not saved because, on some ultimate reckoning of social or economic debits and credits, it may be deemed beneficial.'[886] The Supreme Court also put a strong emphasis on the goal of combating market concentration. The Supreme Court believed that this structural approach is justified by economic theory, and a merger policy is to ensure the situation where there are 'many sellers, none of which has any significant market share.'[887] The Supreme Court held a deep presumption on the anticompetitive effects of a merger with increased market share,[888] and this presumption makes the goal of preventing concentrated power override the potential efficiency gains of the merger. In particular, in this case the Supreme Court did not provide evidence to identify through which mechanism the increased market share would have an anticompetitive impact on the market

---

880 J.B. BAKER and C. SHAPIRO (2007), *supra* n. 698, p. 3.
881 W. KOLASKY and A. DICK (2003), *supra* n. 697, p. 210; C.W. CONRATH and N.A. WIDNELL (1999), *supra* n. 824, p. 688.
882 R.A. SKITOL (1999), *supra* n. 25, p. 244.
883 *Brown Shoe Co., Inc. v. United States*, 370 U.S. 294, 344 (1962).
884 Cited by M.N. BERRY (1996), *supra* n. 312, p. 522.
885 *United States v. Philadelphia National Bank*, 374 U.S. 321, 363 (1963), cited by W. KOLASKY and A. DICK (2003), *supra* n. 697, p. 211.
886 Cited by W. KOLASKY and A. DICK (2003), *supra* n. 697, p. 211.
887 *United States v. Philadelphia National Bank,* 374 U.S. 321, 363 (1963), cited by J.B. BAKER and C. SHAPRIO (2007), *supra* n. 698, p. 2.
888 *United States v. Philadelphia National Bank,* 374 U.S. 321, 363 (1963): 'a merger which produces a firm controlling an undue percentage share of the relevant market, and results in a significant increase in the concentration of firms in that market is so inherently likely to lessen competition substantially that it must be enjoined in the absence of evidence clearly showing that the merger is not likely to have such anticompetitive effects.' Cited by J.B. BAKER and C. SHAPIRO (2007), *supra* n. 698, p. 2.

performance. Market concentration was treated negatively per se for its potential influence on the anticompetitive effects.[889]

The structural approach has also been applied to other merger cases in the 1960s, for example *United States v. Von's Grocery Co.*[890] and *United States v. Pabst Brewing Co.*[891] In these two cases, the efficiency goal was not taken into account, and at that time, a merger could be rejected even though the market share that it created was extremely low.[892] In the *Von's Grocery* case, after the merger, the combined market share for the two grocery chains only accounted for 7.5 percent.[893] In *United States v. Pabst Brewing Co*, after the merger, the firm held 4.49 percent of the sales.[894] In the FTC's decision in *Procter & Gamble* case[895] in 1967, the Commission argued that efficiency gains could not be 'a defense to a merger's illegality'.[896] Justice Douglas from the Supreme Court held that: 'possible economies cannot be used as a defense to illegality. Congress was aware that some mergers which lessen competition may also result in economies but it struck the balance in favor of protecting competition.'[897] These decisions can better be explained by the political goals pursued by the Supreme Court of combating the rising concentrated economic power.[898] Nevertheless, efficiency arguments were recognized in some cases. For example, in *United States v. United States Gypsum Co.*,[899] economic efficiency was mentioned as the procompetitive benefit of a merger, whereas in *Northern Pacific Railway Co. v. United States*,[900] economic efficiency was accepted as 'one of the principal goals' of antitrust law.

4.4.2. Cautiously Accepted Efficiency Claims

The role of efficiency claims starts to change in the Supreme Court decision in *United States v. General Dynamics Corp.*,[901] in 1974, in which the Supreme Court challenged the structural determinate role in merger assessment by arguing the

---

[889] D.I. BAKER and W. BLUMENTHAL (1983), *supra* n. 326, p. 316.
[890] *United States v. Von's Grocery Co.*, 384 U.S. 270 (1966).
[891] *United States v. Pabst Brewing Co.*, 384 U.S. 546 (1966).
[892] W.E. KOVACIC and C. SHAPIRO (1999), *supra* n. 319, p. 11.
[893] J.B. BAKER and C. SHAPIRO (2007), *supra* n. 698, p. 2.
[894] J.B. BAKER (2010), 'Market Concentration in the Antitrust Analysis of Horizontal Mergers', <http://papers.ssrn.com/sol3/papers.cfm?abstract_id=1092248>, p. 4.
[895] Cited by A.A. FISHER and R.H. LANDE (1983), *supra* n. 707, pp. 1593, 1594.
[896] Cited by W. KOLASKY and A. DICK (2003), *supra* n. 697, p. 211.
[897] *FTC v. Procter & Gamble Co.*, 386 U.S. 568, 580 (1967), cited by D.I. BAKER and W. BLUMENTHAL (1983), *supra* n. 326, p. 342.
[898] R. PITOFSKY (1979), *supra* n. 797, p. 1070.
[899] *United States v. United States Gypsum Co.*, 438 U.S. 422 (1978), cited by M.N. BERRY (1996), *supra* n. 312, p. 525.
[900] *Northern Pacific R. Co. v. United States*, 356 U.S. 1 (1958), cited by M.N. BERRY (1996), *supra* n. 312, p. 525.
[901] *United States v. General Dynamics Corp.*, 415 U.S. 486, 497, 498 (1974).

level of concentration has been calculated incorrectly.[902] It was for the first time that market concentration was rebutted by other factors in the decision on whether a merger will 'substantially lessen competition'.[903] By taking an opposite view than the Warren Court in the 1960s, the Burger Court argued that the level of market concentration should only be considered as the starting point for a more comprehensive investigation concerning the potential anticompetitive effects of a merger.[904] Although in this case the largest four firms' market shares reached 75.2 percent, the Supreme Court argued that market share should not be taken as a 'conclusive indicator', and the post-merger firm's 'future power to compete' should be considered more important than the level of market share.[905] This case gives a positive signal towards a reform on merger policy by taking broader aspects of the competitive effects of a merger into account, instead of narrowly focusing on the market shares.[906] From the 1970s, the influence of the 'populist' thinking on antitrust at the Supreme Court therefore decreased.[907]

In *United States v. Marine Bancorporation, Inc.*,[908] another case decided by the Supreme Court in 1974, the Supreme Court stated that the concentration ratios were 'unreliable indicators of actual market behavior', and did not reveal the 'economic characteristics' of the market.[909] In *United States v. Citizens & Southern National Bank*,[910] a case decided by the Supreme Court in 1975, the Supreme Court held that the defendant should be allowed to show that market share could 'give an inaccurate account' of the potentially competitive effects of the merger.[911]

Following the Supreme Court's decision in *United States v. General Dynamics Corp*, lower courts also gave counter-arguments to challenge the dominance of deciding merger cases by assessing the market concentration. For example, in *United States v. Waste Management, Inc.*,[912] the Second Circuit held that the level of the market concentration has to be balanced with the market entry. In the DC Circuit case *United States v. Baker Hughes, Inc.*,[913] market concentration had to be weighed by several other factors and it no longer played a decisive role in merger decisions.[914] After the Hart-Scott-Rodino Act (the amendment of the

---

[902]   J.B. BAKER and C. SHAPRIO (2007), *supra* n. 698, p. 3.
[903]   W. KOLASKY and A. DICK (2003), *supra* n. 697, p. 214.
[904]   R.A. SKITOL (1999), *supra* n. 25, p. 247; Skitol cited the decision in *United States v. General Dynamics Corp.*, 415 U.S. 486 (1974).
[905]   S.M. EDWARDS *et al.* (1981), *supra* n. 832, p. 1552.
[906]   J.B. BAKER and C. SHAPIRO (2007), *supra* n. 698, p. 4.
[907]   R.A. SKITOL (1999), *supra* n. 25, p. 248.
[908]   *United States v. Marine Bancorporation, Inc.*, 418 U.S. 602 (1974).
[909]   S.M. EDWARDS *et al.* (1981), *supra* n. 832, p. 1552.
[910]   *United States v. Citizens & Southern National Bank*, 422 U.S. 86 (1975).
[911]   S.M. EDWARDS *et al.* (1981), *supra* n. 832, p. 1552.
[912]   *United States v. Waste Management, Inc.*, 743 F. 2d 976 (2d Cir. 1984).
[913]   *United States v. Baker Hughes, Inc*, 908 F. 2d 981 (D.C. Cir. 1990).
[914]   J.B. BAKER and C. SHAPIRO (2007), *supra* n. 698, p. 5 cited the decision written by Clarence Thomas and Ruth Ginsburg: 'evidence of market concentration simply provides a convenient starting point for a broader inquiry into future competitiveness.'

Clayton Act) was enacted in 1976, the enforcement of merger rules has moved forward to follow a more 'regulatory' approach, which focuses on the investigation of the competitive effects of a merger.[915]

Upgrading the efficiency claims from a 'factor' to a 'defense' was driven by the *LTV/Republic Steel* merger, which pushed the DOJ to broaden the understanding on efficiency.[916] In this case, the Court argued that efficiencies not only have cost-saving effects, more importantly, efficiencies will increase the competitiveness of the firm which gives them an advantage in international trade.[917] In *Federal Trade Commission v. University Health, Inc.*,[918] the 11th Circuit accepted efficiency as one of the important factors to consider the potential effects in the relevant market after the concentration. This factor can be in deciding whether this merger will lessen competition.[919] However, the Court did not accept an efficiency defense which applies efficiency to offset the anticompetitive effects. The defendant in this case failed because it did not raise sufficient evidence to prove efficiency.

5. INTEGRATING EFFICIENCY GOAL IN THE EU COMPETITION POLICY

5.1. INTRODUCTION

The EU merger control policy was not explicitly included in the Treaty of Paris, nor in the Treaty of Rome. The EC Merger Control Regulation, as a separate legal act was after a long debate adopted in 21 December 1989 and came into force in 1990.[920] All concentrations that have an 'EU dimension' will come under the control of this regulation.[921] There are several reasons for the prolonged debate on the enactment of a merger policy in the EU. One reason was that some firms argued that merger policy was not needed because maintaining the size of the firm was important when it competes against the firms from the US and

---

[915] R.A. SKITOL (1999), *supra* n. 25, p. 247.

[916] W. KOLASKY and A. DICK (2003), *supra* n. 697, p. 219.

[917] *United States. v. LTV Corp.*, 1984 WL 21973, 14 (D.D.C. 2 August 1984): 'To achieve savings in cost through efficiencies which will enable the surviving company to compete more effectively both here and in export markets.' Cited by W. KOLASKY and A. DICK (2003), *supra* n. 697, p. 219.

[918] *Federal Trade Commission v. University Health, Inc.*, 938 F. 2d 1206 (11th Circuit 1991) at 1222.

[919] Cited by W.J. KOLASKY (2001), 'Lessons from Baby Food: The Role of Efficiencies in Merger Review', *Antitrust*, vol. 16, p. 87.

[920] Council Regulation (EEC) No 4064/89 of 21 December 1989 on the Control of Concentrations between Undertakings [1989] OJ L 395/1, amended by Council Regulation (EC) No 1310/97 of 30 June 1997 [1997] OJ L 180/1.

[921] Any concentration 'creates or strengthens a dominant position as a result of which effective competition would be significantly impeded in the common market or in a substantial part of it.'

Japan.[922] Another reason was that horizontal agreements are less dangerous to impose obstacles on cross-border trade. Therefore, they attracted less attention from the Commission when the competition law system was formulated in the 1950s.[923] The third reason was that national competition authorities were concerned to preserve their competences in merger enforcement.[924]

The 1989 Merger Regulation did not clarify the application of efficiency arguments. Article 2(1)(b) of the merger regulation sets two general principles. The first is that consumers must benefit from the 'technical and economic progress'. The second principle is that this 'technical and economic progress' should not impede competition. These two principles seem to indicate that the goal of promoting efficiency is subordinate to the goals of protecting consumers, as well as promoting competition. If the efficiency gains cannot be passed on to consumers, these gains will not be recognized. Moreover, efficiency claims cannot be taken into account in the merger assessment before the identification of its dominant position in the relevant market.

During the initial period of the 1989 Merger Regulation, the methodology that the Commission staff applied was rather a structural approach, and the starting point for a merger analysis was defining the relevant market.[925] It remained an ambiguous issue how the antitrust agencies will treat efficiency claims, and whether a merger with a dominant position can be exempted by efficiency reasons.[926]

In the 1990s, the Commission often took a negative view on efficiency claims, and efficiency arguments were often taken as a factor which will strengthen the dominant position of the merging enterprises.[927] This negative view has been gradually changed after the Merger Regulation was revised in 2004,[928] as well as the implementation of the first Horizontal Merger Guidelines.[929] The Commission's changed attitude towards efficiency has also been revealed in the

---

[922] B. LYONS (2008), 'An Economic Assessment of EC Merger Control: 1957–2007', Center for Competition Policy Working Paper 08–17, available at <http://ssrn.com/abstract=1114128> p. 9; *see also* F. ILZKOVITZ and R. MEIKLEJOHN, 'European Merger Control: Do We Need an Efficiency Defence?', in F. ILZKOVITZ and R. MEIKLEJOHN (eds.), *European Merger Control, do we need an Efficiency Defence?*, Edward Elgar 2006, p. 51; *see* Report on the Communication from the Commission on the European Aerospace Industry – Meeting the Global Challenge (COM(97)0466 – C4–0547/97), 13 October 1998, European Parliament, p. 22: 'European competition law, and in particular merger regulation, must now be interpreted in the context of international competitiveness within increasingly globalised markets.'

[923] D.J. GERBER (1994a), p. 112.

[924] B. LYONS (2008), *supra* n. 922, p. 10.

[925] N. LEVY (2005), 'Mario Monti's Legacy in EC Merger Control', *Competition Policy International*, vol. 1, no. 1, p. 102.

[926] N. LEVY (2005), *supra* n. 925, p. 118.

[927] N. LEVY (2005), *supra* n. 925, p. 119.

[928] Council Regulation (EC) No 139/2004 of 20 January 2004 on the Control of Concentrations between Undertakings (the EC Merger Regulation) [2004] OJ L 24/1.

[929] B. LYONS (2008), *supra* n. 922, p. 27.

mission statements in the annual reports of DG Comp.[930] The first DG Competition's Annual Report was issued in 2004. The annual report of 2004 and 2005 did not mention the words of 'efficiency' or 'efficiencies' in the section on mergers.[931] The 2006 annual report described that the efficiency defense was applied in three mergers.[932] In the 2007 annual report, it was stated that the mission of the DG Comp was to 'ensure markets operate as efficiently as possible'.[933]

5.2. MERGER REGULATION

5.2.1. Merger Regulation 4064/89

Merger Regulation 4064/89 defines that a merger will be prohibited when it impedes competition 'in the common market or in a substantial part of it.'[934] The assessment of merger effects is based on a two-step test, and the first step is to investigate whether the merger would create or enhance a market dominant position,[935] and the second step is to assess within the relevant market, whether the increased market power would affect the effective competition.[936] Under the 1989 Merger Regulation, it was not clear whether an efficiency defense was allowed, or completely ruled out, although the legislative background of the 1989 Merger Regulation seems to support the view that an efficiency defense was excluded. Moreover, during the first decade, efficiency considerations have not been explicitly mentioned in the decisions by the EC Commission.[937] One hint

---

[930]   B. Lyons (2008), *supra* n. 922, p. 27.

[931]   B. Lyons (2008), *supra* n. 922, p. 28.

[932]   B. Lyons (2008), *supra* n. 922, p. 28.

[933]   DG Competition Annual Management Plan 2007, 22 December 2006, European Commission, available at <http://ec.europa.eu/competition/publications/annual_management_plan/amp_2007_en.pdf>, p. 4: 'The mission of the Directorate General for Competition is to enforce the competition rules of the Community Treaties, in order to ensure that competition in the EU market is not distorted and that markets operate as efficiently as possible, thereby contributing to the welfare of consumers and to the competitiveness of the European economy.'

[934]   '[C]reate or strengthen a dominant position as a result of which effective competition would be significantly impeded in the common market or in a substantial part of it.'

[935]   According to Van den Bergh and Camesasca, the meaning of a 'dominant position' has been clarified by the Commission as the 'ability to act to an appreciable extent independently of its competitors, customers, and, ultimately, its consumers': R. Van den Bergh and P.D. Camesasca (2006), *supra* n. 18, pp. 345–346.

[936]   C.S. Goldman, Q.C. *et al.* (2003), *supra* n. 824, p. 114.

[937]   M. Motta (1999), 'EC Merger Policy, and the Airtours Case', available at< http://people.exeter.ac.uk/maf206/motta_1999.pdf>, pp. 9–10; *see* OECD (1995), 'Policy Roundtables: Competition Policy and Efficiency Claims in Horizontal Agreements, Contribution from the European Community', OCDE/GD(96) 65, available at <www.oecd.org/competition/mergers/2379526.pdf>, p. 53: 'There is a clear limit for the efficiency defence: the elimination of competition'. However, it was made clear by the first Commissioner Sir Leon Brittan, QC,

regarding the treatment of efficiencies can be found in Article 2. Article 2(1) of the Merger Regulation in 1989 mentioned several factors to be included in the analysis of merger effects, and one of the factors was the 'development of technical and economic progress', under the condition that this progress will not 'to consumers' advantage', and does not create an 'obstacle to competition'. Therefore, there are two criteria which have to be satisfied if the merger generates technical and economic efficiencies: the first requirement is that consumers will benefit from the efficiency gains; the second requirement is that the improved efficiency will not form any 'obstacle to competition'.[938]

In 2001, the Commission invited public opinions and a review of the Merger Regulation, followed by the publication of a Green Paper in December 2002.[939] This Green Paper specifically addressed the issue of the role of efficiency considerations in merger control. Most parts of this paper responses that the Commission received support the view of taking efficiency into account in merger case analysis.[940] These discussions on efficiency have been incorporated in the 2004 EC Horizontal Merger Guidelines, which specify efficiency in three categories: benefits to consumers, merger specificity and verifiability.[941]

5.2.2.   2004 EC Merger Regulation (ECMR)

The 2004 EC Merger Regulation ('ECMR'), together with the first merger guidelines issued in 2004, opened a new page for the merger policy in the European Union. In the 2004 Merger Regulation, efficiency was formally accepted as a positive factor, because efficiencies generated by the merged parties are beneficial for consumers.[942] Compared with the merger policy in the US, the

---

the suggestion of offsetting the creation of dominant position by efficiency claims was rejected. See SIR LEON BRITTAN, Q.C., 'Principles and Practice of the Merger Regulation', speech at the Center for European Policy Studies, 24 September 1990, Commission Press Release IP/90/751, available at <http://europa.eu/rapid/press-release_IP-90–751_en.htm?locale=en>. N. LEVY (2005), *supra* n. 925, p. 118.

[938] C.S. GOLDMAN, Q.C. *et al.* (2003), *supra* n. 867, p. 114.

[939] Green Paper on the Review of Council Regulation (EEC) No. 4064/89, COM (2001) 745, 11 December 2001.

[940] R. PITOFSKY (2007), *supra* n. 717, p. 1420.

[941] Guidelines on the Assessment of Horizontal Mergers under the Council Regulation on the Control of Concentrations between Undertakings [2004] OJ C 31/03, paras 77, 78, 84.

[942] Council Regulation (EC) No 139/2004 of 20 January 2004 on the Control of Concentrations between Undertakings (the EC Merger Regulation) [2004] OJ L 24/1, recital 29, para 77: 'This will be the case when the Commission is in a position to conclude on the basis of sufficient evidence that the efficiencies generated by the merger are likely to enhance the ability and incentive of the merger entity to act pro-competitively for the benefit of consumers, thereby counteracting the adverse effects on competition which the merger might otherwise have.' 'In order to determine the impact of a concentration on competition in the common market, it is appropriate to take account of any substantiated likely efficiencies put forward by the undertakings concerned. It is possible that the efficiencies brought about by the concentration counteract the effects on competition, and in particular the potential harm to consumers,

EU merger rules indicate a clear consumer welfare standard, without explicitly rejecting the total welfare criterion (such as acknowledging that efficiencies will benefit producers as well).[943]

Section 7 of the Horizontal Merger Guidelines consists of 12 articles, which regulate in detail how efficiency will be treated in merger assessment. There are three preconditions for efficiency to be accepted: first, it must be beneficial to consumers; second, it must be merger-specific; and third, it must be verifiable. However, the guideline does not further specify how efficiencies can be evaluated and verified, for example, paragraph 84 of the Horizontal Merger Guidelines states that 'it is highly unlikely that a merger leading to a market position approaching that of a monopoly, or leading to a similar level of market power, can be declared compatible with the common market on the ground that efficiency gains would be sufficient to counteract its potential anticompetitive effects.'[944]

5.3.   CASE LAW

5.3.1.   Negative View on Efficiency Claims

In the 1990s, the Commission took a negative view on the efficiency claims in a few cases.[945] Efficiency arguments were rejected to offset the anticompetitive harm due to the increased dominant position. The logic behind this reasoning was that the Commission applied a 'dominance test', and an efficiency-enhancing merger could extend its market share and further strengthens its dominant position by forming an efficiency base.[946] This reasoning is also referred to as 'efficiency offence'.[947] For example, in *Danish Crown/Vestjyske Slagterier*, the Commission stated: 'the creation of a dominant position in the relevant markets, means that the efficiencies argument put forward by the parties cannot be taken into account in the assessment of the present merger.'[948] In *AKZO Chemie BV v. Commission*,[949] the ECJ defined that a merger with a market

---

that it might otherwise have and that, as a consequence, the concentration does not create or strengthen a dominant position as a result of which effective competition would be significantly impeded in the common market or in a substantial part of it. The Commission should publish guidance on the conditions under which it may take efficiencies into account in the assessment of a concentration.'

[943]   R. Pitofsky (2007), *supra* n. 717, p. 1420.

[944]   Cited by N. Levy (2005), *supra* n. 925, p. 120.

[945]   The selection of these cases is based on N. Levy (2005), *supra* n. 925, p. 119.

[946]   B. Lyons (2008), *supra* n. 922, p. 27.

[947]   B. Lyons (2008), *supra* n. 922, p. 27.

[948]   *Danish Crown/Vestjyske Slagterier* (Case No IV/M 1313) Commission Decision of 9 March 1999, para 198. Cited by N. Levy (2005), *supra* n. 925, p. 119.

[949]   Case C-62/86, *AKZO Chemie BV v. Commission* [1991] ECR I-3359.

share of 50 percent would be considered to have obtained dominance.[950] Efficiency arguments were rejected by the Commission in *Accor/Wagons-Lits*,[951] *Mercedes-Benz/Kässbohrer*,[952] *Nordic Satellite Distribution*,[953] Commission Decision *At&T/NCR*,[954] *British Telecom/MCI (II)*,[955] *Smith & Nephew/Beiersdorf/ JV*,[956] and *MSG Media Service*.[957] In some cases, the European Commission had treated efficiencies as an offense, instead of as a defense.[958] Efficiency arguments could hardly be accepted when the evidence of the merger's strengthened dominant position is robust.[959] For example, the Commission rejected the efficiency claims in *Bertelsmann/Kirch/Premiere*[960] merger because the merger would obtain a dominant position in the pay-TV market.[961] The same reasoning was found in *Aerospatiale-Alenia/de Havilland*,[962] where the Commission rejected the efficiency claims regarding the potential cost savings and the improved management of the merger, because the proposed merger will strengthen a dominant position in the relevant market.[963]

5.3.2. Cautiously Accepted Efficiency Claims

The Commission's hostile attitude towards efficiency has been gradually changed after the enactment of the Merger Regulation in 2004.[964] The 2004 Merger Regulation, as well as the first Horizontal Merger Guideline which was implemented in 2004, accepted that merger-specific efficiencies are desirable.[965] The most prominent benefit of efficiency gains, according to the Merger Regulation, is that it reduces marginal costs and prices, which will benefit consumers.[966] In 2006, DG Competition published three merger cases which

---

[950]   C.S. GOLDMAN, Q.C. *et al.* (2003), *supra* n. 824, p. 114.
[951]   *Accor/Wagons-Lits* (Case No IV/M 126) Commission Decision of 28 April 1992, para 26(2)(f).
[952]   Mercedes-Benz/Kässbohrer (Case IV/M.477) Commission Decision of 14 February 1995, para 66.
[953]   *Nordic Satellite Distribution* (Case No IV/M 490) Commission Decision of 24 March 1995, paras 145–152.
[954]   *At&T/NCR* (Case No IV/M 050) Commission Decision of 18 January 1991, para 30.
[955]   *British Telecom/MCI (II)* (Case No IV/M.856) Commission Decision of 14 May 1997 para 58.
[956]   *Smith & Nephew/Beiersdorf/JV* (Case No COMP/JV 54) Commission Decision of 30 January 2001.
[957]   *MSG Media Service* (Case IV/M 469) Commission Decision of 9 November 1994.
[958]   C.S. GOLDMAN, Q.C. *et al.* (2003), *supra* n. 867, p. 115.
[959]   T.L. GREANEY (2000), *supra* n. 865, p. 891.
[960]   *Bertelsmann/Kirch/Premiere* (Case No IV/M 993) Commission Decision of 27 May 1998.
[961]   C.S. GOLDMAN, Q.C. *et al.* (2003), *supra* n. 867, p. 115.
[962]   *Aerospatiale-Alenia/de Havilland* (Case No. IV/M053) Commission Decision of 2 October 1991.
[963]   T.L. GREANEY (2000), *supra* n. 865, p. 891.
[964]   B. LYONS (2008), *supra* n. 922, p. 27.
[965]   B. LYONS (2008), *supra* n. 922, p. 27.
[966]   B. LYONS (2008), *supra* n. 922, p. 27.

have applied the efficiency defense.[967] Efficiencies were accepted by the Commission in *Korsnas/AD Cartonboard*, and the Commission acknowledged that the efficiency gains had satisfied the 'pass-through' requirement.[968] Efficiency claims in *Inco/Falconbridge*, however, were rejected because the Commission argued that these gains will not be passed through to consumers.[969] In *Metso/Aker Kvaerner*, it was argued that the efficiency gains were not sufficient to offset the adverse competitive effects.[970]

6. CONCLUSION

This chapter followed the discussion in the previous chapters concerning the goals of antitrust law. The central question in this chapter was that how the efficiency goal has been integrated in the merger policies in the US and the EU. In particular, how different focus on the goals of merger policy would affect the case decisions. The study on the development of the merger policy in the US and in the EU shows that the understanding of the efficiency goal was gradually developed, and this long process was to a large extent influenced by the development of economic theory, and the understanding on efficiency among judges, legislators and policy makers. In the US, economic theories on merger effects include the Harvard School, the Chicago School, and the Williamson tradeoff diagram developed in 1968 offered a criterion which can be applied to weigh the cost and benefit of a merger. In Europe, with the strong influence of the Ordoliberal School, mergers are assessed more from the perspective of whether they will impede competition. Moreover, the goals of merger policies in Europe have not been narrowed down to economic goals only. Therefore, economic goals, such as consumer welfare and total welfare, have to be balanced in merger decisions against other social and political goals, such as market integration, and the freedom to compete.

Another finding of this chapter is that the merger cases that were prohibited in the 1960s in the US would have a different result today. This is because different views on market concentrations have meanwhile changed. Harvard School scholars had a strong belief that concentrations would impede competition, and mergers which increase market concentration level must be examined under scrutiny. This finding gives theoretical support to examine the effects of a merger based on the market structure, and non-structural factors, such as efficiency arguments, could only be taken into account in 'exceptional

---

[967] DG Comp Annual Report 2006, cited by B. LYONS (2008), *supra* n. 922, p. 28.
[968] B. LYONS (2008), *supra* n. 922, p. 28.
[969] B. LYONS (2008), *supra* n. 922, p. 28.
[970] B. LYONS (2008), *supra* n. 922, p. 28.

circumstances'.[971] It was believed that concentration of power would negatively affect economic performance; as a result, the goal of merger rules is to 'deconcentrate' economic power. Starting from the late 1970s, the Chicago School developed economic theories on concentrations, and consequently the market concentration level was no longer the only baseline in merger decisions. Since the 1982 Horizontal Merger Guidelines, non-structural factors have gradually been recognized and adopted in the analysis of the competitive effects of a merger. After the development of the last twenty years, efficiency arguments have been accepted as an important factor in deciding whether a merger is anticompetitive. The case which is decided for the reason of 'increasing concentration level' would have a different decision from the perspective of 'increasing efficiency'. Nevertheless, a consensus has not been reached to use efficiency as a defense to offset the potential anticompetitive harm. There are still different views on the issue of whether the efficiency goal can override other considerations. These findings on merger policies in the US and the EU will have important implications for merger cases in China. The next chapter focuses on the recent cases in China and explains how policy goals would affect the decisions.

---

[971]   US Department of Justice, 1968 Merger Guidelines.

CHAPTER 5

THE IMPACT OF COMPETITION GOALS ON MERGER CASES: A COMPARATIVE PERSPECTIVE

1.   INTRODUCTION

In the previous chapters, a historical debate on competition goals in the US and the EU has been presented. This evolution generally shows that goals of competition law differ among jurisdictions: in the US competition goals focus on consumer welfare and total welfare, and social and moral judgments on anticompetitive conduct have been largely dismissed. In the EU, economic goals have to be balanced with broader concerns, such as contributing to an integrated common market, and providing equal rights for firms to compete. To add one more layer of complexity to the debate, goals of competition law in China seem to be even broader than the situation in the EU: competition goals in China have been extended from economic welfare to the development of the national economy, as well as to wider social and political considerations.

Another important conclusion of the previous chapters is that throughout the evolution of competition goals, the development of economic theory has played an important role in shaping the understanding of competition law. In line with the development of modern economic techniques, economic goals have gradually been accepted by judges, legislators and policy makers in the US and the EU, although the extent to which economic goals are prioritized over other goals may differ between jurisdictions. For example, as far as merger policy is concerned, the efficiency goal has been treated with much less hostile today in the US and the EU than decades ago. This finding explains why economic analysis has to be taken into account in antitrust cases, and why economic criteria can be taken as a benchmark in analyzing competition policy in different countries.

However, given the long debate on competition goals, the question which interests not only academic scholars but also policy makers and competition practitioners is whether competition goals will indeed matter in antitrust practices, and if so, what impact competition goals have on the analysis of cases. Intuitively, if competition goals differ in jurisdiction, this may lead to a different outcome of antitrust cases. It is particularly astonishing for merger cases, as the authority has to interpret the historical evidence in order to make predictions on the merger effects in the future.[972] This challenging task would require the antitrust authorities both to embrace a solid application of economic theory, and to develop a clear understanding of other non-economic goals if a tradeoff between different goals has to be made. This chapter attempts to investigate whether the impacts of policy goals indeed exist.

This chapter takes economic theories and modern economic techniques as the benchmark, and compares how antitrust authorities in the US, the EU and China apply economic techniques to merger case analysis. Since economic theories have a universal nature, the differences in merger analysis may well explain the impact of competition goals on horizontal merger decisions.[973] This chapter draws attention to several substantive issues in merger control policy, and attempts to investigate the extent to which competition policy goals have influenced the implementation of merger policy in the US, the EU and China. It first presents a brief overview of the merger decisions published by the MOFCOM (section 2). It discusses the main features of these cases and briefly analyzes how competition goals might affect MOFCOM's decisions. To deepen the analysis, the third section summarizes economic theories and techniques that can be applied in merger analysis. Economic theories will be applied as a benchmark for a comparative study of merger decisions between the US, the EU and in China. The fourth section investigates how merger policy can be affected by the competition goals. It is composed of two aspects – the first aspect is the investigation of empirical evidence concerning how merger policy is enforced differently in the US, the EU and China. The second aspect is how this difference can be examined through a comparative case study. In this section, two merger cases that were notified at the same time to the antitrust authorities in the US, the EU and China will be studied. The difference in the cases decisions may reflect whether competition goals in each jurisdiction would play an important role. The fifth section discusses to what extent competition policy goals would matter, and if so, whether there are policy implications that could be drawn for competition policy makers in China. The last section concludes.

---

[972]   A. Lindsay (2006), *supra* n. 756, p. 67.
[973]   This research specifically focuses on horizontal mergers, and the reason for this has been stated in the introduction chapter.

2. AN OVERVIEW OF MERGER CASES IN CHINA

2.1. MERGER POLICY IN CHINA: FIVE YEARS' IMPLEMENTATION

Merger policy was frequently enforced after the AML came into force. Until the end of September 2009, among all formally notified transactions, 23 transactions were between domestic enterprises, 55 transactions were between foreign enterprises, and 9 transactions were between domestic and foreign enterprises.[974] Multinational companies were involved in 40 cases, comprising 69 percent of the total cases.[975] From August 2008 to June 2010, 140 mergers were notified and 95 percent of them were approved unconditionally.[976] In 2011, 160 merger reviews were completed and 151 cases were cleared without condition. In the four cases approved under certain conditions, a behavioral remedy was imposed in three cases and a structural remedy was imposed in one case. In 2002, 154 merger reviews were completed with 142 merger cases were cleared without condition. In the six merger cases approved under certain conditions, four of them received a behavioral remedy, in one case a structural remedy was imposed, and in another case a combined remedy was imposed. As of June 2013, the MOFCOM has received 754 notifications, with 690 cases have been reviewed. In the 643 cases in which a decision was issued, 624 were approved without conditions, 18 were approved with restrictions and one was prohibited.[977] From August 2008 to June 2013, only the *Coca Cola/Huiyuan* merger was blocked by the MOFCOM. Among all the 18 cases that were granted remedies, nine received structural remedies, seven received behavioral remedies, and two received combined structural and behavioral remedies.[978] As it is shown in the two graphs below, from August 2008 to August 2013, around 97 percent notified mergers in China were cleared without conditions (Figure 1), and most conditionally approved mergers were imposed behavioral remedies (Figure 2). Until 2013, none of the MOFCOM merger case decision has been reviewed by a court in China, and the role of the court in Chinese merger control remains unclear.

---

[974] X. WANG (2009), 'New Development of China's AML-from Merger Control Perspective', December 2009, presentation at the 5th Annual Asian Competition Law Conference 2009, available at <www.asiancompetitionforum.org/asianfile_091207.html>.

[975] Ministry of Commerce, Press Conference on 17 August 2009, available at <http://sousuo.mofcom.gov.cn/query/queryDetail.jsp?articleid=20090806462392&query=%E5%8F%8D%E5%9E%84%E6%96%96%AD>.

[976] D. HEALEY (2010), 'Anti-Monopoly Law and Mergers in China: An Early Report Card on Procedural and Substantive Issues', *Tsinghua China Law Review*, vol. 3, p. 58.

[977] Y. ZHOU (2013), 'MOFCOM Has Investigated 643 Mergers over last Five Years, Only Coca Cola/Huiyuan was Prohibited' (商务部五年完成643起并购审查, 仅可口可乐购汇源被禁), *ChinaNews.com* (中国新闻网), 1 August 2013, available at <www.chinanews.com/gn/2013/08-01/5113388.shtml> accessed 07.04.2014.

[978] Y. ZHOU (2013), *supra* n. 977.

Figure 1. MOFCOM Merger Decisions (August 2008 to August 2013): Conditional Approval versus Unconditional Approval[979]

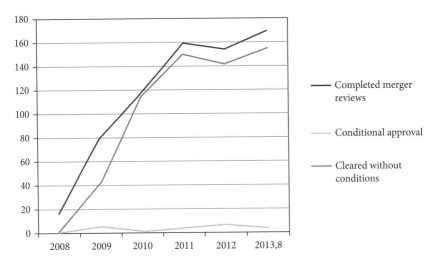

Figure 2. MOFCOM Merger Decisions: Structural Remedies, Behavioral Remedies and Combined Remedies (August 2008 to August 2013)[980]

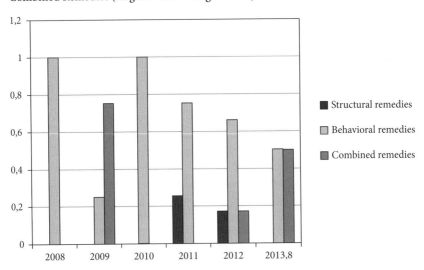

---

[979] Sources: Xɪɴʜᴜᴀ Nᴇᴡꜱ (2009), 'Merger Cases Has Increased since the Promulgation of the AML' (反垄断法实施以来我国反垄断案件呈逐年增长之势), *Xinhua News*, 21 September 2011, available at <www.gov.cn/jrzg/2011–09/21/content_1953353.htm> accessed 10.12.2013; Xɪɴʜᴜᴀ Nᴇᴡꜱ (2011), 'Most Concentrations Were Unconditionally Approved in 2010' (2010年我国绝大部分经营者集中案件无条件通过审查), *Xinhua News*, 5 January 2011, available at <http://money.163.com/11/0105/19/6PLKQ97N00253B0H.html> accessed 16.12.2013; Xɪɴʜᴜᴀ Nᴇᴡꜱ (2013), 'MOFCOM: 97% of Concentration Cases were Unconditionally Approved' (商务部:97%经营者集中反垄断案件无条件通过审查), *Xinhua News*, 23 May 2013, available at <http://news.xinhuanet.com/legal/2013–05/23/c_115886393.htm> accessed 20.12.2013.

[980] MOFCOM website <http://fldj.mofcom.gov.cn/article/ztxx/>.

2.2. A BRIEF OVERVIEW OF MOFCOM'S MERGER DECISIONS

2.2.1. An Overview of the MOFCOM Published Cases

Since 2008, the MOFCOM has published decisions on their website for mergers that are cleared with conditions. From August 2008 to 27 August 2013, the MOFCOM published 21 case decisions, and all these cases were approved with conditions. In this section, an overview of the 21 cases will be presented. By taking a first look at all the published merger decisions (see Table 1 below), several quick conclusions can be drawn. First of all, most conditionally approved mergers were between foreign companies,[981] and only four published cases were between a foreign and a domestic company: *Coca Cola/Huiyuan, GE/Shenhua Group JV, Henkel Hongkong/Tiande Chemical*, and *Walmart/Niuhai*. The merger *GE/Shenhua Group JV* involves both a foreign company and a SOE. Until August 2013, no merger between two domestic companies was cleared with restrictions by the MOFCOM. According to a press release published by the MOFCOM in November 2012,[982] 90 percent of the unconditionally approved cases were between foreign companies. To explain the low percentage of merger cases involving domestic firms, it might be possible that some domestic mergers failed to notify to the MOFCOM, for example the merger between China Telecom and China Unicom was not filed.[983] According to Mario Mariniello, from October 2012 to September 2013, only 15 percent of the notified mergers in China were between domestic enterprises.[984] This percentage is comparatively low because among all the reviewed mergers by the EU Commission for the same period, half of them were between domestic companies.[985] Another explanation might be that some domestic mergers were treated in a rather lenient manner and were cleared without conditions.[986]

---

[981] For a comprehensive study on the MOFCOM's decisions on foreign companies from a perspective of extraterritorial effects of the AML, *see* M. Faure and X. Zhang (2013), 'Towards an Extraterritorial Application of the Chinese Anti-Monopoly Law that Avoids Trade Conflicts', *George Washington International Law Review*, vol. 45, no. 3, pp. 501–538.

[982] MOFCOM (2012), 'Statistics of Unconditionally Approved Concentration Cases' (经营者集中反垄断审查无条件批准案件信息统计情况), 16 November 2012, MOFCOM website, available at <http://fldj.mofcom.gov.cn/article/zcfb/201211/20121108437868.shtml> accessed 15.12.2013.

[983] X. Wang and A. Emch (2013), 'Five Years of Implementation of China's Anti-Monopoly Law – Achievements and Challenges', *Journal of Antitrust Enforcement*, vol. 1, no. 2, p. 267; B. Wang (2009), 'Official with MOFCOM confirms that merger of China Unicom and China Netcom is Alleged Illegal', *The Economic Observer*, 30 April 2009.

[984] M. Mariniello (2013), 'The Dragon Awakes: Is Chinese Competition Policy A Cause for Concern?', *Bruegel Policy Contribution*, issue 2013/14, p. 8.

[985] M. Mariniello (2013), *supra* n. 984, p. 8.

[986] X. Wang and A. Emch (2013), *supra* n. 983, p. 268; X. Wang (2012), 'Comparative Overview – China', in A. Emch, J. Regazzini and V. Rudomino (eds.), *Competition Law in the BRICS Countries*, Wolters Kluwer 2012, p. 266.

The second observation is that the published merger cases cover a large range of industries, from consumer goods to pharmaceutical products, and most involved foreign companies are global players which produce and sell products both in China and in the global market. The third finding is that in most conditionally approved mergers behavioral remedies were imposed. Compared with the conditionally approved merger cases in the EU, it seems that the MOFCOM is particularly in favor of behavioral remedies.[987] According to Mario Mariniello, from 2008 to August 2013, 60 percent of MOFCOM's conditionally cleared mergers were imposed behavioral remedies, with 20 percent for structural remedies, and the rest was for combined remedies.[988] For the same period, the EU Commission has imposed structural remedies for 77 percent of the mergers cleared with restrictions, and 7 percent for behavioral remedies.[989] The remaining 16 percent was for combined remedies. The reason why MOFCOM has relied on behavioral remedies might be two-sided: on the one hand, behavioral remedies have an advantage of being flexible, so they are easier to negotiate and to impose on the merging parties;[990] on the other hand, the flexible use of behavioral remedies may give the MOFCOM the opportunity to achieve a broader goal of competition policy,[991] in particular to pay more attention to the role of competitors instead of consumers. In addition, as some commentators observed, both for the proposal and for the implementation of remedies, the MOFCOM tends to rely on the negotiation as well as the voluntary cooperation from the merging parties.[992]

---

[987] M. MARINIELLO (2013), *supra* n. 984, p. 6.

[988] M. MARINIELLO (2013), *supra* n. 984, p. 6.

[989] M. MARINIELLO (2013), *supra* n. 984, pp. 6–7.

[990] M. MARINIELLO (2013), *supra* n. 984, p. 7.

[991] M. MARINIELLO (2013), *supra* n. 984, p. 7.

[992] Q. HAO (2010), 'Merger Remedies in China: Developments and Issues', *Competition Law International*, p. 19.

Table 1. MOFCOM Published Merger Cases (2008–2013)[993]

Date	Merger case	Industry/Product	Buyer country	Target country	Type of merger	Decision	Type of Remedy
18.03.2009	Coca Cola/Huiyuan	Fruit juice beverage	US	China	Foreign/Domestic	Prohibited	No remedy
18.11.2008	InBev/Anheuser-Busch	Beer	Belgium	US	Foreign/Foreign	Conditional approval	Behavioral
24.04.2009	Mitsubishi Rayon/Lucite	Methylmethacrylate ('MMA'), a material for making plastics	Japan	UK	Foreign/Foreign	Conditional approval	Behavioral and structural
28.09.2009	GM/Delphi	Car	US	US	Foreign/Foreign	Conditional approval	Behavioral
29.09.2009	Pfizer/Wyeth	Pharmaceutical products	US	US	Foreign/Foreign	Conditional approval	Behavioral and structural
30.10.2009	Panasonic/Sanyo	Batteries	Japan	Japan	Foreign/Foreign	Conditional approval	Behavioral and structural
13.08.2010	Novartis/Alcon	Ophthalmic anti-inflammatory Compound and contact lens care products	Switzerland	Switzerland	Foreign/Foreign	Conditional approval	Behavioral
02.06.2011	Uralkali/Silvinit	Potash or potassium chloride (fertilizer)	Russia	Russia	Foreign/Foreign	Conditional approval	Behavioral
31.10.2011	Penelope (AlphaV)/Savio	Electronic yarn cleaner	France	Italy	Foreign/Foreign	Conditional approval	Structural

993   Sources: MOFCOM official website: <http://fldj.mofcom.gov.cn/article/ztxx/>. M. MARINIELLO (2013), *supra* n. 984, p. 5; D.J. HEALEY (2012), 'Strange Bedfellows or Soulmates: A Comparison of Merger Regulation in China and Australia', *Asian Journal of Comparative Law*, vol. 7, no. 1, pp. 13–15.

Date	Merger case	Industry/Product	Buyer country	Target country	Type of merger	Decision	Type of Remedy
10.11.2011	GE/Shenhua Group JV	Coal-water slurry gasification technology	US	China	Foreign/Domestic	Conditional approval	Behavioral
12.12.2011	Seagate/Samsung	Hard disk drives	US	Korea	Foreign/Foreign	Conditional approval	Behavioral
10.02.2012	Henkel Hongkong/Tiande Chemical	Chemicals	Germany	China	Foreign/Domestic	Conditional approval	Behavioral
02.03.2012	Western Digital/Hitachi	Hard disk drives	US	Japan	Foreign/Foreign	Conditional approval	Behavioral and structural
19.05.2012	Google/Motorola	Smart mobile terminals and operating systems	US	US	Foreign/Foreign	Conditional approval	Behavioral
15.06.2012	Goodrich/UTC	Manufactured aircraft power systems	US	US	Foreign/Foreign	Conditional approval	Structural
14.08.2012	Walmart/Newheight	B2C online retail business	US	China	Foreign/Domestic	Conditional approval	Behavioral
06.12.2012	Advanced RISC Machines/G&D/Gemalto Joint venture	Trusted Execution Environment		UK, Germany, Netherlands	Foreign/Foreign	Conditional approval	Behavioral
16.04.2013	Glencore/Xstrata	Natural resource	Switzerland	UK	Foreign/Foreign	Conditional approval	Behavioral and structural
23.04.2013	Marubeni/Gavilon	Export market of beans	Japan	US	Foreign/Foreign	Conditional approval	Behavioral
13.08.2013	Baxter Int./Gambro	Medical device (CRRT)	US	Sweden	Foreign/Foreign	Conditional approval	Behavioral and structural
27.08.2013	MediaTek/Mstar Semicondutor	Electronic (LCD)	Taiwan	Taiwan	Taiwan/Taiwan	Conditional approval	Behavioral

2.2.2.   Observation: How Does the MOFCOM Investigate?

Several questions may arise after a closer look at these merger decisions. The first issue is how the MOFCOM investigated each merger case. As most decisions were rather brief, it was unclear how economic analysis of market share, market concentration was calculated.[994] Nevertheless, all of the decisions have mentioned from which sources the MOFCOM collected the information, such as whether it is from government, trade associations, or from downstream firms. As it is presented in the table below (Table 2), all the case decisions have mentioned that the information was collected from government and trade associations.[995] Besides, most cases have mentioned 'downstream firms' and 'experts', and a few cases have mentioned the 'competitors in the same industry'. As far as consumers are concerned, only 'downstream customers' and 'dealers' were mentioned in some cases, but the role of the end-users and consumer associations was ambiguous. A possible explanation might be that the MOFCOM seems to rely more on the information received from producers, governmental agencies and trade associations. The investigation source might imply that industrial policy considerations and other political goals may play an important role in merger analysis.

2.2.3.   Observation: The High Use of Behavioral Remedies

The second issue is that the MOFCOM's use of behavioral remedies tends to be extensive. In several cases, the merging parties were either required to maintain the price and quantity level for a given product in the market, such as in *Uralkali/ Silvinit*, *Henkel Hong Kong/Tiande*, or were prohibited to increase the market power of this product by acquiring other producers or by building new plants, such as in *InBev/Anheuser-Bush*, *Walmart/Newheight*, *Novartis/Alcon* and *Mitsubishi Rayon/Lucite*.[996] The MOFCOM gave several remedies to *InBev/ Anheuser-Busch*, *Mitsubishi Rayon/Lucite*, *GM/Delphi*, *Seagate/Samsung*, and *Google/Motorola*, whereas these mergers were unconditionally cleared by the antitrust authorities in the US and the EU.[997] Some other conditionally approved

---

[994]   It was argued that the accuracy and transparency of MOFCOM decisions have been improved in later cases. *See* X. WANG and A. EMCH (2013), *supra* n. 983, p. 255.

[995]   Trade associations in China are usually established as government agencies which play a role of monitoring a specific industry. D. HEALEY (2010), *supra* n. 976 p. 25. In practice, trade associations would coordinate with ministries or SOE members, and impose political pressure on merger cases. D.D. SOKOL (2013), 'Merger Control under China's Anti-Monopoly Law', *Minnesota Legal Studies Research Paper No. 13–05*, available at <http://papers.ssrn.com/sol3/papers.cfm?abstract_id=2207690>, p. 11.

[996]   M. MARINIELLO (2013), *supra* n. 984, p. 7.

[997]   X. WANG and A. EMCH (2013), *supra* n. 983, p. 254; Y.W. CHIN (2012), 'The High-Wire Balancing Act of Merger Control under China's Anti-Monopoly Law', available at <http://ssrn.com/abstract=2120280> pp. 7, 12.

cases, such as *Uralkali/Silvinit, Penelope (AlphaV)/Savio*, and *Henkel Hongkong/Tiande Chemical* even did not meet the notification requirement in the US and the EU.[998] In almost all the published cases, the MOFCOM did not provide a detailed analysis regarding the economic justifications for the behavioral remedies imposed on these cases. In particular, using behavioral remedies to maintain price and quantity for one product may not be well explained by competition theory. The issue of preventing a merged firm from entering an area of business or from expanding the operation line seems to be more relevant to industrial policy, which should be the concern of a regulator, but not a competition authority.[999]

In several decisions, for example, in *Mitsubishi Rayon/Lucite* and *GM/Delphi*, the MOFCOM has mentioned that the increased 'competitiveness' of the merging party would restrict the access to a product market for other competitors. In *Coca Cola/Huiyuan*, the MOFCOM claimed that the merged firm would squeeze the market space for domestic small and medium-sized fruit juice producers.[1000] However, economic theory of competition generally shows that the enhanced 'competitiveness' of the merging party would benefit consumers by promoting efficiency.[1001] It would only become an 'anticompetitive concern' when the antitrust authority pays particular attention to the competitors.[1002] In this view, it was more likely that merger policy in China was implemented to fulfill industrial policy goals, and in particular to support the development of domestic firms.[1003]

In some other cases, when there was no major domestic competitor involved in that industry, it seems that the MOFCOM imposed behavioral remedies to mitigate the negative effects on the domestic market. For example, in *Seagate/Samsung* and *Western Digital/Hitachi*, the MOFCOM investigated in detail how the hard disk drive (HDD) market functions, such as the issue of how large computer manufacturers bid for the order in HDD procurement, as well as how market entry, capacity usage and innovation affect the development of the HDD industry. In both cases, the MOFCOM has explicitly mentioned the transaction's impact on consumers because China is one of the major consuming countries of personal computers. From the wording of the MOFCOM, it seems that the welfare impact on consumers is assessed from a boarder picture, and it was taken as one of the issues to understand the function of an industry. Moreover, in both cases consumers across the nation were considered as one group, although the MOFCOM recognized that consumers are highly dispersed. It would also be questionable whether the consideration of the development of the market could

---

[998] Y.W. Chin (2012), *supra* n. 997, p. 7.

[999] D. Healey (2010), *supra* n. 976, p. 44.

[1000] MOFCOM's decision on the Coca Cola/Huiyuan case <http://fldj.mofcom.gov.cn/aarticle/ztxx/200903/20090306108494.html>.

[1001] M. Mariniello (2013), *supra* n. 984, p. 7.

[1002] M. Mariniello (2013), *supra* n. 984, p. 7.

[1003] D.D. Sokol (2013), *supra* n. 995, p. 12.

be understood as following a total welfare standard, as in some situations the differences between the development of the 'domestic market' and the development of the 'domestic industry' were still unclear.

In some cases, the consideration of the 'domestic market' has also been extended to markets relying on international trade. In *Glencore/Xstrata* and *Marubeni/Gavilon* two global mergers, the MOFCOM specifically focused on the effects of the transaction on the import market. In *Glencore/Xstrata*, the MOFCOM mentioned that China is the major copper importing country and constitutes 50 percent of the global copper demand. In 2011, the imported copper consists 68.5 percent of the total supply of copper in China. In both cases, the MOFCOM focused on the analysis of the transaction on the import supply of major natural resources. In *Glencore/Xstrata*, as a remedy to mitigate the anticompetitive effects, the MOFCOM imposed a detailed trade requirement on the long-term contract (from 2013 to 31 December 2020) between Glencore and the Chinese buyers. In *Marubeni/Gavilon*, the MOFCOM put emphasis on the merger's effects on the import market of soya beans. MOFCOM's investigation shows that 99 percent of the soya beans operated by Marubeni are exported to China. In 2012, 80 percent of the supply of soya beans in China relies on import. As the bargaining power from domestic firms is low, MOFCOM imposed behavioral remedies to require Marubeni and Gavilon to keep their business in soya beans independent. The MOFCOM expressed similar concerns in *Uralkali/Silvinit*, and in that case the MOFCOM even mentioned that this merger may negatively affect the agricultural development in China. On the one hand, MOFCOM's concern of the importing market could be explained from the goal of promoting domestic economy, as well as the welfare impact on domestic consumers and producers. On the other hand, this concern can be explained by the role of the MOFCOM itself, as it is a bureau that operates under the leadership of the Ministry of Commerce, of which the major responsibility is to deal with commercial affairs involved in the international trade. It is also possible that the MOFCOM staff members have applied their expertise in dealing with other commercial issues to the implementation of a newborn antitrust law.

Another aspect of the extensive use of behavioral remedies is that in some cases, such as in *Novartis/Alcon*, *Seagate/Samsung*, *Uralkali/Silvinit*, *Walmart/ Newheight*, and *Google/Motorola*, the MOFCOM required a monitor to facilitate the implementation of the behavioral remedies. To some scholars, the goal of appointing a monitor is to ensure compliance.[1004] However, to some lawyers who have followed the *Seagate/Samsung* case closely, this requirement was clearly based on industrial policy concerns.[1005] The reason was that although China is

---

[1004]   X. ZHANG and V. Y. ZHANG (2013), 'Revisiting China's Merger Control, Where are We Going After the Three-Year Milestone?', *Dovenschmidt Quarterly*, no. 1, p. 34.
[1005]   D.D. SOKOL (2013), *supra* n. 995, p. 13.

the largest personal computer market, it does not have a competitive Chinese firm in this industry. In their views, it was highly likely that the government wished to learn from the operation of Western competitors through the process of monitoring.[1006]

2.2.4.   Observation: The Focus on Market Share

The third observation concerning MOFCOM's merger decisions lies in the fact that the MOFCOM tends to focus on the market share of the merging firms. It is highly likely for a merged firm to obtain a 'dominant position' when its post-merger market share is high,[1007] and a merger would be considered highly possible to restrain competition if it creates a dominant position. For example, in *Mitsubishi Rayon/Lucite*, the MOFCOM claimed that the post-merger company held 64 percent of the market share in the MMA product, and that this would lead to a 'dominant position', which could restrict the market access for other competitors.[1008] Similar logic was also applied to the merger analysis of *Pfizer/ Wyeth*, where the MOFCOM claimed that the post-merger firm held a market share of 49.4 percent, with the second producer in the market holding 18.35 percent market share.[1009] Most behavioral remedies were imposed by the MOFCOM for the purpose of mitigating the potential anticompetitive effects; however, these decisions did not provide a detailed analysis regarding to what extent the remedies would indeed reduce the anticompetitive effects.[1010] It also remains unclear how to enhance monitoring efforts and how to deal with the situation if the merging party fails to comply.[1011]

2.2.5.   Summary

Summarizing the two above-mentioned aspects, it gives a general impression that the MOFCOM has paid particular attention to domestic producers who operate in the same industry as the merged firm. By reviewing the cases approved under conditions, it seems that non-economic goals may have played a role in MOFCOM's analysis of merger effects.[1012] This finding could be explained by the competition goals of 'protecting the interest of social public', and 'contributing to the development of the socialist market economy' listed in Article 1 of the AML. In addition, the consideration of domestic competitors also indicates that merger policy in China might have been influenced by

---

[1006]   D.D. SOKOL (2013), *supra* n. 995, p. 13.
[1007]   Q. HAO (2010), *supra* n. 992, p. 17.
[1008]   D. HEALEY (2010), *supra* n. 976, p. 46.
[1009]   D. HEALEY (2010), *supra* n. 976, p. 47.
[1010]   Q. HAO (2010), *supra* n. 992, p. 17.
[1011]   Q. HAO (2010), *supra* n. 992, pp. 16–17.
[1012]   Y.W. CHIN (2012), *supra* n. 997.

industrial policy. As no published case was between two domestic companies, it is difficult to compare whether merger policy has been equally applied to domestic and foreign competitors. However, when a merger between two foreign companies is cleared, it seems that it is always a major concern for the MOFCOM to investigate whether this merger will restrain competition for other domestic competitors in the same industry. Therefore, the boundary between competition policy and industrial policy might not be completely clear-cut in China.

The table below (Table 2) will present four issues in the merger decisions which have been mentioned above. The first issue is how the MOFCOM investigates and in particular collects information for case analysis. Secondly, what are the remedies that have been imposed by the MOFCOM? Thirdly, in each case decision, what are the major concerns of the MOFCOM? Lastly, based on the MOFCOM's analysis of cases, what might be the major consideration of competition goals?

Table 2. An Overview of MOFCOM's Decisions: Remedies, Major Concerns and Competition Goals[1013]

Case	Investigation source[1014]	Remedy (main points)	MOFCOM's major concern	Competition goals[1015]
Coca Cola/Huiyuan	Government, trade associations, fruit juice producer, upstream and downstream firms, experts in law, economics and agriculture	No remedy proposed by the merging parties was accepted by the MOFCOM. This merger was prohibited.	The merger would eliminate and restrict competition in the fruit juice market; will increase the entry barrier for potential competitors and would restrain capacities of domestic producers	The sustainable development of the Chinese fruit juice industry; protect national brands
InBev/Anheuser-Busch	Government, beer trade associations, major domestic beer producers, beer raw material producers, and beer dealers	The equity share in Tsingtao and Zhujiang beer shall not be increased; not allowed to acquire shares in Snow or Yanjing Brewery	Enhanced 'competitiveness' of the merging party; mitigate future anticompetitive effects on Chinese beer market	Protect domestic beer industry
Mitsubishi Rayon/Lucite	Trade associations, producers of MMA and PMMA (polymer and plate) product, the merging parties	Divested 50 percent of Lucite's annual MMA production capacity to a third party buyer; Lucite and Mitsubishi must operate MMA business independently; without MOFCOM's approval, the merged firm is not allowed to build new MMA or PMMA (polymer and plate) manufacture plants in China for 5 years	The dominant position of the merged firm may restrict the competitors' access to the MMA market in China	To protect domestic producers and consumers

1013 Sources: MOFCOM official website: <http://fldj.mofcom.gov.cn/article/ztxx/>; M. MARINIELLO (2013), *supra* n. 984, p. 5; J. O'CONNELL (2012), 'The Year of the Metal Rabbit: Antitrust Enforcement in China in 2011', *Antitrust*, vol. 26, pp. 69–72; Q. HAO (2010), *supra* n. 992, pp. 13–21; Y.W. CHIN (2012), *supra* n. 997; Y.W. CHIN (2013), 'The Chinese MOFCOM Enforces Telecoms Regulations in AML Merger Review', *E-Competition*, no. 51263, pp. 1–2, available at <http://ssrn.com/abstract=2260474>; X. WANG and A. EMCH (2013), *supra* n. 983, pp. 251–256.

1014 For each merger decision, the MOFCOM listed the sources which provided the required information. Both the investigation and the analysis of merger effects were based on these sources.

1015 Neither the MOFCOM nor other government agencies have explicitly explained whether their decisions were made to pursue certain competition goals. The author made this preliminary analysis by incorporating comments and criticisms provided in the literature (source mentioned above in footnote 1013).

Case	Investigation source	Remedy (main points)	MOFCOM's major concern	Competition goals
GM/Delphi	Government, trade associations, car producers and the merging parties	Ensure the supplies of Delphi; merging parties are not allowed to illegally exchange confidential information of other domestic automakers; GM is not allowed to favor Delphi over other auto parts producers	Restrict competition in the automobile market and the upstream auto market in China	Industrial policy considerations (to protect other domestic auto parts manufacturers)
Pfizer/Wyeth	Government, trade associations, competitors in the same industry, upstream and downstream firms	Pfizer is required to divest to a Chinese buyer the swine mycoplasma pneumonia vaccine business in China; Pfizer is obliged to provide technique support to the buyer for three years	Given the high market share of the merged firm (49.4%), the merger would raise anticompetitive concern by controlling product prices	Industrial policy considerations (to protect other producers in the swine mycoplasma pneumonia vaccine market)
Panasonic/Sanyo	Government, trade associations; conducted survey to 39 competitors and downstream customers; made telephone interview with some firms; visited Shenzhen for investigation	Divested a part of business in three battery markets; Panasonic is required to reduce its share in the joint venture from 40 percent to 19.5 percent	Both merging parties hold a high market share in three highly concentrated battery markets	Protection of competition (focus on market power and the number of competitors)
Novartis/Alcon	Government, trade associations, competitors in the same industry; conducted telephone interview with certain firms	Novartis is not allowed to relaunch a product under the name of Infectoflam, or to sell compound products under other names for five years.	The MOFCOM has considered the potential coordinative effects	The development of the Chinese market
Uralkali/Silvinit	Government, trade associations; organized meetings with producers, dealers, experts to collect information	Maintain sales of potassium chloride products to Chinese customers	Holds too large share of a product that is 'crucial to the development of Chinese economy'	The development of the national economy (maintain the supply of strategic resource)[1016]

1016   Y.W. Chin (2012), *supra* n. 997, p. 15.

Case	Investigation source	Remedy (main points)	MOFCOM's major concern	Competition goals
Penelope (AlphaV)/ Savio	Government, trade associations, competitors in the same industry, downstream firms	Alpha's equity share in Uster Technologies Co. Ltd has to be transferred to a third party	Because Alpha has equity share in Uster, the transaction may lead to a coordination between Loepfe and Uster	The development of the Chinese market
GE/Shenhua Group JV	Government, trade associations, competitors in the same industry, experts, third party information	After the transaction, it is not allowed to force customers to use the technology from the joint venture, or to raise the technology cost.	The transaction may impede competition by utilizing Shenhua's supply advantage in coal-water slurry gasification	Promote competition in the coal-water slurry gasification technology market
Seagate/Samsung	Government, trade associations, downstream firms; consulted producers, customers and experts regarding products, relevant market, dealing, market structure, the potential of market development	Keep HDD business under Samsung brand independently; Seagate should maintain its current business model in HDD, and should not restrict the supply of HDD heads by TDK China Co. Ltd; Seagate is required to invest in R&D	By reducing the number of competitors, the merger will reduce the competition pressure for other producers and make it more likely for other producers to coordinate	The development of the Chinese market; promoting consumer welfare
Henkel Hongkong/ Tiande Chemical	Government, trade associations, competitors in the same industry, downstream firms	Tiande is not allowed to charge too high prices and Tiande should supply downstream customers on a non-discriminative basis	The joint venture may restrict competition because Tiande could discriminate other monomer producers in the ethyl cyanoacrylate monomer market	Industrial policy considerations (to maintain the access of certain raw material and to support other producers)[1017]
Western Digital/ Hitachi	Government, trade associations, downstream firms; experts were invited to assess the competitive impact	The operation of Viviti should be maintained as independent; the production capacity and volume of Western Digital and Viviti should be reported to the monitor; Viviti's assets in 3.5" HDD should be divested	The merger may increase the risk for the remaining competitors to coordinate their conduct	The development of the Chinese market; promoting consumer welfare

1017   Y.W. CHIN (2012), *supra* n. 997, p. 15.

Case	Investigation source	Remedy (main points)	MOFCOM's major concern	Competition goals
Google/Motorola	Government, trade associations, downstream firms, consulted experts for technical issues	Google will license its Android platform; Google should treat other equipment manufacturers on non-discriminative terms; Google should be obliged to FRAND terms regarding the patents owned by Motorola	The merger might incentivize Google to provide Android to Motorola on favorable terms, and other rivals might in a disadvantaged position	Industrial policy considerations (the interest of domestic manufacturers)
Goodrich/UTC	Government, competitors in the same industry, downstream customers	Goodrich's aircraft power system business should be divested and a contract with the buyer should be signed within six months after the decision; Goodrich and UTC should provide necessary technical support for the buyer	The merged firm has a very high market share (84%) and the post-merger market concentration is high; barrier to entry is significant;	Merger effects on the global market (MOFCOM was the first antitrust authority which completed this review)
Walmart/Newheight	Government, trade associations, and related companies	After the merger, Newheight is not allowed to provide network service by using its platform to others; Walmart is not allowed to launch value added telecoms service by using a VIE structure	The merger will increase the competitiveness of both parties, and would obtain dominant position in 'value added telecoms services'	Protect competition in the 'value added telecoms service' in China
Advanced RISC Machines/G&D/Gemalto JV	Government, trade associations, competitors in the same industry, downstream firms	The post-merger entity should release the necessary information on TEE based on Trustzone technology; the entity should not take the advantage of its IP to reduce the TEE capacity for any third party	The joint venture would leverage its dominant position to discriminate other TEE technology developers	Industrial policy considerations (other TEE technology developer)
Glencore/Xstrata	Government, trade associations, downstream customers, competitors in the same industry, experts; organized several meetings to check information	Glencore's entire copper business in Las Bambas should be divested; a long term contract on copper, zinc and lead supply with Chinese clients should be maintained	As the merger reduces one of the major competitor, Gemalto will significantly increase its market power in copper, zinc and lead supply market	Industrial policy considerations (effects on the import market)

Case	Investigation source	Remedy (main points)	MOFCOM's major concern	Competition goals
Marubeni/Gavilon	Government, trade associations, related companies	Prohibited to exploit synergies that will reduce wholesale costs and increase Marubeni's competitiveness in the supply of soya beans to the Chinese market	The merger will increase the market power of Marubeni on the soya bean market and will negatively affect China's importing market of soya beans	Industrial policy considerations (effects on import market)
Baxter Int./Gambro	Government, trade associations, downstream customers	Baxter should divest its global CRRT business	The merger will increase the market power of both parties in the CRRT market; the merger would make it more likely for the remaining competitors to coordinate	The competitive effects on China's CRRT market
MediaTek/Mstar Semicondutor	Government, trade associations, competitors in the same industry, downstream firms; conducted survey, organized meetings to check information; local agencies assisted the investigation	Required to notify to MOFCOM before conducting business operations	Difficult for potential competitors to compete with the merged party	The development of the Chinese market

To better understand the influence of policy goals, the fourth section of this chapter will investigate to what extent antitrust authorities in China analyze a merger case from a different perspective than the authorities in the US and the EU. As antitrust authorities in three jurisdictions will all apply economic theories and techniques for merger analysis, economic theories could be used as a benchmark for the comparative study. For this reason, the next section will briefly summarize economic theories, as well as the recent development of economic techniques that are used for horizontal merger analysis.

3.   THE ECONOMIC THEORIES AND TECHNIQUES FOR HORIZONTAL MERGER ANALYSIS: A BRIEF SUMMARY

3.1.   MARKET POWER

Horizontal mergers change the market structure by reducing the number of competing firms and by increasing market concentration; therefore, they have two important effects that vertical mergers and conglomerate mergers do not have.[1018] First, after the merger, the number of the competing firms in the relevant market is decreased. The competitive constraints imposed on one or both merging firms will be significantly reduced and for this reason the merged firm may increase the price. This is called unilateral effects (or single firm dominance) of the merger.[1019] The second anticompetitive concern of a horizontal merger is that the reduction of competing firms may make explicit collusions possible, and this situation is referred to as collective dominance or coordinated effects.[1020]

In both situations, the central concern for competition authorities is to what extent the merged firm may exert market power. The concept of 'market power' as defined by economists is broader than that used by antitrust policy makers.[1021] Economists define 'market power' as the ability of the seller to set prices above *marginal costs*, and this definition is made by setting perfect competition as the benchmark.[1022] Firms do not exert market power in a perfectly competitive market, where prices are set equal to marginal cost and no firm can affect market prices.[1023] Both allocative and productive efficiency are achieved in a perfect

---

[1018]   S. Bishop and M. Walker (2002), *The Economics of EC Competition Law: Concepts, Application and Measurement*, Sweet & Maxwell, section 7.16.

[1019]   S. Bishop and M. Walker (2002), *supra* n. 1018, section 7.16.

[1020]   S. Bishop and M. Walker (2002), *supra* n. 1018, section 7.17.

[1021]   D. Neven, R. Nuttall and P. Seabright, *Mergers in Daylight, The Economics and Politics of European Merger Control,* The Centre for Economic Policy Research 1993, p. 17.

[1022]   D. Neven, R. Nuttall and P. Seabright (1993), *supra* n. 1021, p. 17.

[1023]   D. Neven, R. Nuttall and P. Seabright (1993), *supra* n. 1021, p. 17.

competitive market.[1024] According to this benchmark, firms will hold market power as soon as they are able to raise price above marginal costs.[1025] The assessment of market power should therefore be conducted by examining the extent to which firms are able to raise price above marginal costs without losing buyers.[1026] In industrial economics literature, measuring market power by calculating to what extent the price is deviated from the firm's marginal costs is demonstrated by the Lerner Index (P-MC/P),[1027] which was first proposed by Abba Lerner in 1934.[1028]

However, in practice, 'market power' is usually defined as the ability of the seller to set price above the *competitive level* for a significant period of time.[1029] This is because estimating the market power by focusing on the marginal cost may not be realistic in antitrust practices as the marginal cost pricing is based on the ideal perfect competition model.[1030] In reality, almost all firms would exert a certain level of market power if it is defined as the ability of setting the price above the marginal cost.[1031] Hence, the price under competitive conditions is often taken as the practical benchmark.

In merger analysis, the market power of the merged firm can be assessed through an indirect or a direct way.[1032] The indirect approach relies on several indicators, such as market share and the level of market concentration, in order to estimate the market power of the merged firm. The economic reason for this indirect approach is provided by the SCP framework developed by Joe Bain in 1951.[1033] Following his pioneering work, a large volume of empirical studies on the interaction between market performance and structural variables has been conducted among industrial organization scholars.[1034] The empirical work with a strong focus on market structure provided economic justifications for an indirect approach of merger analysis. In particular, by following this approach,

---

[1024] D. NEVEN, R. NUTTALL and P. SEABRIGHT (1993), *supra* n. 1021, p. 17.

[1025] D. NEVEN, R. NUTTALL and P. SEABRIGHT (1993), *supra* n. 1021, p. 17.

[1026] D. NEVEN, R. NUTTALL and P. SEABRIGHT (1993), *supra* n. 1021, p. 17.

[1027] W.M. LANDES and R.A. POSNER (1981), 'Market Power in Antitrust Cases', *Harvard Law Review*, vol. 94, no. 5, p. 939.

[1028] A.P. LERNER (1934), 'The Concept of Monopoly and the Measurement of Monopoly Power', *Review of Economic Studies*, vol. 1, no. 3, pp. 157–175; For a study on the history of the Lerner Index, *see* N. GIOCOLI (2012), 'Who Invented the Lerner Index? Luigi Amoroso, the Dominant Firm Model, and the Measurement of Market Power', *Review of Industrial Organization*, vol. 41, pp. 181–191.

[1029] M. MOTTA (2004), *supra* n. 507, p. 235; *see* for example, US Horizontal Merger Guidelines 1992, para 0.1: 'Market power to a seller is the ability profitably to maintain prices above competitive levels for a significant period of time'. A. LINDSAY (2006), *supra* n. 756, p. 5.

[1030] S. BISHOP and M. WALKER (2002), *supra* n. 1018, section 3.04.

[1031] S. BISHOP and M. WALKER (2002), *supra* n. 1018, section 3.04.

[1032] M. MOTTA (2004), *supra* n. 507, p. 117.

[1033] T.F. BRESNAHAN (1989), 'Empirical Studies of Industries with Market Power', in R. SCHMALENSEE and R.D. WILLIG (eds.), *Handbook of Industrial Organization*, volume 2, p. 1012.

[1034] T.F. BRESNAHAN (1989), *supra* n. 1033, p. 1013.

post-merger firms with a high market share or a large concentration level would be more likely to exert market power.[1035] In recent years, a new trend has been observed in the industrial organization literature which applies econometric techniques to measure the market power in a direct manner. Both indirect and direct approaches in merger analysis will be explained in detail in the following sections.

3.2. INDIRECT ASSESSMENT OF MARKET POWER

Antitrust authorities have traditionally relied on the indirect approach which focuses on the structure of the market and puts emphasis on market share.[1036] This is based on the economic premise that the structure of the market would influence the market performance, and government intervention (such as implementing merger control policy) would have an impact on market structure.[1037] As mentioned in the previous chapter, the causal chain of 'Structure-Conduct-Performance ('SCP')' was initially developed by Harvard School scholars, in particular the seminal work conducted by Joe Bain.[1038] The pioneering work of Bain was refined by a large volume of empirical study on the relationship between market structure and performance.[1039] Although the direct causal chain of the SCP framework was challenged and criticized,[1040] most

---

[1035] J.B. BAKER and T.F. BRESNAHAN (1992), 'Empirical Methods of Indentifying and Measuring Market Power', *Antitrust Law Journal*, vol. 61, p. 4.

[1036] R.J. VAN DEN BERGH and P.D. CAMESASCA (2006), *supra* n. 18, p. 96.

[1037] A. LINDSAY (2006), *supra* n. 756, p. 11.

[1038] J.S. BAIN (1951), 'Relation of Profit Rate to Industry Concentration: American Manufacturing, 1936–1940', *Quarterly Journal of Economics*, vol. 65, pp. 293–324; J.S. BAIN (1956), *supra* n. 362.

[1039] Researchers often apply practical measurements to assess this relationship. There are three commonly used measures to assess market performance: the rate of return (the extent to which one dollar of investment will generate profits); the price-cost margin (the difference between price and marginal cost); and Tobin's Q (the difference between a firm's stock-market value and the replacement cost of the same assets). Carlton and Perloff briefly summarized the empirical findings on the relationship between market structure and these three types of measures, as well as the criticism of these results. D.W. CARLTON and J.M. PERLOFF, *Modern Industrial Organization*, HarperCollins Publishers 1990, Chapter 12, pp. 361, 371–384.

[1040] The most important criticism of the SCP framework is that the relationship between structure and performance is not a one way direction. As Demsetz argued, the success of a firm is not the result of a concentrated market structure, instead it is the outcome of being efficient and the success of the firm may in turn lead to a higher market share. H. DEMSETZ (1973), 'Industry Structure, Market Rivalry, and Public Policy', *Journal of Law and Economics*, vol. 16, pp. 1–10; It was also argued that there are feedback effects between other variables, such as between conduct and structure. A. LINDSAY (2006), *supra* n. 756, p. 11; Bishop and Walker concluded that various industry variables could be interlinked. S. BISHOP and M. WALKER (2002), *supra* n. 1018, section 3.22; For a comprehensive overview of the refinement and criticism of the SCP framework, *see* for example, R. SCHMALENSEE, 'Inter-industry Studies of Structure and Performance', in R. SCHMALENSEE and R.D. WILLIG (eds.), *Handbook of Industrial Organization*, Elsevier 1989, volume 2, Chapter 16, pp. 952–1009; *See also* M. SALINGER, R.E.

scholars agreed to take structural variables into account when the market performance is assessed.[1041]

One of the important measures to assess market structure is the level of industry concentration. Economists generally agree that it is more likely that a merger will lead to an increase of market power in an industry which is more concentrated, than in an industry with a large number of fragmented, small firms.[1042] This is based on the findings of industrial economics models which show that except for mergers between small firms, mergers which do not generate efficiency gains will increase the concentration level of the market, and in this way they may reduce consumer welfare.[1043] This conclusion has been proven by two types of models.[1044] Models with price as the decision variable show that after the merger, the prices of both the merged firm and other outside firms will increase.[1045] Models with quantity as the decision variable prove that the output produced by the post-merger firm will be reduced whereas the output of outside firms will be increased.[1046]

3.2.1.   The Definition of the Relevant Market

The indirect assessment of market power has long relied on defining the relevant market, and the issue of how the relevant market is defined to a large extent affects the decision of whether a merger will be approved.[1047] Although the concept of 'relevant market' has not precisely defined in any industrial organization books,[1048] in practice it usually refers to the 'narrowest market' in which the merging firm may exert market power,[1049] including both the product relevant market and the geographic relevant market. The theme of defining the relevant market is not to collect the products or a set of geographical areas which

---

CAVES and S. PELTZMAN (1990), 'The Concentration-Margins Relationship Reconsidered', *Brookings Papers on Economic Activity. Microeconomics*, vol. 1990, pp. 287–335.

[1041]   A. LINDSAY (2006), *supra* n. 756, p. 12.

[1042]   M. MOTTA (2004), *supra* n. 507, p. 235.

[1043]   M. MOTTA (2004), *supra* n. 507, p. 234; *See also* R. AMIR, E. DIAMANTOUDI and L. XUE (2009), 'Merger Performance under Uncertain Efficiency Gains', *International Journal of Industrial Organization*, vol. 27, p. 265. The study on the welfare effects of mergers were initiated by Joseph Farrell and Carl Shapiro in 1990. *See* J. FARRELL and C. SHAPIRO (1990), 'Horizontal Mergers: An Equilibrium Analysis', *American Economic Review*, vol. 80, pp. 107–126.

[1044]   M. MOTTA (2004), *supra* n. 507, p. 234.

[1045]   M. MOTTA (2004), *supra* n. 507, p. 234; *see for example* R.J. DENECKERE and C. DAVIDSON (1985), 'Incentives to Form Coalitions with Bertrand Competition', *Rand Journal of Economics*, vol. 16, pp. 473–486.

[1046]   M. MOTTA (2004), *supra* n. 507, p. 234. The most prominent study was conducted by Farrell and Shapiro in 1990 on mergers in Cournot oligopoly. J. FARRELL and C. SHAPIRO (1990), *supra* n. 1043, pp. 107–126.

[1047]   R. GRIFFITH and L. NESHEIM, 'Defining Antitrust Markets', in M. NEUMANN and J. WEIGAND (eds.) *The International Handbook of Competition*, 2nd ed., Edward Elgar 2013, p. 207.

[1048]   L. KAPLOW (2011), 'Market Definition and the Merger Guidelines', 'Market Definition and the Merger Guidelines', *Review of Industrial Organization*, vol. 39, p. 114.

[1049]   D. NEVEN, R. NUTTALL and P. SEABRIGHT (1993), *supra* n. 1021, p. 48.

share similar characteristics, but to investigate whether they are imposing constraints on each other in terms of the possibility of increasing the price.[1050] Motta gives the example that the relevant market of bananas is defined through the examination of whether there are other types of fruits, such as pineapples, mangos and papayas, which could be served as substitutes for bananas, therefore could restrain the possibility of increasing the price for bananas.[1051]

The most commonly used economic technique for defining both the geography and the product relevant market is called the SSNIP test ('small but significant and non-transitory increase in prices test', or the 'hypothetical monopolist test').[1052] This test is applied in the following way.[1053] Continuing the example given by Motta, assume a seller of bananas increases the *current*[1054] banana price by 5 percent[1055] in a *non-transitory* way, if this price increase does not lead to a loss of demand but to an increase of profits, it would indicate that consumers do not switch to other products when the price of bananas is increased; therefore, there is no other product which can impose competitive constraints on bananas. In this case, the product market should be defined as bananas.[1056] By contrast, if the price increase does not lead to a gain of profits due to the loss of demand, the test should continue to put bananas and other fruits, for example, kiwi fruits, together and to investigate a price increase of 5 percent of both banana and kiwi would lead to a profitable outcome.[1057] If so, the product relevant market is bananas and kiwi fruits; if not, the test should continue to include other fruits and to test in which market a price increase will lead to an increase in profits.[1058] Applying the same procedure, when a geographic market is defined, the SSNIP test will be implemented to test whether the sellers in place A, will receive profits when the price is increased. If so, place A will be the geographic market. If not, the test should be continued to test whether it is profitable to include sellers in both place A and B, and even larger areas.[1059]

[1050] M. MOTTA (2004), *supra* n. 507, p. 102.

[1051] M. MOTTA (2004), *supra* n. 507, p. 102.

[1052] This test was first introduced by the 1982 Horizontal Merger Guidelines in the US. R.J. VAN DEN BERGH and P.D. CAMESASCA (2006), *supra* n. 18, p. 97.

[1053] This example is given by MOTTA (2004), *supra* n. 507, p. 102.

[1054] If the seller holds a dominant position, the benchmark to be applied should be the *competitive* prices not the current prices. Because if the seller is the monopolist, the price might be set already high enough, and a 5 percent increase will not be profitable. This refers to the famous 'cellophane fallacy' discussed in the *du Pont* case in the US Supreme Court. M. MOTTA (2004), *supra* n. 507, p. 105 (*United States v. E.I. DuPont de Nemours & Co.*, 351 U.S. 377 (1956)).

[1055] The US 1982 Horizontal Merger Guidelines set it 5 percent whereas in the EU, the Commission Notice on the Definition of the Relevant Market defines it as 5–10 percent. For a discussion on the reason why the threshold is 5 percent or 10 percent, *see* R. PITOFSKY (1990), 'New Definitions of Relevant Market and the Assault on Antitrust', *Columbia Law Review*, vol. 90, no. 7, p. 1838.

[1056] M. MOTTA (2004), *supra* n. 507, p. 102.

[1057] M. MOTTA (2004), *supra* n. 507, p. 103.

[1058] M. MOTTA (2004), *supra* n. 507, p. 103.

[1059] M. MOTTA (2004), *supra* n. 507, p. 113.

In this example, bananas, kiwis, mangos and papayas, chosen by the consumers, are considered to be substitutes from the demand side.[1060] On the producer side, it may also be possible for producers to switch production and to supply a different product when the price increases. This is called supply-side substitutability.[1061] Defining the relevant market is highly crucial to evaluate the extent to which the market is concentrated as well as to measure the market share of the firm. When the relevant market is wider, the market share of a firm becomes smaller.[1062]

3.2.2. Market Concentration

Within the relevant market, an economic technique called the Concentration Ratio ('CR') can be applied to assess the market concentration level. The most commonly used measures are the four-firm and eight-firm Concentration Ratio ('CR4' or 'CR8') which calculate the market share of the top four, or the top eight firms. It is worth mentioning that applying the CR as a proxy for calculating the concentration level of the market suffers from a few of deficiencies.[1063] Firstly, it neglects the relative size among the leading firms.[1064] Bishop and Walker gave an example to explain the deficiency of the CR4: it would have the same result both when the top four firms each hold 20 percent market share, and when the top four firms each hold a market share of 55 percent, 20 percent, 4 percent and 1 percent respectively.[1065] However, the competitiveness in these two markets would differ significantly.[1066] The second deficiency of the CR index is that it does not take into account the total number of firms in the market, and it neglects the market share of smaller firms.[1067]

Another way to measure the concentration level is the sum of the squared market share of each individual firm in the market, which is called the Herfindahl-Hirschman Index ('HHI').[1068] This index was developed by Orris Herfindahl and Albert Hirschman independently based on two different studies.[1069] The popularity of the HHI index in the industrial organization field was brought by Herfindahl's doctoral thesis advisor, George Stigler, who argued

---

[1060]   M. MOTTA (2004), *supra* n. 507, p. 103.

[1061]   M. MOTTA (2004), *supra* n. 507, p. 103.

[1062]   J. FARRELL and C. SHAPIRO (2010), 'Recapture, Pass-Through, and Market Definition', *Antitrust Law Journal,* vol. 76, p. 585.

[1063]   S. BISHOP and M. WALKER (2002), *supra* n. 1018, section 3.25.

[1064]   S. BISHOP and M. WALKER (2002), *supra* n. 1018, section 3.25.

[1065]   S. BISHOP and M. WALKER (2002), *supra* n. 1018, section 3.25.

[1066]   S. BISHOP and M. WALKER (2002), *supra* n. 1018, section 3.25.

[1067]   S. BISHOP and M. WALKER (2002), *supra* n. 1018, section 3.25.

[1068]   M. MOTTA (2004), *supra* n. 507, p. 235; S. CALKINS (1983), 'The New Merger Guidelines and the Herfindahl-Hirschman Index', *California Law Review,* vol. 71, no. 2, p. 409.

[1069]   S. CALKINS (1983), *supra* n. 1068, p. 409; See A.O. HIRSCHMAN (1964), *supra* n. 842, pp. 761–762; A.O. HIRSCHMAN(1945), *supra* n. 842; O. HERFINDAHL, *Concentration in the Steel Industry* 1950.

that the HHI index could reflect the fluctuation of the market share, and in this way it could predict the 'likelihood of effective collusion'.[1070] On the legal side, the HHI index was promoted by Richard Posner in 1969[1071] and later it was introduced to the DOJ by Assistant Attorney General William Baxter, who implemented it in the 1982 Horizontal Merger Guidelines.[1072]

Compared with the CR, one advantage of the HHI method is that it counts all the firms in the market, it is therefore not required to decide *a priori* which firms are more significant in the market in order to measure the concentration level.[1073] However, given the fact that the HHI index is calculated as the sum of the squared values of market share, it gives higher weight to firms with a large market share.[1074] Therefore, a small error in calculating the leading firms' market share will make the result very different.[1075] The HHI index used to be applied to define a 'safe harbor'[1076] under the US 1982 Horizontal Merger Guidelines: mergers with the post-merger HHI below 1000 were unlikely to be challenged by the antitrust authority. Moreover, the HHI index was taken as an important threshold in merger analysis, as the higher HHI a merger reaches the more likely it is to be challenged.[1077]

3.2.3.   Market Share

In addition to the measurement of the market concentration level, another important implication of applying the structural approach in merger analysis is that market power of an individual firm can be measured through its market share.[1078] According to Motta, this implication can also be supported by several industrial organization models.[1079] In addition to market share, there are other indicators that should be incorporated in the analysis of the market power, for example, the productive capacities of the existing rivals, as the market power of the merged firm will be restrained if there are powerful rivals in the market from

---

[1070]   S. CALKINS (1983), *supra* n. 1068, p. 409; G. STIGLER (1964), 'A Theory of Oligopoly', *Journal of Political Economy*, vol. 72, p. 55.

[1071]   R. POSNER (1969), 'Oligopoly and the Antitrust Laws: A Suggested Approach', *Stanford Law Review*, vol. 21, pp. 1602–1603; cited by S. CALKINS (1983), *supra* n. 1068, p. 409.

[1072]   S. CALKINS (1983), *supra* n. 1068, pp. 408, 409.

[1073]   S. CALKINS (1983), *supra* n. 1068, p. 405.

[1074]   F.M. SCHERER and D. ROSS, *Industrial Market Structure and Economic Performance*, 3rd ed., Houghton Mifflin Company 1990, p. 72.

[1075]   F.M. SCHERER and D. ROSS (1990), *supra* n. 1074, p. 72.

[1076]   S. CALKINS (1983), *supra* n. 1068, p. 406.

[1077]   S. CALKINS (1983), *supra* n. 1068, p. 407.

[1078]   S. BISHOP and M. WALKER (2002), *supra* n. 1018, section 3.21.

[1079]   M. MOTTA (2004), *supra* n. 507, p. 235; According to Motta, the economic justifications of applying the market share as the indicator for market power are provided by J. FARRELL and C. SHAPIRO (1990), *supra* n. 1043, pp. 107–126; M.K. PERRY and R. PORTER (1985), 'Oligopoly and the Incentive for Horizontal Merger', *American Economic Review*, vol. 75, pp. 219–227; P. MCAFEE and M.A. WILLIAMS (1992), 'Horizontal Mergers and Antitrust Policy', *Journal Industrial Economics*, vol. 40, pp. 181–187.

which the demand from consumers will be satisfied.[1080] The firm's capacity of raising prices after the merger is also dependent on the ease of entry.[1081] The market power of the incumbent firm is to a large extent restrained when there are potential entrants.[1082] The barrier to entry includes technological, administrative, financial factors, as well as the considerations of switching costs and network effects.[1083] Moreover, the market power of the merged firms could also be affected by the buyers' power.[1084] When the buyers have the power to switch the order to another producer, the firm's ability to raise prices will be constrained.[1085]

3.2.4.   The Consideration of Efficiency Gains

In addition to the economic assessment of the relevant market and the market power, another very important aspect in horizontal merger analysis is the evaluation of the efficiency gains of a merger.[1086] As the Williamson model presented in the previous chapter shows, efficiency gains may counterbalance the anticompetitive effects caused by a merger. Most recent economic evidence indicates that a merger may enhance productive efficiency through the increased economies of scale, and through cost savings in distribution, marketing and administration.[1087] By analyzing 264 mergers in unregulated industries from the SDC Mergers and Acquisitions database, in the period 1980 to 2004, the empirical study by Devos, Kadapakkam and Krishnamurthy showed that the primary source for merger synergies comes from the realization of economies of scale and operation synergies, which counted for 8.38 percent.[1088] Their study also supported the economic view that mergers will generate benefits through a better resource reallocation.[1089] In a recent study by Bernile and Lyandres,[1090] their theoretical model and empirical tests show that the operating synergies generated through a horizontal merger not only benefit the merging firms, but also benefit the rivals who compete with the merging firms in product markets, as well as customers and suppliers who operate in the same supply chain of the merging firm.

[1080]   M. MOTTA (2004), *supra* n. 507, p. 236.
[1081]   M. MOTTA (2004), *supra* n. 507, p. 236.
[1082]   M. MOTTA (2004), *supra* n. 507, p. 236.
[1083]   M. MOTTA (2004), *supra* n. 507, p. 237, footnote 20.
[1084]   M. MOTTA (2004), *supra* n. 507, p. 237.
[1085]   M. MOTTA (2004), *supra* n. 507, p. 237.
[1086]   M. MOTTA (2004), *supra* n. 507, p. 238.
[1087]   M. MOTTA (2004), *supra* n. 507, p. 240.
[1088]   E. DEVOS, P. KADAPAKKAM and S. KRISHNAMURTHY (2009), 'How Do Mergers Create Value? A Comparison of Taxes, Market Power, and Efficiency Improvements as Explanations for Synergies', *The Review of Financial Studies*, vol. 22, no.3, p. 1181.
[1089]   E. DEVOS, P. KADAPAKKAM and S. KRISHNAMURTHY (2009), *supra* n. 1088, p. 1194.
[1090]   G. BERNILE and E. LYANDRES (2013), 'The Effects of Horizontal Merger Synergies on Competitors, Customers and Suppliers', <http://papers.ssrn.com/sol3/papers.cfm?abstract_id=2311560>.

The challenge of incorporating efficiency considerations into merger analysis is rooted in the complex interaction between market structure and conduct. The extent to which the increase of market power of a merger should be tolerated tends to become a paradox.[1091] On the one hand, when a merger generates efficiency gains, the benefit of the merger may offset the anticompetitive harm caused by the increased market power; on the other hand, the industrial economics model shows that a merger can hardly be profitable when it does not obtain a substantial market share.[1092] In practice, efficiency arguments are often dealt with caution in the analysis of merger effects. The benefit of scale economies can only be considered when it is 'merger-specific', that is, it cannot be achieved without the merger.[1093] A typical case is when efficiencies require a close integration of the 'hard-to-trade assets' of both parties.[1094] In economic terms, efficiencies which can only be achieved through cooperation and coordination between firms are called synergies.[1095] More precisely, by coordinating the assets, firms are able to produce by following a new production function;[1096] therefore synergies are achieved through restructuring the output/cost function, which cannot be realized without the cooperation of firms.[1097] The concept of synergy has important implications for evaluating whether the benefits created by economies of scale are 'merger-specific', because it may also be possible for firms to increase economies of scale without a merger (such as through internal expansion), but in that case the merger will not impose any change in the function of prices, outputs or costs.[1098]

In addition, the concept of synergy can also be applied to measure the effects of a merger on consumers.[1099] In the Cournot oligopoly model developed by Farrell and Shapiro,[1100] compared with non-synergy mergers, mergers with synergies are to a large extent more beneficial for consumers. The effects on

---

[1091] *See* 'Merger Paradox' defined by S.W. SALANT, S. SWITZER and R.J. REYNOLDS (1983), 'Losses from Horizontal Merger: The Effect of an Exogenous Change in Industry Structure on Cournot-Nash Equilibrium', *Quarterly Journal of Economics*, vol. 98, no. 2, pp. 185–199.

[1092] The symmetric Cournot oligopoly model developed by Salant, Switzer and Reynolds in 1983 shows that with linear demand and costs, a merger will only be profitable when its pre-merger market share exceeds 80 percent. S.W. SALANT, S. SWITZER and R.J. REYNOLDS (1983), *supra* n. 1091, pp. 185–199. Note that other models may show different results, for example, Deneckere and Davidson (1985) examined the Bertrand model with differentiated products and the significant pre-merger market share is not required to make a merger profitable. DENECKERE, R.J. and C. DAVIDSON (1985), *supra* n. 1045, pp. 473–486; *see* R. AMIR, E. DIAMANTOUDI and L. XUE (2009), *supra* n. 1043, p. 264.

[1093] J. FARRELL and C. SHAPIRO (2001), 'Scale Economies and Synergies in Horizontal Merger Analysis', *Antitrust Law Journal*, vol. 68, p. 687.

[1094] J. FARRELL and C. SHAPIRO (2001), *supra* n. 1093, p. 693.

[1095] J. FARRELL and C. SHAPIRO (2001), *supra* n. 1093, p. 693.

[1096] J. FARRELL and C. SHAPIRO (2001), *supra* n. 1093, p. 693.

[1097] J. FARRELL and C. SHAPIRO (2001), *supra* n. 1093, p. 693.

[1098] J. FARRELL and C. SHAPIRO (2001), *supra* n. 1093, p. 693.

[1099] J. FARRELL and C. SHAPIRO (2001), *supra* n. 1093, p. 693.

[1100] J. FARRELL and C. SHAPIRO (1990), *supra* n. 1043, pp. 107–126.

consumers play a very important role in justifying efficiency arguments in merger analysis. For example, under both the US and the EU merger policy, there is a 'pass-on' requirement that implies efficiency arguments can only be accepted when consumers can benefit from the efficiency gains created by the merger.[1101]

3.2.5.   Entry

The issue of entry is one of the very important aspects in the analysis of market power, as the market power of incumbents will be constrained if there are potential entrants.[1102] Before the emergence of game theory, which assesses the interaction between incumbents and entrants in a strategic framework,[1103] the two dominant views on the conditions of entry were held by Bain and Stigler, who have different understandings of the 'barriers to entry'.[1104] By relying on the SCP framework, Bain argues that 'barriers to entry' are established through a series of structural factors, such as economies of scale, product differentiation and cost advantages of the incumbent firm.[1105] Bain's structural analysis of barriers has policy implications for intervention,[1106] whereas the Chicago School scholar Stigler questioned the view of imposing regulations, patents and tariffs to prevent the entry barriers.[1107] For Stigler, the barriers to entry are additional 'long-term costs' which should be borne by the new entrant.[1108] If incumbents had an advantage and were able to enter the market the first, the potential entrants have to make investments to compete. In situations where potential entrants are able to achieve low costs, or to develop differentiated products at lower costs than incumbents, Stigler would disagree with Bain to include factors of 'scale economies', and 'product differentiation' as 'barriers to entry'.[1109]

The recent development of game theory extended the debate on 'barriers to entry' to the 'likelihood of entry'. The strategic approach to entry analysis

---

[1101]   J. FARRELL and C. SHAPIRO (2001), *supra* n. 1093, p. 687.

[1102]   M. MOTTA (2004), *supra* n. 507, p. 120.

[1103]   *See for example*, S.C. SALOP (1979), 'Strategic Entry Deterrence', *The American Economic Review*, vol. 69, no. 2, Papers and Proceedings of the Ninety-First Annual Meeting of the American Economic Association (May 1979), pp. 335–338; J. FARRELL (1987), 'Cheap Talk, Coordination, and Entry', *The RAND Journal of Economics*, vol. 18, no. 1, pp. 34–39.

[1104]   J.B. BAKER (2003), 'Responding to Developments in Economics and the Courts: Entry in the Merger Guidelines', *Antitrust Law Journal*, vol. 71, p. 191; For an overview of the discussion of 'barriers to entry', see for example, R.J. GILBERT (1989), 'Mobility Barriers and the Value of Incumbency', in R. SCHMALENSEE and R.D. WILLIG (eds.) *Handbook of Industrial Organization*, vol. 1, Elsevier 1989, pp. 476–535.

[1105]   J. BAIN (1949), 'A Note on Pricing in Monopoly and Oligopoly', *American Economic Review*, vol. 39, pp. 448–464; cited by R.J. GILBERT (1989), *supra* n. 1104, p. 480.

[1106]   J.B. BAKER (2003), *supra* n. 1104, p. 192.

[1107]   J.B. BAKER (2003), *supra* n. 1104, p. 192.

[1108]   G.J. STIGLER (1968), *The Organization of Industry*, Homewood: Irwin.

[1109]   J.B. BAKER (2003), *supra* n. 1104, p. 193.

focuses on the situations where the entry requires significant sunk costs.[1110] Economists generally agree that sunk costs could deter entry by making entry riskier.[1111]

3.2.6. Buyers' Power

Another factor that needs to be taken into account in the assessment of market power is whether buyers could restrain the seller's ability to raise prices. According to Motta,[1112] the first author who gave attention to buyers' power is John Kenneth Galbraith in 1952.[1113] The implication of the buyers' power argument is that in industries where buyers are to a large extent concentrated, and the investment to enter the market (fixed cost) is high, the bargaining power of the buyers should not be neglected.[1114] The explanation for this is that a seller would be reluctant to make an investment to enter the market if the buyers are dispersed and only a few would switch their order from the incumbent to the new entrant;[1115] by contrast, if there is a commitment from a large, concentrated number of buyers in the market, the new entrant would be more likely to make a decision to invest.[1116] Some examples of these industries are cable television, newspapers, motion pictures and computer software.[1117] The buyer will have market power when it can constrain the market power from the seller and can force the seller to reduce prices for downstream consumers. Like the terminology of monopoly and oligopoly, when the market power comes from one dominant buyer, the buyer becomes a monopsony; when there are several powerful buyers in the market, they become oligopsony.[1118] Similar to the competitive effects of monopoly and oligopoly, in economic literature, the treatment of buyers' power is also two-sided. The buyers' power should be encouraged only when it has a positive impact;[1119] however, economists and lawyers have not reached a consensus regarding whether the market power from the seller and the buyer should be treated symmetrically,

---

[1110] J.B. BAKER (2003), *supra* n. 1104, p. 196.

[1111] R. SCHMALENSEE (2004), 'Sunk Costs and Antitrust Barriers to Entry', *MIT Sloan School of Management Working Paper No. 4457–04*, p. 8.

[1112] M. MOTTA (2004), *supra* n. 507, p. 121.

[1113] J.K. GALBRAITH, *American Capitalism: The Concept of Countervailing Power*, Mifflin 1952. Note that buyers' power mentioned in this chapter is limited to horizontal mergers. For a discussion of buyers' power and vertical integration, *see* F.M. SCHERER and D. Ross (1990), *supra* n. 1074, pp. 517–539.

[1114] M. MOTTA (2004), *supra* n. 507, p. 121–122.

[1115] M. MOTTA (2004), *supra* n. 507, p. 122.

[1116] N. ADILOV and P.J. ALEXANDER (2006), 'Horizontal Merger: Pivotal Buyers and Bargaining Power', *Economic Letters*, vol. 91, p. 308.

[1117] N. ADILOV and P.J. ALEXANDER (2006), *supra* n. 1116, p. 307.

[1118] R.G. NOLL (2005), '"Buyer Power" and Economic Policy', *Antitrust Law Journal*, vol. 72, p. 589.

[1119] R.A. SKITOL (2005), 'Concerted Buying Power: Its Potential For Addressing the Patent Holdup Problem in Standard Setting', *Antitrust Law Journal*, vol. 72, p. 727.

that is, whether the analysis of anticompetitive effects due to refusal to deal, price collusion and barriers to entry should also be extended to the buyer's side.[1120]

3.2.7. Remedies

After the antitrust authorities analyze the merger effects by taking into consideration the definition of relevant market, market power and the assessment of efficiency gains, they may approve or prohibit the merger, or approve the merger under conditions. In the last scenario, the antitrust authorities often impose 'remedies' on the proposed merger. There are two commonly adopted remedies: structural remedies and non-structural remedies, and the latter often refer to behavioral remedies.[1121] Structural remedies in most situations refer to divestiture, meaning divesting a part or the entire assets of the business and transferring the property rights of these assets to an existing competitor or a new firm.[1122] Behavioral remedies are defined as a type of commitment which ensures that after the merger, the competitors will enjoy a 'level playing field' to access the key assets or technologies owned by the merged firm,[1123] and this situation more commonly arises when a merger leads to vertical integration.[1124] Antitrust authorities can also impose a combination of both behavioral and structure remedies on a proposed merger.

In practice, compared with behavioral remedies, structural remedies embody a clear advantage that they do not require the monitoring efforts from the competition authority after the assets have been divested.[1125] However, structural remedies also face a few challenges when they are implemented. First, the merging firms have a strong incentive to choose a buyer which is not a competitive firm in the market, or as Farrell called it, the buyer is often a 'teammate' of the merging firms.[1126] In addition, the merging firms may reduce the value of the assets to be sold through activities such as transferring personnel or disposing of patents or certain brands.[1127] The second problem of the

---

[1120] R.G. NOLL (2005), *supra* n. 1118, p. 590.
[1121] M. MOTTA (2004), *supra* n. 507, p. 265;.
[1122] M. MOTTA (2004), *supra* n. 507, p. 266. For an evolutionary view of the application of merger remedies in the US, *see* D. BALTO (2001), 'Lessons from the Clinton Administration: The Evolving Approach to Merger Remedies', *George Washington Law Review*, vol. 69, pp. 952–977; J.E. KWOKA JR. and D.L. MOSS (2011), 'Behavioral Merger Remedies: Evaluation and Implications for Antitrust Enforcement', <http://papers.ssrn.com/sol3/papers.cfm?abstract_id=1959588>.
[1123] M. MOTTA (2004), *supra* n. 507, p. 268.
[1124] M. MOTTA, M. POLO and H. VASCONCELOS (2002), 'Merger Remedies in the European Union: An Overview', Paper presented at the Symposium on 'Guidelines for Merger Remedies – Prospects and Principles', Ecole des Mines, Paris, January 17–18, 2002, p. 11.
[1125] M. MOTTA, M. POLO and H. VASCONCELOS (2002), *supra* n. 1124, p. 5.
[1126] J. FARRELL (2003), 'Negotiation and Merger Remedies: Some Problems', *Competition Policy Center, University of California, Working Paper No. CPC 03–41*, p. 2.
[1127] M. MOTTA, M. POLO and H. VASCONCELOS (2002), *supra* n. 1124, p. 6.

structural remedy is that there are significant information asymmetries between the seller, the buyer and the competition authority.[1128] The seller has superior information concerning the value of the assets; therefore the seller is incentivized to prepare the entity package which does not include the crucial assets in the industry.[1129] The third risk of structural remedy is that when the buyer is active in the market, the divestiture may help symmetrically distribute the assets, capacities and the market share between the buyer and the seller. Although the divestiture may reduce the single dominance effect of the merged firm, this symmetry may lead to a collusive outcome which impedes competition in the market.[1130] Therefore, if the competition authority chooses to impose a structural remedy, it is important to both mitigate the single dominance problems, as well as to reduce the risk of post-merger collusive behavior.[1131] Nevertheless, the commitment to ensuring the competitors will have 'non-discriminated' access to technology and assets is often difficult to enforce.[1132]

Most of the behavioral remedies require monitoring efforts from the competition authorities, and a successful monitoring may require the authority to have specific knowledge about the industry.[1133] For this reason behavioral remedies are more difficult to implement. It is particular challenging as the antitrust authority often makes decisions on a merger ex ante after a short period of investigation, and it is difficult to predict the changes of the industry structure.[1134] Moreover, unlike industry regulators, competition authorities are not familiar with the specific knowledge of one particular industry as they deal with competition issues in all industries.[1135]

3.3.   DIRECT ASSESSMENT OF MARKET POWER

3.3.1.   Introduction

Since the 1980s, industrial organization economists have devoted large efforts to developing econometric methods to assess market power in a direct way.[1136] Economic models are applied to observe how a firm or an industry responds to the change of economic conditions in the market.[1137] There are two major

---

[1128]   M. MOTTA, M. POLO and H. VASCONCELOS (2002), *supra* n. 1124, p. 6.
[1129]   M. MOTTA, M. POLO and H. VASCONCELOS (2002), *supra* n. 1124, p. 6.
[1130]   M. MOTTA, M. POLO and H. VASCONCELOS (2002), *supra* n. 1124, p. 8.
[1131]   M. MOTTA, M. POLO and H. VASCONCELOS (2002), *supra* n. 1124, p. 9.
[1132]   M. MOTTA, M. POLO and H. VASCONCELOS (2002), *supra* n. 1124, p. 14.
[1133]   M. MOTTA, M. POLO and H. VASCONCELOS (2002), *supra* n. 1124, p. 14.
[1134]   M. MOTTA, M. POLO and H. VASCONCELOS (2002), *supra* n. 1124, p. 16.
[1135]   M. MOTTA, M. POLO and H. VASCONCELOS (2002), *supra* n. 1124, p. 17.
[1136]   J.B. BAKER and T.F. BRESNAHAN (1992), *supra* n. 1035, p. 3.
[1137]   J.B. BAKER and T.F. BRESNAHAN (1992), *supra* n. 1035, p. 3; for an overview of applying econometric models to assess market power, *see* for example, T.F. BRESNAHAN (1989), *supra* n. 1033, pp. 1101–1057.

developments in modern industrial organization theory: one is that the focus on static interaction in the market has been extended to dynamic situations, and particular attention has been paid to the impact of present competitive activities on future market outcomes;[1138] the other is the refining of economic models to assess competitive effects in the situations where products are differentiated.

Dynamic models of competition effects have been adopted in two dimensions:[1139] one refers to extending the static model to the creation of new products, and this type of study is related to the theory of innovation;[1140] the other dimension refers to studying the effects of present activities on future markets.[1141] For the first dimension, both economic theory and empirical evidence do not reach a conclusion concerning how competition policy could be better implemented to facilitate innovation.[1142] For the second dimension, the limitations of the traditional static models have been mitigated when modern techniques were developed, and the most prominent methodologies include game theory models, which simulate the market entry by applying the model of strategic deterrence,[1143] and merger simulation models, which directly predict the extent to which a merger would affect future competition.

The second major development of modern economic techniques is assessing market power when products are differentiated. Product differentiation is common for consumer goods, for example, the name of the 'brand' is important for products such as beer and cereal.[1144] When products are differentiated, the traditional structural approach of measuring market power through defining the relevant market becomes problematic, because the use of market share and market definition does not give correct results when products made by one producer are substitute to each other at different degrees.[1145] To find a solution, econometricians develop the unilateral effects analysis which takes a direct

[1138] D.H. GINSBURG and J.D. WRIGHT (2012), 'Dynamic Analysis and the Limits of Antitrust Institutions', *Antitrust Law Journal*, vol. 78, no. 1, p. 3.

[1139] D.H. GINSBURG and J.D. WRIGHT (2012), *supra* n. 1138, p. 1.

[1140] J.G. SIDAK and D.F. TEECE (2009), *supra* n. 504, pp. 581–631; the economic debate on incorporating innovation in antitrust policy has been mentioned in the section on 'dynamic efficiency' in Chapter 4 of this book.

[1141] D.H. GINSBURG and J.D. WRIGHT (2012), *supra* n. 1138, p. 1.

[1142] D.H. GINSBURG and J.D. WRIGHT (2012), *supra* n. 1138, p. 4.

[1143] S.C. SALOP (1979), *supra* n. 1103, pp. 335–338; D.H. GINSBURG and J.D. WRIGHT (2012), *supra* n. 1138, p. 3.

[1144] J. HAUSMAN, G. LEONARD and J.D. ZONA (1994), 'Competitive Analysis with Differentiated Products', *Annuals of Economics and Statistics*, no. 34, p. 160.

[1145] O. CAPPS JR., J. CHURCH and H.A. LOVE (2003), 'Specification Issues and Confidence Intervals in Unilateral Price Effects Analysis', *Journal of Econometrics*, vol. 113, p. 5. The pioneering work of criticizing the use of market definition when products are differentiated is by Chamberlin in 1950. E.H. CHAMBERLIN (1950), 'Product Heterogeneity and Public Policy', *The American Economic Review*, vol. 40, no. 2, pp. 85–92. For a detailed elaboration on the limitation of applying market definition to industries where products are differentiated, *see* G.J. WERDEN and G.A. ROZANSKI (1994), 'The Application of Section 7 to Differentiated Products Industries: The Market Delineation Dilemma', *Antitrust*, p. 40; G.J. WERDEN (1997),

approach to predict the effects of merger prices and quantities.[1146] In the situations where products are differentiated, the central concern of the competition authority is the 'unilateral effects' of the merger, which refers to the extent to which a merger will lead to an increase of price in one product, and the anticompetitive effects will be assessed by the substitution possibilities between other products owned by the post-merger firm.[1147]

By applying modern economic techniques, there is a trend of moving towards a direct assessment of market power, instead of focusing on the structural variables such as market definition and market share. Countries such as the US which adopted the modern econometric methods tend to rely less on the definition of the relevant market.[1148] The concept of the 'unilateral effects' has been explicitly included both in the 1997 and the 2010 US Horizontal Merger Guidelines. The 2010 US Horizontal Merger Guidelines even made it clear that the merger analysis 'need not start with market definition', because the 'analytical tools used by the agencies to assess competitive effects do not rely on market definition'.[1149] It is also a clear trend to apply a comprehensive economic analysis of mergers in practice. For example, according to Farrell and Shapiro, the economists who work for the DOJ and the FTC, do not 'mechanically rely on concentration and market share', but 'seek flexibly to understand the economics of the industry'.[1150]

For some scholars in the US, in the situation where products are differentiated, the analysis of merger effects should no longer be based on the market share and the market concentration.[1151] The reason is when products are differentiated, the question of how market should not be decided by the market share; rather, it should be based on price elasticities, that is, the proportion of the change of demand for one product given the change of price for another product.[1152] Moreover, according to Hausman and Leonard, the use of the HHI might also be biased even when products are homogeneous, as the real world

---

'Simulating the Effects of Differentiated Products Mergers: A Practical Alternative to Structural Merger Policy', *George Mason Law Review*, vol. 5, no. 3, p. 368.

[1146] O. CAPPS JR., J. CHURCH and H.A. LOVE (2003), *supra* n. 1145, p. 5.

[1147] D. HOSKEN, D. O'BRIEN, D. SCHEFFMAN and M. VITA (2002), 'Demand System Estimation and Its Application to Horizontal Merger Analysis', *Federal Trade Commission Bureau of Economics Working Paper No. 246*, available at <www.ftc.gov/reports/demand-system-estimation-its-application-horizontal-merger-analysis>,p. 1.

[1148] G. DRAUZ, S. MAVROGHENIS and S. ASHALL (2011), 'Recent Developments in EU Merger Control 1 September 2009 – 31 August 2010', *Journal of European Competition Law and Practice*, vol. 2, no. 1, p. 53; J.B. BAKER and C. SHAPIRO (2007), *supra* n. 698.

[1149] US 2010 Horizontal Merger Guidelines, §4.

[1150] J. FARRELL and C. SHAPIRO (2010), 'Antitrust Evaluation of Horizontal Mergers: An Economic Alternative to Market Definition', *The B.E. Journal of Theoretical Economics*, vol. 10, no. 1, p. 4.

[1151] J.A. HAUSMAN and G.K. LEONARD (1997), 'Economic Analysis of Differentiated Products Mergers Using Real World Data', *George Mason Law Review*, vol. 5, p. 323; L. KAPLOW (2011), *supra* n. 1048, pp. 107–125.

[1152] J.A. HAUSMAN and G.K. LEONARD (1997), *supra* n. 1151, pp. 323, 338.

empirical evidence did not give sufficient support for a structural approach of merger analysis.[1153]

3.3.2.   Merger Simulation Techniques

Compared with the traditional indirect approach in merger assessment, which focuses on market definition and market share, merger simulation models have a particular advantage in dealing with the issue of product differentiation when the dynamic effects of mergers on prices are relatively short term.[1154] The issue of product differentiation makes antitrust authorities focus on the unilateral effects, instead of coordinated effects, generated by the merging firm.[1155] The development of applying merger simulation techniques to merger analysis started in the early 1990s in the US.[1156] Merger simulation usually starts from assessing the industry data through a pricing model (usually for a differentiated product it is the Bertrand model), and this model is used to predict the changes in prices and outputs after the merger.[1157] In theory, each firm will decide the prices for each product at the profit-maximization level, and equilibrium will be reached when no firm can increase their profits by charging a higher price for a given product.[1158] When the data is widely available, such as data from a supermarket scanner,[1159] it will be possible to estimate the pre-merger demand structure, in particular for industries of consumer goods.[1160] After the demand function is estimated and the own and cross-price elasticities are calculated, the profit margin for each product can be directly assessed by solving the 'first-order condition' of the pre-merger firms' profit maximization function.[1161] The

---

[1153]   J.A. Hausman and G.K. Leonard (1997), *supra* n. 1151, p. 342.

[1154]   The analysis of merger simulation models often does not include the issue of long-run dynamic effects, such as the effects of innovation and new product development. R.J. Epstein and D.L. Rubinfeld (2004), p. 1.

[1155]   R.J. Epstein and D.L. Rubinfeld (2001), 'Merger Simulation: A Simplified Approach with New Applications', *Antitrust Law Journal*, p. 883.

[1156]   R.J. Epstein and D.L. Rubinfeld (2004), 'Technical Report, Effects of Mergers Involving Differentiated Products', COMP/B1/2003/07, p. 1.

[1157]   R.J. Epstein and D.L. Rubinfeld (2004), p. 1.

[1158]   D.L. Rubinfeld and R.J. Epstein (2001), 'Merger Simulation: A Simplified Approach with New Applications', *Competition Policy Center, University of California, Berkeley, Working Paper No. CPC 01–26*, p. 5.

[1159]   The retail scanner data, in particular the consumer goods sold in supermarkets, drug stores, convenience stores are first collected by two firms A.C. Nielsen and Information Resources Incorporated (IRI) in the US in the mid-1980s. J.A. Hausman and G.K. Leonard (1997), *supra* n. 1151, p. 325; For a detailed introduction, *see* D. Hosken, D. O'Brien, D. Scheffman and M. Vita (2002), *supra* n. 1147, p. 3.

[1160]   J.A. Hausman and G.K. Leonard (1997), *supra* n. 1151, p. 321; J. Hausman, G. Leonard and J.D. Zona (1994), *supra* n. 1144, pp. 159–180.

[1161]   G.J. Werden (1997), *supra* n. 1145, p. 377; D.L. Rubinfeld (2010), 'Economic Issues in Antitrust Analysis', *Journal of Institutional and Theoretical Economics*, p. 68.

estimation of the demand model, the function of elasticities and profit margins, could help to simulate the price changes after the merger.[1162]

Merger simulation can be conducted by choosing different models to estimate the demand function. The simplest way is to apply the linear demand function, but the most commonly used model is the logit demand function, in which the consumer's taste in one product is compared with another randomly chosen product from a set of choices.[1163] The logit demand function has a strict assumption, that is, the cross-price elasticities between the given product and all other products are identical.[1164] The Almost Ideal Demand System ('AIDS') provides a more flexible approach to estimate the choices by consumers through a hierarchy.[1165] For example, this model assumes that consumers first choose the general categories between food and clothing. The second layer of choice is made within the category of food, such as between bread, meet and vegetable. The following choice is made within the specific brand of food.[1166] Proportionality-Calibrated AIDS ('PCAIDS') is a more simplified approach than AIDS. The PCAIDS maintains the same assumption of keeping the cross-price elasticities equal among products, whereas it provides a more flexible way to estimate the demand function.[1167]

In recent years, some economists have developed new methods besides merger simulation to specifically deal with competition issues in industries where products are differentiated. For example, Farrell and Shapiro developed the Upward Pressure on Price ('UPP') index in 2010.[1168] The UPP Index focuses on a merger's upward pressure on price and this index is calculated through a function of diversion ratios, margins and efficiencies. The application of the UPP index has been widely discussed among scholars[1169] and partially integrated when the merger guidelines in the US and the UK were revised in 2010.[1170]

[1162] D.L. Rubinfeld and R.J. Epstein (2001), *supra* n. 1158, p. 6.

[1163] G.J. Werden (1997), *supra* n. 1145, pp. 377–378.

[1164] J.A. Hausman and G.K. Leonard (1997), *supra* n. 1151, p. 322.

[1165] G.J. Werden (1997), *supra* n. 1145, p. 380; As an example, *see* J. Hausman, G. Leonard and J.D. Zona (1994), *supra* n. 1144, pp. 159–180.

[1166] G.J. Werden (1997), *supra* n. 1145, p. 380.

[1167] D.L. Rubinfeld (2010), *supra* n. 1161, p. 71; R.J. Epstein and D.L. Rubinfeld (2004), *supra* n. 1156, pp. 1–87.

[1168] J. Farrell and C. Shapiro (2010), *supra* n. 1150, pp. 1–39.

[1169] For example, J.A. Keyte and K.B. Schwartz (2011), '"Tally-Ho!" UPP and the 2010 Horizontal Merger Guidelines', *Antitrust Law Journal*, vol. 77, pp. 587–650; A. Oldale and J. Padilla (2013), 'EU Merger Assessment of Upward Pricing Pressure: Making Sense of UPP, GUPPI and the Like', *Journal of European Competition Law and Practice*, vol. 4, no. 4, pp. 375–381.

[1170] J.J. Simons and M.B. Coate (2010), 'Upward Pressure on Price (UPP) Analysis: Issues and Implications for Merger Policy', <http://ssrn.com/abstract=1558547>, p. 3.

4. COMPARING MERGER POLICY IN THE US, THE EU AND CHINA

4.1. INTRODUCTION

The previous section has summarized the economic theories and the recent developments of economic techniques that can be used for merger analysis. Although the extent to which economic goals play a role in competition policy may differ in the US, the EU and China, economic theories can be taken as a benchmark to compare merger decisions in different jurisdictions. Since economic theories and techniques have a universal nature, it would be valuable to compare how antitrust authorities in different jurisdictions use economic tools to analyze merger cases. This section conducts a comparative study to investigate whether merger policies are implemented differently in the US, EU and China, and whether these differences could be explained from a perspective of competition goals.

This comparative study is conducted by following three steps. The first step is to discuss from a theoretical point of view, whether a trend of convergence has been observed in merger enforcement in the US and the EU (section 4.2). The second step is to investigate the empirical evidence regarding whether the US, the EU and China have a different focus on merger analysis (section 4.3). The third step is to conduct a comparative case study, and to discuss whether these differences could be indicated from the decisions made by antitrust authorities (section 4.4). The selection of the *Panasonic/Sanyo* and *Seagate/Samsung* cases is based on the fact that these three mergers have been all notified and decided in China, the US and in the EU at the same time. The discussion of the cases focuses on the issue of how these authorities define the relevant market, assess market power, imposing remedies, and apply econometric tools. The differences in the merger analysis may further provide evidence for the influential role of goals of competition policy.

4.2. COMPARING MERGER POLICY IN THE US AND THE EU: A THEORETICAL DEBATE

Although scholars often argue that goals of competition law in the US and the EU are significantly different, before the *GE/Honeywell*[1171] case, it was widely agreed that the implementation of the merger rules in both antitrust jurisdictions

---

[1171] For a detailed analysis of economic reasoning of the *GE/Honeywell* case, see for example, M.L. Katz (2002), 'Recent Antitrust Enforcement Actions by the US Department of Justice: A Selective Survey of Economic Issues', *Review of Industrial Organization*, vol. 21, pp. 380–383.

followed a pattern of substantive convergence.[1172] After *GE/Honeywell* and *Boeing/McDonnell-Douglas*, the debate shifted towards the differences in merger analysis between the US and the EU.[1173] Attention was paid towards the impact of different competition goals on the implementation of merger policy.[1174] For example, Coppi and Walker argued that the overall focus of the merger investigation was different between the US and the EU,[1175] and this concern was centered at the different understandings of the market power (the concept of 'dominance' in the EU competition law).[1176] The reason for this difference is rooted in the debate between the Ordoliberal tradition in Europe and the Chicagoan influence in the US. Hence, the general theoretical debate between the concept of 'monopolization' in the US and the concept of 'dominance' in Europe will first be mentioned (section 4.2.1). As far as the substantive issues in merger control are concerned, Roeller and Wey argued that the conflicts between the US approach and the EU approach are reflected in three aspects: the market definition, the assessment of competitive effects, and the perspectives on merger remedies.[1177] This section will particularly deal with the issue of based on theoretical review, how market definition is defined differently in the US and the EU (section 4.2.2), and the different treatment of econometric techniques in the US and the EU concerning the assessment of competitive effects (section 4.2.3).

4.2.1. The Concepts of 'Monopolization' versus 'Dominance'

Larouche and Schinkel conducted a detailed comparative study[1178] on the concepts of 'monopolization' under the Sherman Act and the concept of 'abuse of

---

[1172] L. COPPI and M. WALKER (2004), 'Substantial Convergence or Parallel Paths? Similarities and Differences in the Economic Analysis of Horizontal Mergers in US and EU Competition Law', *The Antitrust Bulletin,* vol. 49, p. 101.

[1173] L. COPPI and M. WALKER (2004), *supra* n. 1172, p. 101; D.J. GIFFORD and R.T. KUDRLE (2005), 'Rhetoric and Reality in the Merger Standards of the United States, Canada, and the European Union', *Antitrust Law Journal*, vol. 72, p. 424; L. ROELLER and C. WEY (2003), 'Merger Control in the New Economy', *Netnomics*, vol. 5, p. 10; A comprehensive discussion on the contents *GE/Honeywell* and *Boeing/McDonnell-Douglas* case is beyond the scope of this thesis. For a summary of literature on these two cases, *see* P. SCHUMACHER (2013), 'The EU's Flawed Assessment of Horizontal Aspects in GE/Honeywell: Re-visiting the Last Pillar of the European Prohibition Decision', *European Journal of Law and Economics*, vol. 35, p. 212.

[1174] S. SCHMITZ (2002b),'The European Commission's Decision in GE/Honeywell and the Question of the Goals of Antitrust Law', *University of Pennsylvania Journal of International Economic Law*, vol. 23, no. 3, pp. 539–595; G. DRAUZ, S. MAVROGHENIS and S. ASHALL (2011), *supra* n. 1148, p. 52.

[1175] L. COPPI and M. WALKER (2004), *supra* n. 1172, p. 103.

[1176] L. COPPI and M. WALKER (2004), *supra* n. 1172, p. 103.

[1177] L. ROELLER and C. WEY (2003), *supra* n. 1173, p. 13.

[1178] P. LAROUCHE and M. P. SCHINKEL (2013), 'Continental Drift in the Treatment of Dominant Firms: Article 102 TFEU in Contrast to §2 Sherman Act', *Amsterdam Law School Legal Studies Research Paper No. 2013–34* and *Amsterdam Center for Law and Economics Working Paper No. 2013–08.*

dominant position' under Article 102 of the TFEU. It has been extensively argued that the concept of 'dominance' under EU competition law clearly reflects the influence of Ordoliberal thoughts.[1179] This distinctive feature makes EU competition law focus on the protection of the competitive process, and it is important to prevent the 'abuse' of the dominant position, which may lead to a 'hindrance competition'.[1180] More importantly, the Ordoliberal tradition gives competition policy makers in Europe a weak confidence in the robustness of the market.[1181] As the market is not able to self-correct, the authority of the competition policy has responsibility for dealing with the effects of monopolistic conduct.[1182] Their research supports the perspective of understanding the differences in antitrust cases from different competition traditions, in particular the influence of Ordoliberal thoughts in Europe and the Chicago School in the US.

4.2.2. The Definition of Relevant Market

Coppi and Walker argued that in the US defining the relevant market used to be based on the SSNIP test, and after the emergence of unilateral effect theories, together with the development of econometric techniques, the analysis of mergers in the US relied less on market definition.[1183] In the EU, however, defining the relevant market does not solely rely on the SSNIP test, and other factors will also be considered, such as the differences of functional interchangeability in prices as well as in consumer groups will also be taken into account.[1184] The concept of 'substitutability' between products and geographic areas played a more important role in defining the market under EU competition law.[1185] According to Coppi and Walker, when the merging firms produce differentiated products, the US antitrust authority will directly assess to what extent products are competing with each other, whereas in the EU more attention is given to the industry segmentations.[1186]

[1179] P. LAROUCHE and M. P. SCHINKEL (2013), supra n. 1178, pp. 2, 12; see also D.J. GERBER (1987), 'Law and the Abuse of Economic Power in Europe', Tulane Law Review, vol. 62, pp. 57–107; I. ROSE and C. NGWE (2007), 'The Ordoliberal Tradition in the European Union, its Influence on Article 82 EC and the IBA's Comments on the Article 82 EC Discussion Paper', Competition Law International, vol. 3, p. 8.

[1180] P. LAROUCHE and M. P. SCHINKEL (2013), supra n. 1178, p. 11–12.

[1181] P. LAROUCHE and M. P. SCHINKEL (2013), supra n. 1178, p. 12.

[1182] P. LAROUCHE and M. P. SCHINKEL (2013), supra n. 1178, p.13.

[1183] L. COPPI and M. WALKER (2004), supra n. 1172, p. 105. Some of the examples of the econometric techniques which have increasingly been applied in merger analysis in the US include critical loss analysis, diversion ratios, upward pricing pressure. G. DRAUZ, S. MAVROGHENIS and S. ASHALL (2011), supra n. 1148, p. 53.

[1184] L. COPPI and M. WALKER (2004), supra n. 1172, p. 104; Commission Notice on the Definition of Relevant Market for the Purposes of Community Competition Law [1997] OJ C 372.

[1185] J. ELIZALDE (2012), 'A Theoretical Approach to Market Definition Analysis', European Journal of Law and Economics, p. 451.

[1186] L. COPPI and M. WALKER (2004), supra n. 1172, p. 106.

Elizalde argues that by taking different approaches in the analysis of the relevant market, antitrust authorities in the US and the EU often reach different results in defining the markets.[1187] According to Elizalde, the antitrust authority in the EU follows the 'price-increase' approach, which focuses on the extent to which the firm would be able to profitably raise prices if all products in a relevant market would be operated by this firm,[1188] whereas the antitrust authority in the US takes a 'profit-maximization' approach, which considers that within the defined market, a profit-maximization decision made by the firms jointly would lead to at least a 'small but significant' price increase.[1189] In addition, the definition of the relevant market in the US does not count the reactions of other firms outside the given relevant market, whereas in Europe, not only prices but also product characteristics will also be taken into account in the analysis, hence both demand-side and supply-side substitutes will be considered.[1190]

From a normative perspective, the models of competition with differentiated products developed by Elizalde show that when products are differentiated, the relevant market defined by the EU antitrust authority would be wider than it is defined in the US because of the different treatment of the supply-side substitutes.[1191] According to Elizalde, this difference lies in the fact that in the US, defining the relevant market does not consider supply-side substitutes. When the market share is calculated, the supply-side substitutes are counted as market participants. Under the EU competition law, supply-side substitutes are counted for defining the relevant market if suppliers can easily and quickly switch to substitutes without paying a significant sunk cost. Supply-side substitutes are not considered in the calculation of the market share in the EU.[1192]

4.2.3.   The Treatment of Econometric Techniques

According to Coppi and Walker, the strong reliance on market definition makes it difficult to apply econometric techniques in merger analysis in Europe.[1193] According to Ivaldi and Verboven,[1194] the European Commission's practice in merger assessment has long relied on the concept of 'dominance'. The dominant position is assessed based on the factor of market share, the potential competition,

---

[1187]   J. ELIZALDE (2012), *supra* n. 1185, p. 450.
[1188]   J. ELIZALDE (2012), *supra* n. 1185, p. 451.
[1189]   J. ELIZALDE (2012), *supra* n. 1185, p. 450.
[1190]   J. ELIZALDE (2012), *supra* n. 1185, pp. 450, 451.
[1191]   J. ELIZALDE (2012), *supra* n. 1185, p. 450.
[1192]   J. ELIZALDE (2012), *supra* n. 1185, p. 450.
[1193]   L. COPPI and M. WALKER (2004), *supra* n. 1172, p. 108.
[1194]   M. IVALDI and F. VERBOVEN (2005), 'Quantifying the Effects from Horizontal Mergers in European Competition Policy', *International Journal of Industrial Organization*, vol. 23, p. 670.

as well as the extent to which the remaining competition will be restrained.[1195] Even though after 2002 the Commission reformed merger rules to be more in line with economic theory of oligopoly behavior, and showed a convergence towards the US practice in defining the relevant market in the respect of giving more attention to the SSNIP test as well as the factors of demand substitution,[1196] the merger investigation by the EU Commission still to a large extent focuses on the market share, and structural variables such as the barriers to entry, with econometric analysis playing a limited role.[1197] Notably, this situation in Europe has changed in recent years and econometric analysis has been applied in a few merger cases, such as *Friesland Foods/Campina* and *Ryanair/Aer Lingus*.[1198] However, even though econometric techniques have been accepted by the Commission, it was still common to observe that the Commission was reluctant to apply econometric analysis to consider claimed efficiencies.[1199] According to Roeller and Wey, the conflicting view between the US and EU competition authorities may become obvious when a merger leads to substantial efficiency gains.[1200]

4.3.   COMPARING MERGER POLICY IN THE US, THE EU AND CHINA: EMPIRICAL EVIDENCE

4.3.1.   *Comparing Merger Decisions in the US and the EU*

By using a set of explanatory variables, including structural variables such as the post-merger HHI, the post-merger market share, and institutional variables, such as whether the merger enforcement was more stringent or more lenient, Bergman *et al.* compared the hypothetical decisions to actual decisions and gave a few of important findings on the merger decisions in the EU and the US.[1201] Their study shows that for merger cases with low post-merger market share, if the US merger cases were decided by antitrust authorities in the EU, the enforcement in the EU would have been stricter than it was in the US.[1202] When the post-merger market share increases, the difference between the merger enforcement in the EU and the US falls.[1203] In general, by following a dominance

---

[1195]   M. Ivaldi and F. Verboven (2005), *supra* n. 1194, p. 673.

[1196]   M. Ivaldi and F. Verboven (2005), *supra* n. 1194, p. 672.

[1197]   M. Ivaldi and F. Verboven (2005), *supra* n. 1194, p. 670.

[1198]   *Friesland Foods/Campina* (COMP/M5046) Commission Decision of 17 December 2008; *Ryanair/Aer Lingus* (Case No COMP/M 4439) Commission Decision of 27 June 2007; *see* G. Drauz, T. Chellingsworth and H. Hyrkas (2010), 'Recent Developments in EC Merger Control', *Journal of European Competition Law and Practice*, vol. 1, no. 1 p. 25.

[1199]   G. Drauz, T. Chellingsworth and H. Hyrkas (2010), *supra* n. 1198, p. 25.

[1200]   L. Roeller and C. Wey (2003), *supra* n. 1173, p. 17.

[1201]   M.A. Bergman *et al.* (2010a), 'Comparing Merger Policies in the European Union and the United States', *Review of Industrial Organization*, vol. 36, pp. 305–331.

[1202]   M.A. Bergman *et al.* (2010a), *supra* n. 1201, pp. 327–328.

[1203]   M.A. Bergman *et al.* (2010a), *supra* n. 1201, p. 327.

theory, the EU antitrust authorities tend to impose a tougher standard for mergers than the US authorities, and this trend could be observed more clearly when the post-merger market share is below 70 percent.[1204]

In another empirical study on notified mergers in the EU and the US from 1990 to 2007,[1205] Bergman *et al.* argued that in the US, the proposed merger has to meet more comprehensive notification requirements, and therefore there are more filings in the US than in the EU.[1206] However, it was observed that there are more investigations per filing under the EU merger policy and for the given investigation the number of challenged case is higher than the US.[1207] According to their study, among all the notified mergers, about 8 percent will be investigated under the EU regime whereas in the US it was around 2 percent, although the merger policies in the EU and the US share the same basic reporting requirements.[1208]

As far as the application of economic theories is concerned, the empirical analysis conducted by Bergman *et al.* shows that the antitrust authorities in the EU and the US put different emphasis on the use of economic theory.[1209] In the EU, the competition authorities are more likely to challenge merger cases related to market dominance, and are less strict towards mergers which cause coordinated effects.[1210] Moreover, efficiency gains are less accepted by the antitrust authorities in the EU.[1211] In merger cases before 2004, the year that the new Merger Regulation was implemented in the EU, efficiency claims only appeared in 3 percent of the merger cases; and from 2004 to 2007, this number increased to 11 percent.[1212] By contrast, among all the sample cases studied by Bergman *et al.*, efficiency considerations were taken as a key issue in the merger analysis in the US.[1213] This tendency could be observed by reading the reports issued by the Bureau of Competition and the Bureau of Economics at the FTC, in

---

[1204] M.A. BERGMAN *et al.* (2010a), *supra* n. 1201, p. 329.

[1205] M.A. BERGMAN *et al.* (2010b), 'Merger Control in the European Union and the United States: Just the Facts', <http://papers.ssrn.com/sol3/papers.cfm?abstract_id=1565026>, p. 1.

[1206] M.A. BERGMAN *et al.* (2010b), *supra* n. 1205, pp. 1, 12. Although the discussion of procedural issues in merger policy is excluded in this research, it is worth mentioning here that the process of merger notification in the EU, the US and China shares a similar structure. In the first step, when a certain threshold is met, the proposed merging parties are required to go through a notification procedure (it is called 'Preliminary Review' in China, 'Phase I' in the EU, and 'Initial Phase' in the US). Most merger cases will be cleared at this stage. If it is necessary to conduct a more detailed investigation on the proposed merger, the antitrust authority will initiate the second step (it is called 'Further Review' in China, 'Phase II' in the EU and 'Second Request' in the US). A formal decision will be issued at the end of the investigation, and the merger deal should not be undertaken before the issue of the decision.

[1207] M.A. BERGMAN *et al.* (2010b), *supra* n. 1205, p. 1.

[1208] M.A. BERGMAN *et al.* (2010b), *supra* n. 1205, p. 1.

[1209] M.A. BERGMAN *et al.* (2010b), *supra* n. 1205, p. 2.

[1210] M.A. BERGMAN *et al.* (2010b), *supra* n. 1205, p. 2.

[1211] M.A. BERGMAN *et al.* (2010b), *supra* n. 1205, p. 2.

[1212] M.A. BERGMAN *et al.* (2010b), *supra* n. 1205, p. 35.

[1213] M.A. BERGMAN *et al.* (2010b), *supra* n. 1205, p. 35.

which economists gave merit to efficiencies by raising 161 claims, and legal staff raised 80 efficiency claims.[1214] For horizontal merger cases, efficiency claims appear much more frequently in the reports issued by the FTC (83 percent) than by the EU Commission (5 percent).[1215]

Notably, another empirical study published in 1992 by Coate and McChesney showed that among the 70 merger cases decided by the FTC from 1982 to 1987, efficiency gains were not taken into account and the determinant factor of prohibiting a merger was the consideration of entry barriers.[1216] Moreover, Coate and McChesney found evidence to argue that from 1982 to 1987, the opinions from lawyers at the FTC were more influential than from economists.[1217] By contrast, in a more recent published paper, Coate and Heimert investigated 186 mergers from April 1997 to March 2007, during which period the 1997 Horizontal Merger Guidelines were implemented.[1218] The empirical evidence showed that the FTC staff at the Bureau of Competition and Bureau of Economics treated efficiency arguments in a thorough, consistent manner. The analysis of efficiency issues usually provided necessary information for the merger decision makers at the FTC.

By comparing their study with the one published in 2010 by Bergman *et al.*, it could be concluded that it was common for both the US and the EU merger policy that efficiency gains were only slowly taken into account, and it was the same situation for the US and the EU that in the early enforcement of merger policy, structural factors played a more important role and efficiency gains were not considered.

4.3.2. *Empirical Evidence on EU Merger Policy*

As discussed in the previous chapters, the goals of competition policy in the EU are not limited to economic concerns. If the EU competition policy is enforced to pursue multiple goals, it would be important to investigate whether in practice the EU merger decisions are made in accordance to these goals. Bergman, Jakobsson and Razo conducted an empirical study to examine which factor has contributed significantly to the merger decisions.[1219] By studying around 2020 formal decisions by the European Commission from September 1990 to October

---

[1214] M.A. BERGMAN *et al.* (2010b), *supra* n. 1205, p. 35.

[1215] M.A. BERGMAN *et al.* (2010b), *supra* n. 1205, p. 37.

[1216] M.B. COATE and F.S. MCCHESNEY (1992), 'Empirical Evidence on FTC Enforcement of the Merger Guidelines', *Economic Inquiry*, vol. 20, no. 2, pp. 277–293.

[1217] M.B. COATE and F.S. MCCHESNEY (1992), *supra* n. 1216, pp. 277–293.

[1218] M.B. COATE and A.J. HEIMERT (2009), 'Merger Efficiencies at the Federal Trade Commission 1997–2007', *Federal Trade Commission Economic Issues Series Working Paper*, <http://papers.ssrn.com/sol3/papers.cfm?abstract_id=1338738>.

[1219] M.A. BERGMAN, M. JAKOBSSON and C. RAZO (2005), 'An Econometric Analysis of the European Commission's Merger Decisions', *International Journal of Industrial Organization*, vol. 23, pp. 717–737.

2002, they concluded that there are four main factors that strongly influenced the decision on whether a merger will be prohibited by the Commission: the market share of the firms, the increase of market share as a result of the merger, the barriers to entry, and the likelihood of collusion after the merger.[1220] In their study, political factors such as who was the Commissioner and whether the merging firms are based in a large or a small Member State do not have an impact on merger decisions.[1221] However, if one of the merging parties is a US firm, according to their study, the merger is less likely to be prohibited.[1222] Nevertheless they do not interpret such influence as the result of lobbying from the US firms; rather, they perceive this as the positive influence of a longer experience of competition laws in the US, the US firms hence are able to argue their cases better or be more experienced to select merging parties.[1223]

Their findings that the market share and barriers of entry are the determinant factors for a merger decision were also confirmed by the study of Lindsay *et al.*, who took samples of 245 merger cases from 2000 to 2002.[1224] In a later empirical study published in 2008 by Fernandez, Hashi and Jegers,[1225] the barrier to entry remains the central concern of the Commission in deciding whether a merger could be cleared.[1226] Besides barriers to entry, Fernandez, Hashi and Jegers argued that the increase in market share and the level of market concentration are two significant explanatory variables correlating with the Commission's merger decisions.[1227]

The influence of political factors, however, remains ambiguous as the empirical study by Duso, Neven and Roeller[1228] proved that the country where the merging firm is based in does affect the decisions, whereas the study by Aktas *et al.*[1229] rejected such bias. In a paper published by Aktas, de Bodt and Roll in 2007,[1230] it became clearer that political influence, in particular a pattern of protectionism, was significant during the 1990s. They studied 290 merger cases from 1990 to 2000, and evidence showed that at that time it was more likely

---

[1220]   M.A. Bergman, M. Jakobsson and C. Razo (2005), *supra* n. 1219, p. 719.

[1221]   M.A. Bergman, M. Jakobsson and C. Razo (2005), *supra* n. 1219, p. 719.

[1222]   M.A. Bergman, M. Jakobsson and C. Razo (2005), *supra* n. 1219, p. 732.

[1223]   M.A. Bergman, M. Jakobsson and C. Razo (2005), *supra* n. 1219, p. 732.

[1224]   A. Lindsay, *et al.* (2003), 'Econometrics Study into European Merger Decisions Since 2000', *European Competition Law Review*, vol. 24, pp. 673–682.

[1225]   B.M. Fernandez, I. Hashi and M. Jegers (2008), 'The Implementation of the European Commission's Merger Regulation 2004: An Empirical Analysis', *Journal of Competition Law and Economics*, vol. 4, no. 3, pp. 791–809.

[1226]   B.M. Fernandez, I. Hashi and M. Jegers (2008), *supra* n. 1225, p. 805.

[1227]   B.M. Fernandez, I. Hashi and M. Jegers (2008), *supra* n. 1225, p. 807.

[1228]   T. Duso, D. Neven and L.H. Roeller (2007), 'The Political Economy of European Merger Control: Evidence Using Stock Market Data', *The Journal of Law and Economics*, vol. 50, pp. 455–489.

[1229]   N. Aktas, E. de Bodt and R. Roll (2004), 'Market Responses to European Regulation of Business Combinations', *Journal of Financial and Quantitative Analysis*, vol. 39, pp. 731–757.

[1230]   N. Aktas, E. de Bodt and R. Roll (2007), 'Is European M&A Regulation Protectionist?', *The Economic Journal*, vol. 117, pp. 1096–1121.

for the antitrust authority in the EU to intervene when the merger initiated by a foreign bidder (which is based outside the European Community) imposes larger harm on the European competitors.[1231] When they continued this research in 2011 and added another 184 merger cases from 2001 to 2007, the significant influence of the nationality of the merging firms on the likelihood of antitrust intervention disappeared.[1232] The landmark of this behavioral change was the decisions by the European Court of First Instance in 2002,[1233] as well as the reform of merger policy in 2004. At the same time, their evidence showed that compared with the practice in 1990s, in recent years the European Commission has incorporated more economic factors, such as the size and the value of the deal, in merger analysis.[1234]

These two research papers by Aktas *et al.* have remarkable implications for the understanding of merger policy enforcement in the EU. Following a similar trend of incorporating efficiency arguments in merger analysis, the empirical results showed that it was also a slow process to mitigate political influence on merger decisions. In addition, it could be concluded that the changes in the determinants in merger analysis paralleled with the evolution of competition policy, which was to a large extent driven by the debate of policy goals.

In addition to the study by Aktas *et al.*, there is also empirical evidence that shows a similar trend towards the particular political influence from the US. This conclusion was strengthened by Fernandez, Hashi and Jegers,[1235] who specifically analyzed the factors that influenced the Commissions' merger decisions after the implementation of the EU Merger Regulation in 2004, by investigating 50 resolutions on proposed mergers from 1 January 2005 to 31 July 2006.[1236] In their study, the empirical results do not support the argument that

---

[1231]   N. Aktas, E. de Bodt, and R. Roll (2007), *supra* n. 1230, p. 1099.
[1232]   N. Aktas (2011), 'Market Reactions to European Merger Regulation: A Reexamination of the Protectionism Hypothesis', <http://ssrn.com/abstract=2083645>, p. 6.
[1233]   In 2002, the European Commission lost three merger cases in court: *Airtours/First Choice* (Commission Decision M1524, CFI's case T-342/99, 6 June 2002); *Schneider/Legrand* (Commission Decision M2283, CFI's case, T-310/01 and T-77/02, 22 October 2002) and *TetraLaval/Sidel* (Commission Decision M2416, CFI's case T-5/00 and T-80/02, 25 October 2002). In these three cases, the Court of First Instance criticized the Commission's economic arguments. M.A. Bergman *et al.* (2005), *supra* n. 1219, p. 719; In 2004, the Council Regulation No. 4064/89 was amended by Council Regulation No. 139/2004, and one of the goals of the merger reform in 2004 was to achieve 'better, and more consistent' economic analysis. The changes include inviting the Chief Competition Economist together with a team of economists to merger analysis, replacing the 'Dominance Test' (DT) with the 'Significant Impediment of Effective Competition test' (SIEC), as well as accepting efficiency defense. N. Aktas (2011), *supra* n. 1232, p. 11; For a study assessing the economic impact of the 2004 merger reform, *see* T. Duso, K. Gugler and F. Szuecs (2013), 'An Empirical Assessment of the 2004 EU Merger Policy Reform', *The Economic Journal*, pp. 596–619.
[1234]   N. Aktas (2011), *supra* n. 1232, pp. 6, 20.
[1235]   B.M. Fernandez, I. Hashi and M. Jegers (2008), *supra* n. 1225, pp. 791–809.
[1236]   B.M. Fernandez, I. Hashi and M. Jegers (2008), *supra* n. 1225, p. 798.

the Commission is more likely to clear the merger if the firms are US-based.[1237] Compared with the previous study by Bergman, Jakobsson and Razo, it seems that the influence of whether the merging firm is based in the US has been mitigated after the 2004 merger reform. The empirical study by Szuecs confirmed that the 2004 merger reform was the landmark which significantly mitigated the political influences.[1238] Their results showed that after the reform, the factors which influenced the merger intervention in the EU have become more converged with the practice in the US.[1239]

Although the above-mentioned empirical studies showed a clear declining influence of political factors, it remains ambiguous how particular economic theory plays a role in merger analysis by the Commission. For example, by studying 37 published merger cases after the implementation of the 2004 EC Merger Regulation, Roeller[1240] concluded that from 37 published cases from 2004 to 2009, only in five cases did the merging parties have claimed static efficiencies, and the efficiency claims in two out of the five cases were accepted.[1241] Roeller also concluded that dynamic efficiencies were not accepted in any case during the merger assessment.[1242] According to Roeller, the reason why a relatively low percentage of the merging parties claimed efficiencies was that claiming efficiencies may send a 'bad' signal that the merger could increase market power, which may lead to a decision that the merger is anticompetitive.[1243] This recalled the argument of the 'efficiency offence' in merger policy, although the empirical results did not show that the Commission took a *per se* approach towards dynamic efficiencies.[1244]

Another aspect in applying economic theories to merger assessment investigated by Roeller was the definition of the relevant market. Among the 37 published merger cases between 2004 and 2009, for geographic market definition, 103 out of 273 markets were defined as 'national', 41 of the markets were defined as worldwide and 81 markets were defined as EEA-wide.[1245] By presenting the evidence of how the geographic markets were assessed, Roeller concluded that the more factors at the supply side are considered, the wider the geographic market is defined.[1246] At the same time, when the markets are smaller (more local, national or regional), the role of supply-side factors is

---

[1237]   B.M. Fernandez, I. Hashi and M. Jegers (2008), *supra* n. 1225, p. 803.
[1238]   F. Szuecs (2012), 'Investigating Transatlantic Merger Policy Convergence', *International Journal of Industrial Organization*, vol. 30, pp. 654–662.
[1239]   These factors are: market definitions, pre-merger market concentration, entry barriers, R&D expenditures and dividends. F. Szuecs (2012), *supra* n. 1238, p. 660.
[1240]   L. Roeller (2011), 'Challenges in EU Competition Policy', *Empirica*, vol. 38, p. 292.
[1241]   L. Roeller (2011), *supra* n. 1240, pp. 293–294.
[1242]   L. Roeller (2011), *supra* n. 1240, p. 294.
[1243]   L. Roeller (2011), *supra* n. 1240, p. 294.
[1244]   L. Roeller (2011), *supra* n. 1240, p. 295.
[1245]   L. Roeller (2011), *supra* n. 1240, pp. 296–297.
[1246]   L. Roeller (2011), *supra* n. 1240, p. 297.

narrower.[1247] This finding has an important implication for merger decisions, that is, the issue of how wide a market is defined by the EU Commission is affected by the extent to which supply-side substitution is taken into account.[1248]

4.3.3.   Empirical Evidence on Merger Policy in China

Due to the limited number of cases that have been published by the MOFCOM, there was little empirical study on the merger policy in China. In March and April 2012, Sokol conducted a qualitative survey among antitrust lawyers from 87 international law firms in Australia, Brazil, Canada, India, Europe and the US regarding their practical experiences of dealing with merger cases under the AML.[1249] In the view of antitrust lawyers, merger policy in China is implemented differently from the one in the US and the EU, and political factors (such as industrial policy considerations and the influence from other government bodies) have affected the merger analysis.[1250] For many practitioners, the MOFCOM functions in a bureaucratic way and the intellectual resources of industrial organization economics are largely lacking.[1251] Although the MOFCOM has made significant improvement in the past years, there remained a gap between the Chinese approach to the use of economic analysis in merger analysis and the practice in the US and the EU.[1252] In addition, industrial policy considerations and other political goals often prevail over competition goals when other parts of the government (ministries, or local governments) or trade associations intervene in a merger case notified to the MOFCOM.[1253]

To better understand the role of economic analysis in MOFCOM's decisions, it might be practical to further review the contents of these decisions in detail. According to Article 3 of the Measures on the Review of Concentrations between Undertakings issued by the MOFCOM on 29 August 2011,[1254] the effects of a merger will be assessed by the MOFCOM by following six steps. The first step is to define the relevant market, as well as to investigate the merging parties' market share and their controlling power in the relevant market. The second step is to assess the level of market concentration in the relevant market. The third step is to consider the effects of market entry, as well as the influence of technological development. The fourth step is to consider the merger's effect on

---

1247   L. ROELLER (2011), *supra* n. 1240, p. 297.

1248   L. ROELLER (2011), *supra* n. 1240, p. 298.

1249   D.D. SOKOL (2013), *supra* n. 995.

1250   D.D. SOKOL (2013), *supra* n. 995, p. 6.

1251   D.D. SOKOL (2013), *supra* n. 995, p. 8.

1252   D.D. SOKOL (2013), *supra* n. 995, p. 9.

1253   D.D. SOKOL (2013), *supra* n. 995, p. 11.

1254   Shangwubu Guanyu Pinggu Jingyingzhe Jizhong Jingzheng Yingxiang De Zanxing Guiding (商务部关于评估经营者集中竞争影响的暂行规定) [Interim Provisions on Assessing the Impact of Concentration of Business Operators on Competition] (issued by the Ministry of Commerce on 29 August 2011, effective on 5 September 2011).

consumers and other competitors. The fifth step is to analyze the merger's effect on national economic development and the last step is to incorporate other relevant factors that may influence market competition. The first three steps – defining a relevant market, calculating the market concentration, and assessing the market entry – indicate a rather structural approach in merger analysis. Considering the merger's impact on 'competitors', 'technological development' and 'national economic development', however, may imply the influence of non-competition goals. This provision does not mention how to define a relevant market, because in May 2009 the State Council has issued a specific guideline regarding the definition of the relevant market, and in that guideline the SSNIP test was introduced.[1255] As for the measurement of concentration level, it was mentioned in Article 6 of this provision that both the CR Index and the HHI Index could be used to assess the market concentration level. In addition, this provision states that the higher the market is concentrated, the more likely it is that a merger would impede competition in the relevant market.

By reviewing each decision published by the MOFCOM (see Table 3 below), it could be concluded that the decisions have generally followed the above-mentioned steps, although none of them has released the data that has been used for the calculation of a relevant market and the market concentration. The investigation often starts from defining the relevant market, and gives specific attention to the post-merger entity's market share, as well as to what extent the market is concentrated for the given product. The analysis of competition effects of a merger is largely relied on deciding whether a merger would create a dominant position.

Based on the six steps provided by the provision, a closer look at each criterion would give an answer to the question whether economic analysis has played a role in merger decisions. First of all, the question to be answered is how the MOFCOM defines a relevant market. Although it was acknowledged in the guidelines issued by the State Council that both demand and supply substitution should be taken into account, and the SSNIP test was commonly applied in the US and the EU, for the cases before 2011, the MOFCOM took the approach of examining whether the merging parties have overlapping products and services. Supply and demand substitutions, price effects, and even product characteristics were seldom mentioned. In *Mitsubishi Rayon/Lucite*, the MOFCOM found both companies have overlapping products of MMA, and PMMA (polymer and plate). In *GM/Delphi*, the MOFCOM did not find any overlap in products or services provided by both companies. As they have vertical relationships in the upstream and the downstream markets, the relevant market was defined separately for GM

[1255]   Guowuyuan Fanlongduan Weiyuanhui Guanyu Xiangguan Shichang Jieding De Zhinan (国务院反垄断委员会关于相关市场界定的指南) [Guide of the Anti-Monopoly Committee of the State Council for the Definition of the Relevant Market] (issued by the Ministry of Commerce on 24 May 2009).

and Delphi based on their products. No information regarding supply or demand substitution was mentioned. In *Pfizer/Wyeth*, the MOFCOM first examined whether two firms have overlapping products, and in the next step the MOFCOM concluded that for the product of swine mycoplasma pneumonia vaccine, the merger would change the market structure. The product relevant market is therefore defined as swine mycoplasma pneumonia vaccine.

Since *Uralkali/Silvinit* in June 2011, the analysis of the relevant market has been improved by focusing on product characteristics. In *Uralkali/Silvinit*, the MOFCOM mentioned that the relevant market is defined based on product characteristics, and they concluded that potassium chloride cannot be easily substituted by other fertilizer. It was the same method which was applied to define the market for *Penelope (Alpha V)/Savio, Seagate/Samsung, Western Digital/Hitachi,* and *GE/Shenhua Group JV.* In these cases, the MOFCOM did not explain why a particular product cannot be substituted by others, or whether this substitution is considered from the demand side or the supply side. In *Henkel Hongkong/Tiande Chemical*, the MOFCOM clarified that both the supply and demand side have been considered regarding the substitution possibilities. In addition, factors related to product import and export have also been taken into account. In *Goodrich/UTC*, the MOFCOM stated that product characteristics have been investigated from both the supply and the demand side, in addition, the experiences from downstream customers in the bidding procedure have also been considered. In *Walmart/Newheight* and *Marubein/ Gavilon*, the MOFCOM mentioned that besides the supply and demand factors, the scope and characteristics of the operation system of the merging parties have also been considered to define the relevant market. Although the MOFCOM has significantly improved the analysis of supply and demand substitution, in particular in *Media Tek/Mstar Semicondutor*, as of August 2013, the MOFCOM has not mentioned the SSNIP test in their decisions, and it was unclear whether price elasticities have been calculated in any merger decisions.

The second issue is how market concentration has been assessed. An important finding is that it seems the MOFCOM has applied a clear link between market share, market concentration, and competitive effects. In several merger cases, such as *Mitsubishi Rayon/Lucite*, it was made clear that if a post-merger entity reaches a high market share (whether it is 'high' enough usually depends on the market share of the second and the third market players), it will naturally lead to a conclusion that this entity would hold a dominant position. Next, this dominant position would have negative effects because it will eliminate or restrict competitors in that market. In some cases, such as *Uralkali/Silvinit*, market dominance is indicated by the merging parties' increased control of resource supply, production and sales. In economic terms, this would refer to productive efficiency (economies of scale) as a clear benefit of the merger. However, efficiency arguments have rarely been mentioned by the MOFCOM in the published cases, and the increased control of resources is often taken as evidence to define a 'dominant position'.

The third issue is how other factors, such as the impact on competitors, technological development and the effects on the national economy have been incorporated in merger analysis. In several cases, the impact of a merger on domestic competitors has been emphasized. It was particularly the case for a merger involving a 'leading' global player, or targeting a 'leading' domestic player. For the former case, the MOFCOM has expressed worries for the *GM/ Delphi* merger concerning the negative impact on other domestic auto parts manufacturers. The decision mentions that as both companies are the 'leading' global players in the auto industry, the concentration may make it difficult for other manufacturers to provide auto parts for GM. In *Pfizer/Wyeth*, the MOFCOM concluded that the merger between two leading producers in the swine mycoplasma pneumonia vaccine market may impose high entry barriers for other competitors, given their comparative advantage in technology and innovation. For the latter concern, the MOFCOM mentioned in the *Coca Cola/ Huiyuan* decision that the merger will increase Coca Cola's market power by controlling two 'leading national brands' (Huiyuan and Meizhiyuan). Given this increased market power, the merger will increase the entry barrier for other competitors to enter the fruit juice market. As for the factor of merger's impact on technological development, the issue of innovation, R&D and patents are often taken as entry barriers, instead of an indicator for dynamic efficiency. In *GE/Shenhua Group JV* and *Google/Motorola*, it was concluded that the merging parties' advantage in technology and R&D capacities increases the entry barriers for the product market.

The fourth issue is how the MOFCOM interpreted and applied economic techniques. By reviewing the decisions, it remains unclear whether the MOFCOM has indeed studied the recent development in industrial organization economics. For example, one of the major developments in merger analysis in recent years is the research on unilateral and coordinated effects. In several cases, the MOFCOM has mentioned that the merger would reduce the number of competitors and therefore will impose a risk for the remaining competitors to coordinate. In *Novartis/Alcon*, MOFCOM mentioned that the post-merger entity will obtain 20 percent market share in the market of contact lens care products. The post-merger entity may coordinate with Haichang, a domestic contact lens company with the largest market share of 30 percent, because Novartis has a contract with Haichang in 2008 regarding sales and distribution. This analysis was rather from a policy perspective and was not based on the economic analysis of coordinative effects.

To conclude, by reviewing the economic analysis of MOFCOM's merger decisions, it gives the impression that the MOFCOM has relied on a rather structural approach to investigate the merger effects. For the issue of market definition, the MOFCOM tends to examine product characteristics, and the production line of each merging parties. Price elasticities of each product, as well as the supply and demand substitution between products, were rarely mentioned. For the assessment of market concentration, it seems that the market power of the merging parties to a large extent depends on their market shares. The MOFCOM also tends to examine coordinative effects based on whether the merging parties have built relationships with other firms through contracts or negotiations, instead of applying oligopolistic game theory models to assess the likelihood of the price increase. In all above-mentioned aspects, it could be observed that the MOFCOM has been reluctant to analyze the price effects of a merger. The welfare gains or losses created by a merger are discussed more from the perspective of the changes of the market structure, instead of calculating the possibilities of price increases. From a policy goal perspective, this structural approach may indicate that the MOFCOM tends to investigate the effects of a merger by incorporating various factors and to focus on the merger effects on the Chinese market (or the Chinese industry) as a whole. From an institution perspective, it is also likely that the MOFCOM particularly has an advantage in dealing with policies regarding structural changes in the industry instead of dealing with price issues. Historically, the NDRC is responsible to maintain a stable market price and after the promulgation of the AML, the NDRC became the enforcement agency dealing with price-related cases.

In the table below (Table 3), the economic analysis of MOFCOM's decisions on the 21 conditionally approved cases will be presented. Particular attention will be given to five aspects. The first issue is how the MOFCOM defines product market, and the second issue is how the MFCOM defines geographic market. The third issue is how market share is calculated. The fourth is how market concentration is assessed, and the last issue is whether other factors have been explicitly mentioned in the analysis of merger effects.

Table 3. Economic Analysis in MOFCOM's Merger Decisions[1256]

Case	Product market	Geographic market	Market share	Market concentration	Other factors
Coca Cola/Huiyuan	Fruit juice market	No information	No information	Coca Cola holds a dominant position in the carbonated soft drink market and it may leverage this market power to fruit juice market	After the merger, Coca Cola may increase its market power by controlling famous brands (Meizhiyuan and Huiyuan)
InBev/Anheuser-Busch	No information	No information	No information	No information	This decision did not provide any information regarding the analysis of merger effects
Mitsubishi Rayon/Lucite	The analysis is based on whether the product and service of two merging parties are overlapping. Both companies produce MMA, PMMA (polymer and plate)	Chinese market (no information regarding the economic analysis)	Post-merger entity may have 64% market share in the MMA market, much higher than the second and the third market player	The post-merger entity holds a dominant position because of the high market share; by holding the dominant position, it would eliminate or restrict competitors	The merger would restrict competition in the downstream market (no economic analysis was provided)
GM/Delphi	The merging firms do not have overlapping products and services at horizontal level, but have vertical relationship; the relevant market was defined separately for each firm based on their products.	Chinese market (no information regarding the economic analysis)	No information; it was mentioned that both GM and Delphi are the 'leading' market players in the auto industry	The merger may affect the supply of auto parts to car companies in China; the merger may provide GM information held by Delphi regarding the technology, car design and other information of domestic car manufacturers; the merger may increase the barrier for other manufacturers to supply auto parts to GM	Major concern was the vertical foreclosure in the upstream auto manufacturing market

1256 Sources: MOFCOM website <http://fldj.mofcom.gov.cn/article/ztxx/>; Y.W. CHIN (2012), *supra* n. 997; X. ZHANG and V.Y. ZHANG (2013), 'Revisiting China's Merger Control, Where are We Going After the Three-Year Milestone?', *Dovenschmidt Quarterly*, no. 1, pp. 26–35.

Case	Product market	Geographic market	Market share	Market concentration	Other factors
Pfizer/Wyeth	First examined whether two firms have overlapping products, and then investigated which overlapping product may change the market structure	Chinese market (no information regarding the economic analysis)	For product of swine mycoplasma pneumonia vaccine, the post-merger entity will hold 49.4% market share (much larger than other market players)	The post-merger HHI is 2,182, the increased HHI is 336; market is highly concentrated and the merger may eliminate or restrict competition.	The merger may restrain the development of other competitors by increasing the entry barrier (due to the high investment for innovation)
Panasonic/Sanyo	The analysis was based on in which product market the merger would change the market structure	Global market	61.6% (coin-type lithium batteries), 46.3% (nickel-hydrogen batteries for civil use), 77% nickel-hydrogen batteries for vehicles	The merger will increase market concentration by reducing the number of competitors	The purchasing strategy of the downstream buyers has been extensively considered; the buyers' power has been investigated
Novartis/Alcon	No information regarding economic analysis	Chinese market	Ophthalmic anti-inflammatory compound (60%) and contact lens care products (20%)	No information regarding market concentration and dominance	Coordinated effects (in contact lens care product market, post-merger firm obtains the second largest market share, and it may coordinate with the largest producer (Haichang))
Uralkali/Silvinit	According to the specific product characteristics, potassium chloride cannot be easily substituted	Not clear (the effects on the global market and on the Chinese market both mentioned)	After the merger the entity will have obtain over 1/3 of the global market in potassium chloride supply	The market power will be significantly increased due to the better control of production, supply and export	The importing market of potassium chloride; the impact of this merger on agricultural development in China
Penelope (AlphaV)/ Savio	Based on product characteristics	Not clear (the effects on the global market and on the Chinese market both mentioned)	Loepfe (47.7%) and Uster (52.3%)	Loepfe and Uster are the only two electronic yarn cleaner producers; the market is highly concentrated	Coordinated effects; economies of scale has been mentioned for the analysis of market entry

Case	Product market	Geographic market	Market share	Market concentration	Other factors
GE/Shenhua Group JV	Based on the particular characteristics of coal-water slurry gasification technology	Chinese market (the operation of the joint venture is limited within China, and the customers for this technology are only in China)	No information	Only three major competitors, the market is highly concentrated	Market entry (technological barriers, patents, high R&D investment)
Seagate/Samsung	Based on product characteristics	Global market (because HDD is produced and sold globally)	Seagate 33%, Samsung 10%	Highly concentrated (only five major competitors in the HDD market)	Considered the purchase strategy of the large computer manufacturers, buyers power, innovation, and impact on consumers
Henkel Hongkong/ Tiande Chemical	Product characteristic, supply and demand substitution, and other factors in product import and export	Global market (the effects on the Chinese market have also been considered)	In ethyl cyanoacetate market, each merging party holds 40% to 50% market share	Ethyl cyanoacetate market is highly concentrated (HHI>4,050)	The environmental regulation is taken as a major entry barrier
Western Digital/Hitachi	Based on product characteristics	Global market (because HDD is produced and sold globally)	Western Digital holds 29%, Hitachi holds 18% in both the Chinese and the global HDD market	Highly concentrated market	Considered the purchase strategy of the large computer manufacturers, buyers' power, innovation, and impact on consumers
Google/Motorola	Based on product characteristics	Effects on the global market and on the Chinese market were both considered	Google Android platform holds 73.99% of the market share in China	Highly concentrated (the major three competitors have 97.19% market share)	Entry barriers; the preferences from consumers; patents and R&D capacities
Goodrich/UTC	Product characteristic, the characteristics in supply and demand; experience from downstream customers	Global market (products are supplied and sold globally; the pricing are similar in all regions)	In the market of aircraft power system Goodrich holds 72%, UTC holds 12%	Highly concentrated, post-merger HHI = 7,158; the increase HHI = 1,728	Market entry (high investment in R&D, technological barriers)

Case	Product market	Geographic market	Market share	Market concentration	Other factors
Walmart/Newheight	The scope and pattern of the operation system; supply and demand substitution	Chinese market (considering consumer preferences, transportation, and tariff)	No information on the number of market share	After the transaction, Walmart's market power will be extended to online retail business	The features in the operation system of both merging parties has been considered
Advanced RISC Machines/G&D/ Gemalto IV	No information	No information	No information	The market power is exerted through the control of IP; downstream producers rely on use of trustzone technology	IP was considered as the major factor which increases entry barriers
Glencore/Xstrata	The overlapping product and services provided by the two merging parties	The effects on both the global market and the Chinese market have been mentioned	the post merger entity holds 7.5% (copper production); 9.3% (copper supply)	The merger will enhance the control of resources, improve production chain and the network for sales	The major concern was China's importing market, various factors were considered
Marubeni/Gavilon	The characteristic of the operation system; demand and supply characteristics	Chinese market (considered situations in trade, consumer preferences, transportation and tariff)	99% of the soya beans business operated by Marubeni's targets China's importing market	Marubeni will enhance its dominance by utilizing Gavilon's operating network in North America	The major concern was China's importing market of soya beans, various factors have been considered
Baxter Int./Gambro	The overlapping product provided by the two merging companies; price, technology characteristic of the product, the ease of transferring IP	The effects on the global market and the Chinese market have been both investigated (considered tariff, transportation and factors in import and export)	The Chinese market: the post-merger entity holds market share of 57% (CRRT monitor), 84% (CRRT blood tubing set) and 79% (CRRT dialyzer)	The increase of the HHI in the Chinese market: 1,204 (CRRT monitor), 3,456 (CRRT blood tubing set) and 1,920 (CRRT dialyzer)	The transaction would lead to coordinative effects between the remaining competitors (in particular with Niplo); IP and R&D costs are taken as entry barriers
MediaTek/Mstar Semicondutor	Product characteristics (both supply and demand substitutions have been considered)	Focus on the effects on the Chinese market (for the reasons of cultural preferences, geographical advantage, technology and service, price expectation)	For LCD products, the post-merger entity holds market share of 61% for the global market and 80% in the Chinese market	The HHI in the Chinese LCD market before the merger = 4,533, after the merger = 6,500	The characteristics of the LCD industry have been comprehensively analyzed; factors of IP and R&D are taken as entry barriers

4.3.4.   Conclusion

There are several conclusions that can be drawn by reviewing the empirical studies on comparing merger policy in the US, the EU and China. The first conclusion is that a similar trend can be observed in both the US and the EU that political influence on merger analysis has gradually declined, although given the long history of antitrust development in the US, this trend occurred much earlier in the US than in the EU. Political factors, such as which country the merging firms are based in, used to affect merger decisions by the European Commission. This influence disappeared when the empirical test is conducted again after the 2004 merger reform. The second conclusion is that economic analysis has played a more important role both in the US and the EU. However, the understanding of economic theories may diverge, due to different antitrust traditions, as well as due to the particular competition goals in each jurisdiction. The third finding is that the understanding of economic theories may evolve over time. For example, the European Commission is more reluctant to accept efficiency claims than the US competition authorities. However, as argued in previous chapters, the US antitrust enforcement was in a similar situation in the 1960s, when judges and legislators showed a hostile attitude towards efficiency arguments. As Schmitz once claimed, 'it could be said that European law is close to where US law was twenty-five years ago, although this statement should not be interpreted to mean that European law lags behind'.[1257] Regarding the situation in China, it seems that the MOFCOM's merger analysis reflects some aspects of the antitrust debate in the US and the EU decades ago. Non-competition factors, as well as political influence, do play a role in the MOFCOM's decisions. The application of economic theories and techniques is rather limited, and the MOFCOM tends to focus on structural variables such as market share and market concentration. The effects on unilateral effects, efficiency arguments, the dynamic interaction of market players, as well as other developments in modern industrial economics, are largely neglected.

4.4.   COMPARING MERGER POLICY IN THE US, EU AND CHINA: TWO CASE STUDIES

To better understand the differences in merger analysis between antitrust authorities, it is necessary to investigate the same case which is notified to different jurisdictions. In this section, two global mergers *Seagate/Samsung* and *Panasonic/Sanyo*, which were notified to, as well as investigated by, the MOFCOM, the EU Commission, and the FTC will be studied. The reason for choosing these two cases was the following. As of 27 August 2013, 21 merger

---

[1257]   S. SCHMITZ (2002b), *supra* n. 1174, p. 550.

decisions have been published on the MOFCOM website. Although most of them were global mergers, not many official decisions have been published both by the US, the EU and China, based on which a comparative study could be conducted. Among the total 21 decisions, only *GM/Delphi, Pfizer/Wyeth, Panasonic/Sanyo, Novartis/Alcon, Seagate/Samsung, Google/Motorola,* and *Goodrich/UTC* have been published in three antitrust jurisdictions. *GM/Delphi* and *Google/Motorola* are two vertical mergers and this book focuses on the study of horizontal mergers. *Pfizer/Wyeth* and *Novartis/Alcon* are two cases in the pharmaceutical industry which is subject to specific regulations. The MOFCOM's decision on *Goodrich/UTC* is rather too brief to investigate how economic analysis was conducted. As a result, to focus on the study of competition effects and to exclude the additional influence of other regulations, the merger cases *Seagate/ Samsung* and *Panasonic/Sanyo* are better examples. The *Seagate/Samsung* merger case was approved by the MOFCOM under conditions, but was unconditionally cleared in both the US and the EU.

In this section, a positive study will be conducted to investigate how these jurisdictions apply economic theories to analyze the same merger case, and particular attention will be given to the differences between their merger analysis. Given the fact that it was not possible to exchange information between these antitrust authorities due to the lack of bilateral cooperation agreements,[1258] it could be concluded that these authorities issued their decisions independently. It becomes worthwhile to investigate how antitrust authorities in the three jurisdictions conduct their merger analysis, as these differences may explain whether goals of competition could play a role. In the next section, a normative study will be conducted to investigate whether and to what extent these differences could be explained by competition goals. More importantly, if there are conflicting goals, it will be seen whether policy implications can be drawn to mitigate potential problems.

4.4.1. Panasonic/Sanyo Case

4.4.1.1. Case Summary

Panasonic Corporation and Sanyo Electric Co. are two Japanese international companies providing electronic products. Panasonic's acquisition of Sanyo was notified to the MOFCOM on 21 January 2009 and the investigation started on 4 May 2009. The MOFCOM conditionally approved this concentration and published the decision on 30 October 2009. The concentration was notified to the EU Commission on 11 August 2009 and the EU Commission published its

---

[1258] The extent to which the antitrust authorities in the EU and US can exchange information with MOFCOM remains unclear. G. DRAUZ, S. MAVROGHENIS and S. ASHALL (2011), *supra* n. 1148, p. 52.

decision on 29 September 2009.[1259] This transaction was also investigated by the FTC, with a published decision on 23 November 2009.

4.4.1.2. A Comparative Study on Economic Analysis of Merger Effects

4.4.1.2.1. DEFINING THE RELEVANT MARKET

The MOFCOM defined three relevant product markets: coin-type lithium batteries, nickel-hydrogen batteries for civil use and nickel-hydrogen batteries for vehicles. The geographic market is the global market. The MOFCOM's decision did not explicitly mention how the relevant market was assessed.

The FTC concluded that the relevant market is portable nickel metal hydride ('NiMH') batteries.[1260] Their analysis is based on demand-side substitutability: firstly, the NiMH batteries are particularly suitable for certain products and consumers cannot easily switch to other types of batteries. Secondly, even for products that may also function with other batteries, in response to a 5 to 10 percent price change, evidence has shown that consumers are not willing to switch to alternatives for reasons of cost and performance. For the definition of the geographic market, the FTC concluded that it is a global market because the manufacturing is located in Asia, and the product of portable NiMH batteries is sold to consumers around the world.

In contrast to the FTC's clear and simple approach, the EU Commission's decision on the relevant market starts from the question of what is a battery, and listed all the overlapping products by the merging parties. For each product, the EU Commission investigated both the supply- and the demand-side substitutability. The issues considered for supply-side substitutability include whether the production of a type of battery requires a separate production line and whether it is easy, in the event of a 5 to 10 percent price change, to switch production (the concerns of investment and whether a specific know-how is required). For demand-side substitution, the Commission considered the technical and performance characteristics of each type of battery.

The relevant markets defined by the Commission are broader than those defined by the authorities in the US, including markets for primary cylindrical lithium batteries ('CLB'), rechargeable coin-shaped batteries and portable NiMH batteries. In addition, the EU Commission went beyond the category of batteries and further investigated the impact of the merger on consumer electronic goods (flat-panel televisions, digital projectors, microwave ovens, air conditioners, camcorders, digital still cameras, and other consumer products), although it

---

[1259] *Panasonic/Sanyo* (Case No COMP/M.5421) Commission Decision of 29 September 2009.
[1260] Analysis of Agreement Containing Consent Orders to Aid Public Comment, in the Matter of Panasonic Corporation and Sanyo Electric Co., Ltd.

concluded that for these products the merger would not raise serious doubts. The definition of the geographic relevant market is left open for various products, and the Commission's analysis of the geographic market has largely relied on the market respondents in their investigation.

4.4.1.2.2. ANTICOMPETITIVE EFFECTS

The MOFCOM's assessment of anticompetitive effects relies on the market share and the market concentration level. According to the MOFCOM, the transaction would impede competition because it reduces the number of competitors and hence reduces the choices for downstream customers. In addition, it also becomes more likely for Panasonic to increase prices because such behavior would be welcomed by other producers, and at the same time it would receive little resistance from the consumers due to their weak bargaining power.

According to the FTC, the anticompetitive concerns of the merger are the unilateral effects as Panasonic and Sanyo are the only two high-quality suppliers of portable NiMH batteries. By eliminating a powerful competitor, the merger will make it likely for Panasonic to increase prices and to restrict competition, which would enhance innovation and improve services. The HHI index was applied as a presumption for market power but was not taken as evidence in their decisions.

The EU Commission's investigation on anticompetitive effects starts from calculating the market share of both parties (both in the global and the EEA markets). After calculating the combined market share of the two merging parties in the given relevant market, the Commission did not mention the change of the HHI before and after the merger, but considered how closely these two parties compete, and to answer this question, opinions from other market players were largely incorporated. The Commission also incorporated opinions from other competitors regarding how easily the merging parties could expand their capacities and to what extent new entrants in the global market could prevented from competing.

4.4.1.3. Conclusion

For product market definition, the US authority conducts a clear SSNIP test and only focuses on demand-side substitutability. Consumers' willingness and ability to switch alternatives is the only concern for defining a relevant market. The EU Commission tends to define a relevant market by examining the technology and performance characteristics of a product, and the question whether it is easy to switch production (or purchase) to another product is often answered by incorporating opinions from both producers and consumers. As far as the assessment of anticompetitive effects is concerned, the MOFCOM tends to rely on the evidence from market share and market concentration level. When the market is concentrated and the firms obtain a high market share, it is more likely for the post-merger entity to raise prices, and the situation is worsened when downstream customers have weak bargaining power. For the FTC, the concern of the potential anticompetitive impact was the unilateral effects, and the harm on competition was assessed by the likelihood of raising prices. Neither market share nor market concentration level has been explicitly mentioned in the analysis, although the HHI has been calculated because the US merger guidelines have set the HHI Index as a threshold for the market power. The EU Commission incorporated various factors that may affect the market structure in their merger analysis. The starting point of the anticompetitive effects of the merger is the market share of both parties. When the combined market share of the merging parties is high, the Commission examined how close they competed in the given product market. It seems that the analysis of whether the proposed merger would impede competition by increasing prices is more dependent on the response from other market participants, but not on a theoretical calculation by the Commission itself.

4.4.2.   Seagate/Samsung and Western Digital/Hitachi Case

4.4.2.1. Case Summary

Seagate, Western Digital, Hitachi Storage, Toshiba, and Samsung are the five largest hard disk drive ('HDD') manufacturers in the world. In 2011, two mergers were proposed relatively close together, one being that Seagate proposed an acquisition of Samsung's HDD business, and the other that Western Digital proposed to acquire the HDD business of Hitachi Storage. Both merger cases were notified to the MOFCOM, the FTC and the EU Commission. To compare the merger decisions in the US, the EU and in China, either of these two cases can be used as an example. However, the FTC did not publish decisions on Seagate/Samsung and the EU Commission did not publish the Western Digital/ Hitachi case. To find a solution, the economic analysis in Seagate/Samsung by the MOFCOM and the EU Commission, will be compared with the economic analysis of Western Digital/Hitachi[1261] decided by the FTC. The economic analysis applied in these two cases is comparable, because the involved four companies are in the same product market (HDD business), and these two mergers were notified at almost the same time period. More importantly, by comparing the MOFCOM's decision on Seagate/Samsung and Western Digital/ Hitachi, the economic analysis that is applied in these two cases were almost the same. Therefore, these two cases have been chosen for the comparative study on economic analysis of merger effects.

[1261]   Analysis of Agreement Containing Consent Order to Aid Public Comment, in the Matter of Western Digital Corporation, File No. 111–0122.

4.4.2.2. A Comparative Study on Economic Analysis of Merger Effects

4.4.2.2.1. Defining the Relevant Market

The MOFCOM defined the relevant market based on the product characteristics (volume, price and utilities). Although the MOFCOM acknowledged that the hard disk drives ('HDD') can be further divided into enterprise-used HDDs, desktop computer HDDs, laptop HDDs and HDDs for consumer electronic products, the MOFCOM set HDDs as the relevant market for the Seagate/Samsung case without providing any detailed explanation. The geographic market was defined as the global market due to the fact that HDDs are supplied and purchased on the global market.

The FTC defined the relevant market as desktop HDDs, which refers to HDDs used for non-portable desktop computers or tower personal computers. The reason was that consumers of desktop HDDs look for products with the highest capacity and the lowest price per gigabyte. By taking the SSNIP test, consumers are not willing to switch to other HDDs in case of 5 to 10 percent price increase. Similar to the analysis by the MOFCOM, the FTC also defined the geographic market as the global market, because HDDs are manufactured in Asia but are sold to consumers around the globe.

Compared with antitrust authorities in the US and in China, the EU Commission's approach towards the market definition is much more comprehensive with a detailed analysis of the product characteristics.[1262] Similar to the Panasonic/Sanyo case, the starting point of the analysis was the question of what the hard disk drive ('HDD') is. The Commission points out that the unique feature of the HDD is that it stores data without the need of electronic power. In the next step, the Commission dissected each component of the hard disk drive: the head-disk assembly (includes heads, magnetic media coating, a head positioning mechanism, and a spindle motor), and the printed circuit board assembly. To further understand the characteristics of the HDD, the Commission investigated the HDD manufacturing process, the end-users of the HDD, the upstream makers for HDDs, different HDD customer groups, the trend of innovation and technological development. After the elaboration of the basic characteristics, the Commission examines the demand and supply substitutability of HDDs. Interestingly, the EU Commission did not prove any demand substitution between different end-use applications of HDDs due to the specific technical characteristics of different types of HDDs (such as size, rotational speed, storage capacity and the type of interface).[1263] According to the

---

[1262] *Seagate/HDD Business of Samsung* (Case No COMP/M. 6214) Commission Decision of 19 October 2011.

[1263] *Seagate/HDD Business of Samsung* (Case No COMP/M. 6214) Commission Decision of 19 October 2011, para 32.

Commission, the price gap between different types of hard drives reconfirms the differences in their features. These features can also be observed through different industry dynamics and different supply chain models.

The EU Commission's conclusion on demand substitution significantly contrasts to the finding by the FTC, which excludes all other types of HDDs except for the desktop HDD for the relevant market. The FTC's reasoning was desktop HDD consumers' strong preference towards a HDD with low cost and high storage capacity. This difference indicates that antitrust authorities in the US and the EU have a clear different starting point for the analysis of the relevant market. The US approach gives a strong focus on the price effects on consumers, whereas the EU approach to a large extent focuses on product characteristics.

In addition to the demand-side substitution, the EU Commission also considered the substitutability at the supply side. The Commission concluded that the high technical requirements for each type of hard drive make the switch between different production lines difficult. The Commission concluded that the relevant market is defined as HDDs. As for the geographic market, the Commission followed the same analysis as the FTC and the MOFCOM and agreed to define the market for HDDs as worldwide.

4.4.2.2.2. ANTICOMPETITIVE EFFECTS

Based on the calculation of market share, the MOFCOM concluded that the HDD market is highly concentrated by five major HDD producers (Seagate, Western Digital, Hitachi Storage Technologies, Toshiba and Samsung). MOFCOM's analysis of anticompetitive effect focuses on the downstream computer manufacturers' purchasing pattern. The purchase of HDDs follows a non-public bidding procedure, and major computer manufacturers negotiate the order with HDD producers every three months. In each round of bilateral negotiations, the large computer manufactures often allocate their purchase order to HDD suppliers according to their price and other factors. HDD producers compete with each other to win the largest order, and a merger between Seagate and Samsung would reduce the pressure for such competition. MOFCOM also mentioned that HDD products are highly homogeneous and the HDD market is relatively transparent. It is highly possible to predict another competitor's strategy. In this way, the merger would increase the risk that the remaining competitors would coordinate their activities to impede competition. MOFCOM concluded that to maintain the competition in the HDD market, it is important to keep the current purchasing pattern between computer manufactures and HDD producers. When HDD producers raise prices, this price increase will be transferred to ultimate personal computer users through the computer manufacturers. As China is the largest consuming country for personal computers and consumers do not have sufficient bargaining power to resist the price increase, the merger would impose negative effects on the welfare of domestic consumers. It remains unclear, however, why the MOFCOM specifically focused on the responses from major computer manufacturers as it has also recognized that HDDs can be served to various end-users and there might be other customer groups who purchase HDDs for other uses. For example, the EU Commission has defined the HDD customers as original equipment manufacturers, original design manufacturers, distributors and retailers. The MOFCOM failed to provide a detailed explanation regarding why the preferences of other customers can be neglected, and whether in that case a relevant market should be defined more narrowly.

Similar to the analysis by the MOFCOM, the FTC also raised two anticompetitive effects: the potential risk for coordination and the unilateral effects. It was also acknowledged that HDD products are highly homogeneous and it is possible for the producers to predict the price and output of another competitor. Therefore, it is profitable and also likely for the remaining competitors to coordinate. In contrast to the MOFCOM's analysis of the merger effects on downstream computer manufacturers, the FTC's analysis of unilateral effects focuses on HDD consumers. According to the FTC, HDD customers prefer to have multiple suppliers from which they could choose. The reduction of competitors would reduce the competition pressure and will also reduce the supply choices.

The EU Commission assessed the anticompetitive effects through the merger's impact on non-coordinated effects and on coordinated effects. The Commission explains that non-coordinated effects refer to the situation where the post-merger firm impedes competition by obtaining a dominant position. The increase of market share is often taken as a criterion to assess such dominance. The coordinated effects refer to the extent to which a merger would reduce competitive pressures on the remaining competitors. The reduction of essential competitive constraints should be considered as anticompetitive effects of a merger, even though the coordination between oligopoly members was not likely.[1264] However, for the case of Seagate/Samsung, the Commission did not find that the proposed merger would remove competition constraints and significantly impede competition.[1265] In contrast to the decisions of the FTC and the MOFCOM, the EU Commission did not claim that products are entirely homogenous in the HDD market. For example, it concluded that several factors affect the consumers' choices of the HDDs, such as technical performance (rotation, seek speed), the quality, reliability, and energy consumption. The Commission concluded that HDD products are differentiated in their features. In this regard, the different analysis of coordinated effects between the US, China and the EU may due to the fact that the EU Commission has specifically focused on the different characteristics of each type of HDD. According to the

---

[1264]   Case No COMP/M. 6214 *Seagate/HDD Business of Samsung*, para 314.
[1265]   Case No COMP/M. 6214 *Seagate/HDD Business of Samsung*, para 317.

Commission, the question of whether a merger would remove competitive constraints to a large extent depends on how closely the producers compete. This is assessed not only by the market share, but also by the choices of purchasers. For example, the Commission observed that each HDD producer has specific strengths and weaknesses, and HDD purchasers claimed that the quality of the HDD produced by Samsung was not as good as other leading manufacturers.[1266] Since quality was one of the crucial factors that affected the choices of the HDD buyers, various business respondents confirmed that Samsung was a 'weak competitor'.[1267] For this reason, the Commission concluded that Samsung was not a close competitor to Seagate.[1268]

4.4.2.3. Conclusion

These two cases show that the FTC has consistently applied the SSNIP test for defining a relevant market. The substitutability of a product is only assessed from the demand side, and a relevant market can be defined as soon as consumers are not willing to switch to other products when the price for the given product is increased by 5 to 10 percent. Supply substitution is completely excluded by the FTC in defining the relevant market. Similar to the decision in the Panasonic/Sanyo case, the MOFCOM provided relatively little information on how a relevant market was defined. Although it was mentioned that HDDs can be divided into submarkets according to different end-users, the MOFCOM did not provide further information regarding the demand and supply substitutability of the HDD. Similar to the practice in China, the EU Commission also does not solely rely on the price effects to define a relevant market. The EU Commission often starts the analysis from understanding what the product is. In both the *Seagate/Samsung* case and the *Panasonic/Sanyo* case, the Commission first defines the unique feature of this product (battery, and the hard disk drive), and next starts the investigation into each category or component of the product. It seems that in both cases, the US starts the analysis of the relevant market from the price effects on consumers, the MOFCOM tends to understand the product by investigating the function of the market (or the industry), and the Commission starts the investigation from understanding the product itself.

Regarding the analysis of anticompetitive effects, the FTC tends to focus on the pricing effects after the merger, in particular after the merger, how likely the post-merger entity will increase the price, as well as how likely the remaining competitors will coordinate to increase price. Being consistent with the analysis presented in the previous section, in the case of *Seagate/Samsung*, it seems that

---

[1266] Case No COMP/M. 6214 *Seagate/HDD Business of Samsung*, para 354.
[1267] Case No COMP/M. 6214 *Seagate/HDD Business of Samsung*, para 422.
[1268] Case No COMP/M. 6214 *Seagate/HDD Business of Samsung*, para 356.

the MOFCOM analyzes the merger effects on consumers in a rather indirect way. The MOFCOM paid particular attention to the purchasing system of the major computer manufacturers, and concluded that the solution to mitigate the anticompetitive effects was to maintain the current purchasing pattern. The preferences and behavior from other HDD users and the end-users of personal computers were not explicitly mentioned. The EU Commission's assessment towards non-coordinated effects relies on the extent to which a merger would strengthen a dominant position. Different from the US approach, the EU assessed the coordinated effects not from the likelihood of coordination between oligopoly members, but from the perspective of to what extent the merger would remove the competitive constraints for the remaining competitors. One of the major issues is how closely the two merging firms compete in the relevant market. In *Seagate/Samsung*, for example, the Commission did not prove the coordinated effects because Seagate and Samsung might not be close competitors. The Commission focused on the specific features of the products that they produced and raised the doubt whether these HDD products are differentiated in terms of quality, technical performance and reliability.

4.5.   SUMMARY: WHAT CAN THE EVIDENCE TELL?

In this section, the differences in the implementation of merger policy in the US, EU and China have been investigated. By reviewing the empirical evidence and conducting a comparative study of two cases, there are a few conclusions that can be drawn. First, compared with the US, both antitrust authorities in the EU and in China tend to rely on a few structural variables in the analysis of merger effects, in particular, the combined market share is taken as an important starting point to assess the market power of the post-merger entity. Second, the US authority tends to apply modern economic theories and techniques to measure the merger effects, such as theories on unilateral effects, whereas the EU and the Chinese authorities tend to incorporate various factors, in particular the characteristics of the industry, in their analysis. For example, for the EU Commission and the MOFCOM, product characteristics are taken as a very important factor in defining a relevant market. The issue of how an industry develops or a certain business operates often plays an important role in the analysis of anticompetitive effects. The difference between these two authorities is that the investigation taken by the Chinese authority tends to rely on information from other producers and from governments, whereas for the EU Commission the responses from consumers are also of crucial importance. Taking into account various industrial factors, however, may lead to a broader definition of the relevant market by the EU and China than by the US authority.

Referring to the theoretical debate at the beginning of this section, these differences could to some extent be explained by competition goals in the US,

EU and China. At a first glance, the practice of incorporating more factors in their merger analysis may indicate the multiple goals of the competition policy in the EU and in China. A merger's anticompetitive effects not only need to be assessed from the changes of prices, and therefore the welfare impact on consumers, but also the effects on market structure and the competition effects in the industry. Moreover, the different focus on the merger effects, may also be explained by the different understandings of the function of the market. Influenced by the EU competition law, the merger policy in China also puts emphasis on the concept of 'dominance', and shows a low confidence in the robustness of the market. By relying on structural variables in merger analysis, both antitrust authorities in the EU and in China are reluctant to apply modern econometric techniques, and to accept efficiency gains.

5. DOES GOAL MATTER? A DISCUSSION ON COMPETITION GOALS AND MERGER POLICY

5.1. DIFFERENT GOALS, DIFFERENT RESULTS?

Compared with other competition issues, merger policy has a significant global impact. Mergers between multinational companies are required to be notified to competition authorities in several jurisdictions.[1269] Although companies are obliged to comply with specific merger rules in each country,[1270] it may impose compliance costs on businesses if merger rules are implemented differently in each country due to different concern of policy goals.

By reviewing the decisions in the *Virgin/British Airways* and the *GE/Honeywell* cases, commentators argued that in general the US antitrust authority seems to be less interventionist.[1271] Cento Veljanovski provided the data that in 2000, the probability of intervening by the EU Commission was about ten times higher than the US authority, and it was about nine times more likely to block a merger.[1272] One of the explanations which have been widely agreed was that this difference was due to the lack of consensus regarding the ultimate aim of the antitrust law.[1273] The US antitrust law has developed for over a century and since

---

[1269] G. NIELS and A. KATE (2004), 'Introduction: Antitrust in the US and the EU – Converging or Diverging Paths?', *Antitrust Bulletin*, vol. 49, p. 1.
[1270] G. NIELS and A. KATE (2004), *supra* n. 1269, p. 1.
[1271] G. NIELS and A. KATE (2004), *supra* n. 1269, p. 7.
[1272] C. VELJANOVSKI (2004), 'EC Merger Policy after *GE/Honeywell* and *Airtours*', *The Antitrust Bulletin*, vol. 49, p. 156.
[1273] S. STEVENS (2002), 'The Increased Aggression of the EC Commission in Extraterritorial Enforcement of the Merger Regulation and Its Impact on Transatlantic Cooperation in Antitrust', *Syracuse Journal of International Law and Commerce*, vol. 29, pp. 284–285; C. VELJANOVSKI (2004), *supra* n. 1272, p. 162.

the mid-1980s, the antitrust policy in the US has been framed under the strong influence of the Chicago School.[1274] In contrast, the European approach has a strong focus on the concept of dominance, and therefore tends to follow a legalistic approach.[1275] If a firm holds a dominant position, its effects on competition in the given market, or in another market (through 'leveraging' the market power), must be treated with caution.[1276] The concerns of preventing the abuse of dominant position and protecting the competition process reflect the influence of the Ordoliberalism.[1277] Seeing the different decisions for *GE/Honeywell* as well as *Boeing/McDonnell Douglas* made by the antitrust authority in the US and the EU, some commentators criticized the EU approach was to 'protect competitors'.[1278] The divergent views on competition goals may bring difficulties in harmonizing antitrust practice among jurisdictions,[1279] which would add transaction costs for global business operators, and impose deterrence effects on the efficiency-enhancing mergers.[1280]

Besides the perspective of competition goals, the differences can also be explained from other angles. Timothy J. Muris, the former chairman of the FTC, has pointed out that there are different types of differences that should be understood.[1281] For example, some conduct may be allowed in the US but is prohibited in the EU, due to the varying theories on the competitive harm that have been applied in the enforcement decisions.[1282] Moreover, the same business transaction may impose different levels of harm, as business activities may operate in a different scope in each market, for the reason of local regulation, transportation costs, or the feature of the product.[1283] Even in the situations where business activities and the theories of harm are the same in both

---

[1274]   G. NIELS and A. KATE (2004), *supra* n. 1269, p. 11.

[1275]   G. NIELS and A. KATE (2004), *supra* n. 1269, p. 12.

[1276]   G. NIELS and A. KATE (2004), *supra* n. 1269, p. 13.

[1277]   S. SCHMITZ (2002a), 'How Dare They? European Merger Control and the European Commission's Blocking of the General Electric/Honeywell Merger', *University of Pennsylvania Journal of International Economic Law*, vol. 23, p. 338. For a detailed discussion on Ordoliberlism, see section 3.5.1 of Chapter 3.

[1278]   W.J. KOLASKY (2004), 'What is Competition? A Comparison of US and European Perspectives', *The Antitrust Bulletin*, vol. 49, p. 30; T.L. BOEDER (2000), 'The Boeing-McDonnell Douglas Merger', in S.J. Evenett, A. LEHMANN, and B. STEIL (eds.) *Antitrust Goes Global: What Future for Transatlantic Cooperation?* Brookings Institution Press and Chatham House, pp. 142–143; P. KARACAN (2004), 'Differences in Merger Analysis Between the United States and the European Union, Highlighted in the Context of the Boeing/McDonnell Douglas and GE/Honeywell Mergers', *The Transnational Lawyer*, vol. 17, p. 234.

[1279]   D.K. SCHNELL (2004), 'All Bundled Up: Bringing the Failed GE/Honeywell Merger in from the Cold', *Cornell International Law Journal*, vol. 37, p. 253.

[1280]   W.J. KOLASKY (2002), 'Conglomerate Mergers and Range Effects: It is a Long Way from Chicago to Brussels', *George Mason Law Review*, vol. 10, p. 547.

[1281]   T.J. MURIS (2001), 'Merger Enforcement in a World of Multiple Arbiters', Brookings Institution, Roundtable on Trade and Investment Policy, Washington, DC, 21 December 2001, p. 3.

[1282]   T.J. MURIS (2001), *supra* n. 1281, p. 3.

[1283]   T.J. MURIS (2001), *supra* n. 1281, p. 3.

jurisdictions, antitrust authorities may have different opinions on how to interpret the evidence.[1284] In this situation, the differences might not be surprising as even within the antitrust authority in one jurisdiction, lawyers and economists may disagree with each other.[1285]

In addition, the differences could be understood by reviewing the historical evolution of antitrust theory. The US antitrust law has developed for over a century and it has a much longer history than EU competition law or the Chinese Anti-Monopoly Law. Throughout the evolution of antitrust development and the development of economic theory, the goal of protecting small business, fairness, and other social and political goals were gradually faded away.[1286] Only since the late 1980s have economic goals with clear welfare standards prevailed in modern antitrust analysis. Therefore, competition policy makers in China may also have to go through a similar learning process, and the different results of merger cases may reflect different stages of antitrust development in each jurisdiction.

Furthermore, as the US antitrust law has developed towards a more mature stage, the US antitrust authorities have cooperated with a much larger group of professional economists.[1287] Industrial Organization experts play a crucial role in merger analysis in the US.[1288] Since 2004, the EU Commission has significantly improved the quality of economic analysis of mergers by inviting PhD-trained economists to the Merger Task Force. Compared with the US and the EU, the antitrust authority in China is in need of professional expertise. Hence, the different results of mergers may also indicate the level of professional support that an antitrust agency can seek.

5.2. MOVING TOWARDS ECONOMIC GOALS?

Since the 1980s, economic goals have gained popularity in the US and the view of prioritizing economic goals has also been exported from the US to Europe.[1289] Seeing the change from populist goals towards promoting efficiency in the US, there was an increasing debate in Europe concerning whether EU competition policy should be enforced based on economic goals,[1290] as the Competition Commissioner Neelie Kroes once claimed, 'I think that competition policy evolves as our understanding of economics evolves. In days gone by, "fairness" played a prominent role in Section 2 enforcement in a way that is no longer the

---

1284   T.J. MURIS (2001), *supra* n. 1281, p. 3.
1285   T.J. MURIS (2001), *supra* n. 1281,p. 3.
1286   D.S. EVANS and M. SALINGER (2002), 'Competition Thinking at the European Commission: Lessons from the Aborted GE/Honeywell Merger', *George Mason Law Review*, vol. 10, p. 527.
1287   W.J. KOLASKY (2002), *supra* n. 1280, p. 549.
1288   D.S. EVANS and M. SALINGER (2002), *supra* n. 1286, p. 528.
1289   E.M. FOX (2006), 'Monopolization, Abuse of Dominance, and the Indeterminacy of Economics: The U.S./E.U. Divide', *Utah Law Review*, no.3, p. 725.
1290   E.M. FOX (2006), *supra* n. 1289, p. 727.

case. I don't see why a similar development could not take place in Europe.'[1291] According to Roeller, the recent increasing use of economics is regarded as one of the most 'significant trends' in EU competition policy.[1292] The goal of promoting consumer welfare under the EU competition law has been emphasized during the promotion of a 'more economic approach' and an 'effect-based' analysis of competition issues, which focuses on the competitive effects on the market and on consumers.[1293]

Although it was observed that EU competition law follows a trend of shifting from the integration goal towards economic goals,[1294] given the long pluralist tradition of the EU competition law, there are still challenges remaining in incorporating economic analysis into the interpretation of the competition rules.[1295] On the one hand, economic theories must be integrated to a more comprehensive welfare analysis, including dealing with legal issues such as inequality and legal uncertainty, in order to be acceptable for competition lawyers.[1296] On the other hand, economic analysis may only provide valuable policy recommendations if a broader economic framework could be used, such as incorporating modern theories of innovation, dynamic competition, and transaction cost economics.[1297] More importantly, there are various tools available to achieve the same policy goal, such as consumer welfare; economic tools can be applied to achieve any policy goal. If competition authorities in the EU and in China wish to immediately apply modern economic techniques and models, without going through the stage of learning from the Chicago School thoughts,[1298] there might be a danger of stepping back to 'pre-Chicago considerations', but 'dressed up in post-Chicago clothing'.[1299] In this aspect, economic analysis may serve as an instrument in the development of competition policy; however, relying on economic analysis does not solve the conflict and controversies between various policy goals.[1300] The task of clarifying and defining competition goals often requires efforts from policy makers and judges, who may make the decision by referring to economic theories on competition.

[1291]   N. KROES (2005), 'Tackling Exclusionary Practices to Avoid Exploitation of Market Power: Some Preliminary Thoughts on the Policy Review of Article 82', *Fordham International Law Journal*, vol. 29, no. 4, p. 596; *see also* E.M. FOX (2006), *supra* n. 1289, p. 727.

[1292]   L. ROELLER (2011), *supra* n. 1240, p. 289.

[1293]   L. ROELLER (2011), *supra* n. 1240, p. 289.

[1294]   C. KIRCHNER (2007), 'Goals of Antitrust and Competition Law Revisited', in D. SCHMIDTCHEN, M. ALBERT and S. VOIGT (eds.), *The More Economic Approach to European Competition Law*, Mohr Siebeck 2007, p. 7.

[1295]   R. VAN DEN BERGH (2007), *supra* n. 486, p. 33.

[1296]   R. VAN DEN BERGH (2007), *supra* n. 486, p. 33.

[1297]   R. VAN DEN BERGH (2007), *supra* n. 486, p. 33–34.

[1298]   G. NIELS and A. KATE (2004), *supra* n. 1269, p. 16.

[1299]   C. AHLBORN, D. S. EVANS and A.J. PADILLA (2004),'The Antitrust Economics of Tying: A Farewell to Per Se Illegality', *The Antitrust Bulletin*, vol. 49, p. 317 G. NIELS and A. KATE (2004), *supra* n. 1269, p. 16.

[1300]   R. VAN DEN BERGH (2007), *supra* n. 486, p. 35.

5.3.   IMPLICATIONS FOR CHINESE POLICY MAKERS

The five years of experience of merger policy in China tends to show that the competition authority in China gives particular attention to domestic players[1301] and the decisions seems to be more in line with industrial policy considerations.[1302] Moreover, as the AML has listed five competition goals, the ultimate aims that competition policy in China attempts to achieve are beyond the classic debate in the US and the EU, such as on consumer welfare, total welfare, and freedom to compete. For the Chinese antitrust agency, it is more likely to assess the merger through the effects on the overall development of the national economy.

The first implication that this study wishes to draw for competition policy makers in China is that, as it was discussed both in the US and the EU during the past decades, a consumer-oriented competition law, not a competitor-oriented law, might be more consistent with economic theory and therefore should be promoted. As both the US and the EU have adopted a consumer welfare goal for merger assessment, it would be a significant step for the Chinese competition policy makers to give consumer welfare an increasing role in merger analysis.[1303] As was widely criticized, competition policy should not be applied to protect individual competitors.[1304] Although industrial policy considerations have also been incorporated in the AML and the merger policy in China, for example, Article 27 of the AML indeed included the factors of the effects on competitors in the analysis of the competitive effects, and the concern of protecting domestic enterprises has been supported by the public,[1305] using competition policy to protect certain industries or domestic producers may not be aligned with economic theory.

Moreover, there are also potential risks to focusing on the gains to the competitors in merger analysis. The first risk of emphasizing the goal of protecting producers is that it may raise the question of whether producers have involved in an effective lobbying.[1306] Secondly, by moving away from economic analysis, enforcing merger policy to achieve political goals may be criticized for protecting 'national champions'[1307] or as a form of economic 'nationalism'.[1308]

[1301]   M. MARINIELLO (2013), *supra* n. 984, p. 11.

[1302]   M. MARINIELLO (2013), *supra* n. 984, p. 11.

[1303]   M. MARINIELLO (2013), *supra* n. 984, p. 11.

[1304]   D. HEALEY (2010), *supra* n. 976, p. 45; P.J. WANG, H.S. HARRIS, M.A. COHEN and Y. ZHANG, 'Coca-Cola/Huiyuan Deal is First Acquisition Blocked by China Antitrust Review', Jones Day, March 2009 <www.jonesday.com/Antitrust-Alert--Coca-Cola--Huiyuan-Deal-is-First-Acquisition-Blocked-by-China-Antitrust-Review-03-19-2009/> accessed 28.03.2014.

[1305]   Y. HUANG (2008), *supra* n. 3, p. 122.

[1306]   A. McGINTY and K. NICHOLSON, 'Coca-Cola/Huiyuan: Ministry's Prohibition Sparks Controversy', International Law Office, 2 February 2009, available at <www.internationallawoffice.com/newsletters/detail.aspx?g=76ff3c8f-0c3c-48c0-84e6-feaaf11f863c> accessed 28.03.2014.

[1307]   Y.W. CHIN (2010), 'M&A under China's Anti-Monopoly Law: Emerging Patterns', *Business Law Today*, The ABA Business Law Section's Online Resource p. 4; D. WEI (2011), *supra* n. 29, p. 817; Y.W. CHIN (2012), *supra* n. 997, p. 12.

[1308]   D. WEI (2011), *supra* n. 29, p. 818.

This may negatively affect the credibility of the MOFCOM as the decisions of *Coca Cola/Huiyuan* and *InBev/Anheuser-Busch* received severe criticism around the globe.[1309] It was also the case for the EU Commission, when the decision of *GE/Honeywell* was criticized by the American counterparts as 'protectionist' and 'misguided'.[1310] Protecting a group of producers (such as small and medium-sized firms) from the competition from another group of producers (such as big firms) used to gain popularity in the US in the 1960s. As it was discussed in detail in the third chapter, the populist goals was criticized by Chicago School scholars in the late 1970s as 'protecting small welfare', and since then this view has been dismissed in the antitrust community in the US. The reason was, the meaning of 'competition' from an economic perspective does not refer to maximizing the number of the rivals; rather, it refers to an efficient market outcome[1311] – a market can be perfectly competitive even there is only one firm in the market.[1312] The experience in the US shows that if there is no sound economic evidence, regulating the activities of individual firm may take a risk of destroying competition, although the initial purpose was to protect competition.[1313]

Even though competition policy in China incorporates the goal of industrial policy, as claimed by the EU Competition Commissioner Neelie Kroes in 2007, the 'protectionist goal' was 'old-fashioned' for an industrial policy because it would only be beneficial when the 'competitiveness' of an industry is enhanced.[1314] According to Commissioner Kroes, the goal of industrial policy and competition policy may converge as they both promote competitiveness, but not to protect a certain group of producer. Given the evolution of competition goals in the US and

---

[1309] S. Tucker, P. Smith and J. Anderlini, 'China Blocks Coke's Bid for Huiyuan', 19 March 2009 *Financial Times* <www.ft.com/cms/s/0/5c645830–1391–11de-9e32–0000779fd2ac. html#axzz2gNtWgqQK>. 'Beijing Thwarts Coke's Takeover Bid', 18 March 2009 <http://chinadigitaltimes.net/2009/03/beijing-thwarts-cokes-takeover-bid/> (Lester Ross, an attorney in US Law firm Wilmer Hale said: 'I think it was driven by protectionism, fueled by popular resentment against a foreign company acquiring a popular Chinese brand'); P. Chovanec, 'Beijing's Antitrust Blunder', 23 March 2009, *Wall Street Journal Asia* <http://online.wsj.com/article/SB123773830587406651.html> ('China blocked the deal to protect domestic producers from a capable foreign competitor'); T. Young, 'Asia Law Online, Coke-Huiyuan Reaction: Merger Block is Ridiculous', March 2009, available at <www.asialaw.com/Article/2161922/Quote.html> (citing Martin Huckerby, a partner at Mallesons Stephen Jaques in Shanghai: 'It will take a lot of deals where multinationals look to buy high profile Chinese companies off the table, or cause multinationals to look at smaller targets that are less likely to attract criticism and focus more on their regulatory strategy'); *see also* 'China's MOFCOM Imposes Conditions on InBev's Acquisition of Anheuser-Busch' <www.lexology.com/library/detail.aspx?g=01db2126–5c27–4a6f-813e-a7406b6ff169>.

[1310] E.E. Holland (2003), 'Using Merger Review to Cure Prior Conduct: The European Commission's GE/Honeywell Decision', *Columbia Law Review*, vol. 103, no. 1, p. 74.

[1311] W.J. Kolasky (2004), *supra* n. 1278, p. 31.

[1312] W.J. Kolasky (2004), *supra* n. 1278, p. 31.

[1313] W.J. Kolasky (2004), *supra* n. 1278, p. 40.

[1314] N. Kroes (2007), *supra* n. 683, p. 1406.

the EU, the Chinese competition policy makers may draw lessons concerning moving forward from the goal of protecting competitors to protecting competition, and at the same time switching the focus from producers to consumers.

The second implication is that as it was shown both in the US and the EU, economic analysis should be strengthened in merger analysis. On the one hand, economic theory and techniques become more important in analyzing the merger effects; on the other hand, both the antitrust authorities in the US and the EU have invited economists to work together with the investigation team. Compared with the antitrust authorities in the US and the EU, the intellectual resource for China to enforce merger policy is rather insufficient – with only around 30 staff members in the MOFCOM.[1315] More importantly, as a country with rather weak competition culture, it is still a challenging task to improve the quality of the economic analysis in merger cases by training specialized staff. At the time of the centrally planned economy, there were very few professors and students who taught and studied antitrust law. Only in recent years, several research centers for competition law studies have newly been established in universities in Beijing.[1316] The interdisciplinary research on law and economics is still underdeveloped. An official of the SAIC,[1317] another antitrust enforcement agency, once claimed that economics students have rarely been hired since his agency was founded. To overcome this difficulty, foreign antitrust experts are invited to give lectures in universities as well as to train government agencies in economic theories of competition, enforcement methods and their application in different countries. Nevertheless, this training is short-term based and has a strong geographical limitation, due to the existing financial capacity constraints. In the long run, efforts will be made by universities to enhance the cooperation between law faculties and economics faculties. Building a long-term relationship between researchers and policy makers is also planned. In this way scholars will have access to information, as well as the possibility of applying research results in real-life cases. More importantly, the competition agency needs to set up an efficient recruitment system to hire skilled staff. These professionals with an economics background and antitrust enforcement experience must be recruited separately from other staff within the ministry. Gal has emphasized other ways to increase the staff's professional knowledge, and establish a motivated team. These methods include internal training related to investigation procedures, editing guidance manuals, case histories, as well as motivating the staff by relying on the authority director's personality.[1318]

[1315] X. Wang and A. Emch (2013), *supra* n. 983, p. 269.

[1316] For example, University of International Business and Economics (UIBE), Central University of Finance and Economics (CUFE), Peking University (PKU), China University of Political Science and Law (CUPL).

[1317] X. Wang (2004), *supra* n. 71.

[1318] M.S. Gal (2005), 'The Ecology of Antitrust Preconditions for Competition Law Enforcement in Developing Countries', *New York University Law and Economics Research Paper Series*

6. CONCLUSION

As has been explained in detail in the previous chapters, competition goals in the US, the EU and China are to a large extent divergent. To understand whether competition goals may have an impact on the merger policy, this chapter conducted a comparative study by following two steps. The first step is to investigate whether there are differences in merger analysis in the US, the EU and China. The second step is to understand how these differences can be explained by their competition goals.

The comparative study confirms that there are significant differences in the merger policy in three jurisdictions. To start with, by reviewing the merger decisions published by the MOFCOM, it seems the merger analysis in China has been affected by several non-competition factors. One of the major conclusions was that the MOFCOM has paid particular attention to the interest of competitors, and has applied behavioral remedies in a rather extensive way. In MOFCOM's decisions, it was frequently mentioned that the investigation relies on the information received from government, trade associations, producers, and upstream or downstream firms. In the analysis of merger cases, the MOFCOM has extensively discussed the effects on domestic producers and domestic industries. The merger's effects on consumers are considered in a rather indirect way, and the welfare gains or losses of consumers are taken as one aspect of the merger's effects on the domestic market.

The differences in the merger policy between the US, the EU and China were further discussed by investigating the empirical evidence and by conducting a comparative case study. Empirical studies have shown that compared to the antitrust authority in the US, the EU Commission tends to rely more on structural variables in merger analysis, such as market share and market concentration, and is more reluctant to accept efficiency arguments. Economic techniques, for example the SSNIP test, only play a minor role in the merger analysis by the EU Commission, whereas the FTC tends to focus on the price effects of a merger and modern economic techniques have been widely developed to assess the unilateral merger effects. Similar to the practice in the EU, MOFCOM's merger analysis seems to follow a strong structural approach, and a merger is considered as highly likely to restrain competition when the market is concentrated and when the merger has a significant post-merger market share. The application of economic techniques by the MOFCOM, however, remains rather limited as none of the case decisions have mentioned the SSNIP test or the calculation of price elasticities. Regarding the political influence on merger analysis, the empirical studies showed a historical evolution between the US, the EU and China. Political factors used to play a role in the US in the 1960s and in

Working Paper No. 02/03, available at <http://ssrn.com/abstract=665181>.

the EU before 2002, and these influences were both mitigated in recent years. In MOFCOM's decisions, however, various non-competition factors still play a significant role, and this observation might not be surprising given the fact that China's competition law was only promulgated five years ago.

The empirical findings were to a large extent confirmed by the comparative case study on *Panasonic/Sanyo* and *Seagate/Samsung*. In both cases, the FTC has relied on the SSNIP test as well as the price effects of a merger to define the relevant market. The EU Commission focused on product characteristics whereas the MOFCOM started the investigation by understanding how a particular industry operates. For the anticompetitive effects, the FTC focused on how likely the post-merger firm would raise prices. The EU Commission put emphasis on the competitive constraints that the merging parties imposed on other competitors, and this was assessed by how close the two firms compete before the merger. Not only price effects, but also various characteristics of the product and industry were taken into account by the EU Commission. Compared with the US and the EU, the MOFCOM to the least degree relies on the economic techniques in merger analysis. It seems that the MOFCOM starts the investigation by understanding the operation of a particular industry, in which process the responds from other domestic producers are largely incorporated.

Given the differences in merger analysis in the US, the EU and China, it is important to ask the question whether these differences could be explained from the perspective of competition goals. It was widely argued that the EU Commission's structural approach is rooted in the Ordoliberal tradition which gives attention to the 'dominant' firm. By contrast, the Chicagoan influenced US antitrust law focuses on the extent to which a merger would generate efficiency. The legislative history of the Anti-Monopoly Law in China, however, shows a strong concern for protecting domestic companies and promoting the development of domestic industries. This concern might explain why the MOFCOM has incorporated the opinions from domestic producers in several merger decisions.

To conclude, the central question of this chapter is whether goals of competition law matter. In several aspects, the goal of competition law does matter. The first aspect is that the perspective of competition goals provides an important starting point to analyze the differences between competition policies in different jurisdictions. The difference not only lies in the substantive contents of the competition law, but also in the analysis of individual cases. The second aspect is that antitrust authorities in different countries may apply economic techniques to a different degree due to their specific competition goals. In the case of China, economic techniques only play a minor role, and various non-competition factors have to be taken into account in merger analysis to achieve the broader goals of its competition law. Moreover, influenced by the Ordoliberal and the Chicago tradition, the EU and the US competition law also showed a different understanding regarding specific economic concepts and theories. The perspective of competition goals may also well explain their different explanations of a particular concept, which may lead to a different outcome in case decisions. The third aspect is that comparing the merger policy in the US, the EU and China from a perspective of competition goals may draw unbiased policy implications for the Chinese policy makers. As it has been shown in the past decades, the goal of protecting a specific group of producers should not be a major concern of a competition law. In both the US and the EU, competition laws have been enforced to be more in line with economic theories, and the influence of political factors has been largely mitigated. This finding would have valuable implications for competition policy makers in China, who wish to catch up with the development of antitrust enforcement in more mature economies, that the competition policy could be better implemented if the focus on producers could be switched to consumers, and more attention be paid to the economic, not political, perspectives of the merger effects.

CHAPTER 6

CONCLUSIONS

At the end of this book, it could be concluded that competition goals have a critical impact on merger policy in the US, the EU and China. The perspective of competition goals may be taken as an important starting point to analyze why merger policy in China has been formulated and enforced differently than in the US and the EU. By following the four steps that have been mentioned in the introduction, the previous chapters have particularly focused on the issue of different competition goals in the US, the EU and China, as well as on the impact of competition goals on merger policy. This chapter will summarize the main conclusions, and will provide policy implications and highlight a few interesting topics for future research.

1. DIFFERENT GOALS IN THE US, THE EU AND CHINA

The first conclusion that can be drawn is that competition goals in the US, the EU and China are different, and the evolution of competition goals has to a large extent been influenced by the development of economic theories. In the US, from a positive view, the language used by the Sherman Act is broad and is subject to further judicial interpretations.[1319] However, during the last one hundred years, the federal courts in the US have not clarified a single definition or statement regarding the goal of antitrust law which could guide the enforcement of the Sherman Act. The US scholars have provided different views on the principles that the Congress had in mind when the Sherman Act was adopted in 1890. From a normative perspective, the US scholars generally agree that since the 1980s, economic goals have gained popularity in the antitrust debate, although no consensus has been reached with regard to whether consumer welfare or total welfare should be set as the primary goal of the US antitrust law.

The goals of EU competition policy are different from the goals of the US antitrust law in two respects. The first issue is that the EU competition policy has been utilized to achieve broader goals of the European Union. Since the Rome

---

[1319]   See discussion in Chapter 3, section 2.

Treaty, the fundamental goal of the EU competition policy is to achieve an integrated common market. Therefore, competition policy in the EU is considered as a crucial instrument to facilitate the market integration between Member States. The second aspect is that for EU competition policy makers, economic goals are not the only concern. Far beyond the goals of protecting consumer welfare, total welfare, other social objectives have been largely taken into account.

In China, the drafting process of the Anti-Monopoly Law took thirteen years and the legislative process of this law coincided with the market reform in China. During the drafting process of the AML, one of the most debated issues was the opposite attitudes towards mergers between domestic companies and mergers involving foreign investors. On the one hand, there was a willingness to enforce the merger policy towards foreign investors; on the other hand, there was a reluctance to apply competition rules to domestic firms. As a result, the goals of the AML include various social and political considerations. Moreover, the Chinese Anti-Monopoly Law was enacted not only to establish the legal foundations for a competitive market by promoting consumer welfare and total welfare, but also to contribute to the development of a socialist market economy.[1320] As stated in Article 1 of the AML, competition goals in China include restraining monopolistic behavior, protecting competition, promoting efficiency, protecting the interests of consumers and social public, as well as contributing to the development of the socialist market economy. These five goals are repeated in several articles under the AML. For example, Article 4 indicates the goal of 'contributing to the development of the socialist market economy' by stating that competition rules should be implemented to establish a 'united, open, competitive and orderly' market system. In addition, this goal is mentioned in Article 7 which states that industries which are 'crucial for the national economy and the national security' will be protected. Article 31 further states that for concentrations initiated by a foreign investor, an additional examination on national security might be applied. As far as the goal of 'protecting the interest of social public' is concerned, Article 15 states that it will be possible to grant exemptions if the monopoly agreements are signed for the purpose of protecting the environment, or mitigating the loss in economic recessions, or for the justifiable interests in international trade. Furthermore, Article 27 lists six factors that the antitrust authority should consider in the assessment of concentrations. The fifth factor is the impact of the concentration on national economic development.

From a normative perspective, Chapter 2 also discussed how Chinese scholars and policy makers approached the question of what the goals of the AML and merger policies in China should be. The legislative debate in China could show that there was no consensus on the goals that the AML should

---

[1320] See discussion in Chapter 2 for details.

include, although policy makers in China have generally agreed that the primary concern of the competition law in China is not to promote efficiency, but to contribute to the development of a socialist market economy.

2. COMPETITION GOALS AND MERGER ANALYSIS

The second conclusion that can be drawn from this research is that competition goals have a strong impact on merger analysis. Both the empirical evidence and the case studies have shown that in the US, the analysis of merger effects relies more on economic techniques, and it is more likely for antitrust authorities in the US to accept efficiency arguments. By contrast, the EU Commission tends to rely more on structural variables in merger analysis, such as market share and market concentration, and is more reluctant to accept efficiency arguments. In China, the MOFCOM incorporates various non-economic factors in merger analysis, such as the impact of the concentration on competitors and the effects of mergers on the national economy. The recent developments of economic techniques, for example, the SSNIP test or merger simulation techniques, have rarely been mentioned in the MOFCOM decisions. The MOFCOM tends to define the relevant market by examining product characteristics. Market shares are still taken as an important proxy to assess market power. By comparing the case decisions in the US, the EU and China, it could be concluded that a different focus of competition goals may lead to a different result of case decisions. Given the different views on competition goals, for the same merger case that is notified to three jurisdictions at the same time, it is highly possible that three antitrust authorities issue different decisions.

3. LESSONS FOR CHINA

By looking at them from the perspective of competition goals, the history of antitrust in the US and the EU may provide valuable experiences for competition policy makers in China. This research concludes that there are two major lessons that Chinese competition authorities can learn from their counterparts in the US and the EU. The first lesson is that the implementation of competition policy would be improved when the competition authority could move from achieving political goals to pursuing economic goals. As has been debated in the last decades, using competition policy to pursue the goal of 'protecting competitors' cannot be supported by economic theories, and in many situations it distorts market competition. Giving favorable treatments towards domestic firms may negatively affect the credibility of the MOFCOM, as it would be criticized as a form of 'economic nationalism'. From a law and economics perspective, emphasizing the merger effects on producers and relying on the information collected from producers and trade associations, but not from consumers, may also lead to other problems, such as providing incentives for lobbying and hence increasing the danger of regulatory capture.

The second lesson is that as it was shown in the US and the EU, economic analysis has played a vital role in merger analysis. To improve the merger policy in China, economic analysis should be strengthened in merger decisions. Both economic theories and the recent developments of modern economic techniques should be taken into account in merger analysis. In recent years, law and economics scholars have extensively criticized the practice of relying on market shares to assess market power. Modern economic techniques such as merger simulations have been largely developed to assess market power in a direct manner. The competition authority in China should take the developments in industrial economics into account, in order to avoid making biased decisions which would impose distortions on market competition. Meanwhile, as it has been shown in the antitrust debate in the US and the EU, economists should be invited to join the investigation team to analyze merger effects. Learning from the US and the EU, economic analysis in merger decisions would be significantly strengthened if MOFCOM could receive the support from a team of industrial economists. In addition, efforts should be made to train specialized staff by establishing research centers which could facilitate interdisciplinary research on law and economics. Nevertheless, given the limited experience of implementing the AML and merger policy in China, promoting competition culture remains a long-term goal.

4.   FUTURE RESEARCH

This research proposed a perspective of understanding the merger policy in China from the angle of its policy goals. In focusing on the impact of competition goals on merger policy in the US, the EU and China, this research has addressed several critical issues that are valuable for future research.

The first issue is the comparative study of different schools of thought that have influenced the development of competition policy in the US, the EU and China. As was mentioned in the third chapter, the Harvard School, the Chicago School, and the Ordoliberal School can be distinguished by their different views on competition goals. If a new antitrust regime wishes to draw lessons from the experiences of implementing antitrust law in the US and the EU, an important starting point is to understand the role of competition law by reviewing the debate between law and economics scholars who have led a revolution in antitrust thinking in the last decades. More importantly, to improve the competition legal framework in China, a series of comparative studies on the topic of comparing competition goals between the US, the EU and China would be needed. Although many scholars have observed that China has followed a similar structure to the EU in the design of a competition law,[1321] and some have argued that Ordoliberal thinking might be the most relevant intellectual source for China,[1322] the function and the role to achieve a multitude of economic and non-economic goals make the AML distinct from the competition regime in many countries. The goal of competition is a challenging while interesting issue for Chinese scholars who are interested in comparative competition law. The challenging research topics include, for example, how to promote consumer welfare while at the same time achieving a 'socialist market economy', and how to strike a balance between promoting consumer welfare, total welfare and stimulating economic growth.

The second issue is the study on the enforcement instruments of the AML. Classic law and economics literature on the enforcement mechanisms focus on the question of the extent to which a particular enforcement instrument can deter potential infringers at a low cost. For example, criminal sanctions would be preferred to monetary fines if they can better deter cartel conduct. A centralized antitrust authority would be more desirable than a decentralized system if this structure could save enforcement cost and could improve efficiency. However, this research proposes a new perspective, that is, to discuss the enforcement instruments from the view of competition goals. If a competition regime wishes to achieve a multitude of economic and non-economic goals, the question may arise how different enforcement instruments could be combined to reach different goals. In many aspects, the question of clarifying goals could be more important than the issue of saving enforcement costs. For example, after the promulgation of the AML, many commentators have expressed their concerns of improving the enforcement mechanism,[1323] and some have argued that to improve the enforcement of the AML, the current structure (with shared enforcement competence by the SAIC, the MOFCOM and the NDRC) should be changed to a unified, centralized antitrust authority.[1324] By switching the focus to competition goals, however, their arguments would be challenged because even though the structure of the antitrust authority changes, the controversies and challenges in antitrust enforcement would remain if goals

---

[1321] For example, D.J. GERBER (2008), *supra* n. 7, p. 289; S.B. FARMER (2013), *supra* n. 13, p. 20; D. WEI (2011), *supra* n. 29, p. 812; Y.J. JUNG and Q. HAO (2003), *supra* n. 29, p. 124; J.R. SAMUELS (2007), *supra* n. 29, p. 184; W. ZHENG (2010), *supra* n. 29, p. 648.

[1322] J.O. HALEY (2004), 'Competition Policy for East Asia', *Washington University of Global Studies Law Review*, vol. 3, p. 281.

[1323] For example, X. WANG (2008), *supra* n. 12; B.M. OWEN, S. SUN and W. ZHENG (2008), *supra* n. 7; J.A. BERRY (2005), *supra* n. 42; Z. LIU and Y. QIAO (2012), *supra* n. 48; Y. HUANG (2008), *supra* n. 3.

[1324] Y. HUANG (2008), *supra* n. 3, p. 125; X. WANG (2008), *supra* n. 12, p. 145; J.A. BERRY (2005), *supra* n. 42, p. 205; Z. LIU and Y. QIAO (2012), *supra* n. 48, p. 84.

of competition are not clarified. The implication is that, to improve the enforcement of competition law, the primary concern may not be reducing the enforcement cost, but clarifying the goals of competition law. Taking competition goals as the starting point, one important aspect of future research on the topic of antitrust enforcement is how to combine different instruments to achieve various goals.

Lastly, this research is limited to the scope of merger policy. The analysis of competition goals could also be extended to other areas of competition policy, such as designing rules against administrative monopolies in China. Moreover, the discussion on competition goals is a highly philosophical issue, which requires a more comprehensive interdisciplinary research. The enforcement of legal rules in jurisdictions does not follow the same pattern, of course, not only due to the reason that their goals are different. The complex interaction between cultural, political and economic factors may lead to a different interpretation of the role and the meaning of a competition law. To contribute to a better understanding of competition law and policy, it would be desirable to conduct multidisciplinary, integrated research in the future across the disciplines of economics, law, history, and political science.

REFERENCES

ARTICLES AND BOOK CHAPTERS

ADILOV, N. and P.J. ALEXANDER (2006), 'Horizontal Merger: Pivotal Buyers and Bargaining Power', *Economic Letters,* vol. 91, pp. 307–311

AGHION, P. and J. TIROLE (1994), 'The Management of Innovation', *Quarterly Journal of Economics*, vol. 109, pp. 1185–1209

AGHION, P., N. BLOOM, R. BLUNDELL, R. GRIFFITH and P. HOWITT (2005), 'Competition and Innovation: An Inverted-U Relationship', *Quarterly Journal of Economics,* vol. 120, no. 2, pp. 701–728

AHLBORN, C., D.S. EVANS and A.J. PADILLA (2004), 'The Antitrust Economics of Tying: A Farewell to Per Se Illegality', *The Antitrust Bulletin,* vol. 49, no. 1/2, pp. 287–341

AHLBORN, C. and C. GRAVE (2006), 'Walter Eucken and Ordoliberalism: An Introduction from a Consumer Welfare Perspective', *Competition Policy International,* vol. 2, no. 2, pp. 197–217

AHLBORN, C. and J. PADILLA (2007), 'From Fairness to Welfare: Implications for the Assessment of Unilateral Conduct under EC Competition Law', in C.D. EHLERMANN and M. MARQUIS (eds.), *European Competition Law Annual 2007: A Reformed Approach to Article 82 EC*, Hart Publishing

AIGINGER, K., M. MCCABE, D.C. MUELLER and C. WEISS (2001), 'Do American and European Industrial Organization Economists Differ?', *Review of Industrial Organization*, vol. 19, pp. 383–405

AKMAN, P. (2008), '"Consumer Welfare" and Article 82 EC: Practice and Rhetoric', *CCP Working Paper No. 08–25*, ESRC Centre for Competition Policy, University of East Anglia

AKMAN, P. (2009), 'Searching for the Long-Lost Soul of Article 82 EC', *Oxford Journal of Legal Studies*, vol. 29, no. 2, pp. 267–303

AKMAN, P. (2010), '"Consumer" versus "Customer": The Devil in the Detail', *Journal of Law and Society*, vol. 37, no. 2, pp. 315–344

AKTAS, N., E. DE BODT and R. ROLL (2004), 'Market Responses to European Regulation of Business Combinations', *Journal of Financial and Quantitative Analysis*, vol. 39, pp. 731–757

AKTAS, N., E. DE BODT and R. ROLL (2007), 'Is European M&A Regulation Protectionist?', *The Economic Journal*, vol. 117, pp. 1096–1121

AKTAS, N. (2011), 'Market Reactions to European Merger Regulation: A Reexamination of the Protectionism Hypothesis,' <http://ssrn.com/abstract=2083645>

AMIR, R., E. DIAMANTOUDI and L. XUE (2009), 'Merger Performance under Uncertain Efficiency Gains', *International Journal of Industrial Organization*, vol. 27, pp. 264–273

AREEDA, P. (1983), 'Introduction to Antitrust Economics', *Antitrust Law Journal*, vol. 52, pp. 523–538

AREEDA, P. and L. KAPLOW (2004), *Antitrust Analysis, Problems, Text, Cases*, 6th ed., Aspen Publishers

AREEDA, P.A. and D.F. TURNER (1980), *Antitrust Law: An Analysis of Antitrust Principles and Their Application*, Little Brown

ARROW, K.J. (1962), 'Economic Welfare and the Allocation of Resources for Innovation', in R.R. NELSON (eds.), *The Rate and Direction of Economic Activity*, Princeton University Press

ASIAN DEVELOPMENT BANK (2003), 'Private Sector Assessment, People's Republic of China', Publication Stock No. 091003

AUDRETSCH, D.B., W.J. BAUMOL and A.E. BURKE (2001), 'Competition Policy in Dynamic Markets', *International Journal of Industrial Organization*, vol. 19, pp. 613–634

AVERITT, N.W. and R.H. LANDE (2007), 'Using the "Consumer Choice" Approach to Antitrust Law', *Antitrust Law Journal*, vol. 74, no. 1, pp. 175–264

BAGCHI, A. (2005), 'The Political Economy of Merger Regulation', *The American Journal of Comparative Law*, vol. 53, pp. 1–30

BAIN, J. (1949), 'A Note on Pricing in Monopoly and Oligopoly', *American Economic Review*, vol. 39, pp. 448–464

BAIN, J.S. (1951), 'Relation of Profit Rate to Industry Concentration: American Manufacturing, 1936–1940', *Quarterly Journal of Economics*, vol. 65, pp. 293–324

BAIN, J.S. (1956), *Barriers to New Competition*, Harvard University Press

BALTO, D. (2001), 'The Efficiency Defense in Merger Review: Progress or Stagnation?', *Antitrust*, vol. 16, pp. 74–81

BALTO, D. (2001), 'Lessons from the Clinton Administration: The Evolving Approach to Merger Remedies', *George Washington Law Review*, vol. 69, pp. 952–977

BAKER, J.B. and T.F. BRESNAHAN (1992), 'Empirical Methods of Identifying and Measuring Market Power', *Antitrust Law Journal*, vol. 61, pp. 3–16

BAKER, J.B. (2002), 'A Preface to Post-Chicago Antitrust', in A. CUCINOTTA, R. PARDOLESI and R. VAN DEN BERGH (eds.), *Post-Chicago Developments in Antitrust Analysis*, Edward Elgar pp. 60–75

BAKER, J.B. (2003), 'Responding to Developments in Economics and the Courts: Entry in the Merger Guidelines', *Antitrust Law Journal*, vol. 71, pp. 189–206

BAKER, J.B. (2004), 'Efficiencies and High Concentration: Heinz Proposes to Acquire Beech-Nut', in J.E. KWOKA and L.J. WHITE, *The Antitrust Revolution, Economics, Competition and Policy*, 4th ed., Oxford University Press

BAKER, J.B. (2007), 'Beyond Schumpeter vs. Arrow: How Antitrust Fosters Innovation', *Antitrust Law Journal*, vol. 74, pp. 575–602

BAKER, J.B. and C. SHAPIRO (2007), 'Reinvigorating Horizontal Merger Enforcement', *Reg-Markets Center Working Paper No. 07–12*, <http://ssrn.com/abstract=1089198>

BAKER, J.B. (2008), '"Dynamic Competition" Does not Excuse Monopolization', <http://papers.ssrn.com/sol3/papers.cfm?abstract_id=1285223>

BAKER, J.B. (2010), 'Market Concentration in the Antitrust Analysis of Horizontal Mergers', <http://papers.ssrn.com/sol3/papers.cfm?abstract_id=1092248>

BAKER, J.B. (2013), 'Economics and Politics: Perspectives on the Goals and Future of Antitrust', *Fordham Law Review*, vol. 81, pp. 2175–2196

BAKER, D.I. and W. BLUMENTHAL (1983), 'The 1982 Guidelines and Preexisting Law', *California Law Review*, vol. 71, no 2, pp. 311–347

BARNETT, T.O. (2008), 'Maximizing Welfare through Technological Innovation', *George Mason Law Review*, vol. 15, pp. 1191–1204

BASKOY, T. (2005), 'Effective Competition and EU Competition Law', *Review of European and Russian Affairs*, vol. 1, no. 1, pp. 1–21

BAXTER, W. (1985), 'Responding to the Reaction: The Draftsman's View', in E.M. FOX and J.T. HALVERSON (eds.), *Antitrust Policy in Transition: The Convergence of Law and Economics*, American Bar Association

BAI, C., J. LU and Z. TAO (2006), 'The Multitask Theory of State Enterprise Reform: Empirical Evidence from China', *The American Economic Review*, vol. 96, no. 2, pp. 353–357

BERRY, M.N. (1996), 'Efficiencies and Horizontal Mergers: In Search of a Defense', *San Diego Law Review*, vol. 33, pp. 515–554

BERRY, J.A (2005), 'Anti-Monopoly Law in China: A Socialist Market Economy Wrestles with Its Antitrust Regime', *International Law and Management Review*, vol. 2, pp. 129–152

BERGMAN, M.A., M. JAKOBSSON and C. RAZO (2005), 'An Econometric Analysis of the European Commission's Merger Decisions', *International Journal of Industrial Organization*, vol. 23, pp. 717–737

BERGMAN, M.A. *et al.* (2010a), 'Comparing Merger Policies in the European Union and the United States', *Review of Industrial Organization*, vol. 36, pp. 305–331

BERGMAN, M.A. *et al.* (2010b), 'Merger Control in the European Union and the United States: Just the Facts', <http://papers.ssrn.com/sol3/papers.cfm?abstract_id=1565026>

BERNILE, G. and E. LYANDRES (2013), 'The Effects of Horizontal Merger Synergies on Competitors, Customers and Suppliers', <http://papers.ssrn.com/sol3/papers.cfm?abstract_id=2311560>

BESANKO, D. and D. SPULBER (1993), 'Contested Mergers and Equilibrium Antitrust Policy', *Journal of Law, Economics and Organization*, vol. 9, no. 1, pp. 1–29

BISHOP, S. and M. WALKER (2002), *The Economics of EC Competition Law: Concepts, Application and Measurement*, Sweet & Maxwell

BLAIR, R.D. and J.L HARRISON (1991), 'Antitrust Policy and Monopsony', *Cornell Law Review*, vol. 76, pp. 297–340

BLAIR, R. D. and J.S. HAYNES (2011), 'The Efficiencies Defense in the 2010 Horizontal Merger Guidelines', *Review of Industrial Organization*, vol. 39, pp. 57–68

BLAIR, R.D. and D.D. SOKOL (2012), 'The Rule of Reason and the Goals of Antitrust: An Economic Approach', *Antitrust Law Journal*, vol. 78, pp. 471–504

BLAIR, R.D. and D.D. SOKOL (2013), 'Welfare Standards in U.S. and E.U. Antitrust Enforcement', *Fordham Law Review*, vol. 81, pp. 101–145

BLUNDELL, R., R. GRIFFITH and J. VAN REENEN (1999), 'Market Share, Market Value and Innovation in a Panel of British Manufacturing Firms', *Review of Economic Studies*, vol. 66, pp. 529–554

BLODGETT, M.S., R.J. HUNTER JR. and R.M. HAYDEN (2009), 'Foreign Direct Investment, Trade and China's Competition Laws', *Denver Journal International Law and Policy*, vol. 37, pp. 201–232

BOEDER, T.L. (2000), 'The Boeing-McDonnell Douglas Merger', in S.J. EVENETT, A. LEHMANN, and B. STEIL (eds.), *Antitrust Goes Global: What Future for Transatlantic Cooperation?* Brookings Institution Press and Chatham House

BORK, R.H. and W.S. BOWMAN, Jr. (1965), 'The Crisis in Antitrust', *Columbia Law Review*, vol. 65, no. 3, pp. 363–376

BORK, R.H. (1965), 'Contrasts in Antitrust Theory: 1', *Columbia Law Review*, vol. 65, no. 3, pp. 401–416

BORK, R.H. (1966), 'Legislative Intent and the Policy of the Sherman Act', *Journal of Law and Economics*, vol. 9, pp. 7–48

BORK, R.H. (1967), 'The Goals of Antitrust Policy', *American Economic Review*, vol. 57, no. 2, pp. 242–253

BORK, R.H. (1978), *The Antitrust Paradox: A Policy at War with Itself*, Basic Books

BRESNAHAN, T.F. (1989), 'Empirical Studies of Industries with Market Power', in R. SCHMALENSEE and R.D. WILLIG (eds.), *Handbook of Industrial Organization*, volume 2, North-Holland, Chapter 17, pp. 1101–1057

BRODLEY, J.F. (1987), 'The Economic Goals of Antitrust: Efficiency, Consumer Welfare and Technological Progress', *New York University Law Review*, vol. 62, pp. 1020–1053

BROADMAN, H.G. and X. SUN (1997), 'The Distribution of Foreign Direct Investment in China', *Policy Research Working Paper*, The World Bank, China and Mongolia Department Country Operations Division in February 1997, pp. 1–20

BUSH, N. (2005), 'Chinese Competition Policy: It Takes More Than a Law', *China Business Review*, vol. 32, no. 3, pp. 30–35

BUCKLEY, P. J, A.R. CROSS, H. TAN, X. LIU and H. VOSS (2008), 'Historic and Emergent Trends in Chinese Outward Direct Investment', *Management International Review*, vol. 48, no. 6, pp. 715–748

CAO, Y., Y. QIAN and B.R. WEINGAST (1997), 'From Federalism, Chinese Style, to Privatization, Chinese Style', *The William Davidson Institute at the University of Michigan Business School Working Paper No. 126*

CALKINS, S. (1983), 'The New Merger Guidelines and the Herfindahl-Hirschman Index', *California Law Review*, vol. 71, no. 2, pp. 402–429

CAPPS, O. JR., J. CHURCH and H.A. LOVE (2003), 'Specification Issues and Confidence Intervals in Unilateral Price Effects Analysis', *Journal of Econometrics*, vol. 113, pp. 3–31

CARRIER, M.A. (2008), 'Two Puzzles Resolved: Of the Schumpeter-Arrow Stalemate and Pharmaceutical Innovation Markets', *Iowa Law Review*, vol. 93, pp. 393–450

CARLTON, D.W. and J.M. PERLOFF (1990), *Modern Industrial Organization*, HarperCollins Publishers

CARTON, D.W. and R. GERTNER (2003), 'Intellectual Property, Antitrust and Strategic Behavior', in A.B. JAFFE, J. LERNER and S. STERN (eds.) *Innovation Policy and Economics*, volume 3, MIT Press, pp. 29–60

CARTON, D.W. 'Antitrust Policy Toward Mergers when Firms Innovate: Should Antitrust Recognize the Doctrine of Innovation Markets?', Testimony before the Federal Trade Commission Hearings on Global and Innovative-Based Competition, 25 October 1995, available at <www.ftc.gov/opp/global/carlton.htm>

CARLTON, D.W. (2004), 'Using Economics to Improve Antitrust Policy', *Columbia Business Law Review,* vol. 2004, pp. 283–333

CARLTON, D.W. (2007), 'Does Antitrust Need to Be Modernized?', *Journal of Economic Perspectives,* vol. 21, no. 3, pp. 155–176

CHAMBERLIN, E.H. (1950), 'Product Heterogeneity and Public Policy', *The American Economic Review,* vol. 40, no. 2, pp. 85–92

CHIN, Y.W. (2010), 'M&A under China's Anti-Monopoly Law: Emerging Patterns', *Business Law Today,* The ABA Business Law Section's Online Resource, pp. 1–5

CHIN, Y.W. (2012), 'The High-Wire Balancing Act of Merger Control under China's Anti-Monopoly Law', <http://ssrn.com/abstract=2120280>

CHIN, Y.W. (2013), 'The Chinese MOFCOM Enforces Telecoms Regulations in AML Merger Review', <http://ssrn.com/abstract=2260474>

COATE, M.B. and F.S. McCHESNEY (1992), 'Empirical Evidence on FTC Enforcement of the Merger Guidelines', *Economic Inquiry,* vol. 20, no. 2, pp. 277–293

COATE, M.B. (2005), 'Efficiencies in Merger Analysis: An Institutionalist View', *Supreme Court Economic Review,* vol. 13, pp. 189–240

COATE, M.B. and A.J. HEIMERT (2009), 'Merger Efficiencies at the Federal Trade Commission 1997–2007', *Federal Trade Commission Economic Issues Series Working Paper,* <http://papers.ssrn.com/sol3/papers.cfm?abstract_id=1338738>

COHEN, N.B. and C.A. SULLIVAN (1983), 'The Herfindahl-Hirschman Index and the New Antitrust Merger Guidelines: Concentrating on Concentration', *Texas Law Review,* vol. 62, pp. 453–508

COHEN, W.M. and R.C. LEVIN (1989), 'Empirical Studies of Innovation and Market Structure', in R. SCHMALENSEE and R.D. WILLING (eds.), *Handbook of Industrial Organization,* North-Holland, Chapter 18, pp. 1060–1107

CONRATH, C.W. and N.A. WIDNELL (1999), 'Efficiency Claims in Merger Analysis: Hostility or Humility?', *George Mason Law Review,* vol. 7, no. 3, pp. 685–706

COPPI, L. and M. WALKER (2004), 'Substantial Convergence or Parallel Paths? Similarities and Differences in the Economic Analysis of Horizontal Mergers in US and EU Competition Law', *The Antitrust Bulletin,* vol. 49, pp. 101–152

CRANE, D.A. (2008), 'Technocracy and Antitrust', *Texas Law Review,* vol. 86, no. 6, pp. 1159–1222

CSERES, K.J. (2005), *Competition Law and Consumer Protection,* Kluwer Law International

CURRIE, J.M., J.A. MURPHY and A. SCHMITZ (1971), 'The Concept of Economic Surplus and Its Use in Economic Analysis', *The Economic Journal,* vol. 81, no. 324, pp. 741–799

CLARK, J.M. (1940), 'Toward a Concept of Workable Competition', *The American Economic Review,* vol. 30, no. 2, pp. 241–256

CLARKE, D.C. (2003), 'China's Legal System and the WTO: Prospects for Compliance', *Washington University Global Studies Law Review,* vol. 2, pp. 97–120

DARAI, D., D. SACCO and A. SCHMUTZLER (2010), 'Competition and Innovation: An Experimental Investigation', *Experimental Economics,* vol. 13, pp. 439–460

DEBOW, M.E. (1991), 'The Social Costs of Populist Antitrust: A Public Choice Perspective', *Harvard Journal of Law and Public Policy,* vol. 14, pp. 205–224

DEMSETZ, H. (1973), 'Industry Structure, Market Rivalry, and Public Policy', *Journal of Law and Economics*, vol. 16, pp. 1–10

DENECKERE, R.J. and C. DAVIDSON (1985), 'Incentives to Form Coalitions with Bertrand Competition', *Rand Journal of Economics*, vol. 16, pp. 473–486

DELURY, J. (2008), 'Harmonious in China', *Policy Review*, vol. 148, pp. 35–44

DENG, F., A. EMCH and G.K. LEONARD (2009), 'A Hard Landing in the Soft Drink Market – MOFCOM's Veto of the Coca-Cola & Huiyuan Deal', *Global Competition Policy*, April (2), pp. 1–17

DEVOS, E., P. KADAPAKKAM and S. KRISHNAMURTHY (2009), 'How Do Mergers Create Value? A Comparison of Taxes, Market Power, and Efficiency Improvements as Explanations for Synergies', *Review of Financial Studies*, vol. 22, no. 3, pp. 1179–1211

DING, M. (2011), 'On the Functions and its' Optimization of Antitrust Law' (反垄断法的目标选择及其功能优化刍议), *Journal of Tianjin University of Finance and Economics* (天津财经大学学报), no. 8, pp. 123–129

DIXIT, A. and J. STIGLITZ (1977), 'Monopolistic Competition and Optimum Product Diversity', *American Economic Review*, vol. 67, no. 3, pp. 297–308

DRAUZ, G., T. CHELLINGSWORTH and H. HYRKAS (2010), 'Recent Developments in EC Merger Control', *Journal of European Competition Law and Practice*, vol. 1, no. 1, pp. 12–26

DRAUZ, G., S. MAVROGHENIS and S. ASHALL (2011), 'Recent Developments in EU Merger Control 1 September 2009 – 31 August 2010', *Journal of European Competition Law and Practice*, vol. 2, no. 1, pp. 46–61

DUSO, T., D. NEVEN and L.H. ROELLER (2007), 'The Political Economy of European Merger Control: Evidence Using Stock Market Data', *Journal of Law and Economics*, vol. 50, pp. 455–489

DUSO, T., K. GUGLER and F. SZUECS (2013), 'An Empirical Assessment of the 2004 EU Merger Policy Reform', *The Economic Journal*, pp. 596–619

EASTERBROOK, F.H. (1984), 'The Limits of Antitrust', *Texas Law Review*, vol. 63, no. 1, pp. 1–40

EASTERBROOK, F.H. (1986), 'Workable Antitrust Policy', *Michigan Law Review*, vol. 84, pp. 1696–1713

EISNER, M.A. and K.T. MEIER (1990), 'Presidential Control versus Bureaucratic Power: Explaining the Reagan Revolution in Antitrust', *American Journal of Political Science*, vol. 34, no. 1, pp. 269–287

EDWARDS, S.M. *et al.* (1981), 'Proposed Revisions of the Justice Department's Merger Guidelines', *Columbia Law Review*, vol. 81, no. 8, pp. 1543–1581

ELIZALDE, J. (2012), 'A Theoretical Approach to Market Definition Analysis', *European Journal of Law and Economics*, vol. 34, pp. 449–475

EVANS, D.S. and K.N. HYLTON (2008), 'The Lawful Acquisition and Exercise of Monopoly Power and Its Implications for the Objectives of Antitrust', *Competition Policy International*, vol. 4, no. 2, pp. 203–241

EUCKEN, W. (1950), *The Foundations of Economic History and Theory of Economic Reality*, William Hodge & Company

EMCH, A. (2011), 'Antitrust in China – the Brighter Spots', *European Competition Law Review*, vol. 3, pp. 132–138

EPSTEIN, R.J. and D.L. RUBINFELD (2004), 'Technical Report: Effects of Mergers Involving Differentiated Products', COMP/B1/2003/07

EPSTEIN, R.J. and D.L. RUBINFELD (2001), 'Merger Simulation: A Simplified Approach with New Applications', *Antitrust Law Journal*, vol. 69, no. 3, pp. 883–919

EVANS, D.S. and M. SALINGER (2002), 'Competition Thinking at the European Commission: Lessons from the Aborted GE/Honeywell Merger', *George Mason Law Review*, vol. 10, pp. 489–532

FARMER, S.B. (2013), 'Recent Developments in Regulation and Competition Policy in China: Trends in Private Civil Litigation', in M. FAURE and X. ZHANG (eds.), *The Chinese Anti-Monopoly Law, New Developments and Empirical Evidence*, Edward Elgar, pp. 15–72

FAURE, M. and X. ZHANG (eds.) (2011), *Competition Policy and Regulation, Recent Developments in China, the US and Europe*, Edward Elgar

FAURE, M. and X. ZHANG (eds.) (2013), *The Chinese Anti-Monopoly Law, New Developments and Empirical Evidence*, Edward Elgar

FAURE, M. and X. ZHANG (2013), 'Towards an Extraterritorial Application of the Chinese Anti-monopoly Law that Avoids Trade Conflicts', *George Washington International Law Review*, vol. 45, no. 3, pp.501–538

FARRELL, J. and C. SHAPIRO (1990), 'Horizontal Mergers: An Equilibrium Analysis', *American Economic Review*, vol. 90, pp. 107–126

FARRELL, J. (1987), 'Cheap Talk, Coordination, and Entry', *Rand Journal of Economics*, vol. 18, no. 1, pp. 34–39

FARRELL, J. and C. SHAPIRO (2001), 'Scale Economies and Synergies in Horizontal Merger Analysis', *Antitrust Law Journal*, vol. 68, pp. 685–710

FARRELL, J. (2003), 'Negotiation and Merger Remedies: Some Problems', *Competition Policy Center, University of California, Working Paper No. CPC 03–41*

FARRELL, J. and C. SHAPIRO (2010), 'Recapture, Pass-Through, and Market Definition', *Antitrust Law Journal*, vol. 76, pp. 585–604

FARRELL, J. and C. SHAPIRO (2010), 'Antitrust Evaluation of Horizontal Mergers: An Economic Alternative to Market Definition', *The B.E. Journal of Theoretical Economics*, vol. 10, no. 1, pp. 1–39

FELS, A. (2012), 'China's Antimonopoly Law 2008: An Overview', *Review of Industrial Organization*, vol. 41, pp. 7–30

FERNANDEZ, B.M., I. HASHI and M. JEGERS (2008), 'The Implementation of the European Commission's Merger Regulation 2004: An Empirical Analysis', *Journal of Competition Law and Economics*, vol. 4, no. 3, pp. 791–809

FISHER, A.A. and R.H. LANDE (1983), 'Efficiency Considerations in Merger Enforcement', *California Law Review*, vol. 71, no. 6, pp. 1580–1696

FISHER, A., F. JOHNSON and R. LANDE (1985), 'Mergers, Market Power and Property Rights: When will Efficiencies Prevent Price Increases?' unpublished manuscript, *FTC Working Paper No. 130*

FISHER, F.M. (1987), 'Horizontal Mergers: triage and treatment', *Journal of Economic Perspectives*, vol. 1, pp. 23–40

FISHER, F.M. and D.L. RUBINFELD (2000), '*United States v. Microsoft*: An Economic Analysis', in *Did Microsoft Harm Consumers? Two Opposing Views*, AEI-Brookings Joint Center for Regulatory Studies

Fox, E.M. (1981), 'The Modernization of Antitrust: A New Equilibrium', *Cornell Law Review*, vol. 66, pp. 1140–1192

Fox, E.M. (1986), 'Consumer Beware Chicago', *Michigan Law Review*, vol. 84, pp. 1714–1720

Fox, E.M. (1986), 'Monopolization and Dominance in the United States and the European Community: Efficiency, Opportunity and Fairness', *Notre Dame Law Review*, vol. 61, pp. 981–1020

Fox, E.M. and L.A. Sullivan (1987), 'Antitrust – Retrospective and Prospective: Where are We Coming From? Where are We Going?', *New York University Law Review*, vol. 62, pp. 936–988

Fox, E.M. (2006), 'Monopolization, Abuse of Dominance, and the Indeterminacy of Economics: The U.S./E.U. Divide', *Utah Law Review*, vol. 3, pp. 725–740

Fox, E.M. (2007), 'Economic Development, Poverty, and Antitrust: The Other Path', *Southwestern Journal of Law and Trade in the Americas*, vol. 13, pp. 211–236

Fox, E.M. (2008) 'An Anti-Monopoly Law for China – Scaling the Walls of Government Restraints', *Antitrust Law Journal*, vol. 75, pp. 173–194

Fox, E.M. (2013), 'Against Goals', *Fordham Law Review*, vol. 81, pp. 2157–2161

FTC (1996), 'Anticipating the 21st Century: Competition Policy in the New High-Tech Global Marketplace', Report by Federal Trade Commission Staff, May 1996, available at <www.ftc.gov/system/files/documents/reports/anticipating-21st-century-competition-policy-new-high-tech-global-marketplace/gc_v1.pdf>

Galloway, J. (2007), 'The Pursuit of National Champions: The Intersection of Competition Law and Industrial Policy', *European Competition Law Review*, vol. 28, no. 3, pp. 172–186

Galbraith, J.K. (1952), *American Capitalism: The Concept of Countervailing Power*, Mifflin

Gal, M.S. (2005) 'The Ecology of Antitrust Preconditions for Competition Law Enforcement in Developing Countries', *New York University Law and Economics Research Paper Series Working Paper No. 02/03*, <http://ssrn.com/abstract=665181>

Gao, H. and Dong, X. (2008), 'The Goal and the Values of the AML' (论我国反垄断法的价值目标及其实现), *Socialism Studies* (社会主义研究), serial no. 180, no. 4, pp. 95–100

Gavil, A.I., W.E. Kovacic and J.B. Baker (2008), *Antitrust Law in Perspective: Cases, Concepts and Problems in Competition Policy*, 2nd ed., West

Gerber, D.J. (1987), 'Law and the Abuse of Economic Power in Europe', *Tulane Law Review*, vol. 62, pp. 57–107

Gerber, D.J. (1994a), 'The Transformation of European Community Competition Law?', *Harvard International Law Journal*, vol. 35, no. 1, pp. 97–148

Gerber, D.J. (1994b), 'Constitutionalizing the Economy: German Neo-liberalism, Competition Law and the "New Europe"', *The American Journal of Comparative Law*, vol. 42, pp. 25–84

Gerber, D.J. (1998), *Law and Competition in Twentieth Century Europe: Protecting Prometheus*, Clarendon Press

Gerber, D.J. (2008), 'Economics, Law and Institutions: The Shaping of Chinese Competition Law', *Journal of Law and Policy*, vol. 26, pp. 271–299

Intersentia

GERADIN, D. and I. GIRGENSON (2011), 'Industrial Policy and European Merger Control – A Reassessment', in Fordham Competition Law Institute, *International Antitrust Law and Policy*, Chapter 14

GREANEY, T.L. (2000), 'Not for Import: Why the EU Should not Adopt the American Efficiency Defense for Analyzing Mergers and Joint Ventures', *Saint Louis University Law Journal*, vol. 44, pp. 871–894

GILBERT, R.J. (1989), 'Mobility Barriers and the Value of Incumbency', in R. SCHMALENSEE and R.D. WILLIG (eds.) *Handbook of Industrial Organization*, vol. 1, Elsevier, pp. 476–535

GILBERT, R.J. and S.C. SUNSHINE (1995), 'Incorporating Dynamic Efficiency Concerns in Merger Analysis: The Use of Innovation Markets', *Antitrust Law Journal*, vol. 63, no. 2, pp. 569–601

GILBERT, R.J. and M.L. KATZ (2001), 'An Economist's Guide to *U.S. v. Microsoft*', *Journal of Economic Perspectives*, vol. 15, pp. 25–44

GILBERT, R.J. (2006), 'Looking for Mr. Schumpeter: Where are we in the Competition-Innovation Debate', in A.B. JAFFE, J. LERNER and S. STERN (eds.), *Innovation Policy and the Economy*, volume 6, MIT Press

GILBERT, R.J. (2006), 'Competition and Innovation', in W.D. COLLINS (ed.), *Issues in Competition Law and Policy*, American Bar Association Antitrust Section

GIFFORD, D.J. and R.T. KUDRLE (2005), 'Rhetoric and Reality in the Merger Standards of the United States, Canada, and the European Union', *Antitrust Law Journal*, vol. 72, pp. 423–469

GIOCOLI, N. (2012), 'Who Invented the Lerner Index? Luigi Amoroso, the Dominant Firm Model, and the Measurement of Market Power', *Review of Industrial Organization*, vol. 41, pp. 181–191

GINSBURG, D.H. (1979), 'Antitrust, Uncertainty and Technological Innovation', *The Antitrust Bulletin*, vol. 24, pp. 635–686

GINSBURG, D.H. and J.D. WRIGHT (2012), 'Dynamic Analysis and the Limits of Antitrust Institutions', *Antitrust Law Journal*, vol. 78, no. 1, pp. 1–21

GOLDSTEIN, K.B. (2011), 'Reviewing Cross-border Mergers and Acquisitions for Competition and National Security: A Comparative look at How the United States, Europe, and China Separate Security Concerns from Competition Concerns in Reviewing Acquisitions by Foreign Entities', *Tsinghua China Law Review*, vol. 3, no. 2, pp. 215–256

GOLDSCHMIDT, N. (2012), 'Alfred Müller-Armack and Ludwig Erhard: Social Market Liberalism', *Freiburg Discussion Papers on Constitutional Economics No. 04/12*

GOLDMAN, C.S., Q.C. *et al.* (2003), 'The Role of Efficiencies in Telecommunications Merger Review', *Federal Communications Law Review*, vol. 56, no. 1, pp. 87–154

GREENSTEIN, S. and G. RAMEY (1998), 'Market Structure, Innovation and Vertical Product Differentiation', *International Journal of Industrial Organization*, vol. 16, pp. 285–311

GRIFFITH, R. and L. NESHEIM (2013), 'Defining Antitrust Markets', in M. NEUMANN and J. WEIGAND (eds.), *The International Handbook of Competition*, 2nd ed., Edward Elgar, pp. 207–220

GUO, Y. and HU, A. (2004), 'The Administrative Monopoly in China's Economic Transition', *Communist and Post-Communist Studies*, vol. 37, no. 2, pp. 265–280

HALEY, J.O. (2004), 'Competition Policy for East Asia', *Washington University of Global Studies Law Review*, vol. 3, pp. 277–284

HAO, Q. (2010), 'Merger Remedies in China: Developments and Issues', *Competition Law International*, pp. 13–21

HAMP-LYONS, C. (2009), 'The Dragon in the Room: China's Anti-Monopoly Law and International Merger Review', *Vanderbilt Law Review*, vol. 62, no. 5, pp. 1577–1622

HAN, L. (2004), 'The Opportunity to Establish a Competition System – Foreign M&A as the External Pressure for the AML' (创建反垄断制度的契机-对外资并购催生我国反垄断法的思考), *International Trade* (国际贸易), no. 1, pp. 42–45

HARRIS JR., H.S. (2006), 'The Making of an Antitrust Law: The Pending Anti-Monopoly Law of the People's Republic of China', *Chicago Journal of International Law*, vol. 7, pp. 169–230

HAWK, B.E. (1972), 'Antitrust in the EEC – the First Decade', *Fordham Law Review*, vol. 41, pp. 229–292

HAYEK, F.A. (1948), 'The Meaning of Competition', in *Individualism and Economic Order*, University of Chicago Press

HAYEK, F.A. (1978), 'Competition as a Discovery Procedure', in *New Studies in Philosophy, Politics, Economics and the History of Ideas*, Routledge & Paul

HAYEK, F.A. (2007), *The Road to Serfdom: Text and Documents*, edited by B. CALDWELL, University of Chicago Press

HAY, D. (2011), 'The Assessment: Competition Policy', *Oxford Review of Economic Policy*, vol. 9, no. 2, pp. 1–26

HAUSMAN, J., G. LEONARD and J.D. ZONA (1994), 'Competitive Analysis with Differentiated Products', *Annuals of Economics and Statistics*, pp. 159–180

HAUSMAN, J.A. and G.K. LEONARD (1997), 'Economic Analysis of Differentiated Products Mergers Using Real World Data', *George Mason Law Review*, vol. 5, pp. 321–346

HEYER, K. (2006), 'Welfare Standards and Merger Analysis: Why not the Best?', *Economic Analysis Group Discussion Paper, EAG 06-8*

HEALEY, D. (2010), 'Anti-Monopoly Law and Mergers in China: An Early Report Card on Procedural and Substantive Issues', *Tsinghua China Law Review*, vol. 3, pp. 17–58

HEALEY, D.J. (2012), 'Strange Bedfellows or Soulmates: A Comparison of Merger Regulation in China and Australia', *Asian Journal of Comparative Law*, vol. 7, no. 1, pp. 1–40

HERFINDAHL, O. (1950), *Concentration in the Steel Industry*, Dissertation at Columbia University

HITTINGER, C.W. and J.D. HUH (2007), 'The People's Republic of China Enacts its First Comprehensive Antitrust Law: Trying to Predict the Unpredictable', *New York University Journal of Law and Business*, vol. 4, pp. 246–284

HIRSCHMAN, A.O. (1945), *National Power and the Structure of Foreign Trade*, University of California Press

HIRSCHMAN, A.O. (1964), 'The Paternity of an Index', *American Economic Review*, vol. 54, pp. 761–762

HICKS, J.R. (1935), 'Annual Survey of Economic Theory: The Theory of Monopoly', *Econometrica*, vol. 3, no. 1, pp. 1–20

HOTELLING, H. (1938), 'The General Welfare in Relation to Problems of Taxation and of Railway and Utility Rates', *Econometrica*, vol. 6, no. 3, pp. 242–269

HOPPMANN, E. (1988), *Wirtschaftsordnung und Wettbewerb*, Nomos

HOWELL, T.R., A.W. WOLFF, R. HOWE and D. OH (2009), 'China's New Anti-Monopoly Law: A Perspective from the United States', *Pacific Rim Law and Policy Journal*, vol. 18, no. 1, pp. 53–96

HOFSTADTER, R. (1955), *The Age of Reform: from Bryan to F. D. R.*, Knopf

HOVENKAMP, H. (1982), 'Distributive Justice and the Antitrust Laws', *George Washington Law Review*, vol. 51, pp. 1–31

HOVENKAMP, H. (1985), 'Antitrust Policy after Chicago', *Michigan Law Review*, vol. 84, no. 2, pp. 213–284

HOVENKAMP, H. (1989), 'Antitrust Protected Classes', *Michigan Law Review*, vol. 88, no. 1, pp. 1–48

HOVENKAMP, H. (1989), 'The Sherman Act and the Classical Theory of Competition', *Iowa Law Review*, vol. 74, pp. 1019–1065

HOVENKAMP, H. (1996), 'The Areeda – Turner Treatise in Antitrust Analysis', *The Antitrust Bulletin*, vol. 41, pp. 815–842

HOVENKAMP, H. (2001), 'Post-Chicago Antitrust: A Review and Critique', *Columbia Business Law Review*, pp. 257–338

HOLLAND, E.E. (2003), 'Using Merger Review to Cure Prior Conduct: The European Commission's GE/Honeywell Decision', *Columbia Law Review*, vol. 103, no. 1, pp. 74–110

HOVENKAMP, H. (2012), 'Competition for Innovation', <http://papers.ssrn.com/sol3/papers.cfm?abstract_id=2008953>

HOSKEN, D., D. O'BRIEN, D. SCHEFFMAN and M. VITA (2002), 'Demand System Estimation and Its Application to Horizontal Merger Analysis', *Federal Trade Commission Bureau of Economics Working Paper No. 246*, <www.ftc.gov/reports/demand-system-estimation-its-application-horizontal-merger-analysis>

HUANG, Y. (2008) 'Pursuing the Second Best: The History, Momentum and Remaining issues of China's Anti-Monopoly Law', *Antitrust Law Journal*, vol. 75, pp. 117–132

HUANG, H. (2007) ,'China's New Regulation on Foreign M&A: Green Light or Red Flag?', *University of New South Wales Law Journal*, vol. 30, no. 3, pp. 804–814

HYMAN, D. A. and W.E. KOVACIC (2013), 'Institutional Design, Agency Life Cycle, and the Goals of Competition Law', *Fordham Law Review*, vol. 81, pp. 2163–2174

ILZKOVITZ, F. and R. MEIKLEJOHN (2006), 'European Merger Control: Do We Need an Efficiency Defence?' in F. ILZKOVITZ and R. MEIKLEJOHN (eds.), *European Merger Control, do we need an Efficiency Defence?*, Edward Elgar

IVALDI, M. and F. VERBOVEN (2005), 'Quantifying the Effects from Horizontal Mergers in European Competition Policy', *International Journal of Industrial Organization*, vol. 23, pp. 669–691

JACOBS, M.S. (2001), 'Mergers and Acquisitions in a Global Economy: Perspectives from Law, Politics and Business', *Depaul Business Law Journal*, vol. 13, no. 1, pp. 1–14

JAMES, C.A. (1993), 'Overview of the 1992 Horizontal Merger Guidelines', *Antitrust Law Journal*, vol. 61, pp. 447–458

JOERGES, C. and F. RÖDL (2004), '"Social Market Economy" as Europe's Social Model?', *EUI Working Paper, Law, No. 2004/8*

JONES, A. and B. SUFRIN (2010), *EU Competition Law, Texts, Cases and Materials,* 4th ed., Oxford University Press

JUNG,Y. J, and HAO, Q. (2003), 'The New Economic Constitution in China: A Third Way for Competition Regime?', *Northwestern Journal of International Law and Business*, vol. 24, pp. 107–172

KAMIEN, M.I. and N.L. SCHWARZ (1982), *Market Structure and Innovation*, Cambridge University Press

KARACAN, P. (2004), 'Differences in Merger Analysis between the United States and the European Union, Highlighted in the Context of the Boeing/McDonnell Douglas and GE/Honeywell Mergers', *The Transnational Lawyer*, vol. 17, pp. 209–258

KATZ, M.L. (2002), 'Recent Antitrust Enforcement Actions by the US Department of Justice: A Selective Survey of Economic Issues', *Review of Industrial Organization*, vol. 21, pp. 373–397

KAYSEN, C. and D. TURNER (1959), *Antitrust Policy: An Economic and Legal Analysis*, Harvard University Press

KAPLOW, L. and S. SHAVELL (2002), *Fairness versus Welfare*, Harvard University Press

KAPLOW, L. (2011), 'Market Definition and the Merger Guidelines', *Review of Industrial Organization*, vol. 39, pp. 107–125

KAPLOW, L. (2011), 'On the Choice of Welfare Standards in Competition Law', *Harvard John M. Olin Center for Law, Economics and Business Discussion Paper, No. 693, 2011/5*

KAUPER, T.E. (1983), 'The 1982 Horizontal Merger Guidelines: Of Collusion, Efficiency, and Failure', *California Law Review*, vol. 71, no. 2, pp. 497–534

KERBER, W. (2009), 'Should Competition Law Promote Efficiency? – Some Reflections of an Economist on the Normative Foundations of Competition Law', in J. DREXL, L. IDOT and J. MONEGER (eds.), *Economic Theory and Competition Law*, Edward Elgar, pp. 93–120

KEYTE, J.A. and K.B. SCHWARTZ (2011), '"Tally-Ho!" UPP and the 2010 Horizontal Merger Guidelines', *Antitrust Law Journal*, vol. 77, pp. 587–650

KIERKEGAARD, S. (2001), *Soren Kierkegaards Skrifter 18 Journalerne EE FF GG HH JJ KK*, Gads Forlag

KIRKWOOD, J.B. and R.H. LANDE (2008), 'The Fundamental Goal of Antitrust: Protecting Consumers, Not Efficiency', *Notre Dame Law Review*, vol. 84, pp. 191–244

KIRKWOOD, J.B. (2013), 'The Essence of Antitrust: Protecting Consumers and Small Suppliers from Anticompetitive Conduct', *Fordham Law Review*, vol. 81, pp. 2425–2469

KIRCHNER, C. (1998), 'Future Competition Law', in C.D. EHLERMANN and L.L. LAUDATI (eds.), *The Objectives of Competition Policy, European Competition Law Annual 1997*, Oxford, pp. 513–523

KIRCHNER, C. (2007), 'Goals of Antitrust and Competition Law Revisited', in D. SCHMIDTCHEN, M. ALBERT and S. VOIGT (eds.), *The More Economic Approach to European Competition Law*, Mohr Siebeck, pp. 7–26

KITCH, E.W. (1983), 'The Fire of Truth: A Remembrance of Law and Economics at Chicago, 1932-1979', *Journal of Law and Economics*, vol. 26, no. 1, pp. 163–234

KOVACIC, W.E. (1990), 'The Antitrust Paradox Revisited: Robert Bork and the Transformation of Modern Antitrust Policy', *The Wayne Law Review*, vol. 36, pp. 1413–1472

KOVACIC, W.E. (1993), 'Judicial Appointments and the Future of Antitrust Policy', *Antitrust*, vol. 7, pp. 8–13

KOVACIC, W.E. and C. SHAPIRO (1999), 'Antitrust Policy: A Century of Economic and Legal Thinking', *University of California Working Paper No. CPC 99–09*

KOVACIC, W.E. (2003), 'The Modern Evolution of U.S. Competition Policy Enforcement Norms', *Antitrust law Journal*, vol. 71, pp. 377–478

KOVACIC, W.E. and D.A. HYMAN (2012), 'Competition Agency Design: What's on the Menu?', *European Competition Journal*, vol. 8

KOLASKY, W.J. (2001), 'Lessons from Baby Food: The Role of Efficiencies in Merger Review', *Antitrust*, vol. 16, pp. 82–88

KOLASKY, W.J. (2002), 'Conglomerate Mergers and Range Effects: It is a Long Way from Chicago to Brussels', *George Mason Law Review*, vol. 10, pp. 533–550

KOLASKY, W. and A. DICK (2003), 'The Merger of Guidelines and the Integration of Efficiencies into Antitrust Review of Horizontal Mergers', *Antitrust Law Journal*, vol. 71, no. 1, pp. 207–251

KOLASKY, W.J. (2004), 'What is Competition? A Comparison of US and European Perspectives', *The Antitrust Bulletin*, vol. 49, pp. 29–54

KWOKA, J.E. JR and D.L. MOSS (2011), 'Behavioral Merger Remedies: Evaluation and Implications for Antitrust Enforcement', <http://papers.ssrn.com/sol3/papers.cfm?abstract_id=1959588>

KROES, N. (2005), 'Tackling Exclusionary Practices to Avoid Exploitation of Market Power: Some Preliminary Thoughts on the Policy Review of Article 82', *Fordham International Law Journal*, vol. 29, no. 4, pp. 593–600

KROES, N. (2005), 'Preliminary Thoughts on Policy Review of Article 82', speech at the Fordham Corporate Law Institute, 23 September 2005, available at <http://europa.eu/rapid/press-release_SPEECH-05-537_en.htm>

KROES, N. (2005), 'Delivering Better Markets and Better Choices', speech at the European Consumer and Competition Day, 15 September 2005, available at <http://europa.eu/rapid/press-release_SPEECH-05-512_en.htm>

KROES, N. (2006), 'Industrial Policy and Competition Law & Policy', speech at Fordham University School of Law, 14 September 2006, available at <http://europa.eu/rapid/press-release_SPEECH-06-499_en.htm?locale=en>

KROES, N. (2006), 'Competition Policy and Consumers', speech at the General Assembly of Bureau Européen des Unionsde Consommateurs (BEUC), 16 November 2006, available at <http://europa.eu/rapid/press-release_SPEECH-06-691_en.htm? locale=en>

KROES, N. (2007), 'Foreword', in *Report on Competition Policy 2007*, published by the European Commission, COM (2008) 368 final, available at <http://ec.europa.eu/competition/publications/annual_report/2007/en.pdf>

KROES, N. (2007), 'Speech: Industrial Policy and Competition Law and Policy', *Fordham International Law Journal*, vol. 30, pp. 1401–1412

KROES, N. (2008), 'Exclusionary Abuses of Dominance – the European Commission's Enforcement Priorities', speech at the Fordham University Symposium, 25 September 2008, available at <http://europa.eu/rapid/press-release_SPEECH-08-457_en.htm?locale=en>

KROES, N. (2008), 'Consumers at the Heart of EU Competition Policy', speech at the BEUC, 22 April 2008, available at <http://europa.eu/rapid/press-release_SPEECH-08-212_en.htm?locale=en>

KWOKA JR., J.E. and L.J. WHITE (2004), *The Antitrust Revolution, Economics, Competition and Policy*, 4th ed., Oxford University Press

LAGERLOEF, J.N.M. and P. HEIDHUES (2005), 'On the Desirability of an Efficiency Defense in Merger Control', *International Journal of Industrial Organization*, vol. 23, pp. 803–827

LANDES, W.M. and R.A. POSNER (1981), 'Market Power in Antitrust Cases', *Harvard Law Review*, vol. 94, no. 5, pp. 939–996

LANDE, R.H. (1982), 'Wealth Transfers as the Original and Primary Concern of Antitrust: The Efficiency Interpretation Challenged', *Hastings Law Journal*, vol. 34, pp. 65–152

LANDE, R.H. (1988), 'The Rise and (coming) Fall of Efficiency as the Ruler of Antitrust', *The Antitrust Bulletin*, vol. 33, pp. 429–465

LANDE, R.H. (1989), 'Chicago's False Foundation: Wealth Transfers (Not Just Efficiency) Should Guide Antitrust', *Antitrust Law Journal*, vol. 58, pp. 631–644

LANDE, R.H. (2001), 'Consumer Choice as the Ultimate Goal of Antitrust', *University of Pittsburgh Law Review*, vol. 62, pp. 503–526

LANDE, R.H. (2013), 'A Traditional and Textualist Analysis of the Goals of Antitrust: Efficiency, Preventing Theft from Consumers, and Consumer Choice', *Fordham Law Review*, vol. 81, pp. 2349–2403

LASKOWSKA, M. (2010), 'Dynamic Efficiencies and Technological Progress in EC Merger Control', <http://works.bepress.com/magdalena_laskowska/1> and <http://papers.ssrn.com/sol3/papers.cfm?abstract_id=2336956>

LAROUCHE, P. and M.P. SCHINKEL (2013), 'Continental Drift in the Treatment of Dominant Firms: Article 102 TFEU in Contrast to §2 Sherman Act', *Amsterdam Law School Legal Studies Research Paper No. 2013–34* and *Amsterdam Center for Law and Economics Working Paper No. 2013–08*

LEWIS-BECK, M.S. and J.R. ALFORD (1980), 'Can Government Regulate Safety?', *American Political Science Review*, vol. 74, pp. 745–756

LETWIN, W.L. (1956), 'Congress and the Sherman Antitrust Law: 1887–1890', *University of Chicago Law Review*, vol. 23, no. 2, pp. 221–258

LEIBENSTEIN, H. (1966), 'Allocative Efficiency vs. "X-Efficiency"', *American Economic Review*, vol. 56, no. 3, pp. 392–415

LEVIN, R.C., W.M. COHEN and D.C. MOWERY (1985), 'R&D Appropriability, Opportunity, and Market Structure: New Evidence on Some Schumpeterian Hypotheses', *American Economic Review*, vol. 75, pp. 20–24

LEVY, N. (2005), 'Mario Monti's Legacy in EC Merger Control', *Competition Policy International*, vol. 1, no. 1, pp. 99–132

LERNER, A.P. (1934), 'The Concept of Monopoly and the Measurement of Monopoly Power', *Review of Economic Studies*, vol. 1, no. 3, pp. 157–175

LAU, L. J., QIAN, Y. and ROLAND, G. (2000), 'Reform without Losers: An Interpretation of China's Dual-track Approach to Transition', *Journal of Political Economy*, vol. 108, no. 1, pp. 120–143

LIN, Y.F., F. CAI and Z. LI (1998), 'Policy Burdens, and State-owned Enterprise Reform', *American Economic Review*, vol. 88, no. 2, pp. 422–427

LIN, P. and J. ZHAO (2012), 'Merger Control Policy Under China's Anti-Monopoly Law', *Review of Industrial Organization*, vol. 41, pp. 109–132

Lin, P. (2009), 'Balancing Competition Policy and Industrial Policy under China's AML', presentation at the 5th Summer Workshop on Industrial Organization and Management Strategy, Tsinghua University, Beijing

Li, G. and A. Young (2008), 'Competition Laws and Policies in China and Hong Kong: A Tale of Two Regulatory Journeys', *Journal of International Trade Law and Policy*, vol. 7, no. 2, pp. 186–202

Liu, Z. and Y. Qiao (2012), 'Abuse of Market Dominance under China's 2007 Anti-Monopoly Law: A Preliminary Assessment', *Review of Industrial Organization*, vol. 41, pp. 77–107

Liu, H. (1998), 'Law Regulating Foreign M&As in China' (略论外资并购中国企业的法律规制途径), *Modern Law Science* (现代法学), vol. 2, pp. 77–80

Lianos, I. (2013), 'Some Reflections on the Question of the Goals of EU Competition Law', *CLES Working Paper Series 3/2013*

Lowe, P. (2008), 'The Design of Competition Policy Institutions for the 21st Century – The Experience of the European Commission and DG Competition', *Competition Policy Newsletter*, vol. 3, pp. 1–11

Lindsay, A. *et al.* (2003), 'Econometrics Study into European Merger Decisions Since 2000', *European Competition Law Review*, vol. 24, pp. 673–682

Lindsay, A. (2006), *The EC Merger Regulation: Substantive Issues*, Sweet & Maxwell

Lv, Z. and Tao, W. (2008), 'The Ultimate Goal of the AML' (浅谈我国反垄断法的终极目标), *Study on China Administration for Industry & Commerce* (中国工商管理研究), no. 4, pp. 25–28

Lyons, B.R. (2002), 'Could Politicians be More Right than Economists? A Theory of Merger Policy', *Centre for competition and regulation, UEA, Working Paper No. 02-01*

Lyons, B.R. (2004), 'Reform of European Merger Policy', *Review of International Economics*, vol. 12, no. 2, pp. 246–261

Lyons, B.R. (2008), 'An Economic Assessment of EC Merger Control: 1957–2007', *Center for Competition Policy Working Paper 08-17*, <http://ssrn.com/abstract=1114128>

Mariniello, M. (2013), 'The Dragon Awakes: Is Chinese Competition Policy A Cause for Concern?', *Bruegel Policy Contribution*, Issue 2013/14, pp. 1–15

Mason, E.S. (1939), 'Price and Production Policies of the Large-Scale Enterprise', *American Economic Review*, vol. 29, pp. 61–74

May, J. (1989), 'Antitrust in the Formative Era: Political and Economic Theory in Constitutional and Antitrust Analysis, 1880–1919', *Ohio State Law Journal*, vol. 50, pp. 257–396

Marshall, A. (1891), *Principles of Economics*, Macmillan and Co.

Markham, J.W. (1974), 'Concentration: A Stimulus or Retardant to Innovation?' in H.J. Goldschmid and H.M. Mann (eds.), *Industrial Concentration: The New Learning*, Little Brown & Co

McAfee, P. and M.A. Williams (1992), 'Horizontal Mergers and Antitrust Policy', *Journal Industrial Economics*, vol. 40, pp. 181–187

McGowan, L. and S. Wilks (1995), 'The First Supranational Policy in the European Union: Competition Policy', *European Journal of Political Research*, vol. 28, pp. 141–169

McCHESNEY, F.S. (1980), 'On the Economics of Antitrust Enforcement', *Georgetown Law Journal*, vol. 68, no. 5, pp. 1103–1111

MEHRA, S.K. and Y. MENG (2009), 'Against Antitrust Functionalism: Reconsidering China's Anti-Monopoly Law', *Virginia Journal International Law*, vol. 49, pp. 379–430

MENG, X. and B. DOLLERY (2005), 'Institutional Constraints and Feasible Reform for State-Owned Enterprises in China', *University of New England, School of Economics, Working Paper Series in Economics No. 2005-17*

MEESE, A.J. (2013), 'Reframing the (false?) Choice between Purchaser Welfare and Total Welfare', *Fordham Law Review*, vol. 81, pp. 2197–2251

MESTMÄCKER, E.J. (2011), 'The Development of German and European Competition Law with Special Reference to the EU Commission's Article 82 Guidance of 2008', in L.F. PACE (ed.), *European Competition Law: The Impact of the Commission's Guidance on Article 102*, Edward Elgar

MINDA, G. (1995), 'Antitrust at Century's End', *Southern Methodist University Law Review*, vol. 48, pp. 1749–1782

MONTINOLA, G., Y. QIAN, and B.R. WEINGAST (1995) 'Federalism, Chinese Style: The Political Basis for Success in China', *World Politics*, vol. 48, no. 1, pp. 50–81

MONTI, M. (2000), 'European Competition Policy for the 21st Century', speech at the Twenty-eighth Annual Conference on International Antitrust Law and Policy, The Fordham Corporate Law Institute, New York, 20 October 2000, available at <http://europa.eu/rapid/press-release_SPEECH-00-389_en.htm?locale=en>

MONTI, M. (2001), 'The Future for Competition Policy in the European Union', speech at Merchant Taylor's Hall, 9 July 2001, available at <http://europa.eu/rapid/press-release_SPEECH-01-340_en.htm>

MONTI, M. (2001), 'Foreword', *XXXth Report on Competition Policy 2000*, European Commission 2001

MONTI, M. (2002), 'Foreword', *XXXIInd Report on Competition Policy 2002*, European Commission

MONTI, M. (2002), 'Europe's Merger Monitor', *The Economist*, 7 November 2002, available at <www.economist.com/node/1429439> accessed 05.04.2014

MONTI, M. (2004), 'A Reformed Competition Policy: Achievements and Challenges for the Future', speech at the Center for European Reform in Brussels, 28 October 2004, available at <http://europa.eu/rapid/press-release_SPEECH-04-477_en.htm?locale=en>

MOTTA, M. (1999), 'EC Merger Policy, and the Airtours Case', available at <http://people.exeter.ac.uk/maf206/motta_1999.pdf>

MOTTA, M. (2004), *Competition Policy, Theory and Practice*, Cambridge University Press

MOTTA, M., M. POLO and H. VASCONCELOS (2002), 'Merger Remedies in the European Union: An Overview', Paper presented at the Symposium on 'Guidelines for Merger Remedies – Prospects and Principles', Ecole des Mines, Paris, 17–18 January 2002

MURIS, T.J. (2001), 'Merger Enforcement in a World of Multiple Arbiters', Brookings Institution, Roundtable on Trade and Investment Policy, Washington, DC, 21 December 2001

MURIS, T.J. (2001), 'GTE Sylvania and the Empirical Foundations of Antitrust', *Antitrust Law Journal*, vol. 68, no. 3, pp. 899–912

Neven, D., R. Nuttall and P. Seabright (1993), *Mergers in Daylight: The Economics and Politics of European Merger Control,* The Centre for Economic Policy Research

Neven, D. and L.H. Roller (2000), 'Consumer Surplus versus Welfare Standard in a Political Economy Model of Merger Control', *WZB Working Paper FS IV 00-15*

Nickell, S. (1996), 'Competition and Corporate Performance', *Journal of Political Economy*, vol. 104, pp. 724–746

Niels, G. and A. Kate (2004), 'Introduction: Antitrust in the US and the EU – Converging or Diverging Paths?', *Antitrust Bulletin*, vol. 49, pp. 1–28

Noll, R.G. (2005), '"Buyer Power" and Economic Policy', *Antitrust Law Journal*, vol. 72, pp. 589–624

Oldale, A. and J. Padilla (2013), 'EU Merger Assessment of Upward Pricing Pressure: Making Sense of UPP, GUPPI and the Like', *Journal of European Competition Law and Practice*, vol. 4, no. 4, pp. 375–381

O'Connell, J. (2012), 'The Year of the Metal Rabbit: Antitrust Enforcement in China in 2011', *Antitrust*, vol. 26, pp. 65–77

Owen, B.M., S. Sun and W. Zheng (2005), 'Antitrust in China: The Problem of Incentive Compatibility Antitrust in China', *Journal of Competition Law and Economics,* vol. 1, no. 1, pp. 123–148

Owen, B.M., S. Sun and W. Zheng (2008) 'China's Competition Policy Reforms: The Anti-monopoly Law and Beyond', *Antitrust Law Journal*, vol. 75, pp. 231–266

Odudu, O. (2010), 'The Wider Concerns of Competition Law', *Oxford Journal of Legal Studies*, vol. 30, pp. 599–613

Orbach, B.Y. (2011), 'The Antitrust Consumer Welfare Paradox', *Journal of Competition Law and Economics*, vol. 7, no. 1, pp. 133–164

Orbach, B.Y. (2013), 'How Antitrust Lost Its Goal', *Fordham Law Review*, vol. 81, pp. 2253–2277

Orbach, B.Y. (2013), 'Foreword: Antitrust' Pursuit of Purpose', *Fordham Law Review*, vol. 81, pp. 2151–2156

OECD (1995), 'Policy Roundtables: Competition Policy and Efficiency Claims in Horizontal Agreements, Contribution from the European Community', OCDE/GD(96)65, available at <www.oecd.org/competition/mergers/2379526.pdf >

OECD (2003), 'Trends and Recent Developments in Foreign Direct Investment', Directorate for Financial, Fiscal and Enterprise Affairs, available at <www.oecd.org/dataoecd/52/11/2958722.pdf>

Østbye, S.E. and M.R. Roelofs (2013), 'The Competition-Innovation Debate: Is R &D Cooperation the Answer?', *Economics of Innovation and New Technology*, vol. 22, no. 2, pp. 153–176

Page, W.H. (2008), 'The Ideological Origins and Evolution of U.S Antitrust Law', in W.D. Collins and J. Angland (eds.), *Issues in Competition Law and Policy*, American Bar Association Section of Antitrust Law, volume 1

Pan, C. (2008), 'The Loss of State Assets in Foreign M&As' (论外资并购中国有资产流失问题及法律规制), *Journal of Sichuan Economic Management Institute* (四川经济管理学院学报), vol. 65, no. 3, pp. 23–24

Peng, M.W. (2006), 'Making M&A Fly in China', *Harvard Business Review*, pp. 1–3

Perry, M.K. and R. Porter (1985), 'Oligopoly and the Incentive for Horizontal Merger', *American Economic Review,* vol. 75, pp. 219–227

PITOFSKY, R. (1979), 'The Political Content of Antitrust', *University of Pennsylvania Law Review*, vol. 127, no. 4, pp. 1051–1075

PITOFSKY, R. (1990), 'New Definitions of Relevant Market and the Assault on Antitrust', *Columbia Law Review*, vol. 90, no. 7, pp. 1805–1864

PITOFSKY, R. (2007), 'Efficiency Consideration and Merger Enforcement: Comparison of US and EU Approaches', *Fordham International Law Journal*, vol. 30, pp. 1413–1425

PITTMAN, R.W. (2007), 'Consumer Surplus as the Appropriate Standard for Antitrust Enforcement', *Competition Policy International*, vol. 3, no. 2, pp. 205–224

POGUE, R.A., H.M. REASONER, J.H. SHENEFIELD and R.A. WHITING (1985), '60 Minutes with J. Paul McGrath – interview', *Antitrust Law Journal*, vol. 54, pp. 131–152

POSNER, R.A. (1969), 'Oligopoly and the Antitrust Laws: A Suggested Approach', *Stanford Law Review*, vol. 21, pp. 1562–1606

POSNER, R.A. (1976), *Antitrust Law: An Economic Perspective*, The University of Chicago Press

POSNER, R.A. (1979), 'The Chicago School of Antitrust Analysis', *University of Pennsylvania Law Review*, vol. 127, no. 4, pp. 925–948

POSNER, R.A.(2001), *Antitrust Law*, 2nd ed., The University of Chicago Press

PRIEST, G.L. (2009), 'The Limits of Antitrust and the Chicago School Tradition', *Journal of Competition Law and Economics*, vol. 6, no. 1, pp. 1–9

RHOADES, S.A. (1993), 'The Herfindahl-Hirschman Index', *Federal Reserve Bulletin*, vol. 79, no. 3, pp. 188–189

ROBERTSON, J.R. (2008), 'Symposium: The Anti-Monopoly Law of the People's Republic of China Editor's Note', *Antitrust Law Journal*, vol. 75, pp. 67–72

ROELLER, L. and C. WEY (2003), 'Merger Control in the New Economy', *Netnomics*, vol. 5, pp. 5–20

ROELLER, L. (2011), 'Challenges in EU Competition Policy', *Empirica*, vol. 38, pp. 287–314

ROSE, I. and C. NGWE (2007), 'The Ordoliberal Tradition in the European Union, its Influence on Article 82 EC and the IBA's Comments on the Article 82 EC Discussion Paper', *Competition Law International*, vol. 3, pp. 8–12

RÖPKE, W. (1942), *The Social Crisis of Our Times*, Transaction Publishers

RUBINFELD, D.L. and R.J. EPSTEIN (2001), 'Merger Simulation: A Simplified Approach with New Applications', *Competition Policy Center, University of California, Berkeley, Working Paper No. CPC 01–26*, pp. 1–43

RUBINFELD, D.L. (2008), 'On the Foundations of Antitrust Law and Economics', in R. PITOFSKY (ed.), *How the Chicago School Overshot the Mark- The Effect of Conservative Economic Analysis on U.S. Antitrust*, Oxford University Press, pp. 51–73

RUBINFELD, D.L. (2010), 'Economic Issues in Antitrust Analysis', *Journal of Institutional and Theoretical Economics*, pp. 62–77

SACCO, D. and A. SCHMUTZLER (2011), 'Is There a U-Shaped Relation between Competition and Investment?', *International Journal of Industrial Organization*, vol. 29, pp. 65–73

SALANT, S.W., S. SWITZER and R.J. REYNOLDS (1983), 'Losses from Horizontal Merger: The Effect of an Exogenous Change in Industry Structure on Cournot-Nash Equilibrium', *Quarterly Journal of Economics*, vol. 98, no. 2, pp. 185–199

SAMUELS, J.R. (2007), '"Tain't What You Do" Effect of China's Proposed Anti-monopoly Law on State Owned Enterprises', *Pennsylvania State International Law Review*, vol. 26, pp. 169–202

SALOP, S.C. (1977), 'The Noisy Monopolist: Imperfect Information, Price Dispersion, and Price Discrimination', *Review of Economic Studies*, vol. 44, no. 3, pp. 393–406

SALOP, S.C. (1979), 'Strategic Entry Deterrence', *The American Economic Review*, vol. 69, no. 2, pp. 335–338

SALOP, S.C. (2010), 'Question: What is the Real and Proper Antitrust Welfare Standard? Answer: The *True* Consumer Welfare Standard', *Loyola Consumer Law Review*, vol. 22, no. 3, pp. 336–353

SALINGER, M., R.E. CAVES and S. PELTZMAN (1990), 'The Concentration-Margins Relationship Reconsidered', *Brookings Papers on Economic Activity. Microeconomics*, vol. 1990, pp. 287–335

SCITOVSKY, T. (1951), 'The State of Welfare Economics', *American Economic Review*, vol. 41, no. 3, pp. 303–315

SCHUMPETER, J.A. (2008), *Capitalism, Socialism and Democracy*, Harper Perennial Modern Thought

SCHERER, F.M. (1967), 'Market Structure and the Employment of Scientists and Engineers', *American Economic Review*, vol. 57, pp. 524–531

SCHERER, F.M. (1967), 'Research and Development Resource Allocation under Rivalry', *Quarterly Journal of Economics*, vol. 81, no. 3, pp. 359–394

SCHERER, F.M. and D. ROSS (1990), *Industrial Market Structure and Economic Performance*, 3rd ed., Houghton Mifflin Company, Chapter 14, pp. 517–539

SCHWARTZ, L.B. (1979), '"Justice" and Other Non-Economic Goals of Antitrust', *University of Pennsylvania Law Review*, vol. 127, no. 4, pp. 1076–1081

SCHWEITZER, H. (2007), 'Competition Law and Public Policy: Reconsidering an Uneasy Relationship. The Example of Article 81', *European University Institute (EUI) Working Papers, Law, No. 2007/30*

SCHMALENSEE, R. (1989), 'Inter-industry Studies of Structure and Performance', in R. SCHMALENSEE and R.D. WILLIG (eds.) *Handbook of Industrial Organization*, Elsevier, volume 2, Chapter 16, pp. 952–1009

SCHMALENSEE, R. (2004), 'Sunk Costs and Antitrust Barriers to Entry', *MIT Sloan School of Management Working Paper No. 4457–04*

SCHUMACHER, P. (2013), 'The EU's Flawed Assessment of Horizontal Aspects in GE/ Honeywell: Re-visiting the Last Pillar of the European Prohibition Decision', *European Journal of Law and Economics*, vol. 35, pp. 211–240

SCHMIDT, A. (2001), 'Non-Competition Factors in the European Competition Policy: The Necessity of Institutional Reforms', *Center for Globalization and Europeanization of the Economy, Georg-August-Universitaet Goettingen, Discussion Paper 13*

SCHMITZ, S. (2002a), 'How Dare They? European Merger Control and the European Commission's Blocking of the General Electric/Honeywell Merger', *University of Pennsylvania Journal of International Economic Law*, vol. 23, no. 2, pp. 325–384

SCHMITZ, S. (2002b), 'The European Commission's Decision in GE/Honeywell and the Question of the Goals of Antitrust Law', *University of Pennsylvania Journal of International Economic Law*, vol. 23, no. 3, pp. 539–595

SCHNELL, D.K. (2004), 'All Bundled Up: Bringing the Failed GE/Honeywell Merger in from the Cold', *Cornell International Law Journal*, vol. 37, pp. 217–262

SHANG, M. (2009), 'Antitrust in China – A Constantly Evolving Subject', *Competition Law International*, vol. 5, pp. 4–11

SHAN, W. (2000), 'Towards a New Legal Framework for EU-China Investment Relations', *Journal of World Trade*, vol. 34, no. 5, pp. 137–179

SHAN, P., G. TAN, S.J. WILKIE and M.A. WILLIAMS (2011), 'China's Anti-Monopoly Law, What is the Welfare Standard', *University of South California(USC), Center in Law, Economics and Organization, Research Paper Series No. C11-18*, and *USC Legal Studies Research Paper No. 11-25*

SIDAK, J.G. and D.J. TEECE (2009), 'Dynamic Competition in Antitrust Law', *Journal of Competition Law and Economics*, vol. 5, no. 4, pp. 581–631

SINGLETON, R.C. (1997), 'Competition Policy For Developing Countries, A Long-run, Entry-based Approach', *Contemporary Economic Policy* vol. 15, no. 2, pp. 1–11

SIMONS, J.J. and M.B. COATE (2010), 'Upward Pressure on Price (UPP) Analysis: Issues and Implications for Merger Policy', <http://ssrn.com/abstract=1558547>

SKITOL, R.A. (1999), 'The Shifting Sands of Antitrust Policy: Where it Has Been, Where it is Now, Where it Will be in its Third Century', *Cornell Journal of Law and Public Policy*, vol. 9, pp. 239–266

SKITOL, R.A. (2005), 'Concerted Buying Power: Its Potential For Addressing the Patent Holdup Problem in Standard Setting', *Antitrust Law Journal*, vol. 72, pp. 727–744

SØRENSEN, F., J. MATTSSON and J. SUNDBO (2010), 'Experimental Methods in Innovation Research', *Research Policy*, vol. 39, pp. 313–322

SOKOL, D.D. (2013), 'Merger Control under China's Anti-Monopoly Law', *Minnesota Legal Studies Research Paper No. 13-05*, <http://papers.ssrn.com/sol3/papers.cfm?abstract_id=2207690>

STIGLER, G.J. (1964), 'A Theory of Oligopoly', *Journal of Political Economy*, vol. 72, pp. 44–61

STIGLER, G.J. (1965), *Essays in the History of Economics*, University of Chicago Press

STIGLER, G.J. (1968), *The Organization of Industry*, Homewood: Irwin

STIGLER, G.J. (1987), *The Theory of Price*, Macmillan

STEVENS, S. (2002), 'The Increased Aggression of the EC Commission in Extraterritorial Enforcement of the Merger Regulation and Its Impact on Transatlantic Cooperation in Antitrust', *Syracuse Journal of International Law and Commerce*, vol. 29, pp. 263–302

STUCKE, M.E. (2011), 'Antitrust 2025', *University of Tennessee College of Law Legal Studies Research Paper Series No. 135*

STUCKE, M.E. (2012), 'Reconsidering Antitrust Goals', *Boston College Law Review*, vol. 53, pp. 551–630

STUCKE, M.E. (2013), 'Should Competition Policy Promote Happiness?', *Fordham Law Review*, vol. 81, pp. 2575–2645

STEWART, J. JR. and J.S. CROMARTIE (1982), 'Partisan Presidential Change and Regulatory Policy: The Case of the FTC and Deceptive Practices Enforcement, 1938–1974', *Presidential Studies Quarterly*, vol. 12, pp. 568–573

SULLIVAN, E.T. and J.L. HARRISON (2003), *Understanding Antitrust and Its Economic Implications*, 4th ed., LexisNexis

Sullivan, E.T., H. Hovenkamp and H.A. Shelanski (2009), *Antitrust Law, Policy and Procedures: Cases, Materials and Problems,* 6th ed., LexisNexis

Song, B. (1995), 'Competition Policy in a Transitional Economy: The Case of China', *Stanford Journal of International Law,* vol. 31, pp. 387–422

Solow, R.M. (1957), 'Technical Change and the Aggregate Production Function', *Review of Economics and Statistics,* vol. 39, no. 3, pp. 312–320

Sullivan, E.T., H. Hovenkamp and H.A. Shelanski (2009), *Antitrust Law, Policy and Procedures: Cases, Materials and Problems,* 6th ed., LexisNexis

Szuecs, F. (2012), 'Investigating Transatlantic Merger Policy Convergence', *International Journal of Industrial Organization,* vol. 30, pp. 654–662

Thorelli, H. (1955), *The Federal Antitrust Policy: Organization of an American Tradition,* Johns Hopkins Press

Turner, D.F. (1987), 'The Durability, Relevance, and Future of American Antitrust Policy', *California Law Review,* vol. 75, no. 3, pp. 797–815

UNCTAD (United Nations Conference on Trade and Development) (2006), 'World Investment Report 2006: FDI from Developing and Transition Economies: Implications for Development', United Nations: New York and Geneva, available at <http://unctad.org/en/docs/wir2006_en.pdf>

UNCTAD (United Nations Conference on Trade and Development) (2011), 'World Investment Report 2011, Non-equity Modes of International Production and Development', United Nations: New York and Geneva, available at <http://unctad.org/en/docs/wir2011_embargoed_en.pdf >

Ulen, T.S. (2011), 'The Uneasy Case for Competition Law and Regulation as Decisive Factors in Development: Some Lessons for China', in M. Faure and X. Zhang (eds.), *Competition Policy and Regulation, Recent Developments in China, the US and Europe,* Edward Elgar, pp. 13–44

Vanberg, V.J. (2009), 'Consumer Welfare, Total Welfare and Economic Freedom – on the Normative Foundations of Competition Policy', *Freiburg Discussion Paper on Constitutional Economics 09/3*

Van den Bergh, R. and P.D. Camesasca (2006), *European Competition Law and Economics – A Comparative Perspective,* Thomson/Sweet & Maxwell

Van den Bergh, R. (2006), 'The Economics of Competition Policy and the Draft of the Chinese Competition Law', in T. Eger, M.G. Faure and N. Zhang (eds.), *Economic Analysis of Law in China,* Edward Elgar

Van den Bergh, R. (2007), 'The "More Economic Approach" and the Pluralist Tradition of European Competition Law (comment)', in D. Schmidtchen, M. Albert and S. Voigt (eds.), *The More Economic Approach to European Competition Law,* Mohr Siebeck, pp. 27–36

Van den Bergh, R. and M. Faure (2011), 'Critical Issues in the Enforcement of the Anti-Monopoly Law in China: A Law and Economics Perspective', in M. Faure and X. Zhang (eds.), *Competition Policy and Regulation, Recent Developments in China, the US and Europe,* Edward Elgar, pp. 54–72

Veljanovski, C. (2004), 'EC Merger Policy after *GE/Honeywell* and *Airtours*', *The Antitrust Bulletin,* vol. 49, pp. 153–194

Voigt, S. and A. Schmidt (2005), *Making European Merger Policy More Predictable,* Springer

WALKER, M. (2005), 'The Potential for Significant Inaccuracies in Merger Simulation Models', *Journal of Competition Law and Economics*, vol. 1, no. 3, pp. 473–496

WANG, B. (2009), 'Official with MOFCOM confirms that merger of China Unicom and China Netcom is Alleged Illegal', *The Economic Observer*, 30 April 2009

WANG, X (2004), 'Challenges/Obstacles Faced by Competition Authorities in Achieving Greater Economic Development through the Promotion of Competition', Speech at the OECD Global Forum on Competition, Centre for Co-operation with Non-members Directorate for Financial, Fiscal and Enterprise Affairs, 9 January 2004

WANG, X. (2009), 'New Development of China's AML – from Merger Control Perspective', December 2009, 5th Annual Asian Competition Law Conference 2009, available at <www.asiancompetitionforum.org/asianfile_091207.html>

WANG, X. (2008), 'Highlights of China's New Anti-Monopoly Law', *Antitrust Law Journal*, vol. 75, pp. 133–150

WANG, X. (2012), 'Comparative Overview – China', in A. EMCH, J. REGAZZINI and V. RUDOMINO (eds.), *Competition Law in the BRICS Countries*, Wolters Kluwer 2012

WANG, X. and A. EMCH (2013), 'Five Years of Implementation of China's Anti-Monopoly Law – Achievements and Challenges', *Journal of Antitrust Enforcement*, vol. 1, no. 2, pp. 247–271

WEI, D. (2011), 'China's Anti-Monopoly Law and Its Merger Enforcement: Convergence and Flexibility', *Journal of International Economic Law*, vol. 14, no. 4, pp. 807–844

WEI, D. (2013), 'Antitrust in China: An Overview of Recent Implementation of Anti-monopoly Law', *European Business Organization Law Review*, vol. 14, no. 1, pp. 119–139

WERDEN, G.J. and G.A. ROZANSKI (1994), 'The Application of Section 7 to Differentiated Products Industries: The Market Delineation Dilemma', *Antitrust*, vol. 8, pp. 40–43

WERDEN, G.J. (1997), 'Simulating the Effects of Differentiated Products Mergers: A Practical Alternative to Structural Merger Policy', *George Mason Law Review*, vol. 5, no. 3, pp. 363–386

WILLIAMS, B. (2001), 'The Influence and Lack of Influence of Principles in the Negotiation for China's Accession to the World Trade Organization', *George Washington International Law Review*, vol. 33, pp. 791–847

WILLIAMS, M. (2005), *Competition Policy and Law in China, Hong Kong and Taiwan*, Cambridge University Press

WILLIAMS, M. (2009), 'Foreign Investment in China: Will the Anti-Monopoly Law be a Barrier or a Facilitator?' *Texas International Law Journal*, vol. 45, no. 1, pp. 127–156

WHINSTON, M.D. (2001), 'Exclusivity and Tying in *U.S. v. Microsoft*: What We Know and Don't Know', *Journal of Economic Perspectives*, vol. 15, pp. 63–80

WOOD, B.D. and ANDERSON, J.E. (1993), 'The Politics of U.S. Antitrust Regulation', *American Journal of Political Science*, vol. 37, no. 1, pp. 1–39

WRIGHT, J.D. and D.H. GINSBURG (2011), 'Dynamic Analysis and the Limits of Antitrust Institutions', *Antitrust Law Journal*, vol. 78, pp. 1–23

WRIGHT, J.D. and D.H. GINSBURG (2013), 'The Goals of Antitrust: Welfare Trumps Choice', *Fordham Law Review*, vol. 81, pp. 2405–2423

WU, Z. (2008), 'Perspectives on the Chinese Anti-Monopoly Law', *Antitrust Law Journal*, vol. 75, pp. 73–116

Wu, H. and Wei, W. (2005), 'The Value and Goals of the AML' (论反垄断法的价值目标), *The Jurist* (法学家), no. 3, pp. 92–98

Wu, H. and Jin, S. (2009), 'The Social Goals of the AML' (论《反垄断法》的社会公共目标-以《反垄断法》的实施为契机), *Journal of Capital Normal University* (首都师范大学学报), vol. 188, no. 3, pp. 41–46

Xu, L. C. (2000), 'Control, Incentives and Competition: The Impact of Reform on Chinese State-owned Enterprises', *Economic Transition*, vol. 8, no. 1, pp. 151–173

Xu, C. (2011), 'The Fundamental Institutions of China's Reforms and Development', *Journal of Economic Literature*, vol. 49, no. 4, pp. 1076–1151

Yang, J. (2002), 'Market Power in China: Manifestations, Effects and Legislation', *Review of Industrial Organization*, vol. 21, no. 2, pp. 167–183

Yao, D. and Dahdouh, T.N. (1993), 'Information Problems in Merger Decision Making and Their Impact on Development of an Efficiencies Defense', *Antitrust Law Journal*, vol. 61, pp. 23–45

Yu, D. (2012), 'A Study on the Choose of Welfare Standards in Merger Antitrust Control' (横向并购反垄断控制的福利标准选择研究), *Fudan Journal* (复旦学报), no. 6, pp. 94–104

Zhang, X. and V.Y.Zhang (2007), 'The Anti-Monopoly Law in China: Where Do We Stand?', *Competition Policy International*, vol. 3, no. 2, pp. 185–201

Zhang, X. and V. Y. Zhang (2013), 'Revisiting China's Merger Control, Where are We Going After the Three-Year Milestone?', *Dovenschmidt Quarterly*, no. 1, pp. 26–35

Zhang, G. (2008), 'Controls on the Admission of Customs and Anti-Monopoly of Foreign Mergers and Acquisitions of Domestic Enterprises: A Review of the Regulations Governing Mergers and Acquisitions of Domestic Enterprises by Foreign Investors' (外资并购的准入管制和反垄断管制 – 评《关于外国投资者并购境内企业的规定》), *Journal of Nanjing Normal University* (南京师大学报), November 2008, no. 6, pp. 21–26

Zhang, M. (2005), 'The Target of the AML' (反垄断'剑指何处), *Foreign Investment in China* (中国外资), 2005 no. 1

Zheng, W. (2010), 'Transplanting Antitrust in China: Economic Transition, Market Structure and State Control', *University of Pennsylvania Journal of International Law*, vol. 32, no. 2, pp. 643–721

Zou, H. and P. Simpson (2008), 'Cross-border Mergers and Acquisitions in China: An Industry Panel Study: 1991–2005', *Asia Pacific Business Review*, vol. 14, no. 4, pp. 491–512

OFFICIAL DOCUMENTS, GUIDELINES AND REPORTS

CHINA

Guomin Jingji He Shehui Fazhan Diqige Wunian Jihua (1986–1990) (国民经济和社会发展第七个五年计划) [The Seventh Five Year Plan for National Economic and Social

Development] (approved by the Fourth Session of the Sixth National People's Congress on 12 April 1986)

Guomin Jingji He Shehui Fazhan Dishige Wunian Jihua Gangyao (国民经济和社会发展第十个五年计划纲要) [The Tenth Five Year Plan for National Economic and Social Development] (approved by the Fourth Session of the Ninth National People's Congress on 15 March 2001)

Guomin Jingji He Shehui Fazhan Di Shierge Wunian Jihua Gangyao (国民经济和社会发展第十二个五年计划纲要) [The Twelfth Five Year Plan for National Economic and Social Development] (approved by the Fourth Session of the Eleventh National People's Congress on 16 March 2011)

Guowuyuan Bangongting Guanyu Yinfa Guojia Gongshang Xingzheng Guanli Zongju Zhuyao Zhize Neishe Jigou He Renyuan Bianzhi Guiding De Tongzhi (国务院办公厅关于印发国家工商行政管理总局主要职责内设机构和人员编制规定的通知) [The State Council Notice on Major Duties, Internal Organization and Administration of the SAIC] 11 July 2008

Guowuyuan Bangongting Guanyu Guowuyuan Fanlongduan Weiyuanhui Zhuyao Zhize He Zucheng Renyuan De Tongzhi (国务院办公厅关于国务院反垄断委员会主要职责和组成人员的通知) [Notice of the General Office of the State Council on the Main Functions and Members of the Anti-Monopoly Commission of the State Council] (issued by the General Office of the State Council on 28 July 2008, effective on 28 July 2008)

Guowuyuan Guanyu Jingyingzhe Jizhong Shenbao Biaozhun De Guiding (国务院关于经营者集中申报标准的规定) [Provisions of the State Council on Thresholds for Prior Notification of Concentrations of Undertakings] (adopted at the 20th Executive Meeting of the State Council on 1 August 2008, effective on 3 August 2008)

Guowuyuan Fanlongduan Weiyuanhui Guanyu Xiangguan Shichang Jieding De Zhinan (国务院反垄断委员会关于相关市场界定的指南) [Guide of the Anti-Monopoly Committee of the State Council for the Definition of the Relevant Market] (issued by the Ministry of Commerce on 24 May 2009)

Guowuyuan Bangongting Guanyu Jianli Waiguo Touzizhe Binggou Jingnei Qiye Anquan Shencha Zhidu De Tongzhi (国务院办公厅关于建立外国投资者并购境内企业安全审查制度的通知) [Notice of the General Office of the State Council on the Establishment of the Security Review System for Mergers and Acquisitions of Domestic Enterprises by Foreign Investors] (issued by the General Office of the State Council on 3 February 2011, effective on 3 March 2011)

Shangwubu Fanlongduanju Guanyu Jingyingzhe Jizhong Shenbao Wenjian Ziliao De Zhidao Yijian (商务部反垄断局关于经营者集中申报文件资料的指导意见) [Guiding Opinions of the Anti-Monopoly Bureau of the Ministry of Commerce on the Declaration Documents and Materials of the Concentration of Business Operators] (issued by the Ministry of Commerce on 5 January 2009, effective on 5 January 2009)

Shangwubu Guanyu Pinggu Jingyingzhe Jizhong Jingzheng Yingxiang De Zanxing Guiding (商务部关于评估经营者集中竞争影响的暂行规定) [Interim Provisions on Assessing the Impact of Concentration of Business Operators on Competition] (issued by the Ministry of Commerce on 29 August 2011, effective on 5 September 2011)

Shangwubu Guanyu Shishi Jingyingzhe Jizhong Zichan Huo Yewu Boli De Zanxing Guiding (商务部关于实施经营者集中资产或业务剥离的暂行规定) [Interim Provisions on the Divestiture of Assets or Business in the Concentration of Business Operators] (issued by the Ministry of Commerce on 5 July 2010, effective on 5 July 2010)

Shangwubu Shishi Waiguo Touzizhe Binggou Jingnei Qiye Anquan Shencha Zhidu Youguan Shixiang De Zanxing Guiding (商务部实施外国投资者并购境内企业安全审查制度有关事项的暂行规定) [Interim Measures on Relevant Matters Concerning the Implementation of Security Review of Mergers and Acquisitions of Domestic Enterprises by Foreign Investors] (issued by the Ministry of Commerce on 4 March 2011, effective on 5 March 2011),

Jiushi Niandai Guojia Chanye Zhengce Gangyao (90年代国家产业政策纲要) [Outline of State Industry Policies for the 1990s] (promulgated by the State Council 25 March 1994, effective on 25 March 1994)

Jinrongye Jingyingzhe Jizhong Shenbao Yingye'e Jisuan Banfa (金融业经营者集中申报营业额计算办法) [Measures for Calculating the Turnover for the Declaration of Business Concentration in the Financial Industry] (issued by the China Banking Regulatory Commission, the China Insurance Regulatory Commission, the China Securities Regulatory Commission, the Ministry of Commerce, and People's Bank of China, on 15 July 2009, effective on 15 August 2009)

Jingyingzhe Jizhong Shenbao Banfa (经营者集中申报办法) [Measure for the Undertaking Concentration Declaration] (promulgated by the Ministry of Commerce on 21 November 2009, effective on 1 January 2010)

Jingyingzhe Jizhong Shencha Banfa (经营者集中审查办法) [Measure for the Undertaking Concentration Examination] (issued by the Ministry of Commerce 24 November 2009, effective on 1 January 2010)

Jingyingzhe Jizhong Fanlongduan Shencha Banshi Zhinan (经营者集中反垄断审查办事指南) [Working Guidelines of the Anti-Monopoly Bureau of the Ministry of Commerce on Concentrations of Undertakings] (issued by the Ministry of Commerce on 11 March 2010)

Waiguo Touzizhe Binggou Jingnei Qiye Fanlongduan Shenbao Zhinan (外国投资者并购境内企业反垄断申报指南) [Guide for the Anti-Monopoly Declaration by a Foreign Investor in the Merger or Acquisition of a Domestic Enterprise] (promulgated by the Ministry of Commerce, 8 March 2007, effective on 8 March 2007)

Waishang Touzi Chanye Zhidao Mulu (外商投资产业指导目录) [Category of Industries Guiding Foreign Investments] (promulgated by the Ministry of Foreign Trade and Economic Cooperation, the State Development and Reform Commission, the State Economic and Trade Commission, 31 December 1997, effective on 1 January 1998)

Wei Yifa Shenbao Jingyingzhe Jizhong Diaocha Chuli Zanxing Banfa (未依法申报经营者集中调查处理暂行办法) [Interim Measures for Investigating and Handling Failure to Legally Declare the Concentration of Business Operators] (issued by the Ministry of Commerce on 30 December 2011, effective on 1 February 2012)

Zhongguo Gongchandang Dishiyijie Zhongyangweiyuanhui Disanci Quantihuiyi Gongbao (中国共产党第十一届中央委员会第三次全体会议公报) [Communiqué of the Third Plenary Session of the 11th Central Committee of the CPC] (adopted at the Third Plenary Session of the 11th Central Committee of the Communist Party of China on 22 December 1978)

Zhidao Waishang Touzi Fangxiang Zanxing Guiding (指导外商投资方向暂行规定) [Provisional Regulations on Direction Guide to Foreign Investment] (promulgated by the Ministry of Civil Affairs, the State Development and Reform Commission, the State Economic and Trade Commission, 20 June 1995, effective on 28 June 1995)

Zhonggongzhongyang Guanyu Jianli Shehuizhuyi Shichangjingjitizhi Ruoganwenti de Jueding (中共中央关于建立社会主义市场经济体制若干问题的决定) [Decision of the Central Committee of the Communist Party of China on a Number of Issues about the Establishment of the Socialist Market Economy] (adopted by the Third Plenary Session of the 14th Central Committee of the Communist Party of China on 14 November 1993)

EU

Communication from the Commission: *Guidelines on the Application of Article 81(3) of the Treaty* [2004] OJ C101/97

Communication from the Commission: *Guidance on the Commission's Enforcement Priorities in Applying Article 82 of the EC Treaty to Abusive Exclusionary Conduct by Dominant Undertakings* [2009] OJ C45/7

Communication from the Commission: *Guidelines on the Application of Article 81(3) of the Treaty* [2004] OJ C101/97

Commission Communication: *Industrial Policy in an Enlarged Europe* [COM (2002) 714 final]

Communication from the Commission: *Fostering Structural Change: an Industrial Policy for an Enlarged Europe* [COM (2004) 274 final]

Communication from the Commission: *A Pro-active Competition Policy for a Competitive Europe* [COM (2004) 293 final]

Communication from the Commission to the Council and the European Parliament: *Some Key Issues in Europe's Competitiveness – Towards an Integrated Approach* [COM (2003) 704 final]

Communication from the Commission: *An Integrated Industrial Policy for the Globalisation Era Putting Competitiveness and Sustainability at Centre Stage* [COM (2010) 614]

Communication from the Commission: *Europe 2020 A Strategy for Smart, Sustainable and Inclusive Growth* [COM (2010) 2020 final]

Communication from the Commission to the European Parliament and the Council: *The Strategy for Europe's Internal Market* [COM (99) 624 final]

Communication of the Commission to the Spring European Council: *Working Together for Growth and Jobs: A New Start for the Lisbon Strategy* [COM (2005) 24]

Commission Notice: *Guidelines on Vertical Restraints* [2000] OJ C 291/1

Commission Notice on the Definition of the Relevant Market for the Purposes of Community Competition Law [1997] OJ C 372

DG Competition Annual Management Plan 2007, 22 December 2006, European Commission, available at <http://ec.europa.eu/competition/publications/annual_management_plan/amp_2007_en.pdf>

Green Paper on the Review of Council Regulation (EEC) No. 4064/89, COM (2001) 745, 11 December 2001

Guidelines on the Assessment of Horizontal Mergers under the Council Regulation on the Control of Concentrations between Undertakings [2004] OJ C 31/03

Press Release IP/06/610, European Commission, *Mergers: Commission approves acquisition of AD Cartonboard by Korsnäs*, 12 May 2006, available at <http://europa.eu/rapid/press-release_IP-06–610_en.htm>

Report of the Heads of Delegation to the Ministers of Foreign Affairs (the 'Spaak Report') (original in French: Rapport des chefs de delegation aux Ministres des Affaires Etrangeres), Intergovernmental Committee on European Integration, 21 April 1956, available at <http://aei.pitt.edu/996/1/Spaak_report_french.pdf>

Report on the Communication from the Commission on the European Aerospace Industry – Meeting the Global Challenge (COM (97)0466-C4–0547/97), 13 October 1998, European Parliament

White Paper on Modernisation of the Rules Implementing Articles 85 and 86 of the EC Treaty [1999] OJ C 132/1

XXVth Report on Competition Policy 1995, European Commission, Published in Conjunction with the 'General Report on the Activities of the European Union – 1995', available at <http://ec.europa.eu/competition/publications/annual_report/1995/en.pdf>

MEDIA AND INTERNET RESOURCES

CHOVANEC, P. (2009), 'Beijing's Antitrust Blunder', *Wall Street Journal Asia,* 23 March 2009, available at <http://online.wsj.com/article/SB123773830587406651.html> accessed 06.12.2013

CHEN, Y. (2008), 'Uneasy Road for SOEs' (国有经济一路走来不容易), *XinHuaNet News* (新华网), 3 October 2008, available at <http://news.xinhuanet.com/mrdx/2008–10/03/content_10144853.htm> accessed 03.04.2014

GUO, X. (2007), 'Economic Constitution Prohibiting Monopolistic Conduct' ("经济宪法" 剑指垄断行为), *Legal Daily* (法制日报), 26 August 2007, available at <www.npc.gov.cn/npc/oldarchives/cwh/common/zw.jsp@hyid=0210029_____&label=wxzlk&id=370729&pdmc=flzt.htm> accessed 28.03.2014

LAN, X. (2007), 'State Seeks Control of Critical Industries', *Beijing Review,* 11 January 2007, available at <www.bjreview.com.cn/print/txt/2007–01/09/content_52480.htm> accessed 28.03.2014

McGINTY, A. and K. NICHOLSON (2009), 'Coca-Cola/Huiyuan: Ministry's Prohibition Sparks Controversy', *International Law Office,* 2 April 2009, available at <www.internationallawoffice.com/newsletters/detail.aspx?g=76ff3c8f-0c3c-48c0–84e6-feaaf11f863c>accessed 10.12.2013

MOFCOM (2011), 'The Responsibilities of the MOFCOM', 13 June 2011, available at <http://fldj.mofcom.gov.cn/article/gywm/200809/20080905756026.shtml> (in Chinese) and <http://english.mofcom.gov.cn/departments/fldj2/> (in English) accessed 03.04.2014

MOFCOM (2012), 'Statistics of Unconditionally Approved Concentration Cases' (经营者集中反垄断审查无条件批准案件信息统计情况), 16 November 2012, MOFCOM website, available at <http://fldj.mofcom.gov.cn/article/zcfb/201211/20121108437868.shtml> accessed 15.12.2013

NEUMANN, P. (2003), 'The Slow Boat to Antitrust Law in China', *Faegre Baker Daniels*, 23 December 2003, available at <www.faegrebd.com/4709> accessed 24.03.2014

NING, S. and R. YIN (2011), 'Formal Establishment of Anti-Monopoly Commission Office within MOFCOM Approved', 17 June 2011, *King & Wood Mallesons, China Law Insight*, available at <www.chinalawinsight.com/2011/06/articles/corporate/antitrust-competition/formal-establishment-of-antimonopoly-commission-office-within-mofcom-approved/> accessed 22.03.2014

PEOPLE'S DAILY (2005), 'China has Socialist Market Economy in Place', *People's Daily Online*, 13 July 2005, available at <http://english.people.com.cn/200507/13/eng20050713_195876.html> accessed 05.04.2014

SHANG, M. (2005), 'The Development and Legislation of Competition Policy in China' (发展中的中国竞争政策与立法), MOFCOM website, 27 April 2005, available at <http://tfs.mofcom.gov.cn/aarticle/dzgg/f/200504/20050400081489.html> (in Chinese) accessed 28.03.2014

TUCKER, S., P. SMITH and J. ANDERLINI (2009), 'China Blocks Coke's Bid for Huiyuan', 19 March, 2009 *Financial Times*, available at <www.ft.com/cms/s/0/5c645830–1391–11de-9e320000779fd2ac.html#axzz2gNtWgqQK>

THE NEW YORK TIMES (2009), 'China Explains Rejection of Coke's Bid for Juice Maker', *The New York Times World Business*, 25 March 2009, available at <www.nytimes.com/2009/03/26/business/worldbusiness/26coke.html?_r=0> accessed 15.02.2014

THE WALL STREET JOURNAL (2009), 'Beijing Thwarts Coke's Takeover Bid', *The Wall Street Journal*, 18 March 2009, available at <http://chinadigitaltimes.net/2009/03/beijing-thwarts-cokes-takeover-bid/> accessed 07.04.2014

TANG, Y. (2007), 'Interview: Director Cao Kangtai', *Outlook Weekly* no. 50 2007, available at <http://lw.xinhuanet.com/htm/content_2362.htm> accessed 28.03.2014

WANG, X. (2004), 'Interview: Shang Ming: Anti-Monopoly Law is not only for Multinational Companies', *XinHua Net*, 23 December 2004, available at <http://expo2010.china.com.cn/news/txt/2004–12/23/content_5736697.htm> accessed 05.04.2014

WANG, X. (2006), 'The Relationship between Antitrust Enforcement Agencies and Industry Regulators' (论反垄断法执法机构与行业监管机构的关系), 23 September 2006, 中国民商法律网 (*civillaw.com.cn*), available at <www.civillaw.com.cn/article/default.asp?id=28604> (in Chinese) accessed 04.04.2014

WANG, P.J., H.S. HARRIS, M.A. COHEN and Y. ZHANG (2009), 'Coca-Cola/Huiyuan Deal is First Acquisition Blocked by China Antitrust Review', March 2009, *Jones Day*, available at <www.jonesday.com/Antitrust-Alert--Coca-Cola--Huiyuan-Deal-is-First-Acquisition-Blocked-by-China-Antitrust-Review-03–19–2009/>

WTO (2001), 'WTO News: 2001 Press Releases: WTO Successfully Concludes Negotiations on China's Entry', 17 September 2001, available at <www.wto.org/english/news_e/pres01_e/pr243_e.htm> accessed 20.03.2014

WU, J. (2006), 'Looking Back at the Tortuous Path of the Socialist Market Economy Development' (回望社会主义市场经济的曲折路径), *People.com*, 15 July 2006, available at <http://theory.people.com.cn/GB/49154/49155/4594081.html> (in Chinese), accessed 28.03.2014

Wu, Q. (2006), 'China Regulates Foreign Mergers for More Investment', 11 September 2006, *Embassy of the PRC in the USA*, available at <www.china-embassy.org/eng/gyzg/t271391.htm> accessed 20.03.2014

Xinhua News (2007), 'AML's Equal Treatment of Domestic and Foreign Mergers' (国务院法制办:《反垄断法》不影响企业正当并购), *Xinhua Net*, 10 September 2007, available at <http://news.xinhuanet.com/newscenter/2007–09/10/content_6699043.htm> accessed 21.01.2014.

Xinhua News (2007), 'Business Week: China Makes Remarkable Progress in Civil Law Making', 4 December 2007, *Xinhua Net*, available at <http://en.ce.cn/National/Local/200712/05/t20071205_13816882.shtml#> (in English) accessed 28.03.2014

Xinhua News (2008), 'Coke offer for Huiyuan Triggers Widespread Worry in China', *Xinhua News*, 4 September 2008, available at <www.chinadaily.com.cn/china/2008–09/04/content_6999559.htm> accessed 15.12.2013

Xinhua News (2009), 'Merger Cases Has Increased since the Promulgation of the AML' (反垄断法实施以来我国反垄断案件呈逐年增长之势), *Xinhua News*, 21 September 2011, available at <www.gov.cn/jrzg/2011–09/21/content_1953353.htm> accessed 10.12.2013

Xinhua News (2011), 'Most Concentrations Were Unconditionally Approved in 2010' (2010年我国绝大部分经营者集中案件无条件通过审查), *Xinhua News*, 5 January 2011, available at <http://money.163.com/11/0105/19/6PLKQ97N00253B0H.html> accessed 16.12.2013

Xinhua News (2013), 'MOFCOM: 97% of Concentration Cases were Unconditionally Approved'(商务部:97%经营者集中反垄断案件无条件通过审查), *Xinhua News*, 23 May 2013, available at <http://news.xinhuanet.com/legal/2013–05/23/c_115886393.htm> accessed 20.12.2013

Young, T. (2009), 'Coke-Huiyuan Reaction: Merger Block is Ridiculous', March 2009, *Asia Law Online*, available at <www.asialaw.com/Article/2161922/Quote.html> accessed 20.12.2013

Zhao, H. (2006), 'China Names Key Industries for Absolute State Control', *China Daily*, 19 December 2006, available at <www.chinadaily.com.cn/china/2006–12/19/content_762056.htm> accessed 28.03.2014

Zhao, X. (2008), 'The Nature, Characteristics, and Institutional Concepts of the Anti-Monopoly Law' (反垄断法的性质、地位、特征及其主要制度理念), 29 August 2008, available at <http://jjs.ndrc.gov.cn/gzdt/200808/t20080829_233729.html> (in Chinese) accessed 03.04.2014

Zhang, Y. (2004), 'The Submitted Version of the Anti-Monopoly Law has been formed' (我国《反垄断法》送审稿已形成), *Xinhua Net*, 27 October 2004, available at <http://news.xinhuanet.com/legal/2004–10/27/content_2146394.htm> accessed 23.03.2014

Zhang, L. (2005), 'Three Ministries Fight The Enforcement Competence of the AML' (三部委争立反垄断法, 主管者缺位致今年出台无望), *Beijing Morning Post* (北京晨报), 11 January 2005, available at <http://finance.sina.com.cn/roll/20050111/06181283920.shtml>accessed 22.03.2014

ZHOU, Y. (2013), 'MOFCOM Has Investigated 643 Mergers over last Five Years, Only Coca Cola/Huiyuan was Prohibited' (商务部五年完成643起并购审查, 仅可口可乐购汇源被禁), *ChinaNews.com* (中国新闻网), 1 August 2013, available at <www.chinanews.com/gn/2013/08–01/5113388.shtml> accessed 07.04.2014

MOFCOM DECISIONS

MOFCOM Announcement Number 22 of 2009, the Antitrust Investigation Decision of Prohibiting Coca Cola Acquisition of Huiyuan (中华人民共和国商务部公告[2009年]第22号, 商务部关于禁止可口可乐公司收购中国汇源公司审查决定的公告), 18 March 2009, <http://fldj.mofcom.gov.cn/aarticle/ztxx/200903/20090306108494.html>

MOFCOM Announcement Number 95 of 2008, the Antitrust Investigation Decision of Conditionally Approve InBev Acquisition of Anheuser Busch Companies Inc. (中华人民共和国商务部公告[2008]第95号), 18 November 2008, <http://fldj.mofcom.gov.cn/article/ztxx/200811/20081105899216.shtml>

MOFCOM Announcement Number 28 of 2009, the Antitrust Investigation Decision of Conditionally Approve Mitsubishi Rayon Company Acquisition of Lucite (中华人民共和国商务部公告, 2009年第28号), 24 April 2009, <http://fldj.mofcom.gov.cn/article/ztxx/200904/20090406198805.shtml>

MOFCOM Announcement Number 76 of 2009, the Antitrust Investigation Decision of Conditionally Approve GM Merge with Delphi (中华人民共和国商务部公告2009年第76号), 28 September 2009, <http://fldj.mofcom.gov.cn/article/ztxx/200909/20090906540211.shtml>

MOFCOM Announcement Number 77 of 2009, the Antitrust Investigation Decision of Conditionally Approve Pfizer Merge with Wyeth (中华人民共和国商务部[2009年]第77号公告, 关于附条件批准辉瑞公司收购惠氏公司反垄断审查决定公告), 29 September 2009, <http://fldj.mofcom.gov.cn/article/ztxx/200909/20090906541443.shtml>

MOFCOM Announcement Number 82 of 2009, the Antitrust Investigation Decision of Conditionally Approve Panasonic Company Acquisition of Sanyo (中华人民共和国商务部[2009年]第82号公告, 关于附条件批准松下公司收购三洋公司反垄断审查决定的公告), 30 October 2009, <http://fldj.mofcom.gov.cn/article/ztxx/200910/20091006593175.shtml>

MOFCOM Announcement Number 53 of 2010, the Antitrust Investigation Decision of Conditionally Approve Novartis Joint-Stock Company Acquisition of Alcon (中华人民共和国商务部 [2010年]第53号公告, 关于附条件批准诺华股份有限公司收购爱尔康公司反垄断审查决定的公告), 13 August 2010, <http://fldj.mofcom.gov.cn/article/ztxx/201008/20100807080639.shtml>

MOFCOM Announcement Number 33 of 2011, the Antitrust Investigation Decision of Conditionally Approve Uralkali Joint-Stock Company Acquisition of Silvinit Joint-Stock Company (中华人民共和国商务部[2011年]第33号公告, 关于附条件批准乌拉尔开放型股份公司吸收合并谢尔维尼特开放型股份公司反垄断审查决定的公告), 2 June 2011, <http://fldj.mofcom.gov.cn/article/ztxx/201106/20110607583288.shtml>

MOFCOM Announcement Number 73 of 2011, the Antitrust Investigation Decision of Conditionally Approve Penelope (Alpha V) Acquisition of Savio (中华人民共和国商务部公告2011年第73号, 关于附条件批准佩内洛普有限责任公司收购萨维奥纺织机械股份有限公司反垄断审查决定的公告), 31 October 2011, <http://fldj.mofcom.gov.cn/article/ztxx/201111/20111107855585.shtml>

MOFCOM Announcement Number 74 of 2011, the Antitrust Investigation Decision of Conditionally Approve the Establishment of Joint Venture by GE and Shenhua Group (商务部公告2011年第74号, 关于附条件批准通用电气（中国）有限公司与中国神华煤制油化工有限公司设立合营企业反垄断审查决定的公告), 10 November 2011, <http://fldj.mofcom.gov.cn/article/ztxx/201111/20111107855595.shtml>

MOFCOM Announcement Number 90 of 2011, the Antitrust Investigation Decision of Conditionally Approve the Seagate Acquisition of the HDD business of Samsung (中华人民共和国商务部公告2011年第90号, 关于附条件批准希捷科技公司收购三星电子有限公司硬盘驱动器业务反垄断审查决定的公告), 12 December 2011, <http://fldj.mofcom.gov.cn/article/ztxx/201112/20111207874274.shtml>

MOFCOM Announcement Number 6 of 2012, the Antitrust Investigation Decision of Conditionally Approve the Establishment of the Joint Venture between Henkel Hongkong and Tiande Chemical (中华人民共和国商务部公告2012年第6号, 关于附加限制性条件批准汉高香港与天德化工组建合营企业经营者集中反垄断审查决定的公告), 10 February 2012, <http://fldj.mofcom.gov.cn/article/ztxx/201202/20120207960466.shtml>

MOFCOM Announcement Number 9 of 2012, the Antitrust Investigation Decision of Conditionally Approve Western Digital Acquisition of Hitachi (中华人民共和国商务部公告2012年第9号, 关于附加限制性条件批准西部数据收购日立存储经营者集中反垄断审查决定的公告), 2 March 2012, <http://fldj.mofcom.gov.cn/article/ztxx/201203/20120307993758.shtml>

MOFCOM Announcement Number 25 of 2012, the Antitrust Investigation Decision of Conditionally Approve Google Acquisition of Motorola (中华人民共和国商务部公告2012年第25号, 关于附加限制性条件批准谷歌收购摩托罗拉移动经营者集中反垄断审查决定的公告), 19 May 2012, <http://fldj.mofcom.gov.cn/article/ztxx/201205/20120508134324.shtml>

MOFCOM Announcement Number 35 of 2012, the Antitrust Investigation Decision of Conditionally Approve UTC Acquisition of Goodrich (中华人民共和国商务部公告2012年第35号 关于附加限制性条件批准联合技术收购古德里奇经营者集中反垄断审查决定的公告), 15 June 2012, <http://fldj.mofcom.gov.cn/article/ztxx/201206/20120608181083.shtml>

MOFCOM Announcement Number 49 of 2012, the Antitrust Investigation Decision of Conditionally Approve Walmart Acquisition of 33.6 percent of Newheight's Equity (中华人民共和国商务部公告2012年第49号, 关于附加限制性条件批准沃尔玛公司收购纽海控股33.6%股权经营者集中反垄断审查决定的公告), 14 August 2012, <http://fldj.mofcom.gov.cn/article/ztxx/201303/20130300058730.shtml>

MOFCOM Announcement Number 87 of 2012, the Antitrust Investigation Decision of Conditionally Approve the Establishment of a Joint Venture by Advanced RISC Machines, G&D and Gemalto (中华人民共和国商务部公告2012年第87号, 关于附加限制性条件批准安谋公司、捷德公司和金雅拓公司组建合营企业经营者集中反

垄断审查决定的公告), 6 December 2012, <http://fldj.mofcom.gov.cn/article/ztxx/201212/20121208469841.shtml>

MOFCOM Announcement Number 20 of 2013, the Antitrust Investigation Decision of Conditionally Approve Glencore International Plc Acquisition of Xstrata plc (中华人民共和国商务部公告2013年第20号, 关于附加限制性条件批准嘉能可国际公司收购斯特拉塔公司经营者集中反垄断审查决定的公告), 16 April 2013, <http://fldj.mofcom.gov.cn/article/ztxx/201304/20130400091222.shtml>

MOFCOM Announcement Number 22 of 2012, the Antitrust Investigation Decision of Conditionally Approve Marubeni Acquisition of Gavilon Holdings, LLC (中华人民共和国商务部公告2013年第22号, 关于附加限制性条件批准丸红公司收购高鸿公司100%股权经营者集中反垄断审查决定的公告), 23 April 2013, <http://fldj.mofcom.gov.cn/article/ztxx/201304/20130400100376.shtml>

MOFCOM Announcement Number 58 of 2013, the Antitrust Investigation Decision of Conditionally Approve Baxter International Inc. Acquisition of Gambro AB (中华人民共和国商务部公告2013年第58号, 关于附加限制性条件批准美国百特国际有限公司收购瑞典金宝公司经营者集中反垄断审查决定的公告), 13 August 2013, <http://fldj.mofcom.gov.cn/article/ztxx/201308/20130800244176.shtml>

MOFCOM Announcement Number 61 of 2013, the Antitrust Investigation Decision of Conditionally Approve Media Tek Acqustion of Mstar Semicondutor (中华人民共和国商务部公告2013年第61号, 关于附加限制性条件批准联发科技股份有限公司吸收合并开曼晨星半导体公司经营者集中反垄断审查决定的公告), 27 August 2013, <http://fldj.mofcom.gov.cn/article/ztxx/201308/20130800269821.shtml>

About the Author

Jingyuan Ma is a PhD researcher at the University of Hamburg, Erasmus University Rotterdam and the University of Bologna, taking part in the European Doctorate in Law and Economics programme (EDLE). She holds an LLM in Law and Economics from the University of Hamburg and the University of Ghent (2010), and a BA in Economics from Beijing Foreign Studies University (2009). Her research and teaching interests include economic analysis of competition law, competition policy in China, and the enforcement of law. She has authored several articles on the issue of enforcing competition law in China.

EUROPEAN STUDIES IN LAW AND ECONOMICS

The European Studies in Law and Economics Series is an initiative of the board of the European Doctorate in Law and Economics programme. It is a peer-reviewed book series for a wide audience, including policy makers, legislators, economists, lawyers and judges. The volumes cover a broad range of topics. Each volume is devoted to promote the understanding of the effects of laws on human behaviour, thus providing the tools for a better assessment of the impact of laws on the economic system.

The European Doctorate in Law and Economics (www.edle-phd.eu) is the academic response to the increasing importance of the economic analysis of law in Europe. It is an excellence programme offered by the Universities of Bologna, Hamburg and Rotterdam and sponsored by the European Commission under the Erasmus Mundus scheme. It offers the unique opportunity to study Law and Economics on a PhD level in three different countries. The programme prepares economists and lawyers of high promise for an academic career in a research field of growing importance or for responsible positions in government, research organizations and international consulting groups.

The editorial board consists of Prof. Dr. Michael Faure (Erasmus University Rotterdam and Maastricht University), Prof. Dr. Luigi A. Franzoni (University of Bologna) and Prof. Dr. Stefan Voigt (University of Hamburg).

The editors also invite authors from outside the European Doctorate in Law and Economics to submit publishing proposals. Please contact Ann-Christin Maak (ac.maak@intersentia.co.uk) for further information.